EXPANDING THE GAZE

Gender and the Politics of Surveill. ___

Edited by Emily van der Meulen and Robert Heynen

From sexualized selfies and hidden camera documentaries to the bouncers monitoring patrons at Australian nightclubs, the ubiquity of contemporary surveillance goes far beyond the National Security Agency's bulk data collection or the proliferation of security cameras on every corner.

Expanding the Gaze is a collection of important new empirical and theoretical works that demonstrate the significance of the gendered dynamics of surveillance. Bringing together contributors from criminology, sociology, communication studies, and women's studies, the eleven essays in the volume suggest that we cannot properly understand the implications of the rapid expansion of surveillance practices today without paying close attention to its gendered nature. Together, they constitute a timely interdisciplinary contribution to the development of feminist surveillance studies.

EMILY VAN DER MEULEN is an associate professor in the Department of Criminology at Ryerson University.

ROBERT HEYNEN is a sessional assistant professor in the Department of Communication Studies at York University.

Expanding the Gaze

Gender and the Politics of Surveillance

Edited by Emily van der Meulen and
Robert Heynen

UNIVERSITY OF TORONTO PRESS
Toronto Buffalo London

ISBN 978-1-4426-3746-7 (cloth)
ISBN 978-1-4426-2896-0 (paper)

Library and Archives Canada Cataloguing in Publication

Expanding the gaze : gender and the politics of surveillance / edited by
Emily van der Meulen and Robert Heynen.

Includes bibliographical references and index.
ISBN 978-1-4426-3746-7 (cloth). – ISBN 978-1-4426-2896-0 (paper)

1. Electronic surveillance – Political aspects. 2. Electronic surveillance –
Social aspects. 3. Electronic surveillance – Sex differences. 4. Feminism.
I. van der Meulen, Emily, 1977–, editor II. Heynen, Robert, 1969–, editor.

HQ1190.E96 2016   323.44'8082   C2015-908250-1

This book has been published with the help of a grant from the Federation
for the Humanities and Social Sciences, through the Awards to Scholarly
Publications Program, using funds provided by the Social Sciences and
Humanities Research Council of Canada.

University of Toronto Press acknowledges the financial assistance to its
publishing program of the Canada Council for the Arts and the Ontario
Arts Council, an agency of the Government of Ontario.

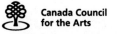

Canada Council   Conseil des Arts
for the Arts   du Canada

ONTARIO ARTS COUNCIL
CONSEIL DES ARTS DE L'ONTARIO
an Ontario government agency
un organisme du gouvernement de l'Ontario

Funded by the   Financé par le
Government   gouvernement
of Canada   du Canada

Canada

Contents

Foreword   vii
SHOSHANA MAGNET

Acknowledgments   xi

Introduction

1 Gendered Visions: Reimagining Surveillance Studies   3
ROBERT HEYNEN AND EMILY VAN DER MEULEN

Gender, Media, and Surveillance

2 Data Doubles and Pure Virtu(e)ality: Headless Selfies, Scopophilia, and Surveillance Porn   35
LARA KARAIAN

3 Living in the Mirror: Understanding Young Women's Experiences with Online Social Networking   56
VALERIE STEEVES AND JANE BAILEY

4 Watch Me Speak: Muslim Girls' Narratives and Postfeminist Pleasures of Surveillance   84
SHENILA KHOJA-MOOLJI AND ALYSSA D. NICCOLINI

5 Profiling the City: Urban Space and the Serial Killer Film   103
JENNY REBURN

Surveillance and Gendered Embodiment

6 Race, Media, and Surveillance: Sex-Selective Abortions in
Canada   135
CORINNE L. MASON

7 Gendering the HIV "Treatment as Prevention" Paradigm:
Surveillance, Viral Loads, and Risky Bodies   156
ADRIAN GUTA, MARILOU GAGNON, JENEVIEVE MANNELL,
AND MARTIN FRENCH

8 Under the Ban-Optic Gaze: Chelsea Manning and the State's
Surveillance of Transgender Bodies   185
MIA FISCHER

Surveillance and the Gendering of Urban Space

9 The Spectacle of Public Sex(uality): Media and State Surveillance of
Gay Men in Toronto in the 1970s   213
ZOË NEWMAN

10 The Surveillance Web: Surveillance, Risk, and Resistance in
Ontario Strip Clubs   240
TUULIA LAW AND CHRIS BRUCKERT

11 Gendering Security: Violence and Risk in Australia's
Night-Time Economies   264
IAN WARREN, KATE FITZ-GIBBON, AND EMMA MCFARLANE

Contributors   290

Index   295

Foreword

SHOSHANA MAGNET

Discussions of surveillance have become commonplace in today's academic and popular culture, structuring our temporal and cultural moment. Such discussions are responses to the increasingly central role surveillance plays in everything from social media to state surveillance and policing. Often these different forms come together – for example, in Canada's Bill C-22 (2011), titled *An Act Respecting the Mandatory Reporting of Internet Child Pornography by Persons who Provide an Internet Service*, and in similar laws in other countries. All of these laws have led to a rash of cases in which people have been sent to jail for sending incriminating selfies (AFP, 2014; Lohr, 2014). Consider the case of the seventeen-year-old American teen who may be prosecuted under child pornography laws for sending nude pictures of himself to his then fifteen-year-old girlfriend. Having sent her photographs of his penis, which were found by his girlfriend's mother, he was arrested by the police. The police planned to inject him with a Viagra-like drug and then photograph his erect penis to see if it matched the selfie, until a public outcry prevented this outcome (AFP, 2014). At the time of writing, the case has yet to be heard. Meanwhile, coverage of it is being structured by the systemic forms of sexism and heteronormativity analysed in this volume. The boy's girlfriend has been rendered without agency and as lacking desire, and the state's violent and voyeuristic gaze on the teenage boy's body is not referenced – indeed, a normative form of acceptable able-bodied masculine sexuality (i.e., an erection) has been invoked as central to proving his guilt or innocence. In this case, as in so much of the analysis of the surveillance that structures our daily lives, and as the editors of this groundbreaking collection argue, the gendered implications of surveillance (and the intersections of gender with race, class, disability, and sexuality) remain undertheorized.

This book is a key text in the burgeoning field of "feminist surveillance studies" (Dubrofsky & Magnet, 2015). Its chapters reflect a number of themes in that field. The intersection of surveillance studies with both girls' and gender studies is one focus of this book. In particular, the contributors examine the ways that young women are placed under forms of surveillance that require them to perform their identities in normative gendered ways, as well as the ways they resist these normativizing sexist and racist tropes. The authors address the limits as well as the possibilities of confessional modes of writing. Memoir has been crucial to the production of feminist theory (Cvetkovich, 2012); yet, as the authors in this collection demonstrate, memoir as a genre is not an inherently politically progressive act. As Judy Segal (2007) argues in a courageous article analysing what she terms the overabundance of memoirs, memoir is "so welcome in part because it is unthreatening – unlike, for example, the genre of the protest rally or the diatribe" (p. 17). The chapters here similarly call new forms of technologized autobiographical writing into question. Rather than understanding blogs, Facebook posts, and other contemporary forms of "memoir" as necessarily emancipatory, the authors note the possibilities of confessional modes of writing while simultaneously analysing how the structures of white supremacist capitalist heteropatriarchal surveillance can strip these texts of their radical potential.

Another important theme of this collection is how the relationship between surveillance, criminalization, and inequality is especially centred on the regulation of urban space and practices of embodiment. Indeed, regimes of surveillance are particularly important in shaping the embodied gendered dynamics of urban life. This book reminds us of the central importance of resisting projects that would intensify surveillance and criminalization: the ways surveillance networks facilitate the criminalization, and increasingly the incarceration, of people living with HIV and people with disabilities; the institutionalization of transmisogyny in the cruel and unusual punishment of trans women; the historic surveillance and criminalization of queer communities; the response to the ongoing epidemic of male violence; and the marginalization and stigmatization of sex workers. While this is not addressed directly, these chapters thus demonstrate the importance of penal abolition to feminist movements, especially given that women of colour remain the fastest-growing demographic incarcerated in the prison system (Hing, 2011). Movements organized around the abolition of prisons highlight the parasitic relationship between transnational corporations and government agencies and the ways that relationship results in the "warehousing of the poor" (Herivel & Wright, 2003), people of colour and Indigenous peoples (Smith, 2015), queer, trans, and genderqueer people (Richie, 2005; Vitulli, 2013), people with disabilities (DAWN-RAFH Canada & Brayton, 2014), and other folks excluded from the benefits of capitalism. In revealing how so many surveillance systems facilitate the criminalization of all types of vulnerable bodies, this book adds to the work of other feminist surveillance studies theorists (Smith, 2015) in making an argument that helps reveal the importance of penal abolition to all feminist projects.

Many of these themes are evident throughout the text, but most explicitly in Mia Fischer's searing analysis of the treatment of whistle-blower Chelsea Manning by the United States government (see chapter 8). Here, Fischer describes the ableist, transphobic violence to which Manning was subject. Stripped to her underwear, and prohibited from doing any activity, including exercise, Manning sat in solitary confinement for twenty-three hours a day, every day. Denied even her prescription eyeglasses, without which she cannot see, Manning was placed under hourly surveillance by guards who woke her when she was sleeping if they could not see her face through the window of her cell. Peeling back the skin of the state to reveal the faulty wiring of inequality that continues to structure systems of surveillance, this book calls for an urgent examination of gender in surveillance studies as a field, while also calling for an end to sexist, racist, trans- and homo-phobic, ableist, and classist forms of surveillance. I hope very much the call this book makes is heeded, by surveillance studies scholars and by state institutions alike.

REFERENCES

AFP (2014, 18 July). US teenager faces jail for sending girlfriend nude selfie. *The Telegraph*. http://www.telegraph.co.uk/news/worldnews/ northamerica/usa/10977677/US-teenager-faces-jail-for-sending-girlfriend-nude-selfie.html

Cvetkovich, A. (2012). *Depression: A public feeling*. Durham, NC: Duke University Press. http://dx.doi.org/10.1215/9780822391852

DAWN-RAFH Canada and B. Brayton (2014, 14 February). The criminalization of women with disabilities: An interview with Bonnie

Brayton from the DisAbled Women's Network of Canada. http://ckutnews.
wordpress.com/2014/02/14/the-criminalization-of-women-with-
disabilities-an-interview-with-bonnie-brayton-from-the-disabled-womens-
newtork-of-canada/

Dubrofsky, R. E. , & Magnet, S. A. (2015). Feminist surveillance studies:
Critical interventions. In R. E. Dubrofsky & S. A. Magnet (Eds.), *Feminist
surveillance studies* (pp. 1–20). Durham, NC: Duke University Press. http://
dx.doi.org/10.1215/9780822375463-001

Herivel, T., and Wright, P. (2003). *Prison nation: The warehousing of America's
poor.* New York, NY: Routledge.

Hing, J. (2011, 8 August). Jezebels, welfare queens – and now, criminally bad
black moms. *Color lines: News for Action.* http://www.colorlines.com/
articles/jezebels-welfare-queens-and-now-criminally-bad-black-moms

Lohr, D. (2014, 6 February). Virginia teen girl accused of posting nude selfies,
arrested for child porn. *Huffington Post.* http://www.huffingtonpost.
com/2014/02/06/nude-teen-selfies-twitter_n_4737810.html

Richie, B. E. (2005). Queering the anti-prison project. In. J Sudbury (Ed.),
Global lockdown: Race, gender, and the prison-industrial complex (pp. 73–85).
New York, NY: Routledge.

Segal, J. (2007). Breast cancer narratives as public rhetoric: Genre itself and the
maintenance of ignorance. *Linguistics and the Human Sciences, 3*(1), 3–23.

Smith, A. (2015). Not seeing: State surveillance, settler colonialism, and gender
violence. In R. E. Dubrofsky & S. A. Magnet (Eds.), *Feminist surveillance
studies* (pp. 21–38). Durham, NC: Duke University Press. http://dx.doi.
org/10.1215/9780822375463-002

Vitulli, E. W. (2013). Queering the carceral: Intersecting queer/trans studies
and critical prison studies. *GLQ: A Journal of Lesbian and Gay Studies, 19*(1),
111–123.

Acknowledgments

All edited collections are collaborative endeavours, and this one is no exception. We are deeply grateful to the many people who have inspired and supported our work over the years, but we would like to specifically recognize those who have contributed more directly to this publication, and without whom this book would not exist. First, we would like to thank Doug Hildebrand and the rest of the staff at the University of Toronto Press; Doug in particular made the long process of academic publishing a smooth and enjoyable venture. Amanda Glasbeek was involved in the early stages of this book, and we would like to acknowledge her contributions in helping shape the collection in its initial form. Stephan Dobson created the index, and on this and other projects he has been an important source of intellectual support and encouragement. The office of the Dean of Arts, Ryerson University, provided the grant for the index. The feedback received from the two anonymous reviewers was very beneficial, and their comments and critiques have produced a stronger and more thorough collection. Emily would also like to acknowledge the Social Sciences and Humanities Research Council for funding her research on women's experiences with CCTV, which provided the initial inspiration for this book.

Finally, this book has only been made possible through the hard work, patience, and dedication of the chapter authors themselves – we thank each of them for entrusting us with their words and their work; their insights and innovations promise to make profound contributions to expanding the gaze of surveillance studies.

Introduction

Chapter 1

Gendered Visions: Reimagining Surveillance Studies

ROBERT HEYNEN AND EMILY VAN DER MEULEN

Surveillance has become ubiquitous in contemporary society. From government and corporate programs for collecting information to the interpersonal forms of watching embedded in social media, surveillance structures our lives in fundamental ways. While many of these surveillance practices have long histories in Euro-Western contexts, dating at least back to the late eighteenth century, most commentators would agree that there has been a dramatic increase in the scope of surveillance in recent decades, especially with the advent of digital technologies. Revelations by WikiLeaks and Edward Snowden of the massive scale of state and corporate surveillance as well as everyday worries over privacy and access to information have led some to argue that George Orwell's fears of an all-seeing Big Brother, as articulated in his influential novel *1984*, have now been realized. While surveillance is the subject of much anxiety, though, a host of films and TV shows ranging from *CSI* to *Person of Interest* and *Homeland* celebrate surveillance, suggesting that for many people, surveillance offers a sense of safety and security. Perhaps more significantly, surveillance and data collection are integral to most forms of the digital communication technologies we use every day. Contemporary society has indeed become, in that sense, a "surveillance society" (Murakami Wood, 2009).

The pervasiveness of surveillance is particularly evident when we think of its many forms. Visual surveillance technologies like closed-circuit television (CCTV) cameras and the integrated surveillance systems of border policing are among the most common examples, but new forms of social media also need to be understood as part of an incredibly powerful if heterogeneous set of surveillance regimes in which vast arrays of data are collected, stored, and organized. Surveillance is performed by states, corporations, police, employers, and schools and universities, as well as individuals, and it serves a wide range of divergent and sometimes contradictory goals, which include managing populations, facilitating commerce, enabling "security," and maintaining interpersonal relationships, in addition to a host of other functions. In collecting, organizing, and mobilizing information, though, these surveillance practices are deeply implicated in relationships of power and inequality. Thus, critics have stressed not only issues of privacy in the collection of data but also the role surveillance plays in "social sorting" (Lyon, 2003) – that is, the differentiation of populations in the service of systems of management and control. This social sorting is perhaps most evident in discourses and practices of national security, where often highly racialized and classed forms of identification target particular populations, but it is in many respects even more pervasive in commercial practices. In a host of different ways, surveillance is central to contemporary forms of neoliberal governance, both in the top-down management of people and economic systems and in the inculcation of forms of self-surveillance (Lyon, 2006, 2007; Hier & Greenberg, 2009; Haggerty & Samatas, 2010). For all the focus on these repressive dimensions, though, others have argued that we need to see surveillance as more "participatory" (Albrechtslund, 2008) and as enabling new forms of sociality and pleasure. Linking these divergent approaches is a shared sense that surveillance is increasingly woven into the fabric of our societies in complex and differentiated ways.

Over the past three decades, writing on surveillance has coalesced into the distinct, if fluid and contested, field of surveillance studies (for key overviews, see Lyon, 2007; Ball, Haggerty, & Lyon, 2012). As with many new fields, however, significant gaps remain, perhaps the most substantial of which is a limited systematic attention to gender. This book aims to contribute to a growing body of scholarship that engages critically with the gendered nature of surveillance in its many forms (see, for example, Ball, Green, Koskela, & Phillips, 2009; Conrad, 2009; Monahan, 2009; Magnet, 2011; Koskela, 2012; Abu-Laban, 2015; Dubrofsky & Magnet, 2015). Incorporating gender into surveillance studies means more than simply adding women (which is often the default when speaking of gender) to an existing framework. Instead, bringing gender into studies of surveillance promises a fundamental reimaging of the field that will open up a range of new and important avenues of inquiry. Gendering the field involves thinking about surveillance practices as socially located as embodied and as having differential impacts.

This perspective also brings longer histories into view, offering a corrective to the more present-centric tendencies that see surveillance as dramatically new. Gendered social practices, subjectivities, bodies, and experiences are also not discrete; gender intersects with a host of other identity forms and social processes, including race, sexuality, ability, and class. Starting from the perspective of gender, we contend, opens up rich and diverse perspectives for our understanding of practices of surveillance, both building on and challenging foundational concepts and approaches. As with much of the field, this book centres on and explores the Western context, a perspective that offers the virtue of focus but that can only ever be partial. An important avenue for further research lies in broadening the field to account more fully for the differential global impacts of surveillance, in particular in Africa, Asia, and Latin America. If gender brings new forms of surveillance into view, much more work is needed to bring globally differentiated experiences of surveillance into its studies.

In what follows, we build on existing work on gender and surveillance as well as other critical work that, while not explicitly addressing surveillance, offers resources for a rethinking of the field. This involves engaging with longer traditions of feminist scholarship and with historical and contemporary social practices that are often not seen as forms of surveillance. In doing so, we begin this introduction with an opening section that provides both a critical overview of surveillance studies and an account of some of the key contemporary works on gender and surveillance that are beginning to transform the field. The next three sections mirror the organizational structure of the book itself, each addressing key areas of focus: gender, media, and surveillance; surveillance and gendered embodiment; and surveillance and the gendering of urban space. In each of the three areas we in fact find a well-developed feminist scholarship that, while often not directly related to or taken up by scholars of surveillance studies, speaks to the key questions in the field. The different areas (media, bodies, urban space) are deeply interconnected, with the themes cutting across the sections of this introduction and, more importantly, linking the various chapters in intriguing and complex ways. Thus, woven through our discussion below is an attempt to bring to bear a range of interdisciplinary perspectives that, we argue, can enrich our understandings. What emerges is less a definitive statement on gender and surveillance and more a set of questions for further research, setting the context in turn for the provocative interventions presented in the subsequent chapters.

Gendering Surveillance Studies

Accounts of contemporary surveillance practices tend to begin in the same place, with Michel Foucault (1977) and his theorization of the panopticon. The panopticon was the term used by Jeremy Bentham in the late eighteenth century to describe a proposed prison architecture in which prisoners would be incarcerated in cells arrayed around a central guard tower, visible to the guards, but with the latter invisible to the prisoners (Bentham, 1798). Bentham's idea was that prisoners, unsure of whether or not they were being watched, would begin to self-surveil, monitoring their own behaviour in case a guard was present. It was this notion that Foucault took up, arguing that over the course of the late eighteenth and nineteenth centuries "a whole type of society emerges" (Foucault, 1977, p. 216), with this panoptic form of discipline dominating a range of institutions from the military to education. The juvenile penal colony of Mettray, France, which was built without walls and opened in 1840, was the first fully developed expression of this project; the "disciplinary technique exercised upon the body had a double effect: a 'soul' to be known and a subjection to be maintained" (Foucault, 1977, p. 295). Rather than the public spectacles of earlier periods of European history, where the many watched the few, Foucault argued that modern society was one in which the few surveilled the many. Surveillance was thus at the heart of modern forms of power and subjectivity, with power in this reading emerging as productive, not simply repressive.

The impact of Foucault's approach can be seen in a variety of concepts developed by surveillance studies scholars to explain the growing ubiquity of contemporary forms of "panoptic surveillance" (Elmer, 2003). Early works conceptualizing new surveillance practices coined terms like the "superpanopticon" (Poster, 1990); analyses often focused on the "panoptic sort" (Gandy, 1993), in which the information gathering by states and corporations served to aggregate, differentiate, and manage populations, a process that David Lyon (2003) has called "social sorting." Where Foucault focused on state institutions like the prison, panoptic surveillance today takes different forms. The automation of surveillance is one aspect of this shift, one that involves a risk management perspective based on aggregations of data. Didier Bigo (2006) describes this as a shift to a "ban-opticon" whereby the "state of emergency" legitimizing state surveillance is normalized, becoming invisible and routinized. Mark Andrejevic (2007a) argues that systems of surveillance have expanded dramatically as a result. We are now in a time of "digital enclosures": "If the creation of enclosures such as those of the prison, the factory, and the asylum ... facilitated the disciplinary monitoring of inmates and workers, that of the digital enclosure extends the monitoring gaze beyond such institutional walls to encompass spaces of leisure, consumption, domesticity, and perhaps all of these together" (p. 301; see also Andrejevic, 2007b). Foucault's work is reconsidered in significant ways in these accounts, but they all suggest that contemporary societies continue to be governed in important ways by a quasi-panoptic logic.

Interestingly, while Foucault has been widely taken up in critical ways by feminist scholars (e.g., Diamond & Quinby, 1988; Butler, 1990, 1993), they have tended to turn to other of Foucault's works in theorizing the emergence of modern subjects. For them, the carceral model of the panopticon, one that in the historical experience of the prison implied primarily male watchers and watched, did not prove as compelling as Foucault's genealogies of sexuality or medicine. Indeed, many others in surveillance studies have expressed a disquiet with the institutional and unidirectional model of surveillance entailed by the panopticon, arguing that contemporary society is characterized more by a "liquid surveillance" (Bauman & Lyon, 2013). For Stéphane Leman-Langlois (2003), even in the realm of policing what we have is more of "a 'myopic' panopticon, one that sees what it can, when it can, and barely manages to meet minimum conventional expectations of police-imposed order" (p. 2). Perhaps the best-known challenge to Foucault's model has come from Gilles Deleuze (1992), who argued that *"societies of control* ... are in the process of replacing disciplinary societies" (p. 4, emphasis in original). A Deleuzian perspective is evident in Kevin D. Haggerty and Richard V. Ericson's (2000) influential work on what they call the "surveillant assemblage"; their article has become a touchstone in surveillance studies, and this introduction and many of the subsequent chapters will return to it at different points. Haggerty and Ericson argue that in their ubiquity and heterogeneity, contemporary surveillance practices constitute a constantly shifting and adapting assemblage of practices rather than the product of a singular locus of power. Haggerty (2006) himself has returned to Foucault for an alternative approach, arguing that his theory of governmentality offers a potentially more fruitful avenue for rethinking contemporary surveillance practices than does the panopticon. The panoptic model, Haggerty contends, is unable to adequately acknowledge the diverse forms and experiences of surveillance, including potentially pleasurable ones.

The shift away from a repressive model owes much to Thomas Mathiesen's (1997) critique of the panopticon. He argued that contemporary society is marked as much by "synoptic" practices as by panoptic ones, the former involving the media and characterized by the many watching the few. Contemporary media, he suggested, have initiated a return to the politics of the spectacle that, in Foucault's account, had been superseded by the emergence of the panoptic model. Indeed, it is especially in media and communication studies that the panoptic model has been challenged most directly, in particular in studies of new media. Social networking, webcams, digital photography, and many other practices enable "participatory surveillance" (Albrechtslund, 2008) – a form of surveillance that, in more optimistic accounts, allows for the democratization of surveillance as entertainment (Albrechtslund & Dubbeld, 2005; Senft, 2008), or, in more concretely political challenges to panoptic power, that "enabl[es] those who are normally the object of surveillance to turn the lens and reverse its power" (Fiske, 1996, p. 127). Where Mathiesen saw the synoptic and the panoptic working in tandem, Hille Koskela (2006) goes further in arguing that "people do not submit to the passive role of 'the observed' that surveillance offers them but, instead, play various active roles with 'surveillance' equipment" (p. 175). This entails "hijacking surveillance," and means that "the present deeply synoptic condition has hardly any qualities which would resemble the panopticon" (Koskela, 2009, p. 163). It is here that a gendered approach has proven especially influential, with feminist theorists contending that unidirectional understandings of the gaze are important in recognizing gendered forms of looking, but that, especially in mass media contexts, we need to go further in examining political challenges, the ambivalent pleasures of looking, and forms of agency and self-production that potentially escape the panoptic logic.

These approaches offer an important challenge to the panopticon, although at times they risk becoming excessively celebratory of the possibilities of new media, losing track in the process of Mathiesen's claim that synoptic and panoptic systems work in tandem. This is especially evident in relation to the commercial logic of social media, which is built on networks of participatory surveillance integrated into panoptic systems in which massive databases of information are mined in order to facilitate advertising and the commodification of our online activity (Fuchs et al., 2012). While these practices may be participatory, they in fact produce forms of "lateral surveillance" (Andrejevic, 2005) that often mimic rather than disrupt "top down" surveillance. Encompassing not only such commercial activity but also a broad range of state and other institutional forms of data collection, the proliferation of surveillance produces what Haggerty and Ericson (2000) have called a "data double" (p. 606), a collection of data directly related to, but distinct from, our "real world" selves. We thus exist in the contemporary world as a doubled self – that is, an informational *and* a material self. As we will see, though, this data double is a fraught concept, in particular when we consider it from a gendered perspective.

It is in thinking through the complex and contradictory nature of contemporary forms of surveillance that a gender-based approach has made some of the most significant contributions to surveillance studies. Koskela's (2002, 2003, 2012) work is especially interesting in this regard, as she was one of the first to bring gender into surveillance studies in a significant way. Her research on the gendered nature of CCTV, for example, stressed that while seemingly important for increasing women's security in potentially dangerous public spaces, cameras can conversely be experienced by women as increasing *insecurity* (for similar findings, see van der Meulen & Glasbeek, 2013). At its most basic, Koskela argues, surveillance is often about men watching women, a dynamic left largely unaddressed in most accounts (see also Norris & Armstrong, 1999). Certainly in Foucault's work this was not explicitly addressed, despite the very different gendered dynamics operative in each of the panoptic institutions he studied. Prisons, education systems, and the military were historically predominantly or exclusively male-dominated, with men watching other men. Different in this respect were psychiatric and medical institutions, with both men and women surveilled by male medical professionals, but with women subjected to special scrutiny. Especially in asylums, where we find the "female malady" (Showalter, 1985) of hysteria becoming a key diagnosis, surveillance itself became a gendered public spectacle, with predominantly female inmates paraded for scientific entertainment (Didi-Huberman, 2003). Here we can see particularly clearly the simultaneous working of the panoptic and synoptic modes, with the latter in this instance by no means emancipatory in nature. The history of asylum practices demonstrates the extent to which both panoptic and synoptic systems promoted internalized forms of self-surveillance through which gender norms were taught. These did not go uncontested, however; much feminist activism over the last century or more has challenged the ways in which myriad forms of self-surveillance have produced such gendered subjects, both masculine and feminine.

Drawing on, expanding, and reimagining gender in surveillance studies involves a critical consideration of some of the broader implications of these gendered practices and histories. Below, we thus draw again on works in the field of surveillance studies that examine gender, but we also return to other feminist and critical traditions that can help us rethink contemporary surveillance, including historical work tracing the emergence of gendered "ways of seeing" (Berger, 1972). Indeed, much feminist writing in a wide range of disciplines, as well as critical work around sexuality, race, class, and disability, is highly attentive to how ways of seeing are central to the emergence of gendered subjects and other social practices. This is reflected also at the methodological level, with feminist approaches promising to open new avenues of inquiry, including a focus on "human interdependence and the moral value of care and caring relations" rather than simply studies of control (Abu-Laban, 2015). Given the importance placed on vision in feminist scholarship, it is striking that few of these scholars have been taken up more widely within surveillance studies. One aim of this introductory chapter is, therefore, to highlight the potential of these fruitful interdisciplinary connections for future research. In the three sections that follow, as well as in the intersections between those different discussions, we draw out the complex and interconnected ways in which feminist scholarship can help us engage more deeply with practices of surveillance; we also introduce the reader to the structure of the collection and to the scholarly work developed around our key areas of focus. In each case, we argue, existing work in surveillance studies offers important resources on which the authors in this collection draw. At the same time, a gendered perspective challenges us to reimagine the approaches that have dominated the field.

Gender, Media, and Surveillance

Vision is central to much feminist writing. This is especially evident in media studies, but it is rooted in a longer perspective that emphasizes the extent to which social and political life, in Western history and culture in particular, has been constituted by stark gendered dichotomies. On the one hand, reflecting exclusions from or unequal access to employment, the political realm, public space, and power, feminists have argued that women are often invisibilized, hidden in the private sphere, or banished to the margins of representations. The rational Enlightenment subject emerged through the suppression of a feminized irrationality founded on the visual metaphors of light and dark. The bourgeois public sphere in turn was constituted through a series of exclusions in which ideas of "rationality" were deployed to exclude or invisibilize women, racialized people, disabled people, the working class, and other "Others" (Fraser, 1992). Conversely and simultaneously, women have also long been marked by a hypervisibility, emerging as the object of a vision that is implicitly masculinized. Most commonly this involves the foregrounding of woman as body, and enables the policing of women's presence in public space, issues that will be explored throughout this book. This paradoxical in- and hyper-visibility is in many respects what structures the practices of gender in contemporary society, although its specific forms have changed historically and vary significantly across the globe. Feminist scholarship and activism has sought to critique and undo the binary structures of vision through which gendered dynamics operate.

The focus of much feminist critique of these gendered visual relations has been on art and the media, with the latter particularly prominent today. It is in the media in particular that we can see this dual process of invisibility/hypervisibility in clear ways, with women underrepresented in many areas but excessively represented (albeit in homogenizing and reductive ways) in others. Here the relationship to surveillance studies is clear, with Mathiesen's work on panoptic and synoptic power especially relevant, although gender has rarely been considered in much depth. The idea of the "male gaze" that comes out of feminist film studies is extremely fruitful, if contested, in helping us think critically about gendered forms of vision. The term originates with Laura Mulvey's (1975) psychoanalytic account of film's scopophilia, the visual pleasure of looking characteristic of the medium. She argued that women have been configured in film through a "to-be-looked-at-ness" (p. 63), with "the image of woman as (passive) raw material for the (active) gaze of man" (p. 17). Women are in effect barred from looking; as Linda Williams (1992) argued of early melodramatic film, "the frustration of the woman's 'look' in the silent melodrama ... is a frustration necessary for the male regime of voyeuristic desire" (p. 563).

The gendered structuring of the gaze in film takes on both panoptic and synoptic dimensions, especially if we consider the space of the theatre. Here panoptic forms of self-surveillance work to produce gendered subjects, both male and female (Friedberg, 1993, pp. 17–20), but we also find a synoptic spectacle. The male gaze operates in complex ways in these accounts, with Mulvey, for example, stressing that women too can occupy the position of the spectator. The risk, though, is that this conception of the male gaze and its internalization in a form of gendered "soul training" becomes reductive and totalizing. Mulvey's work has thus been challenged for its monolithic character, with bell hooks (1992) famously arguing that what she is describing is more specifically a *white* male gaze, with Black women rarely appearing in front of the camera (or behind, for that matter). When they do appear, it is not as the object of the gaze (which remains the white woman), and their subsequent invisibility or denigration means that Black women as spectators develop what hooks calls an "oppositional gaze." Ultimately, Mulvey's account risks missing key dynamics like race; it also risks reinscribing the gendered binary that she is ostensibly critiquing, ignoring the extent to which gender itself is performative – constituted, as Judith Butler (1990, 1993) argues, through the repetition of gendered norms. The male gaze itself can also be queered, undermining the binary system of gender (Halberstam, 2005). From these perspectives, gender systems seek to produce stable identities but are in fact contradictory, fragmented, changing, and intersecting with race, sexuality, disability, class, and a host of other social relations and practices. Gender is also thus embodied, a perspective we develop in the next section.

While focused on film, the work of Mulvey and hooks has influenced feminist media studies more broadly. It has recently been taken up, for example, in studies of gender and surveillance on Twitter (Dubrofsky & Wood, 2014). Social media are arguably rather different from film, though, in particular given the diffuse nature of digital communication. In that sense, social media offer the possibility of more participatory forms of surveillance characterized by "subjectivity that takes part in its own surveillance" (Albrechtslund, 2012, p. 196). Many of the debates around gender and new media (but also "old" media) are precisely about the extent to which the rather monolithic notion of the male gaze is conceptually useful. What is clear, though, is that stereotypical gender norms continue to shape people's social media experiences and that young men and women use social media in distinctive ways (Bailey et al., 2013). These gendered distinctions are reinforced in advertising, with cellphone ads, for example, presenting profoundly gendered images of users that actively legitimize surveillance, in particular of teen girls, situating them again as the object of the gaze (Vickery, 2014). Despite these powerfully gendered dimensions of digital practices, many accounts of new media, identity, and surveillance continue largely to ignore gendered analyses (e.g., Jansson & Christensen, 2014).

To what extent the potentially more open, diffuse, and participatory nature of these new media enables the subversion of hegemonic relations of looking remains a point of debate, and is a theme that runs through the present book.

What is clear from these debates is that a gendered analysis opens up very different perspectives on media and surveillance. Girls and women remain oversurveilled, especially in terms of the formal and informal policing of perceived gender deviance, either in terms of gender identity itself (something that impacts especially strongly on intersex and trans people [see Magnet & Rodgers, 2012; Jakubowska, 2014]) or in terms of sexuality (Biber & Dalton, 2009). At the same time, taking gender as the lens through which to examine surveillance highlights many important ways in which forms of resistance, pleasure, entertainment, and performance have been enabled through new media and social media (Senft, 2008; Bell, 2009). One critique of Mathiesen's notion of the synopticon is that it tends to read the media in top-down fashion, ignoring practices of resistance that emerge especially in new media (Doyle, 2011). Indeed, key themes running through this book are the interplay between panoptic and synoptic dynamics, but also the ways in which young women in particular resist and subvert the male gaze produced through both panoptic and synoptic practices. Especially groundbreaking is the attention to the various dynamics at play in gendered surveillance practices, taking up race, sexuality, and gender expression in particular. The contributions, which thereby move beyond much of the early feminist theorization of gender and the media, strongly suggest that we need to deploy multiple models and theoretical perspectives in order to fully engage with the politics of surveillance.

Beginning this book with four chapters that focus on media foregrounds the significant shifts that have occurred in the field of surveillance with the emergence of digital technologies. Those shifts have enabled a multitude of rapidly expanding possibilities for a gendering of the field. In most of the chapters in the first section, we find that while women, and particularly young women, are so often rendered hypervisible and targeted as "at risk" in both dominant discourse and media, they are in fact by no means passive objects of the masculine surveillant gaze. It is with young women, these chapters suggest, that some of the most significant critical engagements with surveillance practices are emerging. Thus, Lara Karaian's chapter takes up the ways in which young women negotiate sexuality through self-produced and shared "selfies," a pervasive new form of digital, sexual self-expression.

Challenging the frequent configuration of young women's sexuality as in need of control and/or protection, Karaian looks to the *Dr. Phil* show to complicate adults' voyeuristic surveilling of teen sexters. In Valerie Steeves and Jane Bailey's contribution, we find that young women's accounts of their use of online social media are revealing insofar as they recount engaging in complex negotiations between a desire to see and be seen online, and attempts to avoid overvisibility and gendered scrutiny. Their work also considers the formation of masculine subjectivity, moving beyond an account of representation to one in which gender is structured by how we use media. Shenila Khoja-Moolji and Alyssa Niccolini likewise stress the active and agentic role young women play in constructions of sexuality, pleasure, and desire, in this case looking specifically at Muslim girls and young women's confessional texts. Here Muslim girls' subjectivities are constituted not only in relation to gendered and racialized discourses but also through pervasive regimes of surveillance targeting Muslims more broadly; in this regard, the chapter throws a powerful light on the role of surveillance in gendered and racialized conceptions of the American nation. Jenny Reburn's chapter turns to film, specifically serial killer films, to examine the ways in which portrayals of both the killers and the detectives reflect and legitimate cultures of surveillance. Reburn argues that while the killer and the detective are depicted as engaged in practices of surveilling, these films tend to reassert a benevolent and protective conception of heavily masculinized police surveillance over a passive and feminized social body under threat. The idea of the male gaze in this context retains a significant explanatory power.

Surveillance and Gendered Embodiment

Increasingly, large-scale collections of data are tied to visual markers, with various surveillance practices producing a connection between our data doubles and our material bodies. Especially with biometrics – that is, the practice of reading identity from bodily markers like fingerprints, faces, or eyes – we find the body "positioned as an indicator of truth and authenticity about the individual" (Ball, 2006, p. 297; see also Aas, 2006; Gates, 2011), as unproblematically readable for meaning. While in this context the surveilled body is configured as fixed, contemporary bodies are also often understood as fluid and malleable, a perspective evident in fields as disparate as cosmetic surgery and genetic engineering (Heyes, 2007; Rose & Rose, 2012). In genetic engineering as in biometrics, though, "there is no clear point where bodily matter first becomes information" (van der Ploeg, 2003, p. 70), meaning that, regardless of whether the body is produced as fixed or fluid, the relationship between the data double and the material body is profoundly unstable.

One virtue of a gendered approach to surveillance is that it brings to the fore the longer histories of technologies like biometrics and genetics, as well as the ways in which those gendered practices articulate dynamics of race, sexuality, ability, and health. In many respects, this has involved constituting bodies as "normal" and "abnormal," a tendency that is deeply rooted in modern, capitalist cultures. Part of this process has been a gendering of bodies; indeed, it was only in the eighteenth century that European science came to see gender as a biologically rooted form of difference that permeated bodies as a whole – a difference elaborated in medical and scientific imaging so as to buttress the gendered Enlightenment dichotomization of body and mind (Callen, 1998; Amoore & Hall, 2009). Women in particular were conceived of primarily *as* bodies, a development reflected as well in the "tendency in traditional sociology to over-corporealize women" (Ball, 2006, p. 303). Critiques of the Cartesian mind–body dualism have come from a variety of perspectives, with the phenomenological approach of Maurice Merleau-Ponty (1958) – which stresses the body as the ground of perception and cognition – especially important in the development of contemporary sociologies of the body. This focus on the body is crucial as well for the development of a critical theory of gender and surveillance. But such a critical theory needs to simultaneously resist and remain attentive to the overcorporealization of women in the Enlightenment tradition. These seemingly contradictory demands reflect the contradictions of the gendered nature of vision itself and its production of women as both invisibilized and hypervisible.

At the heart of the surveillance society has been the production of normative notions of embodiment, practices built on elaborate surveillance systems that have long privileged the body as a site of both meaning and intervention. Nineteenth- and early-twentieth-century European and North American programs of eugenics and social hygiene, for example, sought to read the "health" of the nation or the race through the surveillance of populations (Withers, 2012; Heynen, 2015), while criminological practices of fingerprinting, physiognomy, and other forms of bodily measurement prefigured contemporary biometrics (Sekula, 1986). As Simone Browne (2010, 2012) argues, many of these early forms of surveillance derived from practices applied to slaves in the United States, with everything from pass systems to branding (itself a biometric practice) enabling control over enslaved bodies. Vision structured slavery in many ways, with slaves themselves denied the "right to look." The legacies of this prohibition extended long into the post-emancipation period, with lynching and other violence against Black men meted out for allegedly looking at white women. In her critique of the idea of the male gaze, hooks argued that white women were rendered hypervisible, with Black women invisibilized in film cultures. In contemporary surveillance it is often Black *men* who are rendered hypervisible, especially when it comes to policing and urban surveillance (Fiske, 1998; Walby, 2006), although certainly Black women are frequent targets of police violence and surveillance as well (Ezekiel et al., 2015).

These forms of racialized and gendered surveillance were at the heart of long histories by which bodies were produced through systems of surveillance as either "normal" or "deviant," often buttressed through scientific practice. We saw this already with eugenics and criminology, but it was also evident in medicine. In the United States, for example, government efforts to screen for tuberculosis in the mid-twentieth century "entailed the institution of a public medical surveillance system ... [that] functioned as a kind of *collective* prophylaxis, making identifiable the disease in its early stages and thus facilitating surveillance and separation of the tubercular subject from family or community" (Cartwright, 1995, p. 150, emphasis in original). Women in this context were configured as vectors of disease and hence as a potential threat to national health. Similar, indeed more virulent, processes of stigmatization and surveillance were later directed at gay men, racialized people, and injection drug users in relation to HIV and AIDS; their bodies were constituted as threats to a heteronormative masculinized national body. This kind of prophylactic surveillance was rooted in medicine and also in older conceptions of national security – a telling point of contact between medicalizing and securitizing forms of surveillance. In Canada and elsewhere, gay men were identified as threats in Cold War discourses and practices of national security, and elaborate technologies were developed to read the bodies and minds of government workers in an effort to uncover hidden sexual deviance (Kinsman & Gentile, 2010).

Given these historical contexts, it is no surprise that feminist scholars have developed extensive critiques of the gendered nature of scientific vision and the surveilling of bodies. Donna Haraway (1991) has been especially influential in this respect, most notably in her arguments about the need to develop radically new forms of objectivity and rationality capable of challenging dominant scientific practice. A feminist politics of vision, she argues, needs to begin from subjugated standpoints "because they seem to promise more adequate, sustained, objective, transforming accounts of the world" (1991, p. 191). This vision "from below" challenges what we might call the techno-scientific male gaze evident, she says, in projects like President Ronald Reagan's Strategic Defence Initiative. Haraway's work prefigured much recent critical writing on American military and secret service surveillance, which, growing out of the notorious "Total Information Awareness" program (Singel, 2003; Whitaker, 2006), has expanded into the ubiquitous multiagency system of state surveillance that Edward Snowden has brought into the public eye. Haraway's gendered and embodied analysis of these violent forms of surveillance, which asks "with whose blood were my eyes crafted?" (1991, p. 192), is often missing from more recent accounts, however. More broadly, Haraway's critical project has great potential significance for reshaping how we understand the wide range of surveillance practices touched on here.

Interestingly, in their influential article on the surveillant assemblage, Haggerty and Ericson (2000) do discuss Haraway as an important resource, but they do not engage with her analysis of gender or with her insistence on the bodily nature of vision. What, we might ask, is the relationship between the data double produced by the surveillant assemblage and the material body, and how is it gendered? The historical perspectives brought to bear here suggest that this question is not such a new one, although much recent research argues that the emergence of digital technologies has intensified the "informatization of the body" (van der Ploeg, 2003, p. 58; see also van der Ploeg, 2012) in ways that are qualitatively new. As Nik Brown and Andrew Webster (2004) argue, with contemporary medical systems "the object of maintenance and care then is no longer simply the individual body, but representations or traces of the body in globalized systems of information and data management" (pp. 80–1). What has happened in some respects is a shift away from state-centred eugenic projects to a "consumer eugenics" (Rose & Rose, 2012, p. 125; see also Haraway, 1997) in line with neoliberal forms of market-based self-governance. We might say that the informatization of the body is not new, but that it has both intensified and shifted in nature.

The notion of the data double is thus useful in understanding these processes, but it also risks reinscribing the dualist understanding of mind and body (or information and body) stemming from the Enlightenment. Rethinking the surveillant assemblage from a gendered perspective, one that also engages with other forms of embodied differences, foregrounds the extent to which surveillance systems themselves in fact generate and sustain these dualities, producing abstracted notions of the body "that both obscure and aggravate gender and other social inequalities" (Monahan, 2009, p. 287). Here we also find connections back to the role of the media in the surveillant assemblage. Thus, for example, the neoliberal undermining of welfare provisions, which involves the punitive surveilling of recipients, has been legitimized in the media and elsewhere by the racialized and gendered image of the "welfare queen" (Kohler-Hausmann, 2007). Media representations in fact serve directly to legitimize and fetishize surveillance practices themselves, with medical and crime television shows especially notable for cementing a male gaze in which women, frequently sex workers, are disproportionately configured as mute bodies, either victims of crime or flesh on which medicalized interventions are performed (Kahle, 2012; Steenberg, 2013).

In the contemporary context, biometrics offers us an especially interesting window into the processes we have been examining here. Biometrics is built upon a myth of scientific objectivity and truth, a biopolitical technology in the sense that it intervenes at the level of the body, of life itself, in order to regulate and shape populations (Ajana, 2013). As Shoshana Magnet (2011) argues, however, no biometric system boasts a 100 per cent accuracy rate, although the ideological and material power of biometrics relies on a myth of omniscient vision (Gates, 2011). Failure is endemic to such systems, but, Magnet contends, this failure is itself productive. There is a paradox at the heart of biometrics in which "biometric technologies succeed even when they fail ... [and] fail even when they succeed" (Magnet, 2011, p. 3). Often these failures are the result of what is called a "failure to enrol," that is, the inability of biometric systems to "read" certain bodies. This may involve surveillance systems calibrated to register white skin and hence not recognize other tones, or the "problem" that people in a host of different occupations lose fingerprint definition. Disabled bodies in particular can be unread or misread, stigmatized as "failed" bodies (Magnet, 2011, pp. 29–31). Trans and other gender nonconforming people experience particular problems with biometric and human border security (Conrad, 2009;

Magnet & Rodgers, 2012), their subjectivity read as deceptive (Beauchamp, 2009). Non-normative bodies and subjects, then, are produced as both invisible and hypervisible, thereby rendering them accessible for various forms of state and extra-state intervention.

It is precisely these themes that are taken up in the second section of this book. Here we have three chapters that examine the ways in which certain bodies are made visible to a surveillant gaze, processes that serve not only to reinforce normative conceptions of embodiment but also to reinforce hegemonic social norms. Corinne Mason looks at the question of reproduction, examining the role of surveillance in the gendered and racialized politics of abortion. She contends that a rhetoric of care for the fetus is mobilized to produce Canadian national subjects as white and that this, through a paternalist saviour narrative, legitimates the enhanced surveillance of racialized subjects in the name of protecting women. Adrian Guta, Marilou Gagnon, Jenevieve Mannell, and Martin French look specifically at the medical and public health surveillance of people living with HIV. By focusing on the recent growth of the "treatment as prevention" paradigm and the increased pressure to test for HIV, they show that the gendered dimensions of this approach have disproportionate effects on already stigmatized bodies. Mia Fischer further develops the analysis of the role of surveillance in stigmatizing particular bodies, examining the US government's surveillance of trans bodies through a study of Chelsea Manning, whose case, Fischer argues, highlights the intersections between regimes of surveillance directed at non-normative sexualities and bodies, and questions of state security.

Surveillance and the Gendering of Urban Space

A central dimension of our above discussion of bodies and surveillance had to do with borders and the role of bodily surveillance in the constitution of national space. Often this national space is highly racialized and is tied directly to the reproduction of what, in older discourses of eugenics, was conceived of as the racial or national body. The contemporary security state, with its obsession with maintaining the integrity of borders, is where we can see these spatial dimensions of surveillance most explicitly. But there are complex intersections between these national-scale forms of surveillance and more localized urban surveillance, something that is highlighted explicitly in the all too frequent police killings of unarmed Black and other racialized men (among others), which have drawn wide public attention to racial profiling and the militarization of urban policing in the United States and elsewhere.

Much urban planning around the globe has, over the past several decades, been shaped by "an unprecedented tendency to merge urban design, architecture, and the police apparatus into a single, comprehensive security effort" (Davis, 1990, p. 224). CCTV cameras are among the most visible form of surveillance in this regard (Leman-Langlois, 2003), but built space itself has come to reflect a surveillant desire. Such securitization is evident in the virtual realm as well, connecting up with our earlier discussion of digital media. Online spaces are increasingly conceived of as analogous to urban or national space and as similarly under threat and in need of border security. The spatial nature of these processes is captured by Mark Andrejevic's (2007a) notion of "digital enclosure," which evokes early capitalist land enclosure and expropriation as a way of theorizing digital corporate surveillance. However, with the exception of studies of CCTV (Koskela, 2002; Wright, Heynen, & van der Meulen, 2015), feminist approaches to the gendered structuring and securitization of urban public space have remained largely absent in surveillance studies. Attention has more often (and in many ways justifiably) focused on how urban surveillance targets other marginalized communities. For example, as Sean P. Hier, Kevin Walby, and Josh Greenberg (2006) argue with respect to CCTV, "the surveillance gaze overwhelmingly falls upon individuals occupying morally laden categories of suspicion: youth, homeless persons, street traders and black men" (p. 232). This is a form of moral governance, they argue, that regulates urban space and can also be read back onto the embodied nature of surveillance discussed above.

Haggerty and Ericson (2000) situate their analysis of the surveillant assemblage in relation to the *flâneur*, the precariously bourgeois male observer who in the late nineteenth century moved on the margins of the commercialized spaces of the emerging modern European metropolis, and who became a prominent allegorical figure of modernity through the work of Walter Benjamin (1983). This figure, they argue, represented a kind of individualized gaze that was the exception to the increasingly tight networks of surveillance within which modern subjects were held; they offer him up as a valuable resource in thinking critically about surveillance. But as with so many discussions of the *flâneur*, who represented a profoundly *masculine* occupation of urban space, a consideration of gender is largely absent from their analysis. Women's occupation of public space in nineteenth-century Europe was much more precarious than that of men (Buck-Morss, 1986; D'Souza & McDonough, 2006). Indeed,

> the privilege of passing unnoticed in the city, particularly in the period in which the *flâneur* flourished – that is, the mid-nineteenth to the early twentieth century – was not accorded to women, whose presence on the streets would certainly be noticed. Not only that – as many historians of the period have pointed out, women in public, and particularly women apparently wandering without aim, immediately attract the negative stamp of the "non-respectable." It is no accident that the prostitute appears as the central female trope in the discourse of modernity. (Wolff, 2006, p. 19)

The figuring of women in public space as sexualized threat remains a staple of contemporary Western culture and highlights again the point made earlier – namely, that gendered relations of vision have rendered women both hyper- and in-visible (Massey, 1994). Much urban surveillance has been informal and enacted through the threat and practice of sexual assault, and as Gill Valentine (1989) has argued of the contemporary context, the resulting fear has structured women's gendered experience of public space (see also Mason & Magnet, 2012). Formal sanctions were also ever-present, with police and middle-class reform groups in the nineteenth century surveilling women in public spaces using a series of laws, in particular those targeting sex workers, as a mechanism for regulating women's access to public space (Walkowitz, 1992; van der Meulen, Durisin, & Love, 2013). The regulation of urban space was central to the broader projects for social hygiene detailed above. It was precisely on the grounds of maintaining bourgeois notions of property and propriety (Bannerji, Mojab, & Whitehead, 2001) that these gendered practices of urban life were instituted. When we look at surveillance practices in the city, therefore, we need to understand them as deeply and necessarily implicated in complex symbolic and material relations that constitute gendered social relations, rather than as practices through which gender-neutral forms of power are spatially (re)produced.

The literature on CCTV demonstrates this gendering of urban public space most explicitly, with research showing that women in fact often experience such "security" measures as deepening gender inequities just as much as they alleviate them (Koskela 2002, 2012). This is evident particularly in relation to marginalized women, with sex workers, for example, experiencing CCTV as especially repressive in its effects (Wright, Heynen, & van der Meulen, 2015). Many of the same concerns that prompted late-nineteenth-century projects for urban moral governance thus continue to hold sway. As surveillance studies scholars note, CCTV "works" – or is perceived to "work" – insofar as it is harnessed to a larger neoliberal project of transforming public, urban spaces from sites of heterogeneity (and, therefore, risk) into predictable, ordered, and homogeneous spaces of consumerism (Ruddick, 1996; Norris & Armstrong, 1999; Huey, Ericson, & Haggerty, 2005; Ruppert, 2006; Leman-Langlois, 2009). In this context, the lives of marginalized communities, identified as potentially "risky," are rendered especially precarious, their marginalization produced in part through practices of surveillance. In social contexts where fears about crime and public disorder are rife, the symbolic function of CCTV in *displaying* an attempt at crime control is arguably paramount, especially given that research shows that CCTV tends to simply displace crime to areas less visible to the camera's gaze (Leman-Langlois, 2008). When scholars do address the gendered nature of public camera surveillance, they tend to homogenize the experiences of women, seeing women as more accepting of surveillance on the grounds of safety. As Emily van der Meulen and Amanda Glasbeek (2013) have noted, however, women's experiences in fact vary depending on class, race, age, and social location, and have much to do as well with conditions of labour (see also Glasbeek & van der Meulen, 2014).

While women's public presence has been rendered especially hypervisible to the surveillant gaze, masculinity is also produced in part through gendered forms of urban surveillance, both informal (or "lateral" in Andrejevic's [2005] terms) and formal. This is perhaps most evident in relation to the surveillance and policing of gay men. The categories "homosexuality" and "heterosexuality" were themselves the product of the same late-nineteenth- and early-twentieth-century projects of moral regulation and social hygiene that we saw earlier, with medical professionals and police driving the emergence of sexual "deviance" as an object of concern and intervention, even as those so labelled were producing other forms of identity and subjectivity challenging social hygienic surveillance (Beachy, 2014). The regulation of same-sex desire produced a specific heterosexualized mode of urban masculinity (Chauncey, 1994; Bell & Valentine, 1995), with the policing of public sex (in parks or bathrooms, for example) the locus of surveillance in many contexts (Dangerous Bedfellows, 1996; Biber & Dalton,

2009; Walby, 2009). Indeed, bathrooms continue to be important for the disciplining of non-normative bodies and forms of sexuality, with formal and informal surveillance of trans and gender nonconforming people especially intense in public restrooms (Cavanagh, 2010).

Surveillance in these contexts is frequently repressive, but we should not lose sight of the multiple challenges and forms of resistance built on the appropriation of the gaze, including the "sousveillance" optimistically discussed in some surveillance studies literature (Mann & Ferenbok, 2013). Feminist activism going back to the nineteenth century has sought to stake a claim to public space, challenging the public/ private divide and the dynamics of the male gaze that have constituted space as threatening. We thus find instances of the *flâneuse* (D'Souza & McDonough, 2006) or the "lesbian *flâneur*" (Munt, 1995), and of artists who challenge the gendered nature of surveillance in public space (Robertson, 2008). We also find that looking and being looked at, while structured by gendered ways of seeing, offer possibilities for mutual pleasure that exceed that repressive structure. As David Bell (2009) puts it, surveillance is sexy, and we need "to think about whether the mobilization of exhibitionism can be read as ways of resisting surveillance" (p. 203). One virtue of the chapters in this book is that these forms of resistance and pleasure are never far from view.

Feminist scholarship and surveillance studies have engaged deeply with urban space, the public and the private, and the policing of identity. It is thus surprising that feminist approaches have remained relatively underdeveloped in surveillance studies. Especially in the final section of the book, but also elsewhere, the contributors offer important new perspectives on gender, surveillance, and urban space. The final three chapters thus trace the various ways in which surveillance increasingly governs urban spaces as well as the highly differentiated ways in which different bodies can occupy those spaces. Zoë Newman's chapter argues that in the surveillance of gay men in Toronto in the 1970s we see the stigmatization of queer sexuality at work but also other dynamics, including class and the demands of property development. This case study, she argues, also helps us rethink the role of media in relation to the surveillance of queer communities and spaces. Tuulia Law and Chris Bruckert turn to low-tech versions of surveillance in examining the experiences of workers in strip clubs and the ways in which their labour is monitored in order to manage risk. Their chapter engages with workers' own experiences with the web of surveillance in such venues and examines how workers themselves negotiate and resist its gendered and raced implications. Finally, Ian Warren, Kate Fitz-Gibbon, and Emma McFarlane focus on masculinity in tracing the workings of surveillance in Australia's night-time economies. They contend that strategies of risk management, implemented through human and technological forms of surveillance, replicate and reinforce normative conceptions of masculinity and violence.

Conclusion

Contemporary societies are shaped in myriad ways by surveillance, and, like all aspects of those societies, these systems of surveillance are deeply gendered. This is not a new insight. As we have shown, critical scholars have long argued that ways of seeing are structured along gendered lines, although in many cases these critics did not conceptualize these practices explicitly in terms of surveillance. Within the field of surveillance studies there is also a growing awareness of the need to bring gender into the heart of the analyses, although as yet these approaches remain somewhat on the margins. This book thus seeks to build on these perspectives, considering as well the ways in which gender is mediated through other forms of identity and subjectivity, such as race, sexuality, and gender expression. This is certainly not a comprehensive book (there are many other areas of surveillance studies where a gendered analysis would be welcome), and its focus on the Western, and especially Anglo-American, world leaves larger transnational and comparative frameworks to be developed. Together, though, the chapters that follow offer profound insights into the gendered dynamics of surveillance through empirical, theoretical, and conceptual case studies. We hope this book represents a significant step towards expanding the gaze.

REFERENCES

Aas, K. F. (2006). "The body does not lie": Identity, risk, and trust in technoculture. *Crime, Media, Culture, 2*(2), 143–158. http://dx.doi.org/10.1177/1741659006065401
Abu-Laban, Y. (2015). Gendering surveillance studies: The empirical and normative promise of feminist methodology. *Surveillance & Society, 13*(1), 44–56.
Ajana, B. (2013). *Governing through biometrics: The biopolitics of identity.* Houndmills, UK: Palgrave Macmillan. http://dx.doi.org/10.1057/9781137290755

Albrechtslund, A. (2008). Online social networking as participatory surveillance. *First Monday, 13*(3). http://dx.doi.org/10.5210/fm.v13i3.2142

Albrechtslund, A. (2012). Socializing the city: Location sharing and online social networking. In C. Fuchs, K. Boernsma, A. Albrechtslund, & M. Sandoval (Eds.), *Internet and surveillance: The challenges of Web 2.0 and social media* (187–197). New York, NY: Routledge.

Albrechtslund, A., & Dubbeld, L. (2005). The plays and arts of surveillance: Studying surveillance as entertainment. *Surveillance & Society, 3*(2/3), 216–221.

Amoore, L., & Hall, A. (2009). Taking people apart: Digitised dissection and the body at the border. *Environment and Planning D: Society and Space, 27*(3), 444–464. http://dx.doi.org/10.1068/d1208

Andrejevic, M. (2005). The work of watching one another: Lateral surveillance, risk, and governance. *Surveillance & Society, 2*(4), 479–497.

Andrejevic, M. (2007a). Surveillance in the digital enclosure. *Communication Review, 10*(4), 295–317. http://dx.doi.org/10.1080/10714420701715365

Andrejevic, M. (2007b). *iSpy: Surveillance and power in the interactive era.* Lawrence, KS: University Press of Kansas.

Bailey, J., Steeves, V., Burkell, J., & Regan, P. (2013). Negotiating with gender stereotypes on social networking sites: From "bicycle face" to Facebook. *Journal of Communication Inquiry, 37*(2), 91–112. http://dx.doi.org/10.1177/0196859912473777

Ball, K. (2006). Organization, surveillance, and the body: Towards a politics of resistance. In D. Lyon (Ed.), *Theorizing surveillance: The panopticon and beyond* (pp. 296–317). Cullompton, UK: Willan Publishing.

Ball, K., Green, N., Koskela, H., & Phillips, D. (2009). Surveillance studies needs gender and sexuality. *Surveillance & Society, 6*(4), 352–355.

Ball, K., Haggerty, K. D., & Lyon, D. (Eds.). (2012). *The Routledge handbook of surveillance studies.* New York, NY: Routledge.

Bannerji, H., Mojab, S., & Whitehead, J. (Eds.). (2001). *Of property and propriety: The role of gender and class in imperialism and nationalism.* Toronto, ON: University of Toronto Press.

Bauman, Z., & Lyon, D. (2013). *Liquid surveillance: A conversation.* Cambridge, MA: Polity Press.

Beachy, R. (2014). *Gay Berlin: Birthplace of a modern identity.* New York, NY: Alfred A. Knopf.

Beauchamp, T. (2009). Artful concealment and strategic visibility: Transgender bodies and the US state surveillance after 9/11. *Surveillance & Society, 6*(4), 356–366.

Bell, D. (2009). Surveillance is sexy. *Surveillance & Society, 6*(3), 203–212.

Bell, D., & Valentine, G. (Eds.). (1995). *Mapping desire.* New York, NY: Routledge.

Benjamin, W. (1983). *Charles Baudelaire: A lyric poet in the era of high capitalism.* London, UK: Verso.

Bentham, J. (1798). *Proposal for a new and less expensive mode of employing and reforming convicts.* London.

Berger, J. (1972). *Ways of seeing.* London, UK: Penguin Books.

Biber, K., & Dalton, D. (2009). Making art from evidence: Secret sex and police surveillance in the tearoom. *Crime, Media, Culture, 5*(3), 243–267. http://dx.doi.org/10.1177/1741659009346048

Bigo, D. (2006) Security, exception, ban and surveillance. In D. Lyon (Ed.), *Theorizing surveillance: The panopticon and beyond* (pp. 46–68). Portland, OR: Willan Publishing.

Brown, N., & Webster, A. (2004). *New medical technologies and society: Reordering life.* Cambridge, MA: Policy Press.

Browne, S. (2010). Digital epidermalization: Race, identity and biometrics. *Critical Sociology, 36*(1), 131–150. http://dx.doi.org/10.1177/0896920509347144

Browne, S. (2012). Everybody's got a little light under the sun: Black luminosity and the visual culture of surveillance. *Cultural Studies, 26*(4), 542–564. http://dx.doi.org/10.1080/09502386.2011.644573

Buck-Morss, S. (1986). The flâneur, the sandwichman, and the whore: The politics of loitering. *New German Critique, NGC, 39*(39), 99–140. http://dx.doi.org/10.2307/488122

Butler, J. (1990). *Gender trouble.* New York, NY: Routledge.

Butler, J. (1993). *Bodies that matter: On the discursive limits of "sex".* New York, NY: Routledge.

Callen, A. (1998). Ideal masculinities: An anatomy of power. In N. Mirzoeff (Ed.), *Visual cultural reader* (pp. 401–414). New York, NY: Routledge.

Cartwright, L. (1995). *Screening the body: Tracing medicine's visual culture.* Minneapolis, MN: University of Minnesota Press.

Cavanagh, S. (2010). *Queering bathrooms: Gender, sexuality, and the hygienic imagination.* Toronto, ON: University of Toronto Press.

Chauncey, G. (1994). *Gay New York: Gender, urban culture, and the making of the gay male world, 1890–1940.* New York, NY: Basic Books.

Conrad, K. (2009). Surveillance, gender, and the virtual body in the information age. *Surveillance & Society, 6*(4), 380–387.

Dangerous Bedfellows. (1996). *Policing public sex: Queer politics and the future of AIDS activism.* Boston, MA: South End Press.

Davis, M. (1990). *City of quartz: Excavating the future in Los Angeles.* London, UK: Verso.

Deleuze, G. (1992). Postscript on the societies of control. *October, 59*, 3–7.

Diamond, I., & Quinby, L. (Eds.). (1988). *Feminism and Foucault: Reflections on resistance*. Boston, MA: Northeastern University Press.

Didi-Huberman, G. (2003). *The invention of hysteria: Charcot and the photographic iconography of the Salpêtrière*. Cambridge, MA: MIT Press.

Doyle, A. (2011). Revisiting the synopticon: Reconsidering Mathiesen's "The Viewer Society" in the age of Web 2.0. *Theoretical Criminology, 15*(3), 283–299. http://dx.doi.org/10.1177/1362480610396645

D'Souza, A., & McDonough, T. (Eds.). (2006). *The invisible flâneuse? Gender, public space, and visual culture in nineteenth-century Paris*. Manchester, UK: Manchester University Press.

Dubrofsky, R. E. & Magnet, S. A. (Eds.). (2015). *Feminist surveillance studies*. Durham, NC: Duke University Press. http://dx.doi.org/10.1215/9780822375463

Dubrofsky, R. E., & Wood, M. M. (2014). Posting racism and sexism: Authenticity, agency, and self-reflexivity in social media. *Communication and Critical Cultural Studies, 11*(3), 282–287.

Elmer, G. (2003). A diagram of panoptic surveillance. *New Media & Society, 5*(2), 231–247. http://dx.doi.org/10.1177/1461444803005002005

Ezekiel, J., Allen, T., Brooks, S., Colvin, D., Graham, D., Graziano, G., … (2015). *Black women's lives matter*. Fairborn, OH: Authors.

Fiske, J. (1996). *Media matters: Race and gender in US politics*. Minneapolis, MN: University of Minnesota Press.

Fiske, J. (1998). Surveilling the city: Whiteness, the black man, and democratic totalitarianism. *Theory, Culture, & Society, 15*(2), 67–88. http://dx.doi.org/10.1177/026327698015002003

Foucault, M. (1977). *Discipline and punish: The birth of the prison* (A. Sheridan, Trans.). New York, NY: Vintage Books.

Fraser, N. (1992). Rethinking the public sphere: A contribution to the critique of actually existing democracy. In C. Calhoun (Ed.), *Habermas and the public sphere* (pp. 109–142). Cambridge, MA: The MIT Press.

Friedberg, A. (1993). *Window shopping: Cinema and the postmodern*. Berkeley, CA: University of California Press.

Fuchs, C., Boersma, K., Albrechtslund, A., & Sandoval, M. (Eds.). (2012). *Internet and surveillance: The challenges of Web 2.0 and social media*. New York, NY: Routledge.

Gandy, O. (1993). *The panoptic sort: A political economy of personal information*. Boulder, CO: Westview.

Gates, K. A. (2011). *Our biometric future: Facial recognition technology and the culture of surveillance*. New York, NY: NYU Press.

Glasbeek, A., & van der Meulen, E. (2014). The paradox of visibility: Gender, CCTV, and crime. In G. Balfour & E. Comack (Eds.), *Criminalizing women: Gender and (in)justice in neoliberal times* (pp. 219–235). Halifax, NS: Fernwood Publishing.

Haggerty, K. D. (2006). Tear down the walls: On demolishing the panopticon. In D. Lyon (Ed.), *Theorizing surveillance: The panopticon and beyond* (pp. 23–45). Portland, OR: Willan Publishing.

Haggerty, K. D., & Ericson, R. V. (2000). The surveillant assemblage. *British Journal of Sociology, 51*(4), 605–622. http://dx.doi. org/10.1080/00071310020015280

Haggerty, K. D. & Samatas, M. (Eds.). (2010). *Surveillance and democracy.* New York, NY: Routledge.

Halberstam, J. (2005). *In a queer time and place: Transgender bodies, subcultural lives.* New York, NY: NYU Press.

Haraway, D. J. (1991). *Simians, cyborgs, and women: The reinvention of nature.* New York, NY: Routledge.

Haraway, D. J. (1997). *Modest_Witness@Second_Millennium.FemaleMan©_ Meets_OncoMouse™: Feminism and technoscience.* New York, NY: Routledge.

Heyes, C. (2007). Cosmetic surgery and the televisual makeover: A Foucaldian feminist reading. *Feminist Media Studies, 7*(1), 17–32. http://dx.doi. org/10.1080/14680770601103670

Heynen, R. (2015). *Degeneration and revolution: Radical cultural politics and the body in Weimar Germany.* Leiden, Netherlands: Brill. http://dx.doi. org/10.1163/9789004276277

Hier, S. P. & Greenberg, J. (Eds.). (2009). *Surveillance: Power, problems, and politics.* Vancouver, BC: UBC Press.

Hier, S. P., Walby, K., & Greenberg, J. (2006). Supplementing the panoptic paradigm: Surveillance, moral governance, and CCTV. In D. Lyon (Ed.), *Theorizing surveillance: The panopticon and beyond* (pp. 230–244). Portland, OR: Willan Publishing.

hooks, b. (1992). *Black looks: Race and representation.* Boston, MA: South End Press.

Huey, L., Ericson, R. V., & Haggerty, K. D. (2005). Policing fantasy city. In D. Cooley (Ed.), *Re-imagining policing in Canada* (pp.140–208). Toronto, ON: University of Toronto Press.

Jakubowska, H. (2014). Gender verification in sport as a surveillance practice: An inside and outside perspective. *Surveillance & Society, 11*(4), 454–465.

Jansson, A., & Christensen, M. (Eds.) (2014). *Media, surveillance, and identity: Social perspectives.* New York, NY: Peter Lang.

Kahle, S. (2012). Reading the body on *House, M.D.*: Medical surveillance as a model of the social. *Communication Review, 15*(4), 274–293. http://dx.doi.org/10.1080/10714421.2012.728423

Kinsman, G., & Gentile, P. (2010). *The Canadian war on queers: National security as sexual regulation.* Vancouver, BC: UBC Press.

Kohler-Hausmann, J. (2007). "The crime of survival": Fraud prosecutions, community surveillance, and the original "welfare queen." *Journal of Social History, 41*(2), 329–354. http://dx.doi.org/10.1353/jsh.2008.0002

Koskela, H. (2002). Video surveillance, gender, and the safety of public urban space: "Peeping Tom" goes high tech? *Urban Geography, 23*(3), 257–278. http://dx.doi.org/10.2747/0272-3638.23.3.257

Koskela, H. (2003). "Cam era" – the contemporary urban panopticon. *Surveillance & Society, 1*(3), 292–313.

Koskela, H. (2006). "The other side of surveillance": Webcams, power, and agency. In D. Lyon (Ed.), *Theorizing surveillance: The panopticon and beyond* (pp. 163–181). Portland, OR: Willan Publishing.

Koskela, H. (2009). Hijacking surveillance? The new moral landscapes of amateur photographing. In K. F. Aas, H. O. Gundhus, & H. M. Lomell (Eds.), *Technologies of insecurity: The surveillance of everyday life* (pp. 147–167). Milton Park, UK: Routledge-Cavendish.

Koskela, H. (2012). "You shouldn't wear that body": The problematic of surveillance and gender. In K. Ball, K. D. Haggerty, & D. Lyon (Eds.), *The Routledge handbook of surveillance studies* (pp. 49–56). New York, NY: Routledge.

Leman-Langlois, S. (2003). The myopic panopticon: The social consequences of policing through the lens. *Policing and Society, 13*(1), 44–58.

Leman-Langlois, S. (2008). The local impact of police video surveillance on the social construction of security. In S. Leman-Langlois (Ed.), *Technocrime: Technology, crime, and social control* (pp. 27–45). Cullompton, UK: Willan Publishing.

Leman-Langlois, S. (2009). Public perceptions of camera surveillance. In W. Deisman et al., (Eds.), *A report on camera surveillance in Canada: Part one* (pp. 41–59). Kingston, ON: Surveillance Camera Awareness Network (SCAN). http://www.sscqueens.org/projects/scan

Lyon, D. (Ed.). (2003). *Surveillance as social sorting: Privacy, risk, and digital discrimination.* New York, NY: Routledge.

Lyon, D. (Ed.). (2006). *Theorizing surveillance: The panopticon and beyond.* Portland, OR: Willan Publishing.

Lyon, D. (2007). *Surveillance studies: An overview.* Cambridge, MA: Polity Press.

Magnet, S. A. (2011). *When biometrics fail: Gender, race, and the technology of identity*. Durham, NC: Duke University Press. http://dx.doi.org/10.1215/9780822394822

Magnet, S.A., & Rodgers, T. (2012). Stripping for the state: Whole body imaging technologies and the surveillance of othered bodies. *Feminist Media Studies*, 12(1), 101–118. http://dx.doi.org/10.1080/14680777.2011.558352

Mann, S., & Ferenbok, J. (2013). New media and the power politics of sousveillance in a surveillance-dominated world. *Surveillance & Society*, 11(1/2), 18–34.

Mason, C., & Magnet, S.A. (2012). Surveillance studies and violence against women. *Surveillance & Society*, 10(2), 105–118.

Massey, D. (1994). *Space, place, and gender*. Cambridge, MA: Polity Press.

Mathiesen, T. (1997). The viewer society: Michel Foucault's panopticon revisited. *Theoretical Criminology*, 1(2), 215–234. http://dx.doi.org/10.1177/1362480697001002003

Merleau-Ponty, M. (1958). *Phenomenology of Perception* (C. Smith, Trans.). London, UK: Routledge.

Monahan, T. (2009). Dreams of control at a distance: Gender, surveillance, and social control. *Cultural Studies, Critical Methodologies*, 9(2), 286–305. http://dx.doi.org/10.1177/1532708608321481

Mulvey, L. (1975). Visual pleasure and narrative cinema. *Screen*, 16(3), 6–18. http://dx.doi.org/10.1093/screen/16.3.6

Munt, S. (1995). The lesbian *flâneur*. In D. Bell & G. Valentine (Eds.), *Mapping desire: Geographies of sexualities* (pp. 114–125). London, UK: Routledge.

Murakami Wood, D. (2009). The "surveillance society": Questions of history, place, and culture. *European Journal of Criminology*, 6(2), 179–194. http://dx.doi.org/10.1177/1477370808100545

Norris, C., & Armstrong, G. (1999). *The maximum surveillance society: The rise of CCTV*. New York, NY: Berg.

Poster, M. (1990). *The mode of information: Poststructuralism and social context*. Cambridge, MA: Polity Press.

Robertson, K. (2008). "Try to walk with the sound of my footsteps": The surveillant body in contemporary art. *Communication Review*, 11(1), 24–41. http://dx.doi.org/10.1080/10714420801888393

Rose, H., & Rose, S. (2012). *Genes, cells, and brains: The Promethean promises of the new biology*. London, UK: Verso.

Ruddick, S. (1996). Constructing difference in public spaces: Race, class, and gender as interlocking systems. *Urban Geography*, 17(2), 132–151. http://dx.doi.org/10.2747/0272-3638.17.2.132

Ruppert, E. (2006). *The moral economy of cities: Shaping good citizens.* Toronto, ON: University of Toronto Press.

Sekula, A. (1986). The body and the archive. *October, 39*, 3–64.

Senft, T. M. (2008). *Camgirls: Celebrity and community in the age of social networking.* New York, NY: Peter Lang.

Showalter, E. (1985). *The Female Malady: Women, Madness, and English Culture, 1930–1980.* New York, NY: Pantheon Books.

Singel, R. (2003, 7 July). Funding for TIA all but dead. *Wired* (magazine). http://archive.wired.com/politics/law/news/2003/07/59606

Steenberg, L. (2013). *Forensic science in contemporary American popular culture: Gender, crime, and science.* New York, NY: Routledge.

Valentine, G. (1989). The geography of women's fear. *Area, 21*(4), 385–390.

van der Meulen, E., Durisin, E.M., & Love, V. (2013). Introduction. In E. van der Meulen, E.M. Durisin, & V. Love (Eds.), *Selling sex: Experience, advocacy, and research on sex work in Canada* (pp. 1–25). Vancouver, BC: UBC Press.

van der Meulen, E., & Glasbeek, A. (2013). *The gendered lens: A report on women's experiences with CCTV in Toronto.* Report, Ryerson University, ON, April.

van der Ploeg, I. (2003). Biometrics and the body as information: Normative issues in the socio-technical coding of the body. In D. Lyon (Ed.), *Surveillance as social sorting: Privacy, risk, and automated discrimination* (pp. 57–73). New York, NY: Routledge.

van der Ploeg, I. (2012). The body as data in the age of information. In K. Ball, K. D. Haggerty, & D. Lyon (Eds.), *The Routledge handbook of surveillance studies* (pp. 176–183). New York, NY: Routledge. http://dx.doi.org/10.4324/9780203814949.ch2_2_d

Vickery, J.R. (2014). Talk whenever, wherever: How the US mobile phone industry commodifies talk, genders youth mobile practices, and domesticates surveillance. *Journal of Children and Media, 8*(4), 387–403. http://dx.doi.org/10.1080/17482798.2014.960436

Walby, K. (2006). Risky spaces, algorithms and signifiers: Disappearing bodies and the prevalence of racialization in urban camera surveillance procedures. *Topia, 16*(Fall), 51–67.

Walby, K. (2009). "He asked me if I was looking for fags ...": Ottawa's National Capital Commission conservation officers and the policing of public park sex. *Surveillance & Society, 6*(4), 367–379.

Walkowitz, J. R. (1992). *City of dreadful delight: Narratives of sexual danger in late-Victorian London.* Chicago, IL: University of Chicago Press. http://dx.doi.org/10.7208/chicago/9780226081014.001.0001

Whitaker, R. (2006). A Faustian bargain? America and the dream of total information awareness. In K. Haggerty & R. Ericson (Eds.), *The new politics of surveillance and visibility* (pp. 141–170). Toronto, ON: University of Toronto Press.

Williams, L. (1992). When the woman looks. In G. Mast, M. Cohen, & L. Braudy (Eds.), *Film theory and criticism: Introductory readings* (4th ed., pp. 561–577). New York, NY: Oxford University Press.

Withers, A. J. (2012). *Disability politics and theory*. Halifax, NS: Fernwood Publishing.

Wolff, J. (2006). Gender and the haunting of cities (or, the retirement of the *flâneur*). In A. D'Souza & T. McDonough (Eds.), *The invisible flâneuse? Gender, public space, and visual culture in nineteenth-century Paris* (pp. 18–31). Manchester, UK: Manchester University Press.

Wright, J., Heynen, R., & van der Meulen, E. (2015). "It depends on who you are, what you are": "Community safety" and sex workers' experiences with surveillance. *Surveillance & Society 13*(2), 265–282.

Gender, Media, and Surveillance

Chapter 2

Data Doubles and Pure Virtu(e)ality: Headless Selfies, Scopophilia, and Surveillance Porn

LARA KARAIAN

Recently, I bought a cardigan that I *really* liked. It's a creamy off-white colour with yellow and black stripes. The written description doesn't do it justice; you need to see it to appreciate it. I particularly like how this cardigan looks on me when paired with a crisp, white, cotton, button-down shirt and tight, dark-blue skinny jeans, tucked into the perfect pair of knee-high leather boots. So does my partner, who describes the ensemble as my "hot for teacher" look. One day, while sporting this outfit (during reading week, what a waste!), I decided to document it using my iPhone and the full-length mirror in one of the washrooms at work. I then, somewhat hesitantly, posted my picture to Facebook. Not prone to self-documenting and sharing so-called "selfies," I briefly worried that my colleagues/Facebook friends would consider me vain and/or unprofessional for having done so. But in the end, and by virtue of some calculus not completely obvious to me, I decided the pleasures I stood to gain outweighed the risks.

"Selfies," such as the one described above, are self-portraits that are usually taken at arms-length or in a mirror, using a cellphone or digital camera, and then posted to social networking sites such as Facebook, Instagram, or Tumblr. They are by no means a new phenomenon, but simply a new manifestation of a long-seated practice of self-portraiture.[1] Fuelled by technological advances (cellphones with forward-facing cameras), new software (on-the-go mobile applications like Snapchat), and the desire to control one's image in an ever-expanding virtual domain, the selfie has become one of the "cultural markers of this generation" (Adewunmi, 2013, n.p.).[2] The selfie has met with mixed responses from those in the blogosphere and the mainstream media (Adewunmi, 2013; BBC News, 2013; Erickson, 2013). More specifically, the production of sexual/ized selfies by teens – referred to by some as "sexting" or "self-produced child pornography" (Leary, 2008) – has been the focus of intense interest and opprobrium among parents, pundits, child protection agencies, and those in the criminal justice system. In this context, where media-hyped concerns about safety and danger have become central, an increasingly instrumental range of policies and practices have developed that are intimately connected to systems of surveillance and that emphasize the protection of children and the extension of control over them, in real time and in virtual environments (Parton, 2006). In this chapter, I focus my gaze on the surveillance of teenagers' self-produced and consensually shared sexual/ized selfies by parents, psychiatrists, and popular culture – specifically, on Dr Phil's sexting segment in his "Crazy Teen Trends" series (2009).[3] I suggest that teenage girls who produce, post, and share sexual/ized selfies, and in particular headless selfies, may arguably and alternatively be viewed as surveillance-savvy agents who are using technology as a tool for performing desires and sexual subjectivity in ways that are informed by surveillance and that fly in the face of surveillance (Weibel, 2002; Koskela, 2004; McGrath, 2004; Andrejevic, 2007). In recognition of the "complex dialectics of watching and being watched" (Lyon, 2006a, pp. 4–5), I argue that teens who employ "safe sexting," in that they actively remove distinguishing features from their selfies, can be seen as mobilizing voyeurism and exhibitionism in resistance to adult, as well as lateral, surveillance practices (Andrejevic, 2005; Bell, 2009). Moreover, I suggest that those who surveil teen sexters can be driven by motivations that lie beyond our (and indeed their own) normal range of perception, such as the erotic pleasure derived from surveillance and the desire to reify certain girls' virtue in real time and in cyberspace.

I should note, however, that the goal of this chapter is not necessarily to condemn adults for deriving pleasure from looking at youths' sexual imagery, any more than it is to condemn the consensual creation or distribution of that imagery by the youth themselves.[4] Rather, the focus of my critique is on surveillance as "a viable mode of social ordering, manag[ing] and control[ling]" (Lyon, 2006b, p. 49) certain adolescent girls' virtu(e)ality. I use this neologism to signify the extent to which adult surveillors have simultaneously deinteriorized teenage girls – by denying that their expressive behaviours may be motivated by sexual desires – and extended their surveillance into the virtual realm. Acknowledging these moves and motivations, I suggest, affords us an opportunity to blur and resist binarized notions of virtuous and wanton, sexual subjects and sexual objects, real and virtual space, and protectionist and punitive policies, as well as vilified and valorized gazes.

To develop my analysis of the surveillance of sexual/ized selfies, I adopt and play with Kevin Haggerty and Richard Ericson's (2000) notion of the surveillant assemblage. Referencing the conceptual tools of Gilles Deleuze and Félix Guattari, Haggerty and Ericson suggest that "we are witnessing a convergence of what were once discrete surveillant systems to the point that we can now speak of an emerging 'surveillant assemblage'" (2000, p. 606). The surveillant assemblage is characterized as "a visualizing device that brings into the visual register a host of heretofore opaque flows of auditory, scent, chemical, visual, ultraviolet and informational stimuli," much of which "pertains to the human body, and exists beyond our normal range of perception" (p. 611). Energized by the desire for order, control, discipline, profit, and voyeuristic entertainment value, these assemblages operate "by abstracting human bodies from their territorial settings and separating them into a series of discrete flows" (p. 606). These flows, they suggest, "are then reassembled into distinct 'data doubles' which can be scrutinized and targeted for intervention" (p. 606), resulting in "a decorporealized body, a 'data double' of pure virtuality" (p. 611).

Drawing on, and admittedly taking liberties with, Haggerty and Ericson's notion of the surveillant assemblage, this chapter begins by analysing an instance wherein parental, psychiatric, and entertainment interests converge to surveil, decorporealize, and discipline adolescent bodies and their digital expression. I suggest that Dr Phil's surveillance of a teenage girl who consensually created and distributed sexual/ized selfies traffics in a similar "aesthetics of desire" (Kincaid, 1998, p. 288) to that which it seeks to condemn, and in doing so makes visible the scopophilia – the "erotic pleasure related to seeing" (Groth, 2012, p. 321) – that may energize and be derived from the scrutinizing and disciplining of such expression.[5] Thus, I suggest that by producing its own set of "data doubles," the *Dr. Phil* show not only brings taboo youth sexuality into the visual register, but also reveals the flow of sexual stimuli that may animate adults' surveillance of adolescent sexual expression, a flow that would otherwise go unacknowledged. The chapter then shifts gears somewhat: I suggest that we take a closer look at teenage girls' headless sexual/ized selfies in order to consider the ways in which they evidence a subversion of the culture of surveillance. To do so I locate "hot and headless" selfies in the context of the "pornification of surveillance" (Bell, 2009) and consider how the "proliferation of porn and porn-like images, practices and aesthetics [makes] available a new idiom that [girls] can … [redeploy] subversively … against normative (and normalizing) surveillance" (Bell, 2009, p. 205).

Dr Phil and the Surveillance of Sexual/ized Selfies

The indisputably controversial status of the sexual/ized selfie is evidenced by the breadth of media coverage peddling hyperbolic constructions of the risks of online sexual expression (Karaian, 2012, 2014; Lee et al., 2013; Hasinoff, 2015; Karaian & Van Meyl, 2015). My earlier examination of the images and texts accompanying news-media, fictional, legal, and child protection/crime control responses to sexting demonstrate that the figure of the "sexter" most often depicted is that of a white, thin, well-dressed, usually blonde or light- and long-haired, feminine teenage girl, and that the message imparted is that these girls should exhibit more self-respect, self-control, self-censor-ship, and ultimately abstinence from sexting as a means of preventing sexting's purported harms (Karaian, 2012, 2014). This demographic of teenage girls is featured on daytime talk shows such as the *Tyra Banks Show* (2009), in dramas such as *Law and Order: SVU* (2009), an in fictional programing aimed specifically at a younger audiences such as in *90210* (2010). In each of these examples, the female sexter is met with some combination of awe and derision. Below I consider how, why, and to what effect Dr Phil's surveillance of teenage sexting merges paternalistic, psychiatric, and media scrutiny of the practice and mimics the aesthetics of the very "child porn" it seeks to cen-sure. In addition, I consider how an acknowledgment of the scopo-philic dimensions of the consumption of, and attempt to control, the eroticised virtu(e)al girl blurs the distinction between the vilified and valorized gaze.

   Dr Phil begins his sexting episode by interviewing the parents of a twelve-year-old, white, middle-class girl who, according to the web-site's description of the episode, "sends risqué text messages." Sitting on stage with Dr Phil, the girl's parents relay having "caught" their daughter after she had taken pictures of herself in a bikini and sent the images to her boyfriend. They also apparently "discovered" text mes-sages including questions such as "Do you really want to kiss?" and "Do you want to [expletive]?" The parents also describe the distribu-tion of an image of their daughter in her bra and panties (which we later learn was taken by a friend while she posed in the school change room) and "a video on her phone where she was dressed up like a prostitute," apparently "with short shorts and her cleavage showing."

Dr Phil begins by asking the girl's father what he thinks about this. Choking back tears, the father laments that he has a twelve-year-old who talks and dresses as "unacceptably" as she does and adds, "even for an eighteen-year-old to be doing these things is ..." He never completes the sentence; rather, he rather trails off, looks down, and shakes his head before eventually admitting he doesn't know how to control the behaviour. When Dr Phil asks the girl's mother what she thinks is going on, she claims that access to a cellphone and requests for pictures make her daughter feel good about herself. She adds that she does not believe her daughter's behaviour is sexual but merely attention-seeking, although it attracts the "wrong" attention, for her daughter has been called a "slut" and a "whore." When Dr Phil asks the parents what their daughter thinks of this, the father claims that the daughter has said, "It doesn't mean what it looks like." Both parents reference her as having claimed, "It's not a big deal," "All the kids are doing it," and "This is just the way people talk now" – claims that are supported to some extent by studies that have found that the prevalence of teens' voluntary involvement in sexting varies from 4 to 30 per cent (Lenhart, 2009; Englander, 2012, p. 2); that girls and boys sext at almost equal rates to one another (Lenhart, 2009; National Campaign to Prevent Teen and Unplanned Pregnancy, 2008; Peskin, 2013); and that the rates of sexting are the same across white, racialized, and ethnic minority youth (Peskin, 2013).[6]

Ultimately, after claiming to have assessed everything the parents provided him with, including her "evaluations" and "that sort of thing" (read *images*?), Dr Phil talks to the daughter one-on-one. Before doing so, however, he informs the viewing audience that this is necessary because of the legal consequences, such as child pornography charges, that may flow from her actions. The camera then cuts to a backstage room, where we see the girl sitting in a blue armchair. Her head and face are not in the frame – to "respect her privacy." Instead we see the tips of her dark brown shoulder-length hair and her exposed white neck and clavicles. She is wearing a loose, green, scoop-necked, short-sleeve shirt and black or dark-blue jeans. The eye is drawn to a small microphone pinned to the neckline of her shirt between her breasts. The camera jumps between images of her headless body seated in a chair and a close-up of her hands clasped together between her legs.

Once the interview begins, the camera angle shifts again so that we are looking at the back of the girl's head and shoulders and at all of Dr Phil, who is seated in a chair facing her.

When Dr Phil asks the girl what she thinks about the issue, she provides a completely different answer from what she had provided to her parents: "I think," she says, "that the pictures that I sent they're not right, but some of them were okay because they were of my face, but other pictures that I sent that they were, like, unacceptable and wasn't right." Dr Phil then asks her to be more specific about why the pictures they're talking about are unacceptable: "The ones where you're not fully dressed. The ones where you're in kind of a sexy pose, or, whatever." At this point, the camera once again cuts to her clasped hands between her legs and rests there while she answers. We can see her chipped red nail polish and an obviously fake diamond-crusted band on one finger. The colour of the polish is brazen. The chipped state of her nails is now "in," as are "visible bra straps [and] glaringly obvious roots" (Ryzik, 2008, n.p.); both signifying, until recently, "drug addiction, manual labor or pure laziness" (n.p.), as well as – most importantly for our purposes – female sexual impropriety. The diamond-crusted ring is gauche, and noticeably not on her ring finger. Contrasted with the smallish, white, female hands, we see "the mixing of the sexual with the nonsexual … adult with child signifiers … work[ing] together to intensify the oxymoronic nature of the subject" (Khan, 2011, p. 304). Soon, a lengthy but revealing exchange ensues between Dr Phil and the girl regarding why her pictures were "inappropriate":

GIRL: Because it shows too much of me, and it looks not appropriate [cut to her father wiping a tear away from one of his eyes].
DR PHIL: Tell me what that means, not appropriate. Why is it not okay to send those?
G.: Because it's illegal, and it's too much and you shouldn't, like, be sending stuff like that when you're younger [cut to her hands between her legs].
D.P.: Why did you do it if you didn't know it was ok?
G.: Because my friend wanted me to.
    […]
D.P.: But you could have said, "Oh my gosh I'm not going to do that. People might see them and think bad things about me." Why did you do it even though you knew it probably wasn't a good idea? Do you

have the ability to tell your friend "No"? [Dr Phil asks with one finger along the side of his face and other resting (lasciviously?) on the inside of his lower lip]

G.: I think that my friend, like. A lot of my friends have a big mouth and they like to use it a lot. Like me. Except for, I mean, they would probably say something about me and I would probably lose that friend.

D.P.: If you wouldn't do what they wanted you to?

G.: Yes [cut to mom rolling her eyes and looking unconvinced].

D.P.: Are you afraid that someone would look at those pictures and think that *you're a bad girl*? [Emphasis added]

G.: Um ... well ... people said that about me in second grade [it is obvious that she keeps speaking here but the rest of what she says it edited out]. [...]

D.P.: Are they [her parents] right?

G.: Yes ... [there is a hint of some other sentiment in this answer, one that I would refer to as hesitation or even disagreement. I believe this prompt's Dr Phil's rephrasing of the question].

D.P.: So you agree with them?

G.: [slightest pause] Yeah.

D.P.: Cause you don't want to be doing this [more of a statement than a question].

G.: Uh uh [shakes her head from side to side].

D.P.: Because once that picture's out there you have no control over it ... If *you weren't involved in it then it wouldn't be out there*. [Emphasis added]

Ultimately, Dr Phil ends the segment by diagnosing the girl as suffering from "poor self-esteem" and "low ego strength." He claims it's good that they're getting to this early enough to intervene. He then delivers the following assessment:

I truly believe that she has some neurological involvement here ... I think the parts of her brain that controls the inhibition centers are probably not as active as they need to be, which is something that could be dealt with. *I strongly believe this: This is not about sex*; I think it is about attention ... I think we need to map her brain, which is not an invasive procedure ... Then I think we need to look at her hormonally, biochemically, and then talk about what needs to happen with her therapeutically. This is one of those things that you can turn around, but you've got to jump on this with both feet. I wouldn't trust her from here to the edge of this stage with a boy or a cell phone until this gets done. [Emphasis in the original]

There is much going on in the above-cited images, exchange, and assessment, not the least of which is a pathologization and a responsibilization of the girl (rather than those who redistributed her image without her consent) for failing to manage the risks of digital sexual expression (see Karaian, 2014; LaMarre & Sutherland, 2014). More interesting, for our purposes, however, is the extent to which the above exchange and its accompanying visuals expose adult anxiety about white, middle-class, good girls being (dis)graced by their sexual impropriety and thus marred as "white trash" (Karaian, 2014; see also Linnemann et al., 2013). This is evidenced in part by the parents' expressed concerns about their daughter looking like a "prostitute" and being called a "whore" and by Dr Phil's concern that others would think she was a "bad girl" (later, he himself deems her uninhibited to the point of being untrustworthy). The girl's parents work diligently with Dr Phil to deny any sexual motivations on the girl's part. The mother refers to the behaviour as driven by a desire for attention, while Dr Phil reframes the girl's behaviours in desexualized medical terms, ultimately scrutinizing her as an object of "surveillance medicine" – a patient "before [her] time" (Elliot, 2009, p. 36) – who is subsequently exposed to additional medical intervention. Indeed, whether or not a sexual motivation informed the daughter's decision to create and share her "provocative" imagery will likely never be known. The girl is never asked if sexual desire was a motivating factor in her decision to sext; indeed, she is described as claiming that her sext "doesn't mean what it looks like" – as denying that her image is sexual and/or her behaviour is sexually motivated. In this context, however, it seems fair to surmise that had sexual desire informed her decision, such an answer would not have been well received. Her claim then may be equally read as one of self-preservation in the face of parental discipline. So in the end, the girl's agreement with her parents and Dr Phil about the inappropriateness of those of her images that depicted more than her face appears more like a last-ditch effort to "save face," having been publicly shamed for digitally displaying her body, if not her desires. Ultimately, however, the episode ends by reframing the girl as having come through this ordeal with her pure virtu(e)ality intact. For instance, just prior to delivering his assessment, Dr Phil claims:

First off, in so many ways, you have absolutely hit the daughter lottery … [W]hat a beautiful *little girl*, I mean, [turns to the studio audience] I'm sorry you all can't see her but this is a *precious* young woman. I mean, she really is.

And, she has a *warmth* about her, and a *vulnerability* about her that is *so good*. I mean ... there's so much more right here than there is wrong. [Emphasis added]

Of course, via Dr Phil's backroom cameras and my own description of the images these cameras produced, we *have* seen the girl whom Dr Phil further desexualizes by describing her in simultaneously childish and paternalistic terms (precious/little/vulnerable/good/warm). In fact, not only have Dr Phil and I provided our respective audiences with a glimpse of the girl, but we have both also trafficked in a similar "aesthetics of desire" (Kincaid, 1998, p. 288) to those which the girl's parents and Dr Phil seek to censor, and which I seek to uncensor. In doing so, we've revealed the paradox that underlies the surveillance of selfies: by obsessively focusing on protecting children, we are "saturat[ing] children with a sexual discourse that inevitably links children, sexuality, and erotic appeal" (Kincaid, 1998, p. 101), all the while denying how "eroticizing exists in symbiotic relationship with sanitizing and ... veiling and ... exposing exist in an encircling doublespeak" (p. 102).[7] Where Dr Phil and I diverge, however, is with regard to our willingness to acknowledge the possibility that the girl is a sexually desiring subject and, moreover, that those who surveil her digital expression may have been motivated by, or derived erotic pleasure from, our respective surveillance of her sexual/ized selfie (or the surveillance of the surveillance of these selfies). That is, I am suggesting that by inciting her parents to describe the content of their daughter's sexual texts and images, by referencing the language in her texts and the content of her images, and, finally, by (re)producing these in a sexually heightened yet unacknowledged (or acknowledged in my case) context – one that eroticizes images of a headless girl with her hands between her legs – this episode unwittingly (and this chapter not so unwittingly) exposes the false assumption that "an a priori split exists between the voyeurism of the many and the voyeurism of the few" (Metzl, 2004, p. 417); between the vilified gaze of the peeping Tom and valorized gaze of the doctor cum entertainer. As Jonathan Metzl (2004) argues, "both American popular culture and American psychiatry would benefit from rethinking the complexity of their positions in relation to each other in the ever-changing dialectic of browser and browsed" (p. 429). But unlike Metzl, who suggests that by focusing on the voyeur's direct observations we lose "a theory for understanding the unseen, the unacknowledged, and other blind spots that [fall] outside of [our] gaze" (2004, p. 425),

I suggest here that such a focus reveals how she who takes pleasure in being seen is condemned and controlled, while her caring middle-class parents and the medical professionals who surveil and subsequently traffic in the same verbal and visual content and aesthetics as her are idealized (see also Khan, 2011).[8]

Hot and Headless: Surveillance Subverted?

The increased surveillance of girls and their sexual/ized selfies is often couched in rhetoric that defines girls as victims of pornonormativity. While sexual expression may indeed be circumscribed by the conventions of mainstream porn, I have suggested above that sexual/ized selfies may also offer evidence of teenage girls' sexual subjectivity and that adults' surveillance of these selfies may expose implicit and unacknowledged stimuli and desires. Here I shift my focus somewhat and suggest that teenage girls' self-produced "hot and headless" selfies can be seen as evidence of both their surveillance savviness and their subversion of the culture of surveillance. In asserting this, I share with David Bell (2009), whose work has influenced this section, that while I, and indeed my readers, may be ambivalent about some of my upcoming claims, such judgment "should not stop us from at least considering the possibilities of a resistance that knowingly deploys the 'master's tools' and which brings to the surface, plays with, contests and resists the voyeurism and exhibitionism argued to be latent in what Tabor calls the 'algebra of surveillance'" (2001, p. 203). As such, I briefly consider the headless selfie as an instance wherein the girl is "shooting back [at the male producers of much mainstream porn]" (Steve Mann, in Bell, 2009, p. 210). In doing so, I argue that she can be seen as both "denaturaliz[ing] and disrupt[ing] the authorized uses and 'flow' of surveillance" (Bell, 2009, p. 210), as well as resisting both the criminalization of culture (Presdee, 2000) and "regimes of shame" (Koskela, 2004, p. 207) that would seek to discipline her and reify her pure virtu(e)ality.

Feminists have long critiqued the exclusion of women's heads from images and artistic representations as evidence of men's sexual objectification of women resulting in a toxic environment wherein girls and women are denied their subjectivity and thus become knowable as violable. Given this, it begs asking whether headless sexual/ized selfies can be seen as anything other than dehumanizing and decorporealizing entities rife for consumption and control. I suggest that they *can* be and that this is possible if we focus our gaze on what has been added to the frame, namely, the girl's outstretched arm. For example, in 2012, a parent from Kansas City took umbrage at a sculpture, titled "Accept or Reject," of a headless woman with exposed breasts snapping a self-portrait of herself. Her opprobrium resulted in a grand jury investigation into whether the city was promoting obscenity to its minors (Jeltsen, 2012). In a blog post about the resulting controversy, Amy Hasinoff (2012) asks, "Why is a statue depicting self-objectification more offensive than artwork objectifying women created by male artists?" Hasinoff astutely suggests that the problem for some stems from the fact that this statue, unlike classic female nudes depicted in a range of artistic media, represents an active sexual subject rather than a passive nude object. "Some news coverage," she writes, "blurs out the statue's exposed breasts, but I don't think that's really what people feel is offensive about it. Instead they should censor the statue's outstretched arm with the camera – the act of choosing to represent herself is what seems to be the problem" (http://amyhasinoff.wordpress.com/category/sexting).

I agree fully with Hasinoff's reading and suggest that the headless sexual/ized selfie is not only a practice of self-representation but also one of re-embodiment and resistance, in opposition to the decorporealizing and desexualizing efforts and effects of the surveillance of girls' digital sexual expression. That is, the inclusion of the arm in the frame of the headless selfie marks the image as one of "user-generated content" and in doing so fills in the absent subjectivity of the decapitated girl.[9] User-generated content can be seen as turning technology into a mirror (Strathern, 2004) (indeed, those who take selfies often aim their technology onto an actual mirror), depicting the photographer as simultaneously object and subject of her self-representation. This is not to suggest that a girl's visual representation offers a false self that is distinguishable from her pure humanity; rather, she, as a sexual subject, is "mediating between the embodied self and the 'I' that is simultaneously present in the virtual realm" (Koskela, 2004, p. 208, citing Higgins et al., 1999, p. 115). The girl who "generates" literally and figuratively poses a challenge to the pure, virtuous, and neurologically challenged girl in the medicalized and pop-cultural panopticism advanced by Dr Phil. With her arm, it can be argued, she refuses modesty and obedience and reveals her private life as well as at least one small aspect of her sexual self.

This contention challenges the more popular move to dismiss girls who expose themselves as suffering from "false consciousness" under patriarchy and late capitalism, or as affected by "whore-envy" brought on by a purportedly hypersexualized culture (Papadopoulos, 2010). And indeed, although both surveillance and our cultural context work to normalize human bodies (Koskela, 2004), a range of post-structural, Third Wave feminist, critical adolescent, and sociological literature also recognizes the agency of youth and their ability to navigate, affect, and appropriate both their environment and its surveillant technologies and techniques through their choices and behaviours. In fact, when we get the rare opportunity to hear what youth think about the practice of sexting, we see that the objectifying image may hold less power than adults endow it with. For instance, when teens participating in focus groups[10] on this topic were asked, "How are texts used differently from photos in sexting?" they responded with the following:

WILLIAM [18, LOWER MERION]: Photo sexting is done more in middle school when you just get this technology and you're horny.

FARRAH [17, LOWER MERION]: As you get older, kids use raunchy texts more. They're things kids wouldn't want to say in person. But they can really send the wrong message.

WILLIAM: If a girl sent me a picture of her boobs, well, obviously I'd like to show it to some friends. But I wouldn't show them a raunchy text from her because that would be awkward. Sexually charged language is more intimate, more private.

ZOE [18, LOWER MERION]: We see virtual images all day long, so if someone sends you an image, it loses the identity of the person. It's just a picture.

WILLIAM: And usually the face is not in it. (*New York Times*, 2011)

Staying for the moment with these comments regarding facelessness and the loss of identity, I suggest that if the inclusion of the girl's arm in the frame of her selfie doesn't persuade you of my argument that girls' sexualized selfies can be seen as resistance to surveillance culture, then maybe her headless torso will. That is, although the headless woman, and by extension the absence of her eyes and face, has long been lamented as proof positive that the male gaze does not want to be challenged, or to be looked back at, I suggest that girls' active omission of their faces and heads from their selfies is its own form of resistance to the surveillant gaze. She is not "looking back" at those who are deriving voyeuristic pleasures from her image; but at the same time, she is denying those same voyeurs their *disciplinary* pleasure (which may itself be eroticized).

Because she has cut off her head and "lost her identity" – as the youth above claim she has done – her selfie is "just a picture" and not a disciplinary tool. The "unthinking" headless girl, who should have known better than to express her sexuality online, becomes knowable as a surveillance-savvy and unpunishable "unidentifiable" sexual subject. She can be seen not as denying her individuality but rather as evading castigation. Because her torso is headless, the selfie taker can be known as resisting the "disappearance of disappearance" (Haggerty & Ericson, 2006, p. 619) – that is, as bucking against the increasing difficulty that individuals face to maintain their anonymity or to escape the monitoring of social institutions. Moreover, by claiming her right to the erotic in an erotophobic or erotonormative culture, she can be understood as "confronting the limits of what is considered morally, ethically or legally acceptable behaviour, [and] asking who gets to decide what is acceptable, and … what's at stake in setting the bounds of acceptability in this way" (Bell, 2009, p. 211).

Surveilling the Surveillors: Sexuali/ized Selfies and Cybertip.ca

Each generation invents new technologies and media, develops new spaces, draws new borders, reimagines the aesthetic and the erotic, and refines notions of sexual agency and subjectivity. This does not happen in neat, linear steps but rather within messy pleasure/power dynamics wherein the erotics of seeing and being seen are politically complex. Central to this dynamic is the role of the media, which amplify and project a variety of new trends and risks facing children. In the case of sexual/ized selfies, this amplification is intensified by the increasing number of anti-sexting child crime control and child protection measures that expressly denounce volitional teenage sexting and encourage the reporting of adolescents who self-produce and share "child pornography" (Karaian, 2012, 2014). Cybertip.ca – Canada's national tip line for reporting the online sexual exploitation of children and a subsidiary of the Canadian Centre for Child Protection (CCCP) – is one key tool for such reporting. Despite Cybertip.ca's original focus on child sexual abuse and exploitation, the CCCP's recent emphasis on anti-sexting initiatives and its adherence to a Criminal Code definition of "child pornography" together mean that consensually produced and shared teenage sexts fall within its protectionist scope. Coupled with new mandatory reporting requirements imposed on Internet providers in 2011,[11] it takes no great stretch of the imagination to predict an increased reporting of consensually produced and shared sexual/ized selfies. In fact, the National Center for Missing and Exploited Children in the United States is now excluding young people who have uploaded their images from its analyses of children identified in illegal images, for self-produced images were distorting their data (SPIRTO, 2013, p. 4).

Cybertip is undoubtedly an important resource for addressing harmful instances of exploitation, but it may also be serving as a tool for discipline and control. By making would-be producers of sexual imagery aware of the risk that they may be reported, potential producers of sexual imagery are being encouraged to self-surveil and self-censor. Indeed, the fact that anyone can anonymously report a person who produces, possesses, or distributes self-produced "child pornography" raises the spectre of synoptic public surveillance – surveillance of the few by the many (Mathiesen, 1997). While the Cybertip website does not explicitly enumerate the potential consequences of reporting, anecdotal evidence suggests that in some instances parents or guardians of youths who self-produce and distribute sexual imagery may be notified and the threat of criminalization used as a means to ensure that youth conform to adults' sexual norms. These threats are all the more egregious given that the CCCP's Internet safety initiatives do not acknowledge the affordances of adolescent sexual expression, nor do they acknowledge the existence of a private use exemption preventing the application of child pornography charges in instances where sexual images are self-produced and shared in ways that meet the exemption's parameters (*R. v. Sharpe*, 2001).

The CCCP has acknowledged receiving tips regarding youths' self-produced sexual imagery, which they refer to as self/peer exploitation. In response they recently released their *Self/Peer Exploitation Resource Guide* (CCCP, 2012), a self-described tool for families, schools, and law enforcement to effectively identify and respond to this "emerging child exploitation issue" (See Karaian, 2015). Having defined self/peer exploitation as synonymous with sexting, consensual or otherwise, the guide, much like the *Dr. Phil* episode considered above, brings taboo youth sexuality into the visual register and raises questions about the scopophilic dimensions of its surveillance. For instance, in an effort to acknowledge variation in instances of "self/peer exploitation," the guide suggests that adult responders determine the nature, intent, and extent of the violations (i.e., the degree of sexual explicitness), whether an impulsive or malicious intent was involved (note that the guide makes no room for reasoned and calculated production and distribution (CCCP, 2012, p. 6). The guide goes on to suggest that, if possible, the responder should not view the images or videos in question (p. 7), but that in order to provide proper support, school personnel ought to select and adapt the questions provided in the guide depending on who they are speaking to. These questions include:

> Can you tell me what you were wearing when the picture(s)/video(s) was taken?
> Can you describe what parts of your body were exposed?
> Were you involved in any type of sexual behaviours when the picture(s)/video(s) was taken? (CCCP, 2012, p. 11)

While this line of questioning is framed as a means to ensure a measured response to the particular circumstances at hand, as has been argued above, the detail required to gauge a response allows for a different, if unacknowledged, intent and effect. As James Kincaid (1998) argues in his now seminal text, *Erotic Innocence: The Culture of Child Molesting*, through these stories of child abuse and (self)-exploitation, "we find ourselves forced (permitted) to speak of just what they [in this case children] are doing; we take a good, long look at what they are doing. We denounce it all loudly but never have done with it, and are back to denouncing it the next day, not ignoring the details. We reject this ... activity with such automatic indignation that the indignation comes to seem almost like pleasure" (p. 7).

Conclusion

In this chapter I have reconsidered the relationship between sexual/ized selfies, scopophilia, and the sexualization of surveillance, as well as binarized notions of virtuous and wanton, sexual subjects and sexual objects, real and virtual space, protectionist and punitive policies, and vilified and valorized gazes. In doing so I have sought to re/view headless selfies, re/present the teens who post and share them, and expose the unacknowledged erotic motivations and pleasures that are potentially derived from surveillance. This chapter can be understood as a product of what porn studies scholar Linda Williams refers to as "on/scenity" – "the gestures by which a culture brings on to its public arena the very organs, acts, bodies, and pleasures that have heretofore been designated ob/scene and kept literally off-scene" (2004, p. 3) – and as a mode of resisting the social ordering, managing, and controlling of adolescent girls' virtu(e)ality.

ACKNOWLEDGMENTS

This work was supported by the Social Science and Humanities Research Council of Canada.

NOTES

1 See http://famousselfportraits.tumblr.com.
2 The term was coined by Jim Krause (2005) in his book *Photo Idea Index*.
3 For the purposes of this chapter, "teenager" refers to youth between the ages of 13 and 17. Alternately, I refer to teenagers as youth, young people, and minors. I use sexual/ized here to draw attention to two key conceptual issues: that sexual/ized selfies are not inherently sexual, nor are they always intended to be sexual by the teens who produce them. Rather, as with any other image, they are polysemic and come to be seen and known as sexual, or alternatively, denied as such, by the adults who surveille and even reproduce the images in different contexts (i.e., the courtroom, popular media). This is evidenced by the widespread and problematic conflation of nudity, and even partial nudity, with sexuality in the legal and extralegal responses to minors' self-produced imagery (Cover, 2003), as well as by the fact that girls who photograph and share images of themselves in bikinis have been deemed "sexually lascivious" and therefore subject to child pornography prosecutions (see Karaian, 2012). I also use the term sexual/ized to highlight the extent to which those who are surveilled by adults are often those who are white, middle-class, heterosexual "good girls." This, I suggest, evidences a popular belief that *subjects* are *sexual* whereas *objects* are *sexualized*. Thus, the use of sexual/ized in this context is meant to suggest a process of sexualization that is political and that reifies some "good girls" as objects of protectionism in opposition to their knowing and exploitable "Other." As will be demonstrated, attention to these distinctions is necessary, given the ambivalent relationship that adult surveillors appear to have with the idea that white, heterosexual, middle-class girls can be sexually desiring agents who may actively

choose to digitally express their sexuality (Karaian, 2012, 2014; Hasinoff, 2015).

4 As Kincaid (1998) writes in *Erotic Innocence*, "The erotic feelings we have towards children are not, in themselves, a problem – or at least not a problem we can't handle. Becoming part of that problem is the solution. Denial does nobody any good and drives the desire into the lying, scapegoating babble, where it thrives and does terrible harm" (p. 288). Indeed, drawing on this contention, there exists a body of critical literature on the harms of child pornography *laws* for both youth and adults (see Adler, 2001), and specifically the constitutionality of the possession of child pornography (excluding images depicting the commission of a sexual crime against a child). See, generally, Persky and Dixon (2001).

5 Scopophilia – also defined as the "love of looking" – has arguably "ushered in yet more surveillance and monitoring," as is suggested by Haggerty and Ericson (2006), who, citing the work of David Lyon (2006b), suggest that the effect of the "intrinsically pleasant act" of viewing is evidenced by "the increasing public prominence of formerly private actions, combined with the cultural conception that the uninhibited scrutiny of others is acceptable" (p. 28).

6 In citing these statistics, however, I fully acknowledge a range of methodological issues that plague statistics on the true prevalence and nature of sexting. See Lounsbury, Mitchell, and Finkelhor (2011).

7 For a consideration of academics' complicity in the proliferation of sites of surveillance, see Haggerty (2009).

8 Here Metzl (2004) is referring to the fact that "the obsession to see is also an act of displacement, in as much as the compulsions of the voyeur are defined as much as what he is not looking at as by what he is" (p. 425).

9 This insight is inspired in part by Khan's (2011) analysis of how the "head-shot" of the novelist, located on the back of the novel *Lullabies for Little Criminals*, comes to fill in the missing subjectivity of a drawn, headless, and torso-less child skipping elsewhere on the same back cover.

10 According to the *New York Times*, teens were interviewed individually and in two focus groups. The first focus group, in Manhattan, was organized by the Anti-Defamation League. The second, with students from Lower Merion, a Philadelphia suburb, was coordinated by Stephanie Newberg, a therapist who works with adolescents, and Paula Singer, a community organizer.

11 Bill C-22, An Act Respecting the Mandatory Reporting of Internet Child Pornography by Persons who Provide an Internet Service, came into force on 8 December 2011. Cybertip.ca became the designated reporting entity.

REFERENCES

Adewunmi, B. (2013, April 2). The rise and rise of the "selfie." *The Guardian*. http://www.guardian.co.uk/artanddesign/2013/apr/02/rise-and-rise-of-the-selfie

Adler, A. (2001). The perverse law of child pornography. *Columbia Law Review*, *101*(2), 209–273. http://dx.doi.org/10.2307/1123799

Andrejevic, M. (2005). The work of watching one another: lateral surveillance, risk, and governance. *Surveillance & Society*, *2*(4), 479–497.

Andrejevic, M. (2007). *iSpy: Surveillance and power in the interactive era*. Lawrence, KS: University Press of Kansas.

BBC News. (2013, June 6). Self-portraits and social media: The rise of the "selfie." http://www.bbc.co.uk/news/magazine-22511650

Bell, D. (2009). Surveillance is sexy. *Surveillance & Society*, *6*(3), 203–212.

CCCP (Canadian Centre for Child Protection). (2012). *Self/peer exploitation resource guide: School and family approaches to intervention and prevention*. https://www.cybertip.ca/app/en/internet_safety-self_peer_exploitation

Cover, R. (2003). The naked subject: Nudity, context, and sexualilzation in contemporary culture. *Body & Society*, *9*(3), 53–72. http://dx.doi.org/10.1177/1357034X030093004

Elliot, C. D. (2009). Kid-visible: Childhood obesity, body surveillance, and the techniques of care. In S. P. Hier & J. Greenberg (Eds.), *Surveillance: Power, problems, and politics* (pp. 33–45). Vancouver, BC: UBC Press.

Englander, E. (2012). Low risk associated with most teenage sexting: A study of 617 18-year-olds. *Massachusetts Aggression Reduction Centre*, Bridgewater State University, MA. http://vc.bridgew.edu/cgi/viewcontent.cgi?article=1003&context=marc_reports

Erickson, C. (2013, 15 February). The social psychology of the selfie. *Mashable*. http://mashable.com/2013/02/15/social-media-and-the-selfie/

Groth, M. (2012). Scopophilia. In M. Kosut (Ed.), *Encyclopedia of gender in media* (pp. 321–322). Thousand Oaks, CA: Sage Publications.

Haggerty, K. D. (2009). Forward: surveillance and political problems. In S. P. Hier & J. Greenberg (Eds.), *Surveillance: Power, problems, and politics* (pp. ix–xviii). Vancouver, BC: UBC Press.

Haggerty, K. D., & Ericson, R. V. (2000). The surveillant assemblage. *British Journal of Sociology*, *51*(4), 605–622. http://dx.doi.org/10.1080/00071310020015280

Haggerty, K. D., & Ericson, R.V. (Eds.). (2006). *The new politics of surveillance and visibility*. Toronto, ON: University of Toronto Press.

Hasinoff, A. A. (2015). *Sexting panic: Rethinking criminalization, privacy, and consent*. Champaign, IL: University of Illinois Press.

Hasinoff, A. A. (2012, 11 June). Statue depicting self-objectification more offensive than artwork objectifying women. https://amyhasinoff. wordpress.com/2012/06/11/statue

Higgins, R., Rushhaija, E., and Medhurst, A. (1999). Technowhores. In *Cutting Edge*, Eds., *Desire by design: Body, territories, and new technologies* (pp. 111–122). London, UK: I. B. Tauris.

Jeltsen, M. (2012, 10 Sept.). "Accept or reject": Bare-breasted "sexting" sculpture triggers obscenity investigation. *Huffington Post*. http:// www.huffingtonpost.com/2012/09/10/ accept-or-reject-sexting-sculpture_n_1870525.html.

Karaian, L. (2012). Lolita speaks: 'Sexting,' teenage girls, and the law. *Crime, Media, Culture, 8*(1), 55–71. http://dx.doi.org/10.1177/1741659011429868

Karaian, L. (2014). Policing "sexting": Responsibilization, respectability, and sexual subjectivity in child protection/crime prevention responses to teenagers' digital sexual expression. *Theoretical Criminology, 18*(3), 282–299. http://dx.doi.org/10.1177/1362480613504331

Karaian, L. (2015). What is self-exploitation? Rethinking the relationship between sexualization and "sexting" in law-and-order times. In D. Egan, E. Renold, & J. Ringrose (Eds.), *Children, sexuality and "sexualisation": Beyond spectacle and sensationalism* (pp. 337–351). London, UK: Praeger.

Karaian, L., & Van Meyl, K. (2015). Reframing risqué/risky: Queer temporalities, teenage sexting, and freedom of expression. *Laws, 4*(1), 18–36. http://dx.doi.org/10.3390/laws4010018

Khan, U. (2011). Prostituted girls and the grown-up gaze. *Global Studies of Childhood, 1*(4), 302–313. http://dx.doi.org/10.2304/gsch.2011.1.4.302

Kincaid, J. R. (1998). *Erotic innocence: The culture of child molesting*. Durham: Duke University Press.

Koskela, H. (2004). Webcams, TV shows and mobile phones: Empowering exhibitionism. *Surveillance & Society, 2*(2/3), 199–215.

Krause, J. (2005). *Photo idea index: Rxploring new ways to capture and create exceptional images with digital cameras and software*. Cincinnati, OH: How Books.

LaMarre, A., & Sutherland, O. (2014). Expert opinion? A micro-analysis of eating disorder talk on Dr. Phil. *The Qualitative Report, 19*: Article 86, 1–20.

Lenhart, A. (2009). Teens and sexting. *A Pew Internet & American Life Project Report*. Retrieved 4 July 2010 from http://pewresearch.org/pubs/1440/teens-sexting-text-message.

Leary, M. (2008). Self produced child pornography: The appropriate societal response to juvenile self-sexual exploitation. *Virginia Journal of Social Policy and the Law, 15*(1), 1–50.

Lee, M., Crofts, T., Salter, M., Milivojevic, S., and McGovern, A. (2013). Let's get sexting: Risk, power, sex, and criminalisation in the moral domain. *International Journal for Crime and Justice, 2*(1), 35–49.

Linnemann T., Hanson, L., and Williams, L. S. (2013). "With scenes of blood and pain": Crime control and the punitive imagination of The Meth Project. *British Journal of Criminology, 53,* 605–623.

Lounsbury, K., Mitchell, K., & Finkelhor, D. (2011). The true prevalence of "sexting" fact sheet. *Crimes against Children Research Centre.* http://www.unh.edu/ccrc/pdf/Sexting%20Fact%20Sheet%204_29_11.pdf

Lyon, D. (Ed.). (2006a). *Theorizing surveillance: The panopticon and beyond.* Cullompton, UK: Willan Publishing.

Lyon, D. (2006b). 9/11, synopticon, and scopophilia: watching and being watched. In R. Ericson & K. Haggerty (Eds.), *The new politics of surveillance and visibility* (pp. 35–54). Toronto, ON: University of Toronto Press.

Mathiesen, T. (1997). The viewer society: Michel Foucault's "panopticon" revisited. *Theoretical Criminology, 1*(2), 215–234. http://dx.doi.org/10.1177/1362480697001002003

McGrath, J. (2004). *Loving big brother: Performance, privacy, and surveillance space.* London, UK: Routledge.

Metzl, J. M. (2004). From scopophilia to survivor: A brief history of voyeurism. *Textual Practice, 18*(3), 415–434. http://dx.doi.org/10.1080/09502360410001732935

National Campaign to Prevent Teen and Unplanned Pregnancy and Cosmo Girl. (2008). Sex and tech: Results from a survey of teens and young adults. https://thenationalcampaign.org/resource/sex-and-tech

New York Times. (2011, 26 March). What they're saying about sexting. http://www.nytimes.com/2011/03/27/us/27sextingqanda.html?_r=0

Papadopoulos, L. (2010). *Sexualisation of young people review.* London: Home Office; http://webarchive.nationalarchives.gov.uk/20100418065544/http://homeoffice.gov.uk/documents/Sexualisation-of-young-people.html.

Parton, N. (2006). *Safeguarding childhood: Early intervention and surveillance in a late modern society.* New York, NY: Palgrave Macmillan.

Persky, S., & Dixon, J. (2001). *On kiddie porn: Sexual representation, free speech, and the Robin Sharpe case.* Toronto, ON: New Star Books.

Peskin et al., (2013). Prevalence and patterns of sexting among ethnic minority urban high school students. *Cyberpsychology, Behavior, and Social Networking, 16*(6): 1–6.

Presdee, M. (2000). *Cultural criminology and the carnival of crime*. London, UK: Routledge.

R. v. Sharpe [2001] 1 S.C.R. 4.

Ryzik, M. (2008, May 22). I love what you didn't do to your chipped nails. *New York Times*. http://www.nytimes.com/2008/05/22/fashion/22SKIN. html?pagewanted=all&_r=0

SPIRTO (2013). Self produced images – risk taking online: Quantitative analysis of identified children data. European Union's Safer Internet Programme Knowledge Enhancement Project. www.spirto.health.ed.ac.uk. 1–19.

Strathern, M. (2004). Forward: The mirror of technology. In E. Hirsch & R. Silverstone (Eds.), *Consuming technologies: Media and information in domestic spaces* (pp. vi–x). New York, NY: Routledge.

Tabor, P. (2001). I am a videocam. In I. Borden, J. Kerr, J. Rendell, & A. Pivaro (Eds.), *The unkown city: Contesting architecture and social space* (pp. 122–137). Cambridge, MA: MIT Press.

Weibel, P. (2002). Pleasure and the panoptic principle. In T.Y. Levin, U. Frohne, & P. Weibel (Eds.), *CTRL[SPACE]: Rhetorics of surveillance from Bentham to Big Brother* (pp. 207–23). Cambridge, MA: MIT Press.

Williams, L. (2004). Porn studies: Proliferating pornographies on/scene: An introduction. In L. Williams (Ed.), *Porn Studies* (pp. 1–23). Durham, NC: Duke University Press.

Chapter 3

Living in the Mirror: Understanding Young Women's Experiences with Online Social Networking

VALERIE STEEVES AND JANE BAILEY

Online social media appear to be ideal tools for developing alternatives to the phallocentric cinema that Mulvey (1975) argued objectified women while subjectivizing men through adoption of the male gaze. Many have theorized that girls' and young women's capacity to use online social media to actively assert when they are available and what can be seen (White, 2003) creates an opportunity for them to exert greater control over their own "to-be-looked-atness" (Mulvey, 1975). It also offers opportunities for representing alternatives to discriminatory stereotypes (Dixon-Scott, 2002; Senft, 2008) and for transgressing socially imposed modesty norms (Koskela, 2004) reflective of discriminatory standards that historically isolated women from participation in the public sphere (Allen & Mack, 1990).

Feminist, critical race, and queer theory scholars (Dworkin, 1974; Lorde, 1984; MacKinnon, 1987; Crenshaw, 1991; hooks, 1992; Butler, 1993; Nussbaum, 1995) have for some time been writing about in/visibility, objectification, and the impact of otherized identities on the status of being watched and intelligible. Yet attending to these issues as something more than an add-on is a relatively recent phenomenon in surveillance studies. We contend that "doing surveillance studies" in a way that builds on past research requires us to heed the rising call in the multidisciplinary and rapidly growing field of surveillance studies to attend to gender and sexuality (Ball, Green, Koskela, & Phillips, 2009; Corones & Hardy, 2009; Koskela, 2012) and intersecting identity categories such as race and Aboriginality (Mason & Magnet, 2012).

It is frequently noted in the surveillance literature that gender affects who is watched and how that person is constructed by the watcher (Hier & Greenberg, 2009, p. 26). Furthermore, there is a growing body of surveillance literature focused on the ways in which axes of discrimination such as gender, race, and sexual identity and their intersections inform heightened state and institutional monitoring of individuals and groups (Parenti, 2003; Zureik & Salter, 2005; Eubanks, 2006; Hier & Greenberg, 2009; Monahan & Fisher, 2011; Monahan, 2010; Gates, 2011; Mason & Magnet, 2012). To some extent, this path-breaking body of literature meshes well with panoptic accounts of surveillance in which the gaze of the empowered few serves to discipline and disempower the objectified many.

But, as Brighenti (2007) notes, surveillance is experienced across a spectrum of visibility, and the panoptic model fails to account for the socially contested nature of the power relations that contextualize the experience of being monitored, especially in online environments, where surveillance is multidirectional and involves both individual and institutional/governmental monitoring (Regan & Steeves, 2010). In this environment, girls' experiences are shaped by competing desires to be seen and to see, on the one hand, and to draw boundaries around what can be seen and how it is interpreted, on the other.

Social media are an especially important area to examine because the gaze that is implicated there is a mediatized one in which the once private social space of bedroom culture (McRobbie, 1978) can be converted into a quasi-public space by commercial interests. Some of the work that has attended to media and gender has focused on the male gaze of the passive female subject within the realm of film and photograph. However, social media constitute an interactive space where female presentation can be actively constructed by the user herself through her interactions with her audience(s). This complicates the concept of girls as passive recipients of the male gaze; it also calls for an interrogation of girls as the producers of images for gendered consumption.

Moreover, watching and being watched in online social media implicates not just the potential for the panoptic gaze of the state and private institutions, but a form of synoptic gaze (Mathiesen, 1997) in which the many are trained to recognize and watch for a few types of performances and to incorporate those into interpersonal watching of others. However, within surveillance studies, it is contested whether interpersonal watching actually constitutes surveillance (Andrejevic, 2005; Hier & Greenberg, 2009). Perhaps this is because it has been presumed that interpersonal watching is somehow neutral in terms of the exercise of power, or at least is of less concern in terms of individual rights and liberties than are state and institutional watching.

For many otherized groups, however, privately exercised forms of non-institutional monitoring and control founded on discriminatory myths and attitudes have proven equally de-liberating and seem likely to interact with and inform state and institution-based forms of watching (Patel, 2012). We therefore echo the call of Monahan (2009) for a "new line of inquiry into gender and surveillance" (p. 287) that more completely accounts for the effects of political exercises of power in all their forms. Such an account would not "artificially abstract bodies, identities, and interactions from social contexts in ways that both obscure and aggravate gender and other social inequalities" (Monahan, 2009, p. 287). From this perspective, the gendering of surveillance is equally distributed throughout all forms of monitoring, whether of the super-visible who are targeted for excessive surveillance or of those whose surveillance recedes into the background because it is normalized and taken for granted.

Our chapter will make an initial contribution to the discussions around surveillance and gender and the increasingly complex inter-weaving of public and private spaces by presenting the findings of a qualitative study that explored girls' and young women's lived experiences of watching and being watched online. We provide a theoretical framework for better understanding the complex negotiation with stereotypes and publicity that this lived experience entails as girls and young women simultaneously pursue social success by embracing the online gaze while avoiding the very real risk of negative social consequences associated with "too much" exposure. Our results suggest that an account of surveillance that incorporates panoptic, synoptic, and interpersonal forms of watching offers greater potential for understanding the surveillant forces that tend to undermine the potential for digital media to rupture the male gaze theorized by Mulvey (1975).

Our Methodology

We held six sixty-minute semistructured interviews with six young women and one sixty-minute focus group discussion with eight young women in the fall of 2010. The interviewees had been recruited by advertisements posted on the University of Ottawa's campus. The ads sought women between the ages of eighteen and twenty-two who used social networking (blogs, online videos) as a regular part of their social activities and were interested in participating in an interview about their online experiences as women, especially regarding privacy and equality and the benefits and risks of online social interaction. Participants were selected on a first-come, first-served basis.

In the interviews and the focus group, we explored, among other things, the types of visual and textual representations the participants used online to express their identity as young women, as well as the interplay between these representations and the mainstream media representations they see around them. We also discussed their understanding of privacy, gender, and equality in the context of their online activities. The interview participants were ethnically very diverse, and included an African Canadian who moved to Canada as a girl, three second-generation Canadians whose families were from Korea, the Middle East, and India respectively, a French Canadian, and an English Canadian of European descent.

With the participants' permission, the interviews and focus group were audiotaped and transcribed by the research assistant for our analysis. All identifying information was removed from the transcripts, and pseudonyms were used to identify participants.

Our Findings

"I enjoy being visible as a girl online ..."

Social media and gender were closely linked for our participants, and many of them felt that being seen as a girl was a key part of their online personas; as Amber noted, "it should be really clear if you're male or female" online. Although they identified a number of signals that separate girls from boys, including pictures of cute things like "puppies," "girlie" mainstream pop culture interests (e.g. *Twilight*), and a heightened interest in both talk and "drama," the most important signal was the photo. As Andrea put it:

> That's the point of Facebook, for people to see who you are ... I do that through my picture. ... Probably the pictures is the biggest thing.

Corrine indicated that maintaining an online presence was socially essential. Andrea suggested that, for some social media users, posting pictures of offline activities lends an air of reality to those offline events, in a sense validating the person who posted them because she becomes visible and her activities become real to others:

Facebook kind of makes it real. Like, if I didn't post pictures up on Facebook, I never really went to the beach last weekend … But it's not just about you; it's about everyone else. I want everyone else to know I was out doing something.

Some of our participants also felt that the visibility afforded by social media brought with it positive opportunities to garner compliments (Corrine), to seek support at low points (Brenda), to maintain existing relationships (Tina; Andrea), to rekindle past relationships (Francesca), and to develop new ones (often at a more rapid pace than might have been the case in real space) (Dawn). However, they also talked about the ways in which online visibility provided a way to present a persona that casts aspects or a version of an authentic self in a favourable light, to "build a picture of themselves as what they want to be perceived as" (Jenna) or, as Francesca put it, to "present myself in a certain fashion, in a way that I can control in person."

"… but it's hard work …"

This kind of identity performance, although sought after, was constrained by three main factors. First, even though participants recognized that online social network users often engaged in persona construction, some, like Francesca, felt that the people who watched these performances did not always draw a distinction between the online persona and the actual person:

So I think it's just become so much a part of our culture, where it's like, you just want people to associate the face that you have kind of posted on Facebook with who you are. And I think it's an aspect of yourself, but it's not like this is me entirely. And I think people miss that and get that confused.

Second, our participants felt that they were responsible for managing the expectations and emotional needs of the various audiences who viewed them online, including family, friends, boyfriends, employers, and men giving them unwanted attention. Since taking steps to shape their online interactions – such as ignoring or rejecting friend requests, limiting the visibility of certain kinds of information to certain groups of people as opposed to others, and defriending people altogether – often resulted in hurt feelings and wounded real-space relationships

(Dawn; Brenda; Andrea; Francesca), their actions were constrained by worries that they might be cast in a negative light. This created a significant burden, calling for careful attention to their online presentation because missteps could require a high level of energy to repair.

The young women we talked to saw this burden as a highly gendered one because they bore a disproportionate responsibility in terms of relationship maintenance as compared to young men. As Francesca described it, "Even for myself, I find it much easier to unfriend guys than girls, because I think girls just naturally fear the repercussions, because there usually are repercussions." Many of them lamented the ways in which they were held to account as young women for things they said or did online, contrasting this high level of social regulation with the relative freedom they perceived their male counterparts to enjoy. Amber summarized this:

> Guys can get away with bloody murder compared to girls in social networking. Because, like, no one expects a guy to care, you know what I mean? But they expect a girl to care, so if a girl doesn't care, they just assume that she's doing it purposely, you know what I mean? ... They'll be like, "Oh. She must hate me," you know what I mean?

Third, online visibility was often shaped by commercial metaphors that privilege a view of the self as commodity and of social interaction as entertainment. For example, Dawn said a Facebook profile is "like a personal ad, yourself. Like, 'I'm a good time; if you're with me, you're going to have fun. Let's go have fun.'" Brenda likened her behaviour online to shopping: "If you're walking down the street, looking in shop windows, and keep going on ... That's how I see it. I do, actually, [think of my Facebook profile as a store about myself]." Tina put it this way: "It's like a reality show, with people you already know." Interestingly, all of our participants indicated that young women's social media sites were more interesting than young men's, precisely because they met the criteria for high entertainment value. Sandra told us, "That is, to be honest, primarily why I go on girls' pages – for that stuff ... Oh, you know, what happened at the club last night, or why so-and-so hates so-and-so."

Given the heavy emphasis these metaphors place on the visual, our participants spent a great deal of time and thought on crafting their online look. Indeed, the visual nature of online media as a whole made it important both to be seen and to not be seen badly. Sometimes "badly" was related to behaviour or activities that could be taken out of context. As Danni explained:

> Generally, if I'm doing something and it really shouldn't be recorded for history to remember, I'll just be like, "No pictures." And I'll give them that look, and they won't take a picture ... I just try to keep it, like, if an employer stumbles upon it, they'll be like, "Oh, she's just a normal person who has fun." Not "Oh, she's a delinquent runaway."

However, most of the time, our participants worried about being seen "badly" when a photo of them posted online was uncomplimentary or highlighted what they saw as their "bad" physical features.

Moreover, all of our participants acknowledged that this focus on looks was highly gendered. Whereas the guys they knew could get away with posting goofy or silly pictures, girls had to be very careful about the image they presented. All but one of our participants told us that they spend a great deal of time selecting profile pictures and other photos to post online to make sure that the photos they post will be well received by others. Some co-opted stereotypical representations of girls and women from mainstream media and reproduced them; others disparaged those who did so. But all of them acknowledged the power associated with a sexualized self-presentation online.

The most commonly referenced image in this discussion was the "duckface," the over-the-shoulder self-portrait profile shot of a girl with cheeks sucked in and lips puckered.[1] A number of our participants explicitly rejected this kind of image. For example, Danni lamented, "Why do you really have to do that to yourself?" While some of our participants thought such online behaviour was "immature" or "stupid," many others described young women who post duckface shots, bikini shots, and sexualized images of themselves as "confident" and "popular."[2] They told us that this kind of identity performance was a way to get "validation" and social success. As Amber put it, this image matches "the typical female – always has her hair done, always has her makeup done, always has, like, matching outfits and still tries to go out partying even though she's 26 and getting married. Whatever."

"... at least for other girls ..."

At the same time that they refrained from problematizing this type of power, treating it as a given, a number of them placed caveats when they talked about this kind of femininity. For example, after a long discussion of why young women choose to portray a narrow stereotypical version of femininity online, Danni backtracked, disclaiming an expertise in this kind of performance because

> my close female friends generally aren't like that … So when I say the stereotypical stuff, it's not so much my own close friends. It's the outside circle of that, where it's just acquaintances I know, or what I've seen online, 'cause there's a website called antiduckface.com or something. It's just people have sent in their own pictures of friends making the face, and then whoever is receiving them is just judging them and being like, "Why?"

Amber distanced herself from this presentation by likening herself to boys: "Guys are a lot more like me in their approach to Facebook, like, it's kind of just there." Interestingly, she placed this caveat almost immediately after admitting that she posts duckface shots on her own social media sites. When trying to explain this apparent contradiction, she linked pressures on girls and women to post sexualized images directly to mainstream media stereotyping:

> And I'll admit, like, sometimes I do it, but just because I don't know what else to do, because everyone else poses this way, so I just assume that I should pose this way …
>
> Question: Is there pressure to be like that on Facebook?
>
> I think that's why they do it, really, quite frankly. But then again, that's why most people do what they do, right? They see models wearing Dolce & Gabbana and they're like, "Oh, D&G!" And then, yeah. They just kind of want to do what they think is cool.

Later in our interview, Amber again linked girls who post a high number of photos of their boyfriends on social media to media stereotypes:

> Hollywood culture's so deeply embedded in females' psyches that I think a lot of them truly believe that they need a boyfriend … But I don't think that it's really that healthy, being in one of those relationships. It's just got the bling and lustre of a Hollywood romance. I think that's what they try to work out in real life, then I think they realize that it doesn't work out. Like, the epitome of this is the sparkly vampire. 'Cause he sparkles … It doesn't matter that he's cold and dead.

"… unless that's inconsistent with my other goals …"

Other participants described how they struggled to distance themselves from this sexualized image of femininity in order to make room for some other kind of self – student, professional, fun girl, or a girl who is "more like, 'Hey, that's cool,' versus, like, 'Hey, that's hot'" (Amber). Natalie's story is particularly evocative in this regard. She prefaced her comments by telling us that when she was a child, no one paid any particular (negative or positive) attention to her or how she looked, and she was free to dream about growing up and becoming a doctor. But things changed when she began to post pictures of herself on Facebook and people posted comments publicly praising her because she was very beautiful. "I was like, 'I want to get these comments, that'd be nice.' I don't think I initially started that way, but once you start getting the comments, you sort of start feeding into that a bit … then it became something I'd be conscious about." Image became so important to her that she would only post photos that had been taken by a professional photographer.

The attention Natalie received because of her physical beauty became a barrier to her other dreams. Before she went through puberty, she "just focused on school. It was never like, 'That's the pretty girl,' or this or that. And then things changed. And so I still had that old mentality of, I want to be a doctor. And it's kind of conflicting." It was only through her reflections during our interview that she began to question this. "I've been asking myself why I never realized that [I could be pretty and a doctor] until now. I think when I was younger, it was always it has to be one or the other; it can't be both."

Natalie's solution was to remove any photos of herself from social media except for group shots and to actively monitor photos in which she was tagged. Also, she did not post information about her relationship status. Others, like Corrine, reported a similar concern about "being perceived as something I'm not" and shared a reluctance to post photos or their relationship status because it was difficult to control how they would be perceived by people who were monitoring their sites.

At the same time, monitoring was both taken for granted and part of the pleasure of social media. There was widespread agreement among our participants (Jenna, Tina, Amber, Danni, Corrine, Brenda) that social media users place one another under a form of surveillance, again often as a form of entertainment. As Jenna put it, with respect to what some referred to as "stalking": "Everyone does it. And we all know that we read each other's profiles." According to Kim, those who post more expose themselves to more surveillance: "The downside, I guess, is really that the more things you post, people will kind of check your profile … These days, everyone says, 'I'm stalking you on Facebook' with kind of a sense of humour."

"… away from family and unwanted male attention …"

The ready visibility of social media also enabled monitoring by family members and made it difficult to maintain an appropriate separation between the various social roles our participants played, from girlfriend, to friend, to employee, to daughter. As Tina noted with respect to being questioned by family members about comments she had posted about breaking up with her boyfriend:

> And I was like, "Oh my goodness, you can't have me on Facebook anymore." This is getting ridiculous, you know? Like, I babysit your kids. This is a part of my life that you shouldn't be seeing.

Online visibility also created the possibility of attracting unwanted male attention. A number of our participants agreed that young women were at greater risk of stalking[3] by unknown older men and, thus, ought to guard their online privacy more carefully than young men (Francesca, Amber, Parvati, Andrea, Corrine). Others, like Francesca, found this "creepy." However, they all reported a high degree of resiliency in this regard, typically unfriending or deleting boys or men they did not know, although a number of them did express concerns for younger girls. As Corrine put it: "And I know, like, my 15-year-old cousins who are really pretty, like, they have Facebook too. That really weirds me out … Guys can just stalk them; can just go through their pictures and look at them … Obviously you're young and really impressionable."

"… and my girlfriends …"

Our participants' greatest concerns about surveillance, though, related to being watched by other girls in their social circle (Corrine, Andrea, Danni, Tina, Francesca), because being watched opened them up to harsh judgment. As Corrine put it, "I hate [Facebook] because you're putting yourself with girls; you're putting yourself out there to be judged all the time. And it's just … I don't know, private things become so public, for you to be judged on it." Interestingly, putting yourself out there was seen as a way to gain validation, but the very act of seeking validation created vulnerabilities. Corrine explained: "I see on Facebook that girls are seeking that attention more, and seeking that approval, and judgment on their looks, more than guys are. And that alone just makes them more vulnerable."

Once again, this dynamic was highly gendered, with girls held to a much higher standard than boys. As Brenda put it: "If a guy cheats on a girl, everyone's going to be like, 'Oh, he's such a dick,' right? But then it kind of fades away. But if a girl cheats on a guy, it's like, 'Oh my God, what a slut, what a whore' – blah, blah, blah. That reputation will follow her for the rest of her life." Moreover, those strategies that were markers of confidence and popularity noted above – the duckface and bikini shots – also opened up the possibility of being labelled a slut, as did having "too many friends," a public profile, or simply displaying attention-seeking behaviour:[4]

> [Girls seem like sluts] if they have, like, a ridiculous amount of friends – also, like, very attention-seeking. So I think guys notice it too ... ["Attention-seeking" and "slut"] are not synonymous, but they often go hand-in-hand, I'd say. (Natalie)

"... so I need privacy ..."

Perhaps as a result, our participants suggested that young women were more likely than young men to have private social networking pages (Andrea) and to spend considerably more time crafting their postings, photos, and online personae (Dawn, Corrine). Because of this, privacy took on heightened importance as a tool for exercising some level of control over both self-presentation and audience interpretation; this allowed them to "pick and choose" who had access to what information about them (Amber, Francesca, Kim) and thereby avoid getting "screwed by what you've posted online" (Brenda).

"... and I have to be more careful than boys ..."

However our participants defined privacy and their related concerns, many quite clearly articulated the struggle to selectively maintain privacy in the context of online social networking. For example, Francesca told us:

It's difficult sometimes, because when you're deciding … what information to post up, you want to be able to kind of keep your friends up to date … But then again, you always have to be – or I try to be cognizant of the fact that other people could be viewing this information. So it's difficult, because I feel like there's kind of a cap on how much you can say, even though this is your page and this is, you know, your domain.

Moreover, our participants felt that this process was more complicated for girls than for boys, for several reasons. Most of our participants believed that girls were likely to be more active on social networking sites than boys (Brenda, Andrea), and more likely to engage in gossip and "drama" online (Vecepia, Tina, Andrea, Kim), as well as likely to disclose more information about and photos of themselves (Brenda) in an effort to "prove" themselves or to gain approval or validation (Brenda, Francesca). As Francesca put it:

I've never encountered a girl that has not had Facebook, ever. Which is surprising. Whereas with guys, it's kind of like black and white, and I'm not that shocked … And I don't know why, but I think girls get trapped into that, and kind of wanting to prove to other girls, I would say, even more than proving to guys, that, you know, "I'm your equal."

Some of our participants speculated that the less emotional or dramatic online social networking practices of young men at least partly explained why young men were less likely both to stalk and to be stalked online by their peers than were young women (Sandra). To the extent that boys were less subject to online scrutiny than girls, Corrine speculated they were much less likely than girls to have to be careful regarding what they posted.

Our participants identified a number of strategies for exercising this care. Corrine sought to maintain a clear boundary between her social networking presence, which was the public part of her life, and her private existence:

I'm really careful about the private part of my life, keeping it separate from the public part of my life … You're not going to see these private parts of my life right on my Facebook. Just like I don't want people seeing me a in a bikini; I'll save that for later. Once you get to know me, maybe you can see me in a bikini.

Indeed, a number of our participants consciously developed their online personae in light of concerns about how different audiences would react to their self-presentations. As Dawn put it:

> I feel like my persona at school or work or socially is different from my persona at home, like, with my parents and stuff. And now what I'll get a lot of is family members adding me on Facebook … So, I'll have a lot of, sometimes, I'll have to go to my friends and be like, "Okay, who can see what?" And then it's like, okay, these people can see everything, these people can see some stuff, these people can see just enough that they don't think I'm hiding anything from them, but not really see anything at all … So, for me, 'cause my online personality feels more like the me that I am every day than the me that I am to my parents, or, like, my extended family sort of thing, I feel that this would be … It's censored me, but it's true me, although it's censored.

Similarly, in light of her concerns about employer monitoring, Francesca worked to "make sure that I always consistently put out a professional representation of myself."

For many of our participants, presenting an online personae involved consciously limiting what they posted, not only on their own pages but also on those of their "friends" (Andrea, Francesca). As Kim articulated: "I really watch what I post … Like, I question myself, like, three times about it, and I see if it's really non-confidential." Others policed content by detagging photographs of themselves or requesting that others do so (Brenda, Andrea, Corrine, Kim). Francesca described a more nuanced form of content control, which effectively limited accessibility without the need for complete self-censorship:

> Sometimes, like, my friends and I will just kind of – not necessarily write stuff in code, but, like, we'll just be very careful about what we say. Like, a lot of times, we just naturally have nicknames for everything … so if I want to write a message about something and I don't necessarily feel like writing a private message, it's still private enough that only this person can understand, which is my goal.

Our participants also identified a number of privacy mechanisms aimed at limiting their audiences, including the following: ignoring or declining new "friend" requests; deleting "friends" (Amber, Sandra, Tina); deleting Facebook altogether (Corrine); maintaining a private profile only (Corrine); and adjusting privacy settings to block certain "friends" from seeing certain kinds of content (Dawn, Amber, Francesca). As Amber noted, in relation to concerns about employer monitoring: "I contemplated taking [my Facebook page] down, deleting it all together, but I decided not to. I kept it. I took down some pictures and things that I thought would incriminate me, like, unacceptable social things. But I keep it private. You can't search me. I 'Googled' myself and nothing really comes up."

Francesca noted that social networking sites can be structured in ways that may complicate individual deliberations about what to post: "I feel like it's so structured for you, and it makes assumptions that you have a favourite quote, et cetera." Similarly, Dawn noted that other than one free text box below the profile picture, "there's always, like, instructions on what you're supposed to be doing there. Like when you go to put a picture up, it's like, do this, do this, do that, do that ..." Very practical considerations may limit the efficacy and attractiveness of these information and audience control strategies. As Kim put it: "Why is it so complicated? ... It's set for default that you're going to show everything. So you really have to go through and check things by yourself – figure it out by yourself before you can, like, be sure about it."

For some of our participants, the complications associated with making these adjustments were not worth the time. As Amber said: "A lot of it is like ... I'm busy. I just can't be bothered to sit down and filter all my pictures and all my friends. It's just too much work. You just kind of put it at the back of your mind. Facebook really for me consists of, like, twenty people constantly, kind of thing. The rest of them are just kind of there."

"... but that doesn't mean I'm being treated unequally ..."

Most of our participants consistently identified the ways in which gender affected privacy and interpersonal watching differently for young women than for young men online. Even so, most of them also felt there was no issue of inequality online, save for the potentially greater exposure to stalking by unknown men (Kim). As Brenda said: "I don't really think I've been treated unfairly online because I'm a girl. I don't really think I've ever been hassled because I'm a girl." Dawn expressed similar sentiments but suggested that the same might not be true for girls living outside the "Western world," who would face greater monitoring.

When probed on what online equality would look like, however, a few of our participants reflected back on the gendered costs of online visibility discussed above and suggested:

> I think online equality would look a lot like, I guess, just regular equality. Where I wouldn't have to spend time thinking about what I could and should put on Facebook, and I could just put on any picture that I think makes me look good ... That, to me, would be online equality, where I wouldn't be thinking about things a million times before I put up a simple picture. (Andrea)

> I would think [that women are less equal than men online], just because I see that we have to try so much harder. Like, everything else in the world, like, I feel like I have to try harder to be perceived as not the ditzy MySpace girl, or try not to be portrayed as the girl who's trying not to be the ditzy MySpace girl, you know? It's really tricky for me. Whereas I feel like my guy friends just created a Facebook account, and it was easy. They don't get judged as much on their stuff. So yeah, I definitely think there's an issue of equality. (Corrine)

> I find [equality online] an interesting question to try and answer, because I've never seen it, so it's hard to kind of, like, really kind of even know where to start ... I really can't even imagine, which is kind of scary. I can't imagine equality online. (Francesca)

Again, the visibility of social media was implicated, because it tended to focus attention on looks and to require girls to choose between being "pretty" and "nice," and being anything else. Natalie put it this way:

> Just as in real world, you know, how a lot of times compliments are nice and welcomed, I think that [the] Facebook equivalent of that, for example, is people commenting on your photos and saying, "You're so pretty; you're so this." It's just another avenue to kind of get that, admiration, I guess I would call it? Which again would feed into their own egos, as opposed to guys who might seek that in other domains and venues.

Discussion

Our findings illustrate the dynamic ways in which young women socially construct their online identities (Phillips, 2009; Bronstein,

2013) and rely on social media to care for and manage their social relationships (Shade, 2008). Our participants approached social media as performative spaces where they could experiment with identities by crafting culturally meaningful, coherent, intelligible, and recognizable narratives, and configure those identities within a network of social relationships (Cover, 2012). Seeing and being seen on social media was consciously embraced as a way to affirm themselves and connect with others.

But in spite of their self-reflexive engagement with online visibility, their performances were shaped and constrained by broader social narratives around femininity, narratives in which "physical beauty, sexual attractiveness, and product consumption supersede intelligence and creativity" (Thiel-Stern, 2005, p. 179). These narratives focus on the sexualized feminine body and draw from media representations that provide what Thiel-Stern calls authoritative knowledge of how girls are supposed to be (Thiel-Stern, 2005). Our findings accordingly suggest that even when young women are the creators of their own online representations, their agency is exercised within a social environment that continues to privilege stereotypical images of how they should see themselves and present themselves to be seen by others, and that this creates a gendered burden that complicates their online interactions.

Certainly, as Brighenti (2007) reminds us, "it is no mystery that the asymmetry between seeing and being seen is a deeply gendered one – often, a sexualized one. In modern western society, typically, the male is the one who looks, while the female is the one who is looked at" (p. 330). The male sexualized gaze is especially potent for girls as they move from childhood to adolescence. Hauge (2009) suggests that a direct negotiation with heteronormative discourses around sexuality is the primary marker of the shift from girl child to young woman. As such, our participants' reading of markers like makeup, clothing, and boyfriends to signal femininity online demonstrates their facility with the heteronormative ideal, as does their ready acknowledgment of the link between the sexualization of this pretty, thin, feminine body and social power (Heilman, 1998). In this sense, the online world duplicates the offline world (van Doorn, van Zoonen, & Wyatt, 2007), in that girls are required to negotiate with the "untroubled" status (Hauge, 2009, p. 301) of the type of body that is assumed to be most privileged by the male gaze.

However, our findings suggest that social media do not simply replicate the centrality of this binary classification (Manago, Graham,

Greenfield, & Salimkhan, 2008); they *amplify* it, in three interrelated ways. First, the commercial surveillance that drives social media intensifies girls' interactions with media representations and restructures the environment in ways that privilege heteronormative performances of girl. Second, the surveillance by family members and peers creates a gendered burden to care for and manage others' expectations; managing this burden is complicated by the ways in which that same surveillance breaks down the boundaries between performances of various identities, particularly because the demands of mainstream performances conflict with other identities they inhabit (such as daughter and employee). Third, social media alienate the feminine body through the hypervisibility of the *image* of the body. This makes the body an object of judgment that is subject to scrutiny by others and the self; it also exacerbates the negative effects of failed performances (Frost, 2001). In the following section, we discuss each of these dynamics in turn.

Commercial Surveillance and the Mediatization of Online Spaces

Our participants' use of styles and fashions to project a feminine identity in online spaces is consistent with research that reports that media images provide the "raw material" (Bovill & Livingstone, 2001, p. 3) with which young people construct their identities. McRobbie (1978) identified the importance of the bedroom as a private social space in which girls appropriate and experiment with this raw material. Steele and Brown suggest (1995) that "for many teens, the bedroom is a safe, private space in which experimentation with possible selves can be conducted" (cited in Bovill & Livingstone, 2001, p. 3). The benefits of bedroom culture are accordingly tied to the ability to retreat from scrutiny and to try on various ways of being, away from the judgments of non-intimate others.

However, McRobbie's early work also emphasized how this experimentation "has been led, exploited even, by powerful commercial interests in the fashion and music industries" (1978, pp. 2–3). Certainly, our participants were aware of, and lamented, the mainstream media representation of the "attractive" female body that saturates entertainment and marketing content (Thiel-Stern, 2005). However, a number of them also readily appropriated and reproduced these images in an effort to make themselves intelligible to others, even as they expressed disdain for their narrow representations of femininity. Moreover, they reproduced these images on social media that are typically programmed to default to "public" and that open up the virtual bedroom – and the performances that take place there – for others to see.

Westlake (2008) suggests that these kinds of "fluid performances, which may look like exhibitionism, are energetic engagements with the panoptic gaze: as people offer themselves up for surveillance, they also resist being fixed as rigid, unchanging subjects" (p. 21). But the ability of the panoptic model, where the few watch the many, to explain on its own this kind of performativity is limited by its disciplinary focus (Hier, 2003), which positions the watched as passive and the gaze as inherently disempowering (Brighenti, 2007). We suggest that our participants' active engagement with media representations can be better understood as a product of the interaction of panoptic and synoptic surveillance, where the many watch the few.

Mathiesen (1997) offered his analysis of the synoptic gaze as a corrective to surveillance theories that fail to take the role of the mass media into the account of surveillance in late modernity. He suggested that the top-down form of panoptic surveillance is mutually constructed with and by a synoptic form of monitoring that habituates the many to "seeing, and thereby contemplating, the actions of the few" (Hier, 2003, p. 404). For our purposes, this model helps account for the monolithic presence of mainstream media representations of femininity in online spaces, because synoptic surveillance encourages large numbers of people to concentrate on something in common. This common focus amplifies the importance of media representations because they come to dominate the visual domain and accordingly act as shared cultural capital that is easily appropriated by and intelligible to others.

However, it is important to note that the panoptic affordances of social media work to reinforce the ways in which the synoptic gaze is encouraged to focus on sexist commercial messages. Social media are structured by commercial imperatives that embed mainstream media images directly into the social environment (Grimes & Shade, 2005; Steeves, 2006). But by seamlessly collecting personal information from and about their users, online platforms not only synoptically privilege heteronormative images of femininity through the ubiquitous placement of advertising and sponsored content; they also monitor how girls respond to these messages and reconstruct the online social environment to magnify their impact. Accordingly, panoptic and synoptic forms of surveillance merge in ways that reinforce existing social relations (Hier, 2003). As our findings illustrate, mainstream representations reproduced in social media thereby take on new life and set the stage for narrow, stereotypical performances of femininity.

To create space for other kinds of identities, our participants were quick to place caveats that distanced them and their friends from these representations. This provided a window into the complicated and contradictory terrain they are required to navigate. They sought to create a sense of self that was socially acceptable and intelligible to others by complying *enough* with the dictates of mediatized images of femininity, but they also feared that space for other kinds of identities would be shut down if they complied *too much*.

This was best exemplified by their narratives around sluts, who were deemed "too much" – they paid too much attention to makeup and clothing, placed too much focus on their boyfriends, were too overt in their sexuality, and were too public online. The fear of overreaching, of trying too hard, of going too far to emulate mainstream tropes, led to our participants walking a tightrope between being sexy enough and being too sexy. They sought to occupy an acceptable feminine subjectivity that incorporated mainstream elements of sexualized display while avoiding the label "whore" (Hauge, 2009, p. 301).

Accordingly, the visibility afforded in online spaces provides an opportunity for identity play, but that visibility is perilous because the line between success and failure is razor thin. As Brighenti (2007) notes, "visibility is a double-edged sword: it can be empowering as well as disempowering ... Concentrations of visibility-as-power always attract their highly visible nemesis of downgrading and 'fall'" (p. 335). Our participants' identity experiments online were therefore fraught with difficulty: they sought to avoid the humiliation that follows when young women fail to fit themselves into the narrow norms associated with mainstream, commercialized tropes.

Interpersonal Surveillance and the Burden of Care

The consequences of failure are also magnified by the surveillant nature of the space. Successful performances by our participants were rewarded with compliments and social support, but at the same time, it was difficult for them to segregate unsuccessful performances because they were seen by so many intended and unintended audiences. The difficulty of segregation encourages the performance of identities that "remain closely related to the binary gender system" (van Doorn, van Zoonen, & Wyatt, 2007, p. 143) because such identities are easier to inhabit and explain to others.

Privacy strategies were accordingly important to our participants because the inability to erect boundaries between audiences detracted from their ability to perform different identities. They found it difficult to deal with family members, who could monitor their relationships – especially with boys – and overreact to behaviours (like the duckface) that were consistent with mainstream tropes. All participants expressed concerns about employers who could misinterpret photos of drinking or partying. They also found it tiring to be held to account by girlfriends, who could take things out of context and create drama.

Privacy regulation fails to respond to young women's needs for control over boundaries because it is preoccupied with the collection of personal information. The point of social media is to make oneself visible by providing a flow of information about oneself; the point of privacy in this context is to assert control over when and how that visibility is interpreted by various audiences. Simple regulatory responses that focus on (non)consensual disclosure of information miss the point.

But compartmentalizing performances was only a partial solution for our participants. The visibility afforded by social media was tiring because it was gendered; they were monitored in ways that their male peers were not, simply because they were girls in the public sphere. Yet being seen badly was equally gendered, in that they were held to account for any missteps where they failed to take others' feelings into account, for as girls, they were expected to respond to and placate the emotions of others. Accordingly, the care and control afforded by surveillance collapsed: monitoring for pleasure and monitoring for control both reinforced performances that conformed to gendered expectations.

The panoptic model of surveillance often struggles to explain this kind of experience, because it has "fostered a disproportional focus on the disciplined individual who lives under the panoptic gaze to the neglect of the observer in the metaphorical inspection tower" (Hier & Greenberg, 2009, p. 22). From this perspective, the panopticon is a "technology of power for society as a whole, regardless of any specific application" (ibid.). However, "power does not circulate equally, and blurring the distinction between the relations of domination and subordination ... has the effect of relativizing historically recurrent asymmetries of power and surveillance at the expense of understanding visualization and perception as relations of power" (p. 23).

Competing models, such as the surveillant assemblage proposed by Haggerty and Ericson (2000), better describe the nodal nature of online information flows. But by equating synopticism with partial democratization (given the way the many can now watch the few), the assemblage overemphasizes the power of the many and fails to fully account for asymmetric monitoring (Hier & Greenberg, 2009, pp. 19–20). Some surveillance scholars have, accordingly, tended to dismiss interpersonal surveillance as an apolitical form of voyeurism, or visibility without consequence. But visibility is "a relational social process ... that is conditioned by vested material interests and desires" (p. 24). As such, theories of surveillance must account for the spectrum of visibility, especially in online spaces, where negotiation of public and private space is increasingly complex and where synoptic, panoptic, and interpersonal forms of surveillance interact and magnify one another.

Visuality and the Body

Brighenti (2007) suggests that surveillance scholarship can move forward by examining the ways in which the field of visibility structures social relations. He argues that visibility lies at the intersection of relations of perception and relations of power (Brighenti, 2007, p. 324). In this sense, visibility is always political. So when "something becomes more visible than before, we should ask ourselves who is acting on and reacting to the properties of the field, and which specific relationships are being shaped" (p. 327).

This is particularly important for members of equality-seeking communities, who have an ambivalent relationship to visibility. Communities that fall below the "fair threshold of visibility" (p. 329) become invisible and are accordingly marginalized (Lorde, 1984). Indeed, this marginalization was the early concern of the feminists who first encountered the Internet as a male-dominated space (Richards & Schnall, 2003). Female participation was seen as the corrective; girls and young women could wrest equality in online spaces by eschewing norms of modesty and making themselves visible (Koskela, 2002, 2004). However, communities that are pushed above the fair threshold of visibility are also at risk (Moreno, 2008), because being super-visible can lead to paralysis and a loss of control over one's own image:

It is a condition of paradoxical double bind that forbids you to do what you are simultaneously required to do by the whole ensemble of social constraints ... Clearly, one's positioning behind or beyond the thresholds of fair visibility raises the problem of the management of one's social image in one's own terms. Therefore, when philosophers and political activists support the claims for recognition put forward by minority groups, one should be aware that the very social relationship producing recognition can produce denial of recognition, too. Distortions in visibility lead to distortions in social representations, distortions through visibility. (Brighenti, 2007, p. 329)

Our participants' experiences suggest that the gendered gaze operating in social media can push young women into the realm of super-visibility, where their performances are easily distorted by the mainstream tropes through which others – and the girls themselves – interpret those performances. Again, the synoptic nature of social media helps exacerbate visibility: the synopticon "embraces the visual in the most emphatic manner because the synopticon is thoroughly visual and visualizing" (Hier, 2003, p. 405).

The emphasis placed on photos amplifies the visual aspect of online performances. Senft (2008) notes that photos are an integral part of gender signification in online spaces. Our participants certainly spent a great deal of time and effort crafting their online self-presentations. The contested nature of the feminine body meant that their displays opened them up to judgment both by others and by themselves. The risk of judgment became something of a disciplinary force as they self-monitored their performances to remain intelligible without crossing the line.

Harper and Tiggemann (2008) note that image sharing encourages girls to think about their bodies from the perspective of a critical observer, in a sense alienating them from their embodiment so they can engage with the image of their body from the perspective of the male gaze. This effect is amplified in social media, which are strongly visual: girls' online identities are crafted for consumption by viewers who read visual cues that are understood within a commercial lexicon. Because of this, photos are less an "expression of a reflexively chosen identity" than a commodity that can be understood within a "consumerist visual representation of society as a catalogue" (Schwarz, 2010, p. 163). Here, we see another effect of interpersonal surveillance in online social media as participants learn to embrace marketing surveillance mechanisms on a micro level (Andrejevic, 2005).

Ringrose and Renold's findings about offline performativity in the United Kingdom apply here:

[Girls] must now perform a "post-feminist masquerade" where they are subject to more intensified technologies of bodily perfection and visual display as "feminine subjects" in a current "fashion and beauty" system that privileges oppressive forms of idealised white femininity. (Ringrose & Renold, 2012, p. 461)[5]

Once again, the potential for a lived equality recedes.

Conclusion

Ironically, the very constraints placed on young women online – the heteronormative tropes embedded in commercialized social space, the gendered nature of the surveillant gaze within interpersonal surveillance, and the overvisibility of the feminine body – were not seen by most of our participants as impinging on their equality. Instead, "the compulsory hypersexual embodiment that dominates popular celebrity culture [was packaged] as a form of sexual, feminine liberation" (Ringrose & Renold, 2012, p. 462), and gender injustices – the heavy management burden described by our participants and the sense that boys "get away with murder" – were reinstated in ways that became invisible to them as matters of equality. Perhaps most importantly, our results suggest that it is urgent to further develop surveillance studies in a way that better accommodates the interrelationships among panoptic, synoptic, and interpersonal modes of watching that coalesce to undermine the emancipatory potential of online social media for girls and young women. Our participants described a world in which the struggle for "the visibility without which [one] cannot truly live" (Lorde, 1984, p. 43) was played out under the spotlight of a commercially crafted white, middle-class, hyperheterosexual gaze that privileges a very circumscribed understanding of girlhood and womanhood. The panoptic and synoptic forces that privilege this gaze and the performances that gaze favours train the watched both to internalize its norms into their understandings and assessments of self (Gandy, 2000) as part of a strategy to remain intelligible, and to interpersonally surveil others according to its norms. Until the relationships between panoptic, synoptic, and interpersonal forms of surveillance are better understood and accounted for, it will be difficult to tailor successful strategies for intervention. Without such strategies, freedom and equality for girls and young women in online environments (as in offline environments) seem highly unlikely to follow.

NOTES

1 Duckface pictures were often associated with bikini shots or "bathroom mirror" shots, and the profile aspect on the shot was seen as a way to look "skinnier."
2 Ironically, the participants in the focus group were also quick to label a girl who did so as a "slut."
3 A notable exception to the idea that young men were unlikely to be stalked was Corrine's speculation about her boyfriend: "[My boyfriend] probably just uses it to watch me. [I guarantee] if there was a guy in a picture with me, he'd probably stalk that guy to find out. I know he has done that before."
4 For a fuller discussion of this dynamic, see Bailey, Steeves, Burkell, and Regan (2013).
5 The findings of Finn (2011) about ordinary Americans' post-9/11 staring at women racialized as South Asian similarly underscore the intersecting influence of race and gender in lateral forms of surveillance.

REFERENCES

Allen, A., & Mack, E. (1990). How privacy got its gender. *Northern Illinois University Law Review, 10*, 441–478.
Andrejevic, M. (2005). The work of watching one another: Lateral surveillance, risk, and governance. *Surveillance & Society, 2*(4), 479–497.
Bailey, J., Steeves, V., Burkell, J., & Regan, P. (2013). Negotiating with gender stereotypes on social networking sites: From "bicycle face" to Facebook. *Journal of Communication Inquiry, 37*(2), 91–112. http://dx.doi.org/10.1177/0196859912473777
Ball, K., Green, N., Koskela, H., & Phillips, D. (2009). Editorial: Surveillance studies needs gender and sexuality. *Surveillance & Society, 6*(4), 352–355.
Bovill, M., & Livingstone, S. (2001). *Bedroom culture and the privatization of media use.* London, UK: London School of Economics, LSE Research Online. <http://eprints.lse.ac.uk/672/>
Brighenti, A. (2007). Visibility: A category for the social sciences. *Current Sociology, 55*(3), 323–342. http://dx.doi.org/10.1177/0011392107076079
Bronstein, J. (2013). Personal blogs as online presences on the internet. *Aslib Proceedings: New Information Perspectives, 65*(2), 161–181. http://dx.doi.org/10.1108/00012531311313989
Butler, J. (1993). *Bodies that matter: On the discursive limits of "sex."* New York, NY: Routledge, Chapman and Hall.

Corones, A., & Hardy, S. (2009). En-gendered surveillance: Women on the edge of a watched cervix. *Surveillance & Society, 6*(4), 388–397.

Cover, R. (2012). Performing and undoing identity online: Social networking, identity theories, and the incompatibility of online profiles and friendship regimes. *Convergence (London), 18*(2), 177–193.

Crenshaw, K. (1991). Mapping the margins: Intersectionality, identity politics, and violence against women of colour. *Stanford Law Review, 43*(6), 1241–1299. http://dx.doi.org/10.2307/1229039

Dixon-Scott, K. (2002). Turbo chicks: Talkin' 'bout my generation: Third-wave feminism is comfortable with contradiction because that's the only way the world makes sense. *Herizons, 16*(2), 16-19.

Dworkin, A. (1974). *Woman hating*. New York, NY: Penguin Group.

Eubanks, V. (2006). Technologies of citizenship: Surveillance and political learning in the welfare system. In T. Monahan (Ed.), *Surveillance and security: Technological politics and power in everyday life* (pp. 89–107). New York, NY: Routledge.

Finn, R. (2011). Surveillant staring: Race and the everyday surveillance of South Asian Women after 9/11. *Surveillance & Society 8*(4), 413–426.

Frost, L. (2001). *Young women and the body: A feminist sociology*. Basingstoke, UK: Palgrave. http://dx.doi.org/10.1057/9780333985410

Gandy, O. (2000). Exploring identity and identification in cyberspace. Annenberg School for Communication, University of Pennsylvania. <https://www.asc.upenn.edu/usr/ogandy/Identity.pdf>

Gates, K. (2011). *Our biometric future: Facial recognition technology and the culture of surveillance*. New York, NY: NYU Press.

Grimes, S. M., & Shade, L. (2005). Neopian economics of play: Children's cyberpets and online communities as immersive advertising in NeoPets. com. *International Journal of Media & Cultural Politics, 1*(2), 181–198. http://dx.doi.org/10.1386/macp.1.2.181/1

Haggerty, K., & Ericson, R.V. (2000). The surveillant assemblage. *British Journal of Sociology, 51*(4), 605–622. http://dx.doi.org/10.1080/00071310020015280

Harper, B., & Tiggemann, M. (2008). The effect of thin ideal media images on women's self-objectification, mood, and body image. *Sex Roles, 58*(9–10), 649–657. http://dx.doi.org/10.1007/s11199-007-9379-x

Hauge, M. (2009). Bodily practices and discourses of hetero-femininity: Girls' constitution of subjectivities in their social transition between childhood and adolescence. *Gender and Education, 21*(3), 293–307. http://dx.doi.org/10.1080/09540250802667625

Heilman, E. E. (1998). The struggle for self: Power and identity in adolescent girls. *Youth & Society, 30*(2), 182–208. http://dx.doi.org/10.1177/0044118X98030002003

Hier, S. (2003). Probing the surveillant assemblage: On the dialectic of surveillance practices as processes of social control. *Surveillance & Society, 1*(3), 399–411.

Hier, S., & Greenberg, J. (2009). *Surveillance: Power, problems, and politics.* Vancouver, BC: UBC Press.

hooks, b. (1992). *Black looks: Race and representation.* Boston, MA: South End Press.

Koskela, H. (2002). Video surveillance, gender, and the safety of public urban space: "Peeping Tom" goes high tech? *Urban Geography, 23*(3), 257–278. http://dx.doi.org/10.2747/0272-3638.23.3.257

Koskela, H. (2004). Webcams, TV shows, and mobile phones: Empowering exhibitionism. *Surveillance & Society, 2,* 199–215.

Koskela, H. (2012). "You should wear that body": The problematic of surveillance and gender. In K. Ball, K. D. Haggerty, & D. Lyon (Eds.), *Routledge Handbook of Surveillance Studies* (pp. 49–56). London, New York: Routledge.

Lorde, A. (1984). *Sister outsider.* Berkeley, CA: Crossing Press.

MacKinnon, C. (1987). *Feminism unmodified.* Cambridge, MA: Harvard University Press.

Manago, A., Graham, M. B., Greenfield, P. M., & Salimkhan, G. (2008). Self-presentation and gender on MySpace. *Journal of Applied Developmental Psychology, 29*(6), 446–458. http://dx.doi.org/10.1016/j.appdev.2008.07.001

Mason, C., & Magnet, S. (2012). Surveillance studies and violence against women. *Surveillance & Society, 10*(2), 105–118.

Mathiesen, T. (1997). The viewer society. *Theoretical Criminology, 1*(2), 215–234. http://dx.doi.org/10.1177/1362480697001002003

McRobbie, A. (1978). Working class girls and the culture of femininity. In Centre for Contemporary Cultural Studies, Women's Studies Group (Ed.), *Women take issue: Aspects of women's subordination (initiated by) Women's Studies Group* (pp. 96–108). London: Hutchinson.

Monahan, T. (2009). Dreams of control at a distance: Gender, surveillance, and social control. *Cultural Studies, Critical Methodologies, 9*(2), 286–305. http://dx.doi.org/10.1177/1532708608321481

Monahan, T. (2010). *Surveillance in a time of insecurity.* New Brunswick, NJ: Rutgers University Press.

Monahan, T., & Fisher, J. (2011). Surveillance impediments: Recognizing obduracy with the deployment of hospital information systems. *Surveillance & Society, 9*(1/2), 1–16.

Moreno, A. (2008). The politics of visibility and the GLTTBI movement in Argentina. *Feminist Review, 89*(1), 138–143. http://dx.doi.org/10.1057/fr.2008.1

Mulvey, L. (1975). Visual pleasure and narrative cinema. *Screen, 16*(3), 6–18. http://dx.doi.org/10.1093/screen/16.3.6

Nussbaum, M. (1995). Objectification. *Philosophy & Public Affairs, 24*(4), 249–291. http://dx.doi.org/10.1111/j.1088-4963.1995.tb00032.x

Parenti, C. (2003). *Cage: Surveillance in America from slavery to the war on terror.* New York, NY: Basic Books.

Patel, T. (2012). Surveillance, suspicion, and stigma: Brown bodies in a terror-panic climate. *Surveillance & Society, 10*(3–4), 215–234.

Phillips, D. (2009). Ubiquitous computing, spatiality, and the construction of identity: Directions for policy responses. In I. Kerr, V. Steeves, & C. Lucock (Eds.), *Lessons from the identity trail: Anonymity, privacy, and identity in a networked society* (pp. 303–318). New York, NY: Oxford University Press.

Regan, P., & Steeves, V. (2010). Kids R Us: Online social networking and the potential for empowerment. *Surveillance & Society, 8*(2), 151–165.

Richards, A., & Schnall, M. (2003). Cyberfeminism: Networking on the net. In R. Morgan (Ed.), *Sisterhood is forever: The women's anthology for a new millennium* (pp. 517–525). New York, NY: Washington Square Press.

Ringrose, J., & Renold, E. (2012). Teen girls, working-class femininity, and resistance: Retheorising fantasy and desire in educational contexts of heterosexualised violence. *International Journal of Inclusive Education, 16*(4), 461–477. http://dx.doi.org/10.1080/13603116.2011.555099

Schwarz, O. (2010). On friendship, boobs, and the logic of the catalogue: Online self-portraits as a means for the exchange of capital. *Convergence (London), 16*(2), 163–183.

Senft, T. (2008). *Camgirls, celebrity, and community in the age of social networks.* New York, NY: Peter Lang.

Shade, L. (2008). Internet social networking in young women's everyday lives: Some insights from focus groups. *Our Schools, Our Selves,* 65–73.

Steeves, V. (2006). It's not child's play: The online invasion of children's privacy. *University of Ottawa Law and Technology Journal, 3*(1), 169–188.

Thiel-Stern, S. (2005). "IM me" – identity construction and gender negotiation in the world of adolescent girls and instant messaging. In S. R. Mazzarella (Ed.), *Girl wide web: Girls, the internet, and the negotiation of identity* (pp. 179–201). New York, NY: Peter Lang.

van Doorn, N., van Zoonen, L., & Wyatt, S. (2007). Writing from experience: Presentations of gender identity on weblogs. *European Journal of Women's Studies, 14*(2), 143–158. http://dx.doi.org/10.1177/1350506807075819

Westlake, E. (2008). Friend me if you Facebook: Generation Y and performative surveillance. *Drama Review, 52*(4), 21–40. http://dx.doi.org/10.1162/dram.2008.52.4.21

White, M. (2003). Too close to see: Men, women, and webcams. *New Media & Society, 5*(1), 7–28. http://dx.doi.org/10.1177/1461444803005001901

Zureik, E., & Salter, M. (2005). *Global surveillance policing.* Portland, OR: Willan Publishing.

Chapter 4

Watch Me Speak: Muslim Girls' Narratives and Postfeminist Pleasures of Surveillance

SHENILA KHOJA-MOOLJI AND
ALYSSA D. NICCOLINI

This chapter analyses the discursive production of muslim[1] girls' sexuality and how it is taken up as an object of surveillance. We inquire into the genre of confessional texts written by muslim women that attempt to disrupt stereotypes around their sexual and national subjectivities and position them in agentic positions of speaking for their own desires, bodies, and sexual practices. In addition to providing muslim women with a form of control over their representations, we argue that these media enrol muslim bodies in complex relations of surveillance through the proliferation and archiving of information about their interior lives. We specifically investigate popular cultural media such as the compilations *Love, InshAllah* (Mattu & Maznavi, 2012) and *Living Islam Out Loud* (Abdul-Ghafur, 2005) and the interactive websites that accompany them. This chapter is in response to the larger call of this collection to heed to the gendered forms that surveillance can take as well as its "role in propagating intersectional forms of oppression" (Monahan, 2011) while also offering sites of participation. As such, we look at these media as complex assemblages that yield particularly gendered forms of social regulation and knowledge production, while also opening up spaces for play, pleasure, and subversion within surveillance practices.

In an age where popular culture tends to invoke Orientalist imaginaries (Said, 1978; Scott, 2007) that depict muslim female bodies as dangerous, fetishized, and hypersexualized, or as oppressed by muslim men and in need of Western protection and liberation (as epitomized by the cultural fascination with the Taliban shooting victim Malala Yousafzai [Khoja-Moolji, 2015]), popular media where muslim women have the opportunity to self-author depictions of their bodies and desires are rare and important indeed. Yet, while we and the editors of *Love,*

InshAllah and *Living Islam Out Loud* see collections like these as sites of empowerment and dialogue, we also acknowledge the problematic ways in which they also contribute to forms of social surveillance. Following Jasbir Puar (2007), we see sexuality and the surveillance of muslim bodies in the wake of 9/11 as inseparably linked in that "discourses of counterterrorism are intrinsically gendered, raced, and sexualized and … illuminate the production of imbricated normative patriot and terrorist corporealities that cohere against and through each other" (p. xxiv). As disruptions of stereotypic depictions of muslim female sexuality and national identity, how might these texts contribute to positioning muslim and feminist bodies as "insurgent"? What archives do they add to and what modes of observation do they invite? What anxieties, surprises, and pleasures around sexuality, gender, and national belonging motivate their readers and contributors?

Seeking to forge lines of contact across affect theory, feminist studies, and surveillance studies, we draw on theories of social surveillance (Albrechtslund, 2008; Marwick, 2012), surveillance as a cultural practice (Monahan, 2011), and postfeminism (Gill, 2007; McRobbie, 2009; Harris, 2012; Ringrose, 2012) to inquire into the discursive and affective incitements in the texts. We note that *Love, InshAllah* and *Living Islam Out Loud*, and their online media, function to demarcate particular sexual, political, and citizenship roles for muslim girls that map onto conceptualizations of postfeminist girlhood. Girls thus engage in self-surveillance (Gill, 2007) to ensure conformity with the script of postfeminism. In addition, the texts serve as records of the interior, hidden lives of muslim women that can be taken up for further surveillance relations through peer-to-peer monitoring (Marwick, 2012). Intentionally crafted to surprise, titillate, and disrupt assumptions, these works also rely particularly on non-muslim readers' affective responses to generate meaning. Yet they are simultaneously affectively invested in the pleasure, excitement, and power inherent in self-display, providing the muslim women authors with a form of what Hille Koskela (2004) calls "empowering exhibitionism." We explore these incitements through our own divergent positionings as a muslim immigrant from Pakistan (Shenila) and an American-born secular non-muslim (Alyssa). These inherently unstable identity markers orient us in shifting and complex ways to the texts as "insiders" and "outsiders." Thus, we highlight the fraught discursive, affective, and ideological work of this genre – work that is underwritten both by cultural anxieties about "who must be watched and who we should attempt to 'know better'" (Oppenheimer,

2012) and simultaneously by the agentic and even "playful" (Albrecht-slund, 2008) pleasures of dispelling stereotypes and articulating new sexualized and national subjectivities for muslim women.

Flexible Citizens and Cultures of Display: Postfeminism and Surveillance

The unabashed forms of display and confession the young women in *Love, InshAllah* and *Living Islam Out Loud* undertake – acts that within particular muslim communities could lead to discipline, ostracization, and even excommunication – take up familiar frames of "postfeminist girlhood" (Gill, 2007; McRobbie, 2009; Ringrose, 2012). Postfeminism signals an entanglement of feminist ideals with neoliberal sensibilities that emphasize individualism, competition, entrepreneurial identity, and self-help. According to Rosalind Gill (2007), postfeminism operates along several dimensions, some of which include the de-emphasis of motherhood as a defining characteristic for women, the maintenance and display of sexy bodies that must be managed and improved, and an increasing emphasis on individual choice and empowerment that requires constant self-surveillance and discipline. McRobbie (2009) argues that today, notional forms of equality in the realms of education and employment are offered to young women so that they can participate in the consumer economy, yet these forms of "access" exist in place of structural changes that might result from a reinvented feminist politics. She thus argues that in the postfeminist social and cultural landscape, feminism is instrumentalized, depoliticized, and un-done. It is taken up by Western governments to mark the boundaries between West and others along the lines of gender and sexual freedoms. The young muslim women in the texts we have named seem to be taking a postfeminist identity (individualization, enactment of personal responsibility and choice, and display of interior lives, including sexual lives) in order to stake their claims to particular forms of American national identity.

In this neoliberal context, young women, such as the authors of these confessional texts, are urged to take personal responsibility for improving their lives, and to speak up and advocate on their own behalves instead of relying on the state. They are positioned as flexible citizens who can survive in today's risk societies through self-invention and personal effort (Gill, 2007). Those who are unable to perform this kind of citizenship are marked as "at-risk" (Harris, 2012) and perhaps even anti-capitalist and un-American. In addition, Anita Harris (2012) notes that "in times of immense change ... some categories of youth are both constructed and overdetermined as worthy of special scrutiny" (p. 146). In recent decades, muslim youth have emerged as a site of cultural panic; on their bodies, anxieties as wide-ranging as terrorism, English language preservation, and national security are debated and discussed. Many of these youth are constructed as insufficiently progressive; they are seen as clinging to their original national and linguistic identities, making claims on the state, and resisting requirements for self-disclosure and personal responsibility (Harris, 2012).

Along the same lines, there is an increasing interest in hearing girls' own voices: they are being encouraged to speak up and disclose their inner selves rather than be spoken *for*. These calls are often structured in the context of youth participation and empowerment. Indeed, Harris (2012) notes that today's "culture of display and confession" (p. 125) promotes the performance of "true" selves and that there is an understanding that young women ought to make their private lives visible for public consumption. Young women engage in what McRobbie (2009) calls the "new sexual contract" (p. 54) according to which it becomes acceptable, as it had earlier been for men, to uncover their bodies, engage in sexual activity outside the bounds of marriage, produce and/or consume porn, get drunk or experiment with drugs, and then discourse or write about it. This "phallic girl" (McRobbie, 2009, p. 83) seems to be deploying a particular form of equality that she has attained in relation to men. In relation to muslim girls, there has been a proliferation of first-person accounts about their private lives, quests for veiling or deveiling, struggles within mosque communities, engagement with faith, or travels from the global South to the global North. We thus see an impetus for girls to expose their thoughts, bodies, and intimate details of their private lives to perform empowerment and/or to simply partake in the culture of display and confession.

We argue that these calls for disclosure and discourse can serve both regulatory and empowering functions. While they extend the circle of surveillance to the interior lives of girls and add to a lively archive tracking the activities and movements of muslim bodies, the authors of the texts strategically tap into surveillatory practices to disrupt limiting cultural scripts. While we recognize that these texts are situated within a postfeminist culture of display and confession that enlists muslim girls in intricate forms of both self- and social surveillance, we also track how they might function as democratic spaces for different kinds of women to come together and engage with one another, and as pedagogies that seek to correct the limiting stereotypes circulating in American culture around muslim women. We see these postfeminist enactments intersecting with Torin Monahan's (2011) conceptualization of surveillance as a cultural practice. Monahan sees surveillance as "embedded within, brought about by, and generative of social practices in specific cultural contexts" (p. 496). This perspective allows us to read the genre of confessional texts written by muslim women as situated within, products of, and producing the surveillance of American muslims' bodies. Rather than a unidirectional form of control and disciplining, we see surveillance as a multidimensional social practice, where objects of surveillance often resist, reformulate, resignify, and reproduce surveillance practices. Albrechtslund (2008) calls this participatory surveillance, wherein surveillance can be seen as a lateral relationship that entails acts of resistance and agency by objects of surveillance. We thus read the confessional texts written by muslim women not only as responses to the widespread surveillance of muslim bodies, but also as forms of surveillance in which these women enrol themselves willingly, for it promises to produce more egalitarian gender relations within and outside muslim communities.

McRobbie (2009), however, cautions precisely against celebrating self-disclosure as a form of empowerment or resistance, or as enactments of agency by the powerless. She argues that the celebratory uptake of oppressed or marginalized women's voices absolves us from critiquing the wider misogynist and racist structures within which this speech is produced in the first place. Yet while the women in *Love, InshAllah* and *Living Islam Out Loud* do engage in postfeminist cultures of display, their inhabitations of these culturally familiar forms work to denaturalize them. If postfeminist girlhood is a symbol of Westernized "progress" – albeit an illusory progress that feminist scholars take to task (Gill, 2007; Ringrose, 2012) – then by taking up these cultural forms, muslim women position themselves within rather than outside the national body. By explicitly addressing larger social inequities (anti-muslim sentiment, sexism, racism, heteronormativity) *by and through* forms of self-display, their narratives intentionally politicize the confessional genre and inevitably exceed neat determinations of surveillance as completely oppressive and of self-exposure as inherently disempowering.

Indeed, muslim women's relationship with surveillance has been made more complex in the post-9/11 world, for many (if not all) have been forced into positions of heightened public and even institutional scrutiny. Muslim women's intentional mobilization of surveillatory impetuses, through inviting others to observe personal and intimate details of their lives, has transformed surveillance from an anxiety-ridden into a pleasurable and even empowering experience. Engaging in peer-to-peer forms of surveillance through the exchange of personal stories within a network of muslim women also works to create affective communities where new forms of affiliation are possible. These women create a warm and non-judgmental space within which surveillance is mobilized to proliferate wider-ranging forms of muslim subjectivities. Here, the affective jolts of terror, fear, and suspicion usually experienced with being surveilled are mitigated, and watching and being watched become sites of excitement, community, and even comfort. This reminds us of Monahan's (2010, 2011) call to inquire into the democratic or empowering functions of surveillance. He notes that surveillance can bring about openness and participation as well as equalize power among social groups.

The texts under consideration are meant to be to be "insurgent," to rise up against normative views about muslim women and create a space for multiple representations of muslim subjectivities. In this way, the texts make voyeuristic journeys possible for both muslim and non-muslim readers and incite and invite a complex constellation of affects – surprise, shock, excitement, interest, disgust, shame, and pleasure – in discovering "the secret lives of American Muslim women" (Mattu & Maznavi, 2012, cover).

Rejecting, Performing, and Enrolling in Surveillance

Edited by two young American muslim women, Nura Maznavi and Ayesha Mattu, *Love, InshAllah* (2012) is a compilation of real-life stories of "dating, longing and sex" (back cover) written by twenty-five women who "self-identify as both American and Muslim" (p. x). Through first-person confessional accounts, *Love, InshAllah* seeks to provide a peek into the previously inaccessible and "secret love lives of American Muslim women" (front cover). The young muslim women in *Love, InshAllah* share stories about exploring their bodies and sexualities, partaking in body modifications, physical intimacy, subcultural groups, dating and courtship, and the selection of spouses with or without the approval of their families. Both books also disrupt heteronormative depictions of female muslim sexuality in cultural imaginaries that position it as always in relation to male desire (either an oppressive muslim male desire or a desiring Occidental gaze) by including stories of queer desire, thus providing an intimate glimpse into a range of sexual subjectivities.

Living Islam Out Loud (2005) is similarly composed of first-person accounts written by American muslim women, who explain their struggles to "creat[e] a distinctly American Muslim culture" (p. 2) and seek to disrupt misconceptions about muslim women. The editor notes that "very rarely do we encounter empowering images of American Muslim women" (p. 3). The text thus features stories about spiritual journeys, identity, and love by "strong" muslim women. It is hoped that through these narratives "the masses of women who fear judgment and condemnation will find permission to claim their own experiences and a self-determined future" (p. 6). The collection has four parts. The section titled "Love," in which the authors engage in conversations about sex and sexuality, will be the focus here. The authors hope the text will function as an impetus for "safe and honest conversation about sex among Muslims at the family and community level … with a sense of personal responsibility and freedom" (p. 52).

Surprising Pleasures

Both the texts invite and anticipate a non-muslim readership. *Love, InshAllah*, for instance, includes a glossary for non-muslim readers. Positioning non-muslim readers in a self-conscious "outsider" position, the glossary gives the text a particular didactic power while also signalling welcome. It also ushers non-muslims into the role of outside surveillor. What does it mean to intentionally invite watching from those who perceive the muslim body as culturally foreign? In many ways, by inviting the gaze of a non-muslim audience, the women in *Love, InshAllah* and *Living Islam Out Loud* are controlling the terms under which their bodies are monitored and watched. Rather than being passive objects of policing eyes, they enact modes of surveillance on their own terms and invite a non-muslim audience to watch them in new ways. As Albrechtslund (2008) argues, this upends the "vertical ways surveillance is often conceptualized in such cultural metaphors as 'Big Brother" and 'Panopticon.'" He notes that "the hierarchical conception of this relation puts the power into the hands of the watcher while the watched is a more or less passive subject of control" (participatory surveillance section, para. 3). Instead, the women authors in these texts establish more "lateral" (Andrejevic, 2005; Albrechtslund, 2008) forms of surveillance where power shifts between the viewer and viewed; they become peers, destabilizing the earlier vertical relationship, and the pleasures of watching and being watched overlap.

As Mattu and Maznavi (2012) write in their introduction, "we wanted to challenge the stereotypes of the wider American audience by presenting stories that are rarely heard" (p. ix). The stories seek to tap into affective stances of interest, curiosity, shock, and surprise from non-muslims. G. Willow Wilson remarks precisely on this in her review, declaring the book "frank, engrossing and refreshingly honest ... a book full of hidden surprises" (review page). Eve Sedgwick (2003) sees surprise as a particularly important affective position and places it in opposition to paranoia. In many ways, the intense surveillance and generalized mistrust of muslims by some Americans is a form of paranoia. Sedgwick (2003) argues that the paranoia rests on a "faith in exposure" (p. 139), describing it as "characterized by placing, in practice, an extraordinary stress on the efficacy of knowledge per se – knowledge in the form of exposure. Maybe that's why paranoid knowing is so inescapably narrative" (p. 138). By producing their own forms of knowledge, the writers in *Love, InshAllah* tap into the narrative hunger of the paranoid as well as the exposure that surveillatory practices demand of muslim bodies. Yet in seeking to "surprise" non-muslim readers with unexpected narratives of muslim subjectivities, their text is also what Sedgwick terms "reparative." Reparative modes, according to Sedgwick (2003), "are more about pleasure" and are "ameliorative" and "reformist" (p. 144); the women authors in these compilations definitely intend to ameliorate negative or narrow conceptions of muslims in America.

Entangled in Social Surveillance

That said, the texts are not utopic; they directly confront the difficulties of being muslim in America. Several authors in *Love, InshAllah* discuss the pressures to be a "good Muslim girl" (p. 96, p. 127) or the "perfect example of a Muslim in America" (p. 132). These pressures come from both an outside (non-muslim) and an inside (familial, communal, or internalized) disciplinary gaze. The texts quietly interrogate (an acknowledged fraught word within post-9/11 discourses) the role surveillance plays in muslim life, and surveillance is thematically prominent in both *Love, InshAllah* and *Living Islam Out Loud*. As

Abdul-Ghafur (2005) writes, "the paradox of September 11, 2001, is that it firmly and forever established Islam and Muslims in the eyes of the West" (p. 2). The authors of both collections play with this enforced visibility. Editor Ayesha Mattu's (2012) narrative "The Opening," recounts living in Boston in the immediate aftermath of 9/11. The event made her hyperaware of "how white Boston really is" and of her own new hypervisibility. She writes about "a friend [who] asked if I would hang an American flag outside my home to prove my patriotism" (p.48) after the attacks. Similarly, Mohja Kahf (Abdul-Ghafur, 2005) in *Living Islam Out Loud* is aware of, and responds to, the overt surveillance of muslim bodies and spaces of worship: "I will not circle my wagons around the mosque, will not yield in fearful worry to the entreaties of the wagon-circlers inside nor to the shouts of the hatemongers outside. I will function within this double bind. I strategize around it with every move I make, every piece I write" (p. 131).

As Kahf illustrates, the surveillance the authors explore is not just from non-muslims. Social surveillance work has "begun to unpack the ongoing eavesdropping, investigation, gossip and inquiry that constitutes information gathering by people about their peers" (Marwick, 2012, p. 379). Many of the women in *Love, InshAllah* recount growing up, as Insiya Ansari does in "Sex by any other Name," "under the watchful eyes of [their] parents" (p. 88) and the larger muslim community. Ansari goes on to characterize this as a "parental enmeshment" in American muslim girls' lives, an enmeshment captured in "a crude maxim in our dialect that essentially means I was 'all up in my parents' armpits'" (p. 88). Lena Hasan in "Cyberlove" escapes her family's watchful eye by chatting with muslim men online. As she narrates, "to my family's eyes, I was hard at work in front of my computer, writing code for my school assignments. In reality, I was crossing swords with Asian men while playing the role of magician in a Multi-User Dungeon" (p. 235). She also describes herself in a surveillatory position as she "eavesdrop[ped] for a few months" (p. 234) on the men at Friday study circle at the mosque, who were separated from the women by "portable partitions, improvised out of bedsheets" (p. 233). The women writers reveal, often with humour, the creative and resourceful lengths they took to elude surveillance even while participating in it. By compiling a collection of diverse and (for some) taboo stories of love and sex, the contributors have found a means to both extend and speak back to these peer-to-peer forms of surveillance.

As in *Love, InshAllah*, many narratives in *Living Islam Out Loud* focus on surveillance. In "My Own Worst Enemy," Manal Omar describes the intense self-surveillance she performed in attempting to be a "good Muslim woman" (p. 66). She anticipated surveillance by other muslims and worked diligently on an acutely gendered self-presentation. In her words, "I internalized the message that being a quiet and demure girl was the path to being a responsible and pure woman" (p. 55). Khalida Saed complicates notions of social surveillance in "On the Edge of Belonging." After coming out as a lesbian to her mother, she feels "extreme loneliness and isolation" (p. 88) and begins more intensely immersing herself in a muslim identity by wearing hijab and starting a Muslim Student Association at her high school. Performing "good muslim girlhood" does not "stop her [from] being queer," however much she wishes it were so (p. 88). The oppressive social surveillance she feels coming from her family and muslim community is very different from the exposure she experiences at a LGBTQ youth group meeting. She recalls how lengthy the process of introducing themselves was since instead of just names, the young people, invigorated by the chance to affirm their queer identities, gushed "out all this information about themselves" (p. 89). Saed describes her own turn and how she struggled with what information she should reveal to the group: "Should I give my real name? Should I state my real age? ... When it was finally my turn, I blurted out everything about myself that I could possibly remember. I think I even included my middle name and place of birth" (p. 89). Here she voluntarily enlists and even revels in exposing intimate details about herself.

Making Interior Lives Visible

Both, *Love, InshAllah* and *Living Islam Out Loud* work to manage the social category of American muslim women by discursively producing a muslim girlhood characterized by postfeminist calls for individualization, personal responsibility and choice, and display of self. Several authors in *Love, InshAllah* signal this independence by sharing stories of their quests for romantic love, and position this search in opposition to the arranged marriages that are prevalent in most Muslim communities. This tension is also observed by Olsen (1997) in her ethnographic work with immigrant youth in California. Olsen found that immigrants "measure[d] their own level of Americanization on a scale with romance at one end and respecting the authority of one's parents and one's tradition at the other" (p. 146). So it is not surprising that self-invention through romantic love is a prominent theme in *Love, InshAllah*. Indeed, only a few authors acquiesced to arranged marriages (p. 9). These enactments of personal choice and independence are in line with contemporary understandings of youth citizenship, which construct young women as ideal new citizens capable of taking personal responsibility in today's risk societies, in which "communal ties and traditional bonds have become looser and less predictable" (Harris, 2004, p. 65). This is in contrast to *Living Islam Out Loud*, where several authors agreed to arranged marriages only to later encounter incompatibility or abuse within those marriages. The authors here recount domestic violence, the inability of husbands to consummate the marriage, and marriages solely in order to obtain an American green card. However, narratives of triumph surround these stories, too, when women decide to leave or divorce their spouses to begin new lives on their own, and not on their parents' or community's terms.

As noted earlier, this incitement to disclose details about private lives is grounded in postfeminist calls for girls' participation, as well as the "talking cure" (deCastell, 2004, p. 54), which insists that hearing silenced voices can fix everything. Intimate thoughts and experiences are shared so that readers can come to know "real," "authentic" muslim women. Through these processes, however, muslim girls enrol themselves in postfeminist scripts of self-surveillance, in which they perform particular kinds of knowledges and narrate a specific orientation towards politics, sexuality, and consumption that aligns with postfeminist characteristics of individuality, personal choice, and girlpower. Any deviation would mark them as "at risk" or, worse, "unpatriotic." The intentional exclusion of non-normative stories by the authors of *Love, InshAllah*, for instance, signifies their understanding of these dynamics. For instance, not many authors produce knowledge about their experiences of racial, social, and economic discrimination, or criticize government policies towards minority populations. Performing such critiques is not part of postfeminist girlhood. The postfeminist script demands self-surveillance and relies on cooperation from objects of surveillance (Bauman & Lyon, 2012).

An Unfolding Archive

In an effort to extend conversations beyond the codex text, *Love, InshAllah* provides a website where the editors and authors blog and visitors can share questions anonymously through an advice column that invites questions about "love and sex and everything in between" (http://loveinshallah.com/advice). In one post, a non-muslim woman asks for advice on dating a muslim man who hides their relationship from his family. On last visit to the site, there were fifty-six comments from both muslims and non-muslims. The comments are remarkably civil in tone; conspicuously absent are the vitriolic anti-muslim rants sadly common to open commentary threads. There is only one comment disparaging an interfaith relationship: "relations between different people is not right." A level-headed respondent asks, "Do you have any interest in expanding on this thought?" Either the site has attracted incredibly well-behaved visitors or there is careful moderation of the content. In either case, it serves to display democratic debate rather than divisiveness around muslim subjectivities. It is also a space where muslim women (and men) construct particular visions of themselves as citizens. Through "subjectivity building" (Albrechtslund, 2008, participatory surveillance section, para. 2), muslim women use the virtual space to depict themselves as agentic women working to debunk negative stereotypes of muslims in America. Here, instead of being oppressed and spoken for, they bandy with men in democratic debate; instead of being sectarian or insular, they welcome dialogue with non-muslims; instead of being lambasted by anonymous anti-muslim commentators, they are addressed by a largely sympathetic and respectful online community of their making.

The website extends the time of the text into a future that invites more stories and perspectives, what Puar (2007) terms an "unfolding" (p. xix) rather than static archive. Here, visitors can "Meet the Ladies of *Love, InshAllah*" through a controlled form of "unveiling." The biographies the women have posted offer varying degrees of access to the viewership – some women provide lengthy histories accompanied by smiling headshots, others include only a profile in hijab or sunglasses, while others, like the pseudonymous Insiya Ansari, offer only a sentence with a headshot where a scarf (not hijab) deliberately conceals all but one eye. In a similar gesture of disguise, the pen-named Nour Gamal substitutes a cartoon image for her photograph. Reflecting the variety of perspectives the collection encompasses, the women invite and elude a range of intimacy and surveillance in online access. All the while, the open space of the Internet invites a wider audience and an accessible archive for the surveillance of muslim bodies and communities. It has been widely noted that the surveillance of online activity is a hallmark of the "War on Terror." Here, the website contributors shape an online space that provides an opportunity for surveillance, but also for stylized "subjectivity-building" (Albrechtslund, 2008).

It is assumed that this disclosure will disrupt stereotypes about muslim women and make possible previously taboo conversations within muslim communities. Indeed, *Love, InshAllah* has received praise from several muslim public intellectuals, who call it a "desperately needed corrective" and position it as embodying the "authentic voices of Muslim women" (advance praise section). Others posit that it will "upend the stereotypes of veiled and abused Muslim women" and give a more representative picture of what America looks like (front page). The texts, in this way, engage in the dual project of freeing muslim women from the discursive tropes that represent them as submissive and voiceless, and defusing the threat of muslim immigration. That muslim women – and not muslim men – have undertaken this task is not surprising. Women have historically borne the burden of upholding communal norms of morality and piety and have been employed as symbols in nationalist, religious, and ethnic struggles (see Devji, 1991; Yuval-Davis, Anthias, & Kofman, 2005; Khoja-Moolji, 2011). Also, during migration, women's bodies, sexual practices, and consumption habits have become signifiers of their group's status and reputation (see Espiritu, 2001). So by enrolling in and evading particular forms of surveillance, the authors are self-stylizing a particular form of Western citizenship.

Intimacy and Transparency

More broadly, the texts and online archives can be read to enact new understandings of intimacy. Gregg (2013) notes that there is a new assumption that intimacy and transparency go hand-in-hand; there is no need for privacy if there is nothing to hide. In this context, revealing and exposing secrets is seen as a productive and healthy thing to do to maintain a relationship – perhaps even a relationship with one's nation. This premise seems to inform the two texts under consideration: the authors see in self-disclosure a promise for better relations among muslims, as well as between muslims and non-muslims. The editors of *Love, InshAllah*, for instance, seek to "challenge the stereotypes of the wider American audience" (p. ix), and the editors of *Living Islam Out Loud* strive to "humanize American Muslim women to our fellow citizens of the world" (p. 6) and hope their stories will allow other muslim women to "find permission to claim their own experiences" (p. 6). There is, thus, an implicit assumption that disclosure will promote intimacy and mutual understanding.

But these self-disclosures can also be read as a response to the West's desire to hear the voices of the marginalized for the sake of its own coherence, authorization, and redemption (Jones, 2004). In the context of colonial and Orientalist legacies, contemporary relationships between muslims and non-muslims include a sense of entitlement on the part of non-muslims to certain kinds of knowledges about muslim women. These include women's voices that highlight the oppressive characteristics of Islam/Muslim men (such as *Infidel* by Ayaan Hirsi Ali; *The Trouble with Islam Today* by Irshad Manji; *A God Who Hates: The Courageous Woman Who Inflamed the Muslim World Speaks Out Against the Evils of Islam* by Wafa Sultan; and *Standing Alone in Mecca: An American Woman's Struggle for the Soul of Islam* by Asra Nomani); those that reveal the struggles of living within the fold of oppressive Islam/Muslim men and then escaping it (such as *I Am Nujood, Age 10 and Divorced* by Nujood Ali; *I am Malala: The Girl Who Stood Up for Education and Was Shot by the Taliban* by Malala Yousafzai; *Sold: One Woman's True Account of Modern Slavery* by Zana Muhsen); and those that give viewers access to muslim women's real, interior lives (such as *Honour, Heels, and Headscarves: Real-Life Stories of Women from Istanbul* by Carla de la Vega; *Princess: A True Story of Life Behind the Veil in Saudi Arabia* by Jean Sasson). Some might argue that disclosures by muslim women do little to destabilize sedimented relations of power and that they can be read, instead, as strategies of neocolonialism, which make possible further surveillance of muslim bodies. There is, for instance, no explicit responsibility for improving the social conditions of muslims/women/queers/youth assigned to those who consume these texts. Performance of these knowledges and individualized explanations for social problems is assumed to be enough.

Pleasure of Being Watched

Throughout this chapter we have problematized any neat engagement with the texts. These stories can be taken up for external surveillance, but they also offer sites of participatory surveillance (Albrechtslund, 2008), where the emphasis is on their playful and social functions. As noted earlier, Albrechtslund (2008) suggests that we move beyond the hierarchical conception of surveillance and look for ways in which surveillance can help build subjectivity. Indeed, the editors of both texts emphasize their own and the authors' choice to write about making sense of the world. The contributors to both texts are acutely aware that divulging stories of sex, sexuality, and marriage may lead to ostracism by the community or accusations of playing into "orientalist fantasy about Muslim women" (Mattu & Maznavi, 2012, p. iv). Yet they strongly value their voices and see their stories as rare, non-normative, and unique, as destabilizing popular conceptions of muslim women while documenting the fraught processes of identity construction. Indeed, online networking through social websites facilitates news ways of constructing identity, for it entails calculated self-disclosures and performances. In the context of the argument made by the authors that limited spaces are available for muslim women to discuss issues of sex and sexuality, the online and textual forums can become empowering. Koskela (2004) has termed the intentional revelation of intimate details "empowering exhibitionism" (p. 199) and notes that people often use the visibility afforded by social media, reality TV, and other avenues to self-construct their identity and thereby "reclaim the copyright of their own lives" (p. 206). Viewing *Love, InshAllah* and *Living Islam Out Loud* through the lens of empowering exhibitionism reveals the authors' agency in terms of reconstructing the image of muslim women in the United States – they are performing for the "gaze" on their own terms. They are engaging in a form of counter-surveillance by circulating narratives and images themselves. In this way, "exhibitionism *plays* with visibility" (Koskela, 2004, p. 209, emphasis original); it seeks to capture the power of the surveillor.

Yet as noted earlier, the images and performances in the text are aligned with postfeminist scripts, which encompass exhibiting one's body and desires, as well as exposing interior lives, in ways that often offer "the perfect heterosexual male fantasy" (Jimroglou, 2001, p. 287). Koskela (2004), however, notes that "there is some voyeuristic fascination in looking, but, reciprocally, some exhibitionist fascination in being seen" (p. 203). Revealing secrets and engaging in conversations around topics marked as taboo can be pleasurable for the authors. There is pleasure in evading what Koskela (2004) calls the "regime of shame" (p. 207), which directs people to keep hidden particular actions and thoughts. In the context of muslim communities, this regime of shame has a gendered dimension. Faisel Devji (1991), for instance, notes that in the legal muslim discourse, the distinctions among the public, private, and domestic spheres entailed the paganization and eroticization of women. Women were "deemed to pose a threat to or denial of the public Muslim patriarchate" (Devji, 1991, p. 145), and this necessitated their seclusion and legitimized various forms of surveillance. Fatima Mernissi (1991), too, draws attention to ways in which women's sexuality was deemed uncontrollable because it could create *fitna* (chaos), again, in the public realm. Thus, the display of the female body and sexual desires in the current text presents a threat to the normative regime of shame within which sexuality and pleasure are regulated. By rejecting this regime, the authors blur the boundaries between the public and private, contest the histories that mark their bodies as shameful, and in doing so partake in pleasures that come with trespassing and transgressive acts. The authors are applauded for doing so – Wajahat Ali, for instance, praises the authors: "this illuminating anthology ... should be applauded ... for its ability to celebrate these utterly normal, healthy, messy, and all-too human discussions about love and sexuality which for too long have been buried under a veil of shame, fear, and self-imposed censorship" (Mattu & Maznavi, p. ii). Thus, the authors are able to model what a moral uprising against this regime of shame might look like, and can inhabit the role of trailblazers.

Conclusions: Difficult Negotiations

Khalida Saed (2005) ends her narrative in *Living Islam Out Loud* by writing: "being young, and being a Muslim immigrant in the post-9/11 era, and being so decidedly American in Muslim society ... it's all so complicated and difficult to negotiate" (pp. 93–4). In this chapter we have argued that, indeed, negotiations of gender, sexuality, and muslim identity are fraught with complexities. The tales in *Love, InshAllah* & *Living Islam Out Loud* offer a range of voices that confound certainties as to what constitutes muslim identity in America. By intentionally playing with surveillance practices, the women in these texts take up regulatory, postfeminist scripts of femininity while simultaneously recasting the narrow structures of what constitutes American identity. By inviting surprise in how we envision muslim women and American identity writ large, they may elicit what Sedgwick (2003) calls a reparative stance, one in which "the reader has room to realize that the future may be different from the present, it is also possible for her to entertain such profoundly painful, profoundly relieving, ethically crucial possibilities as that the past, in turn, could have happened differently from the way it actually did" (p. 146). It is such reparative reading that we extend to those interested in taking up these women's narratives, whether for surveillance or pleasure, or the interesting possibilities of both.

NOTE

1 We choose not to capitalize muslim in this chapter to signal the diversity of interpretations of Islam.

REFERENCES

Abdul-Ghafur, S. (2005). *Living Islam out loud: American Muslim women speak*. Boston, MA: Beacon Press.

Albrechtslund, A. (2008). Online social networking as participatory surveillance. *First Monday*, *13*(3). http://firstmonday.org/ojs/index.php/fm/article/view/2142/1949. http://dx.doi.org/10.5210/fm.v13i3.2142

Andrejevic, M. (2005). The work of watching one another: Lateral surveillance, risk, and governance. *Surveillance & Society*, *2*(4), 479–497.

Bauman, Z., & Lyon, D. (2012). *Liquid surveillance: A conversation*. Cambridge, MA: Polity.

deCastell, S. (2004). No speech is free: Affirmative action and the politics of give and take. In M. Boler (Ed.), *Democratic dialogue in education: Troubling speech, disturbing silence* (pp. 51–56). New York, NY: Peter Lang.

Devji, F. (1991). Gender and the politics of space: The movement for women's reform in Muslim India, 1857–1900. *South Asia*, *14*(1), 141–153. http://dx.doi.org/10.1080/00856409108723151

Espiritu, Y. L. (2001). "We don't sleep around like white girls do": Family, culture, and gender in Filipina American lives. *Signs*, *26*(2), 415–440. http://dx.doi.org/10.1086/495599

Gill, R. (2007). Postfeminist media culture: Elements of a sensibility. *European Journal of Cultural Studies*, *10*(2), 147–166.

Gregg, M. (2013). Spousebusting: Intimacy, adultery, and surveillance technology. *Surveillance & Society*, *11*(3), 301–310.

Harris, A. (2004). *Future girl: Young women in the 21st century*. London, New York: Routledge.

Harris, A. (2012). Citizenship stories. In N. Lesko & S. Talburt (Eds.), *Keywords in youth studies: Tracing affects, movements, knowledges* (pp. 143–152). New York, NY: Taylor and Francis.

Jimroglou, K. M. (2001). A camera with a view: JenniCAM, visual representations, and cyborg subjectivity. In E. Green & A. Adam (Eds.), *Virtual gender: Technology, consumption, and identity* (pp. 286–301). London: Routledge.

Jones, A. (2004). Talking cure: The desire for dialogue. In M. Boler (Ed.), *Democratic dialogue in education: Troubling speech, disturbing silence* (pp. 57–68). New York, NY: Peter Lang.

Koskela, H. (2004). Webcams, TV shows, and mobile phones: Empowering exhibitionism. *Surveillance & Society, 2*(2/3), 199–215.

Khoja-Moolji, S. (2011). Redefining Muslim women: Aga Khan III's reforms for women's education. *South Asia Graduate Research Journal, 20*(1), 69–95.

Khoja-Moolji, S. (2015). Reading Malala: (De)(re)territorialization of Muslim collectivities. *Journal of Comparative Studies of South Asia, Africa, and the Middle East, 35*(3), 539–556.

Marwick, A. E. (2012). The public domain: Surveillance in everyday life. *Surveillance & Society, 9*(4), 378–393.

Mattu, A. (2012). The Opening. In A. Mattu & N. Maznavi (Eds.), *Love, InshAllah: The secret love lives of American Muslim women* (pp. 46–57). Berkeley, CA: Soft Skull Press.

Mattu, A., & Maznavi, N. (2012). *Love, InshAllah: The secret love lives of American Muslim women.* Berkeley, CA: Soft Skull Press.

McRobbie, A. (2009). *The aftermath of feminism: Gender, culture, and social change.* London, UK: Sage Publications.

Mernissi, F. (1991). *Women and Islam: A historical and theological enquiry* (Mary Jo Lakeland, Trans.) Oxford, UK: Basil Blackwell.

Monahan, T. (2010). Surveillance as governance: Social inequality and the pursuit of democratic surveillance. In K. D. Haggerty & M. Samatas (Eds.), *Surveillance and democracy* (pp. 91–110). New York, NY: Routledge.

Monahan, T. (2011). Surveillance as a cultural practice. *Sociological Quarterly, 52*(4), 495–508. http://dx.doi.org/10.1111/j.1533-8525.2011.01216.x

Olsen, L. (1997). *Made in America: Immigrant students in our public schools.* New York, NY: New Press.

Oppenheimer, R. (2012). Surveillance. In N. Lesko & S. Talburt (Eds.), *Keywords in youth studies: Tracing affects, movements, knowledges* (pp. 54–58). New York, NY: Taylor and Francis.

Puar, J. K. (2007). *Terrorist assemblages: Homonationalism in queer times.* Durham, NC: Duke University Press. http://dx.doi.org/10.1215/9780822390442

Ringrose, J. (2012). *Postfeminist education? Girls and the sexual politics of school.* London, UK: Routledge.

Saed, K. (2005). On the edge of belonging. In Abdul-Ghafur, *Living Islam out loud: American Muslim women speak*. Boston, MA: Beacon Press.

Said, E. (1978). *Orientalism*. New York, NY: Vintage Books.

Scott, J. (2007). *Politics of the veil*. Princeton, NJ: Princeton University Press.

Sedgwick, E. (2003). *Touching feeling: Affect, pedagogy, performativity*. Durham, NC: Duke University Press.

Yuval-Davis, N., Anthias, F., & Kofman, E. (2005). Secure borders and safe haven and gendered politics of belonging: Beyond social cohesion. *Ethnic and Racial Studies, 28*(3), 513–535. http://dx.doi.org/10.1080/0141987042000337867

Profiling the City: Urban Space and the Serial Killer Film

JENNY REBURN

The serial killer is understood as a predominantly urban phenomenon: repeat murder somehow belongs in the alienating city, the anonymity imposed by metropolitan spaces apparently facilitating "stranger killing." This concept is articulated in a cycle of movies I refer to as profiler films, in which the city is constructed as an inherently dangerous space that requires surveillance. I argue that these films depict urban space as subject to the monitoring gaze of both the killer and the profiler – a detective figure uniquely equipped to combat the serial killer. Both these figures, the killer and the profiler, are typically white men, who align their surveillance with patriarchal power structures. Yet these types of films rarely problematize male violence; instead, they focus on the killer's ability to remain inconspicuous in the urban sprawl. The movies tend to construct the city as a space that demands regulation and supervision over which these two agents of surveillance fight, with the ultimate success of the profiler dependent on his (and occasionally, her) ability to map urban space.

Depictions of the urban serial killer can be traced as far back as silent cinema (most notably *The Lodger* [Alfred Hitchcock, 1927]), but I am concerned here with the upsurge in American city killer films beginning in the late 1970s and continuing, with interesting modifications, into the 2010s. These films emerged as the United States faced an apparent epidemic of random violence, during which the FBI developed new theories and investigative procedures to deal with serial murder. The FBI's influence over serial killer discourse remains significant despite criticism of these procedures (Seltzer, 1998; Schmid, 2005; Bull, 2013). In particular, the FBI profiler has been constructed as the only defence against the incomprehensible serial killer. The commercial success of Thomas

Harris's Hannibal Lecter novels (Harris, 1981, 1988, 1999) – famously based on the author's research at the FBI (Seltzer, 1998; Schmid, 2005) – and their cinematic adaptations demonstrate the cultural impact of the profiler narrative throughout the 1980s and 1990s.

By the end of the 1990s, the profiler was being superseded to some extent by the forensic specialist, most notably in the television series *CSI: Crime Scene Investigation* (2000–) (Bull, 2013). Traditional representations of the profiler continue to appear in film, but since the late 1990s, the character has just as often been depicted subversively. The profiler is often defeated by the killer or is revealed to be the/another killer. Although these adjustments began before 2001, this development is often ascribed to post-9/11 shifts. The serial killer offers a safer, more familiar figure of fear than the ethnically Other terrorist (Schmid, 2005); the trajectory of the Hannibal Lecter character from terrifying but narratively peripheral to "seductive," charismatic, and plot-defining epitomizes this modification (Picart & Greek, 2007, p. 246). In addition, nationally divisive debates surrounding the use of potentially invasive legal powers and surveillance technology are articulated in torture porn[1] (Tziallas, 2013) and in the television series *Dexter* (2006–2013) (Byers, 2010; Macdonald, 2013). While torture porn often incorporates an unsuccessful profiler figure, *Dexter*'s protagonist is a serial killer who uses his considerable intuitive talent for recognizing other killers, as well as forensic skills developed in his capacity as a police blood analyst, to target other murderers, combining the roles of profiler and killer in a way foreshadowed by Harris's Hannibal Lecter. Despite an academic emphasis on interpreting these developments through a post-9/11 frame, it is likely that the profiler cycle, having begun in the late 1970s and maintained its popularity for two decades, had by 2000 reached a point where playful, subversive reworkings offered longevity to a familiar formula.

This chapter begins by discussing the concept of the monitored city and the influence of discourse surrounding the crimes attributed to Jack the Ripper on the construction of the urban serial killer. The profiler film demonstrates the ways in which contemporary responses to these Victorian crimes – most notably an emphasis on the Gothic and the use of the serial killer threat to monitor female behaviour – are echoed as the serial killer becomes a significant cultural figure in late-twentieth-century America. I show that both the serial killer and the city are depicted as monitoring the population in gendered ways. I then explore cinematic portrayals of the serial killer, arguing that the development of the profiler figure over the past forty years has contributed to a sense of the city as a space in need of masculine supervision. Although these films are more commonly interrogated within the psychoanalytic debates initiated by Mulvey's work on the male gaze (Mulvey, 1990), this chapter uses Foucauldian concepts as a framework. This decision does not undermine the importance of discussions emerging from Mulvey's intervention; instead, it recognizes a body of literature that has not been incorporated into film studies to the same extent as psychoanalytic theory. This work highlights the discursive nature of the serial killer, acknowledging the status of this figure as a real-world phenomenon that is only accessible through representation (Cameron & Frazer, 1987; Caputi, 1988; Seltzer, 1998). Acknowledging this discursive status offers insight into the ways in which the serial killer figure can be used to support dominant ideology. In addition, Foucault's analysis of panoptical surveillance, and feminist responses that critique his gender-blind approach, are useful in exploring the ways in which these films depict urban space as subject to monitoring not just by the killer and the profiler, but also by a more pervasive supervision that sometimes coincides with these two figures. While the films often hint at sinister parallels between the killer and the profiler, connections between the mainly benevolent profiler and the apparently benign but potentially repressive gendering of space remain concealed.

Panoptic Cities, Serial Killing, and the Urban Profiler

Foucault (1977/1991) uses the panopticon – a prison designed to ensure that one unseen guard is able to monitor every convict, with each prisoner always potentially visible to supervision – to argue that power is not limited to repressive state institutions. Following the main goal of the panopticon, which is "to induce in the inmate a state of conscious and permanent visibility that assures the automatic functioning of power" (Foucault, 1991, pp. 200–1), Foucault contends that this condition causes surveillance to be internalized. This surveillance is not self-evidently repressive, for it is built into the social order and has positive features such as increased efficiency and other improvements that benefit society (Foucault, 1991, p. 210). Rather than oppress the population as a mass, the panoptical society exercises a disciplinary power within which identity is constructed, combining "hierarchical surveillance and normalising judgement" in order to "constitute the individual as effect and object of power" (Foucault, 1991, p. 192). Modes of behaviour are not consciously observed; since surveillance is internalized, behaving within culturally defined norms appears natural and instinctive.

This internalization is highlighted in a feminist response to Foucault, which critiques his failure to acknowledge gender. Bartky (2003) argues that surveillance, and the internalized self-surveillance prompted by potentially constant observation, is covertly coded as a masculine gaze, regardless of the individual's gender. She argues that "a panoptical male connoisseur resides within the consciousness of most women: they stand perpetually before his gaze and under his judgement" (2003, p. 34). This surveillance can be experienced as "positive" in that women who adhere to a particular "feminine" role benefit economically, professionally, and socially, despite being locked into culturally determined modes of behaviour and appearance. This analysis has significance in debates around the treatment of women who are subjected to male violence. The idea that women who act or dress "immodestly" are somehow more exposed to sexual harassment or attack suggests that this violence serves as a corrective to inappropriate female behaviour, especially behaviour that relates to sexuality. It is not uncommon for incidents of sexual assault against women to be followed by official advice suggesting that women avoid certain areas and refrain from walking alone, especially at night (Ward Jouve, 1986; Boyle, 2005; Cameron, 2014). This reaction – prompting women to adjust their habits, rather than tackling male behaviour and attitudes – underlines the patriarchal power structures that influence societal ideas around violence. It also implies that public spaces are male spaces, with the female victims of sexual violence serving as an example of the perils of defying traditional gender boundaries.

What is important here is not the existence of these ideas but their widespread acceptance as commonsensical, rational assumptions. As I will explore, these notions are often also evident in serial killers' discussions of their own crimes, but this phenomenon does not so much offer an insight into any peculiarity in these murderers' mindsets as it reinforces the prevalence of this thinking. Killers who target women working as prostitutes, for example, are often understood to be enacting a somehow comprehensible antipathy towards sex workers (Boyle, 2005; Gregoriou, 2011). Even relatively recent true crime investigations of the murders attributed to Jack the Ripper position the killer as punishing his victims for seducing men, spreading sexual diseases, and "flaunting" their sexuality (see, for example, Fido, 1999; Harrison, 1999; Cornwell, 2002). These theories construct male loathing of sex workers as in some way understandable, implicitly condoning misogynistic violence. The victims are positioned as contributing to their own deaths through their "unfeminine" behaviour and their presence in male space. Jack the Ripper's continued celebrity is accompanied by a "'moral' message" that warns "the city is a dangerous place for women, when they transgress the narrow boundaries of home and hearth and dare to enter public space" (Walkowitz, 1982, p. 544). Analysis of the Peter Sutcliffe case – the murders of thirteen women in the north of England between 1975 and 1980 by a man whose claim to be punishing sinful women encountered little scrutiny outside of feminist responses – exposes similarly misogynistic monitoring of female behaviour. The tacit approval of Sutcliffe's attitude towards women is evident in journalistic and true crime accounts of the case, as well as in police and judicial reactions to the murders (Hollway, 1981; Ward Jouve, 1986). As police searched for the killer, attention was focused on the need for women to adjust their habits. This shifted responsibility from the killer and the patriarchal power structures that enabled his violence to the women themselves, who should have avoided making themselves vulnerable (Hollway, 1981; Ward Jouve, 1986). Studies of more recent media representations of misogynistic violence demonstrate that this admonishment of female behaviour was not limited to Victorian London, or even 1970s Britain, but continues to prevail in contemporary accounts of sexual violence (Boyle, 2005). An examination of news reports following the murders by Steve Wright of five women working as sex workers in Ipswich, England, in December 2006 revealed that these murdered women were often criticized for putting themselves in danger and that their drug habits were used to shift blame from Wright to his drug-addicted victims (Gregoriou, 2011).

Barkty's feminist reading of Foucault helps explain why these expectations around female behaviour go largely unchallenged. By understanding surveillance as both internalized and implicitly gendered, we can comprehend this monitoring of female behaviour as ostensibly benign but in reality repressive. Arguably, it is its apparent benevolence that lends this supervision its power, for "the more soft and subtle the panoptic strategies, the more [the panoptic regime] produces the desired docile bodies" (Lyon, 2006, p. 4). Taking apparently logical, straightforward precautions appears sensible and rational until the concepts behind these safety measures are worked through.

Foucault's emphasis on the city as a site of surveillance has also been reframed with greater awareness of gender. Donald (1999) argues that urban space offers the possibility of regulating the population through the manipulation of streets and recreational areas. Urban planners seek to "make the city an object of knowledge and so a governable space ... to render the city transparent" (p. 14). This concept of "benign surveillance and spatial penetration" (p. 14) understands citizens as a group to be categorized, a mass out of which meaning can be constructed in the form of statistics (p. 32). Meaning is also apparent in the division of city space by economic class and gender. Furthermore, city space is "charged and polarised by an avaricious and eroticised gaze which is predominantly gendered male" (p. 114). The city, then, is a panoptical model through which the state can supervise the population, but it is also a thoroughly gendered space in which specific areas offer different experiences that are dependent on gender.

An important figure in this space, particularly as this character developed at the same time as the modern city, is the detective. In nineteenth-century fiction, the detective's investigation parallels his movements through the city (Warwick, 2007); he functions as "the personification of the power to decipher its networks" (Donald, 1999, p. 3). He is able to cross class boundaries, and this allows the increased surveillance of certain individuals (Cunningham, 2007; Walkowitz, 2007). The detective story "stages the city as enigma: a dangerous but fascinating network of often subterranean relationships in need of decipherment" (Donald, 1999, p. 70). This concept of the detective as an urban decoder eventually assimilates the more modern interest in the crime scene but remains tied to the idea of urban space being made legible by certain individuals.

Discourse surrounding Jack the Ripper is significant to both the development of the urban detective (Willis, 2007) and fundamental aspects of serial killer discourse. Although never conclusively identified (or perhaps *because* of this enduring mystery), the killer (or killers) of a contested number of women working as prostitutes in 1888 in London's Whitechapel district remains a significant cultural figure (Caputi, 1988). The complex merging of fact and fiction surrounding these crimes, including the notorious nickname, obscures their misogynistic nature (Boyle, 2005). The cultural power of "Jack the Ripper" is evident in more recent accounts that similarly efface the gendered aspects of this form of violence, which is most notable in the use of the gender-neutral term "serial killer." The serial killer is "everyman and no man" (Rehling, 2009, p. 243), escaping gendered analysis through the status of white masculinity as neutral and universal, invisible through its ubiquity. This status paradoxically both highlights the hazard to *women* and obscures the masculine origin of the violence: he is both "an everyman (he could be anyone, the threat to women was pervasive) and an invisible man (his identity is unknown, the gendered reality of his crimes downplayed)" (Boyle, 2005, p. 58). Despite the archetypal image of Jack the Ripper as a *man* in a long dark coat and face-concealing hat, the patriarchal characteristics of his crimes are rarely discussed outside feminist analysis.

A notable illustration of this phenomenon is provided by the Sutcliffe case. Similarities between Sutcliffe's crimes and those committed in 1888 Whitechapel (his early victims were working as prostitutes, and he left them mutilated and in the open) inspired Sutcliffe's media nickname "the Yorkshire Ripper," underlining the influence of Jack the Ripper as a model for future murderers (Walkowitz, 1982; Caputi, 1990; Boyle, 2005). Other similarities are evident in cultural responses that imbue the serial killer with supervisory power over women and that naturalize the concept of women as victims. The media reactions to both the 1888 murders and the Sutcliffe case positioned female victims as responsible for their own deaths – they walked alone in (male) public spaces and offered sex for money – with no analysis of the social and economic factors contributing to the existence of prostitution (Walkowitz, 1982; Ward Jouve, 1986). This reduces a serial killer's violence to a "mad or bad" dichotomy: either he is an example of aberrant psychology requiring psychiatric but not sociological study, or he is motivated by extreme biological urges, a "product of nature not society" (Hollway, 1981, p. 37). Both explanations distance the killer from normative masculinity while concealing parallels between his perception of sex workers and that of wider society (Ward Jouve, 1986).

This implicit endorsement of the killer's misogynistic monitoring is evident in journalistic accounts that describe aspects of the female victim's behaviour – whether she was drunk, whether she had carelessly wandered alone into an unsafe area – to provoke either sympathy or condemnation depending on the victim's adherence to gendered standards (Gregoriou, 2011). It is also discernable in an interview by television journalist Sylvia Chase with the American killer Henry Lee Lucas in 1984. Lucas describes his stalking of solitary women in public spaces, stating that a lone woman "ain't safe at all." Chase's response, expressing fear as she asserts that she often travels alone, prompts the by now imprisoned Lucas to position his interviewer in the role of vulnerable victim: "What if somebody like me be out there?" Lucas's question suggests that "*all* women are meant to internalise the threat and message of sexual terrorism" (Caputi, 1988, p. 118; emphasis in original).

This monitoring role is also apparent in the insistent focus on the killer rather than his victims. Understanding seriality – the defining element of serial killer narratives (Dyer, 2002) – as an example of pathological collection, Knox (2003) argues that the victims are "abstracted" from their domestic and familial environment, "removed from the utility of work and the context of sociality" (p. 290). The killer's objectification of victims as they are violently abstracted into his series has dark echoes of Foucault's panopticon model. The "dissolution of the victim as subject" (p. 293) clearly goes further than state panoptical surveillance, which controls individuals by codifying rather than destroying their identity, but the parallel highlights the killer's ability to order, monitor, and supervise individuals.

The desire to categorize is echoed by the FBI's promotion of profiling as a response to the serial killer. The FBI's intervention in serial killer discourse in the 1970s has been interpreted as an effort to claim greater financial and jurisdictional resources by "producing the 'official' definition of serial murder" – a response to the serial killer panic that echoes the FBI's control of other apparent threats, such as organized crime (Schmid, 2005, p. 67). The perceived growth of random, seemingly unmotivated, exceptionally violent homicides, amplified by increasingly sensationalized journalism and the use of the serial killer threat by a variety of special interest groups, provided the FBI with an opportunity to claim ownership of the phenomenon (Jenkins, 1994; Schmid, 2005). Profiling uses aspects of the crime (type of victim, location, method of killing) to identify the killer's behavioural characteristics (Keppel & Birnes, 2003). It studies crime scenes and forensic reports in order to classify the killer within existing groups. Its investigative aims and concern with categorization position profiling within state surveillance, yet fictional representations construct the profiler as a more intuitive, maverick figure whose surveillance skills are the only match for the killer.

The prominence of profiling in serial killer discourse is such that this method has been used to reinvestigate the prototypical serial killer case, that of Jack the Ripper, despite the geographical and temporal distance between 1880s Whitechapel and late-twentieth and early-twenty-first-century America. In her effort to identify the murderer, the crime fiction writer Patricia Cornwell (2002) used profiling theories and terminology to examine these real, historical homicides. Similarly, fictional retellings of the Whitechapel crimes anachronistically depict their investigating detective applying profiling concepts, most notably in the film *From Hell* (Hughes Brothers, 2001). Since the late 1970s, profiling has been presented by the FBI as the only defence against the serial killer (Jenkins, 1994; Seltzer, 1998; Simpson, 2000; Schmid, 2005), with Gothic tropes used to depict the battle between the incomprehensibly evil killer and the innately gifted profiler (Surette, 2007), just as the Whitechapel murders were understood through Gothic conventions a century earlier (Boyle, 2005).[2] This use of Gothic, metaphysical framings reflects a contemporaneous shift towards neoconservative ideology (Schmid, 2005; Surette, 2007). Despite the supposedly scientific roots of profiling, profilers are depicted using less rational terms, "constructed as naturally skilled Gothic-like protagonists" (Surette, 2007, p. 221). The penetration of profiler narratives into popular culture can thus be partly explained by their familiarity, in that they echo existing conventions and tropes.

The Killer and Profiler in Film

Since the late 1970s, a group of films has developed that highlight the relationship between the killer and the profiler. These two figures are uncannily doubled, and the films follow the profiler's dangerous immersion in the world of the killer (Halberstam, 1995; Simpson, 2000; Cettl, 2003). The profiler is a special kind of detective: while not always a law enforcement professional, s/he invariably demonstrates skills that allude to surveillance, to a special ability to see more than others and to interpret clues imaginatively. S/he is often a police officer but can also be a writer (*Time After Time* [Nicholas Meyer, 1979]; *The Mean Season* [Philip Borsos, 1985]; *The Raven* [James McTeigue, 2012]), psychic (*Jack's Back* [Rowdy Herrington, 1988], *Hideaway* [Brett Leonard, 1995], *Eye of the Killer* [Paul Marcus, 1999]), or forensic investigator (*Bone Daddy* [Mario Azzopardi, 1998], *The Bone Collector* [Phillip Noyce, 1999]). These activities relate to monitoring and observation, and the films highlight the profiler's instinctive talent for scrutinizing others, tapping into the notion of the expert in surveillance who combats the killer by matching his ability to survey society.

The depiction of a detective figure as the possessor of a special way of seeing is not new: two influential early detectives, Edgar Allan Poe's Dupin and Arthur Conan Doyle's Holmes, both display an extraordinary talent for observation (Gates, 2006; Summerscale, 2008). The profiler echoes these pre-professional detectives as s/he disregards the judicial authorities associated with twentieth- and twenty-first-century detection in favour of intuition and instinct. Although the FBI defines profiling as an administrative procedure, popular understandings of this process privilege a more mystical notion that imbues the profiler with an innate, eerie comprehension of the killer (Jenkins, 1994; Surette, 2007). These unconventional tactics are necessary, for the serial killer's targeting of strangers makes traditional investigation – which focuses on links between killer and victim – ineffective (Stratton, 1996). Serial killing undermines these methods; and in suggesting that a killer can take advantage of the anonymity engendered by urban living, it underlines the concept of serial killing as a modern, metropolitan problem (Dyer, 1997). The profiler film combines the mystical version of profiling with its more administrative form, portraying the profiler as uncannily gifted but also constructing the city as a site requiring categorization. Although some profiler characters are female, I focus here on depictions of men in this role in order to examine the masculine surveillance typical of these films. Female profilers are similarly constructed, but their interest in the killer often takes on romantic overtones that are too complex to explore here (for an analysis of the homoerotic implications of the relationship between the male profiler and the killer, see Kaplan, 1998).

Like the serial killer, the profiler is a complex merging of fact and fiction (Seltzer, 1998; Schmid, 2005; Surette, 2007). The cinematic profiler does not appear after the FBI profiler becomes familiar through news reports; instead, the profiler film precedes by a few years the circulation in popular culture of the FBI-defined profiler concept. The paralleling of the killer with individuals who are not members of traditional law enforcement yet who are uniquely able to tackle the killer is evident in early profiler films such as *Eyes of Laura Mars* (Irvin Kershner, 1978) and *Time After Time* (Nicholas Meyer, 1979). These profilers do not use the administrative, supposedly rational methods of the FBI but instead rely on intuitive talent. Their outsider status makes them more capable of dealing with the killer than the conventional, bureaucratic detective (Cettl, 2003; Simpson, 2000; Bull, 2013).

While later films introduce FBI profiling methods and vocabulary, these procedures rarely help catch the killer, and the seemingly rational terminology of profiling is overtaken by language that suggests intuition and empathy. Each profiler ultimately abandons his/her training in order to cultivate a disturbingly profound understanding of the murderer. However, this formula is not far removed from popular representations of real FBI investigations. Autobiographical accounts by founder profilers Robert Ressler and John Douglas celebrate their own maverick tendencies, depicting their struggles against unwieldy and outmoded FBI procedures and highlighting their need to understand the killer over scientific, technical skills (Ressler, 1992; Douglas & Dodd, 2007). This lone hero trope is hugely popular in American cinema, and it is likely that these films tapped into ideology – American individuality and frontier rhetoric, anti-feminist backlash, distrust of bureaucracy – that was particularly potent at the end of the 1970s (Tasker, 1995; Baker, 2006; Gates, 2006).

These themes can be traced in the profiler film's depiction of the city as an intensively monitored space that is paradoxically conducive to the serial killer's sinister surveillance. It is "depicted as the hub of hidden agenda and intrigue; a personal amusement park for the serial killer to pursue his perverse pleasures" (Macdonald, 2013, p. 40). The profiler film constructs the city as a chaotic labyrinthine space in which disintegration and decay are evident to the profiler but are ignored by other characters except, usually, the serial killer. Crime and corruption are rife and apathy is suggested by the profiler's lone recognition of the threat posed by the serial killer. Many of the films begin with a descent from an opening skyline shot into dark, grimy streets where we witness a murder or the discovery of a body (*Murder by Decree* [Bob Clark, 1979]; *Tightrope* [Richard Tuggle, 1984]; *From Hell*; *The Bone Collector*). This convention plunges us from a relatively safe perspective into the dangerous urban sprawl. Institutional spaces such as police stations and hospitals, places intended to regulate and supervise the population, are chaotic and incapable of tackling the city's problems. Many of the films use disease metaphors to construct the city as a space in need of therapeutic measures, echoing historical attempts to treat social problems by monitoring the city (Donald, 1999). In place of the nineteenth-century social reformer stand the killer and profiler, linked by their awareness of urban squalor and degeneration. The construction of the killer as an exceptional figure originating from and taking advantage of urban isolation and chaos distances the murderer from normative masculinity. His crimes are not linked to gendered power structures but instead are portrayed as an unfortunate and rare but somehow inevitable aspect of modern life; disassociated from patriarchy, the crimes are naturalized and their misogynistic motives effaced (Caputi, 1988; Rehling, 2009).

The First Deadly Sin (Brian G. Hutton, 1980) highlights the disease metaphor through the profiler's ill wife, Barbara (Faye Dunaway), who "embodies the city's illness" (Morgan, 2002, p. 82). The opening scene parallels her operation with a murder: as she is taken into the theatre, the killer moves towards his victim; the surgeon's instruments are noisily set down as the murderer prepares to strike a passer-by; the insistent beeps of a heart monitor bleed over from the theatre scene to the attack, which occurs as the surgeon slices into flesh. Later, as a thunderstorm rages, Barbara's deterioration is doubled with the killer's psychosis. As she gasps for air, he screams and gesticulates violently. Morgan finds that the crosscutting "makes clear that she is in crisis sympathetically with the city, and that her body and the city are affected by the same morbid influence" (Morgan, 2002, p. 83). Both Barbara and the city are in need of specialized male observation and intervention. This interpretation indicates the passive roles to which female characters are usually restricted in these films, with the profiler's wife in this case functioning not as a victim of the killer but as a symbol for the contaminated city.

Films such as this construct the city as necessitating the specialized masculine gaze of the profiler. The profiler is infuriated by apathy and by the bureaucratic procedures that impede beneficial change. He works by instinct rather than administrative investigative procedure, relying on intuition and, most significantly, seeing things others cannot. In a film full of sight metaphors, it is no accident that *Seven*'s (David Fincher, 1995) Detective Somerset (Morgan Freeman) is able to see connections others miss (Dyer, 1999). He links forensic evidence found in a victim's stomach to the crime scene floor, leading him to a poetry excerpt hidden by the killer. Somerset's literary knowledge, emphasized by his productive visit to a library whose labyrinthine passages he efficiently negotiates, allows him to interpret the poem's significance, and his profound understanding of human nature (conveyed to his partner as they discuss the problems of their city) alerts him to the danger posed by the intelligent, methodical killer who is dismissed by others as a typical madman.

The profiler's special gaze is highlighted by his rejection of conventional methods. In *The Bone Collector*, profiler Rhyme (Denzel Washington) instructs his protégé Amelia (Angelina Jolie) not to learn procedures but instead to "trust those instincts you were born with." His breakthroughs are presented as epiphanies rather than traditional detection. As he examines evidence, Rhyme gazes intently towards the mid-distance, suggesting deep thought. A montage sequence juxtaposes intense close-ups of his eyes with images of old photographs and maps, which he visualizes as he uses his specialist knowledge of New York crime history to decipher clues. In a trend that further underlines the profiler's distance from conventional police work and highlights the importance of sight, several psychic profilers experience this phenomenon as visual glimpses of the murders (*Eyes of Laura Mars*; *The Dead Zone* [David Cronenberg, 1983]; *Eye of the Killer*).

Other profilers demonstrate a similarly instinctive capacity for recognizing a serial killer and scrutinizing their city. At the beginning of *From Hell*, a fictionalized version of the Jack the Ripper crimes, Detective Abberline (Johnny Depp) examines the corpse of the first victim before disagreeing with other officers who believe a local gang is responsible. Announcing that they are looking for "a different breed of killer," Abberline is both factually accurate (the serial killer, the film insists, is quite different from the perpetrators of isolated murders) and ironically prophetic, as the film recounts the crimes that have influenced serial killer discourse and tied the serial killer to urban settings. Like the profilers in *Time After Time*, *Cop* (James B. Harris, 1988), *Off Limits* (Christopher Crowe, 1988), and *Jennifer Eight* (Bruce Robinson, 1992) these men are alone in recognizing that a serial killer is active and that they must use their exceptional surveillance skills and extra-judicial methods to tackle the threat.

The profiler film engages with two forms of surveillance – quasi-mystical special insight, and administrative ordering of the urban mass – to depict the profiler as an expert in both modes. The profiler ultimately relies on intuition over more practical skills relating to ordering the city, but both methods highlight his distinctive role as a supervisory observer. In *Seven*, after Somerset has intuitively recognized the type of criminal he is chasing, he resorts to an illegal but productive method to narrow down the search: he pays an FBI agent for library records of books that relate to the crimes. Similarly, in *The First Deadly Sin*, Delaney (Frank Sinatra) instinctively recognizes that he is dealing with a serial killer but is unable to focus on individual suspects until an eccentric museum curator identifies the rare weapon. Delaney then accesses the mailing list of a local supplier, although, like Somerset, he employs unofficial help (the curator and a victim's widow sort through the list to narrow the suspect pool) to categorize individuals effectively.

The profiler's home reflects his unusual visual powers: he often has a skylight that is highlighted through camera angles (*Time After Time*, *The First Deadly Sin*, *The Bone Collector*), suggesting the occupant's privileged vision. In *Jack's Back*, the profiler wakes from a psychic dream of a murder, only to watch from his balcony as police cars race to the scene of the crime. These homes are sanctuaries from the chaotic, crime-ridden city, and in several films (*The Mean Season, Seven*), the profiler plans to leave the city for a more peaceful environment. In *The First Deadly Sin*, for example, Delaney promises his wife that he will buy a seaside cottage for his impending retirement; although she remains in hospital throughout the film, their desire to escape the city is apparent in her idealized paintings of the sea that cover the walls of their apartment. *The Bone Collector*'s bedridden Rhyme, whose paralysis restricts him to one room of his large, open-plan home, gazes at both the skylight above his bed and his computer screensaver, which depicts an animated seaside scene. In both of these films, safe domestic spaces are taken over by the investigation and turned into surveillance hubs. Rhyme's expansive home is filled with police officers and their computers, while Delaney sorts through evidence on his kitchen table; he removes his wife's painting from her easel and replaces it with a board that categorizes crime scene details.

Besides possessing a privileged view, the profiler commands an unusual ability to negotiate urban space and read the networks of the city; this links him to the nineteenth-century detective and underlines his role as guardian of the city. Profilers often dominate the cinema frame, with a background city skyline highlighting their supervisory role. *The Bone Collector* begins with an establishing shot of the familiar New York skyline before a pre-paralysed Rhyme steps into the frame, his face filling the screen and his expression suggesting ease in his surroundings. Deep focus ensures that both he and the skyline remain in focus, giving them equal importance. Publicity posters for *Cop, Righteous Kill* (Jon Avnet, 2008), and *Blitz* (Elliot Lester, 2011) depict the profilers as figures dominating the skyline of their respective cities, emphasizing their responsibility to their territory.

Many of the plot twists in profiler films concern this ability to master space and decipher the labyrinthine city. Profilers who work within law enforcement are entitled to access some private spaces, and they possess a profound understanding of the city as a result of their years monitoring its criminals. Profilers who are amateur detectives rely on innate skills in navigating the city, with psychic abilities sometimes offering them an advantage. The ability to cross boundaries is most notable in *Murder by Decree* and *From Hell*, both of which suggest that powerful politicians and the British monarchy were involved in the

Whitechapel murders. These profilers traverse the poor Whitechapel area as well as wealthy neighbourhoods where the guilty are shielded by their economic and social status. In *Murder by Decree*, Sherlock Holmes (Christopher Plummer) is first seen in a luxurious theatre; he is seated opposite the Royal box, indicating his social prominence. The next scene contrasts this lavish setting: an inebriated prostitute is murdered in a narrow, foggy, dark street. Holmes is equally comfortable in Whitechapel, clinically examining the crime scene while his medically trained assistant Dr Watson (James Mason) looks away in disgust. When Holmes recognizes that he is under surveillance, he adopts a chimney sweep disguise to discreetly visit a potential witness. He negotiates poorer areas with ease, ultimately chasing the killer past industrial spaces to the dockside. Yet Watson is tricked by a potential witness, is almost mugged, and is eventually arrested. Similarly, *From Hell*'s Inspector Abberline is equally comfortable in illicit opium dens, the dangerous Whitechapel streets, and wealthier areas: he even leads Mary Kelly (Heather Graham), a prostitute whose social status restricts her to poor areas, into an art gallery, shocking its wealthy patrons.

Despite this ease in moving through urban spaces, a frequent problem faced by the profiler is accessing the private space of the killer in order to prove his guilt. The films highlight the frustration of the profiler, who cannot obtain a search warrant and must utilize illegal methods to protect his city. In *Cop, The First Deadly Sin,* and *Seven*, the profiler illicitly accesses the killer's home, but this indiscretion is justified by the extraordinary threat posed by the killer and, often, by his cynical use of the law. Other profilers who are not connected to law enforcement must use similarly prohibited methods as they conduct their investigations, but again their manipulations are inconsequential compared to the crimes of the killer.

The most crucial space in the serial killer narrative is the crime scene, and the profiler film focuses on this space as the centre of communication between the killer and the profiler, who acts as a semiotician to decode its meaning (Cettl, 2003). The crime scene functions as "more than just a physical map of the interior of the victim's body; it is also a map of the interior of the killer's mind. It is effectively his mind laid out, his work displayed and signed, a text to be read" (Warwick, 2006, p. 564). This concept underlines Knox's understanding of the abstracting of the victims: firmly fixed in the killer's series, each victim is "retroactively altered by a new identity as a murder victim, and her dead body becomes a new medicalised object" (Warwick, 2006, p. 564). This reference to medical surveillance relates to the autopsy but also implies that there is a therapeutic form of supervision in the profiler's study of the crime scene. The crime scene is the point at which the journeys of the profiler and the killer converge: the profiler often stands in the literal footsteps of the killer as he examines his "text." The victim's suffering is rarely noted beyond any clues it offers to the investigation. That these individuals have been targeted by a *serial* killer further effaces their distinctiveness; they are often not even named once it is established that they are simply another link in the series. Our empathy for the victim is undermined by our awareness of the danger posed to the profiler as he accesses these dangerous scenes. The journey to the scene is long and tense, with the profiler negotiating hazards (it is often dark, sometimes underground, usually in labyrinthine, unfamiliar, industrial spaces, or across waste ground) as he approaches the body.

The killer's ability to prepare these often elaborate scenes suggests an eerie control over space and evokes the serial killer's talent for blending into the background – a common feature of factual and fictional accounts (Seltzer, 1998). These films demonstrate the murderer's skill in traversing the city: he enters private domestic spaces with ease, discreetly abducts individuals from public areas, and moves through urban space unobtrusively, even after a brutal attack. He is often simply a threatening shape until near the end of the film: in *Seven*, John Doe (Kevin Spacey), whose name suggests a lack of identity, is an indistinct shape during a long chase sequence (Dyer, 1999). Several of the films focus on the killer's eyes and portray stalking and attack scenes from his point of view, emphasizing his control of the visual field and maintaining his anonymity. Dyer (1999) finds that *Seven* suggests that modern urban life facilitates serial killing, particularly as Doe and the (unnamed and therefore itself anonymous) city are similarly "characterless" (p. 41). *The Bone Collector* demonstrates a similar parallel in depicting a killer disguised as a taxi driver: he moves around the city and abducts victims with ease as, like white masculinity, the ubiquity of the taxi cab lends anonymity. The taxi blends into the metropolis; its ability to weave undetected through the city indicates the killer's control of urban space. It is impossible to isolate one cab among thousands, so every taxi is potentially dangerous: when the novice profiler Amelia runs home from a disturbing crime scene, sinister music and the appearance of a cab suggest she is threatened. In addition, the reflection of the killer's eyes in the rear-view mirror (which appear in several scenes as well as on the publicity poster) underlines the links among sight, the surveillance of urban space, and the anonymous killer.

Some acknowledgment of the patriarchal origins of the killer's aggression is evident in the profiler film. Rehling (2009) argues that the eerie doubling of the white, male profiler and killer implicitly links the undistinguished, neutral status of white masculinity to the pathology of the serial killer – a point supported by Dyer (2002), who finds that the repetitive, dispassionate efficiency of the serial killer epitomizes white masculinity. This association is enhanced in films in which the profiler role is inhabited by a woman or Black man. In these cases, the profiler is distanced from the killer's violence. Black male and female profilers are not tainted by their ability to understand the killer, their racial and gender difference apparently ensuring that they remain uncorrupted (Gates, 2006; Rehling, 2009). In depicting a white man whose ability to detect the murderer depends on their shared potential for violence, the profiler film provides a limited critique of white male privilege, although the profiler's violence is ultimately positioned as necessary and redemptive – as the only way to stop the killer.

The profiler film more often frames the serial killer as an urban rather than a gendered problem. The films highlight the confusing, chaotic nature of the city and relate the problem of finding the killer to the difficulty of isolating one individual in the bustling urban sprawl. Conventional forms of state surveillance are ineffectual. The killer rarely appears on criminal databases, so obtaining his fingerprints or DNA from the crime scenes is useless and sometimes deceptive (in *Seven* and *The Bone Collector*, the killer leaves a false trail that leads only to the next victim). He avoids CCTV, and the few witness descriptions are vague. Police cars that race through the streets with their lights flashing and sirens blaring are too late to catch the killer; helicopters promise privileged vision with their impressive mobility and searchlights but discern only a blurry figure as it escapes their scrutiny; heavily armed SWAT teams burst through doors but are out-manoeuvred by the intelligent, agile murderer.

The failure of conventional surveillance attributes responsibility for serial violence to modern urban life. The killer is understood to be in some way produced and assisted by "the anonymity of mass societies and the rapidity of urban transport [...] the dissolution of the affective bonds of community and lifelong families" (Dyer, 1997, p. 15). The profiler film's attributing of blame to the city, rather than to male violence, is highlighted in *The Watcher* (Joe Charbanic, 2000), in which Griffin

(Keanu Reeves) stalks young women before killing them in their own homes. Before each murder, he sends a photograph of the victim to the profiler, Campbell (James Spader), giving him a few days to save her. Each picture is featured on television news reports and on flyers handed out by police officers. A city planner narrows down possible locations; takeaway cups and shop signs are identified and linked to potential sites. Despite pervasive urban surveillance, these efforts are fruitless, the homogenization of the municipal landscape and modern consumerism making it impossible to distinguish the victims' identities through the urban environment and chain stores that surround them. We are invited to share concern at the implication that these victims are already "lost" within the city before their deaths. A radio show host asks "how can this happen in the communication age?," while images of bustling streets underline the vast size of the population. Griffin refers to this problem when he taunts Campbell after one killing – "we're all stacked right on top of each other, but we don't really notice each other" – framing the deaths as an urban problem and evading culpability.

Seeing Violence against Women

In framing the killer as an urban rather than a gendered phenomenon, the profiler film naturalizes the concept of women as victims while expunging connections between serial violence and masculinity. When female profilers appear, they are usually mentored by an older man (*The Silence of the Lambs* [Jonathan Demme, 1991]; *Kiss the Girls* [Gary Fleder 1997]; *The Bone Collector*), and they often fail to entirely defeat the killer (*Candyman* [Bernard Rose, 1992]; *Copycat* [Jon Amiel, 1995]; *Hannibal* [Ridley Scott, 2001]). However, a number of these female-led films have been recognized as critiquing patriarchal power structures to varying extents. Most notably, *The Silence of the Lambs* highlights the prejudice and harassment faced by Agent Starling (Jodie Foster). Foster's slight stature is frequently used to visually isolate her from the taller, burlier men of the FBI, singling her out as "a small figure in a male world" (Tasker, 2002, p. 23) and suggesting that while detection may be a masculine field, this limitation is culturally imposed. In addition, both *Kiss the Girls* and *The Bone Collector* depict physically proficient novice female profilers who outrun and outfight their male advisers, demonstrating their superior abilities in negotiating space. *Copycat* begins with an unusually overt recognition of the white, male origins of the typical serial killer, as psychologist Dr Helen Hudson (Sigourney Weaver) confidently announces to a packed lecture theatre the racial and gender statistics of serial violence (Rehling, 2009). This advance is undermined by the next scene, in which Hudson is brutally attacked, a trauma that leads to agoraphobia. The film's detection narrative then parallels her psychological recovery. Helped by a female detective, Hudson investigates the crimes of a killer obsessed with her original attack, slowly regaining command of space as her confidence increases (Tasker, 1998). In these films, the female profilers rely on spatial control in the same way as their male counterparts, and the films often highlight the misogyny they face as an obstacle in the detection process.

Conversely, in the male-led profiler film, women are usually restricted to the domestic sphere, while detection takes place in male spaces. Delaney's substitution of his absent wife's painting for his crime scene analysis in *The First Deadly Sin*, for example, epitomizes this gendering of crime investigation. In addition, although the male profiler is often in physical peril, women are at greater risk. *The Watcher* plays with the urban anonymity concept when Campbell unwittingly shares an elevator with the killer: although Griffin grins, there is no sense that Campbell is in immediate danger. Later, however, as Griffin talks to Campbell's psychiatrist/love interest, sinister music implies a threat. Despite her professional skills, she is alone in her office with an unfamiliar man; she grows uncomfortable as he walks around the room, studying her workspace. The profiler's wife/girlfriend is frequently endangered in these films; the final sequence often features the profiler's desperate chase/fight to rescue his partner. The passivity suggested by this convention is noted by Dyer (1999) in his analysis of *Seven*, in which Tracy (Gwyneth Paltrow), the pretty, blonde wife of Detective Mills (Brad Pitt), is murdered by John Doe. Tracy represents the meaning of "male encounter in the world" (Dyer, 1999, p. 31), in which she functions as a trophy, an object to be fought for and over. This positioning of a threatened woman as a chattel over which killer and profiler battle consolidates the conventional nature of the gendered power structures the profiler film supports.

The profiler and the killer are typically white men, and the victims are usually women or weaker men (Dyer, 1997). This aligns their surveillance with patriarchal power structures. Female vulnerability is stressed in stalking/attack sequences filmed from the killer's perspective. In *The Watcher*, Campbell describes Griffin's crimes as we see grainy footage filmed from outside a window of a woman undressing, oblivious to being watched. That Campbell is describing the killer's activities as we watch them unfold underlines the doubling of killer and profiler. The two men share a desire to observe, which is sanctioned in Campbell's case by his investigative role in tackling the killer, but the parallel is highlighted by the killer's taunting ritual: he sends photographs of future victims to the detective, forcing him to examine these voyeuristic images for clues to the identities of the unsuspecting women. Campbell explains that women who ensure that their curtains are closed at night are often "less careful" in the morning, attributing some blame to the victims. Griffin specifically targets "lone women," and the film alludes to gendered stereotypes in constructing women without male protection as vulnerable. Griffin befriends a shy woman whose isolation is emphasized when, oblivious to Griffin's presence in her home, she wearily answers her telephoning mother's questions about potential boyfriends, preventing Campbell from warning her by phone. Another victim – a busker squatting in an abandoned factory – is warned by a male friend that the police are circulating her picture; when he leaves, she is suddenly vulnerable, and Griffin appears. Each of these women is doomed not by Griffin's misogyny but by her lack of social contacts: there is no one close to her to recognize her photograph in time. Additionally, she lives alone, beyond male surveillance, and is therefore defenceless when Griffin invades her private space.

The threat posed to "lone women" is implied by references to the need for women to be accompanied in public spaces. In both *The January Man* (Pat O'Connor, 1989) and *Blitz*, it is suggested that women should be walked to their front door at night, recalling Walkowitz's discussion of Jack the Ripper's "moral" message. Profiler films often suggest that those who transgress gendered spatial boundaries risk coming to harm. *From Hell* depicts the victims of Jack the Ripper as under constant repressive surveillance: they are watched by men as they walk along the Whitechapel streets, they must hide their activities from the police, and they are threatened by gangs. These women have no private space; they live in temporary, usually shared, accommodation, and their work on the streets exposes them to random violence as well as the threat of the serial killer. Instead of linking these experiences to gender inequalities, however, the film accepts prostitution and its dangers as routine. By explaining the crimes as the result of a conspiracy, *From Hell* explains the killings not as examples of patriarchal violence but rather as an intriguing mystery with a gender-neutral motive (Boyle, 2005).

While not all profiler films focus entirely on female victims, greater attention is paid to attacks on women. In *Blitz*, in which a murderer targets police officers, the shooting of a female officer focuses on her fear and pain to a greater extent than any of the attacks on male victims: an overhead shot depicts her lying alone and clutching her throat, gasping as blood pools around her. Regarding the attacks on men, two excise the victims' deaths and another highlights the killer's rage rather than the victim's suffering (the camera focuses on the killer's face). When a female officer is attacked but saved by a teenager's intervention, she screams helplessly as the boy is beaten. *The Mean Season* and *The Bone Collector* also feature killings of both men and women, but again the camera lingers on the anguish of female victims: men are killed quickly or off-screen, yet we see close-ups of the women as they scream or cry before their deaths.

This naturalization of women as victims corresponds to the depiction of the male profiler as a patriarchal figure who is responsible for his community. Some of these figures are literal fathers whose concern for their daughters amplifies their unease with urban violence (*Cop, Tightrope, Righteous Kill*). In *Frequency* (Gregory Hoblit, 2000) a father and son search for a killer who is targeting their wife/mother, again restricting women to domestic roles. *Righteous Kill* is particularly interesting: the profiler, Turk (Robert De Niro), is a detective suspected of being a serial killer who targets criminals (a twist ending reveals that his partner, Rooster [Al Pacino], is the killer). Turk's paternalistic attitude is stressed through his concern for a young female lawyer who is forced to take part in a sting to catch a drug dealer. He leads her through an abandoned factory into an expansive, gaudy nightclub as he tries to calm her, highlighting the detective's ability to negotiate city spaces. Like *From Hell*, the film suggests that this skill is a gendered one, with a woman able to access different spaces only when accompanied by an older man who enjoys privileged mobility. Turk's fatherly manner is consolidated in the final scene when, now free of suspicion, he discusses his improved relationship with his daughter as he coaches a girls' softball team. Having revealed that Turk is not the killer, the film highlights his benign supervision of the girls (in contrast to the opening scene, in which he fights with fellow officers as they play baseball); a closing crane shot of the diamond as he walks towards the players underscores the sense of closure as he regains his legitimate, and thoroughly gendered, monitoring role.

In depicting a vigilante serial-killing police officer, *Righteous Kill* hints at a less beneficent concept of male surveillance, with Rooster taking advantage of his state-sanctioned authority. Analogies have been made between the serial killer and patriarchal ideology in responses to the Whitechapel and Sutcliffe crimes, with the killings interpreted as "punishment" for female prostitution (Walkowitz, 1982; Ward Jouve, 1986; Macdonald, 2013). Sutcliffe's self-description as a purifying, monitoring figure – the "street cleaner" whose sole concern with the *female* purveyors of prostitution is unremarkable and even acceptable to the police officers searching for the killer (Walkowitz, 1992) – eerily echoes Rooster's claim to be "a street-sweeper." Yet the film downplays the paralleling of the serial killer with state-sanctioned law enforcement by depicting Rooster as a decent man overwhelmed by urban problems and his responsibility to his city. As the investigators debate whether the killer is a cop, they sit in front of a large window with an expansive view of the New York skyline – a view that underscores their professional responsibilities to their city. The victims are denied sympathy: selected because they cannot be prosecuted for serious crimes, they revel in their immunity and their economic advantages (drugs are sold in a dealer's palatial club, a rapist's large television set is admired by the police, a hitman gloats about his expensive car). This framing of violence within class is typical of the profiler film, with *Murder by Decree, From Hell, The First Deadly Sin, Jack's Back, Kiss the Girls,* and *Time After Time* also linking the crimes to the killer's economic privilege.

In addition, *Righteous Kill* depicts the victims as posing a specific threat to women, who must be protected by male guardians. The case that inspires Rooster's killings is the murder of a young girl: her mother provides an alibi for the murderer, her own boyfriend. We later witness the mother, a dishevelled drunk, try to excuse her perjury (she feared violent retribution), leaving no doubt that the only possible justice for the girl is extra-judicial. Another helpless female compels illegitimate retribution when her rapist escapes prosecution because of a legal irregularity: as he swaggers from the courtroom, she weeps. These cases expose disparity in the legal system, but rather than explore wider, entrenched social inequalities, the film offers the vigilante killer as a response to individual instances of injustice. The movie uses the familiar paralleling of profiler and killer to depict Rooster as a well-intentioned man who takes his surveillance responsibilities to extremes. The criticisms of official bureaucracy voiced by various police officer characters underline the profiler's rejection of conventional detection methods, rules, and procedures – a stance that is common to these films. Traditional surveillance is inadequate when dealing not only with serial killers, as *Righteous Kill* suggests, but also with the drug dealers, pimps, paedophiles, and mafia hitmen that Rooster eliminates.

Not all profiler films go as far as *Righteous Kill* in constructing the city as a space in which such repressive surveillance is necessary to protect the vulnerable. The variations in the profiler film can be partly explained by the cycle's duration – beginning in the late 1970s, reaching a peak in the 1990s, and continuing in the 2010s – and by the considerable political changes throughout this time period. While Hollywood cinema of the 1980s is regarded as particularly neoconservative (Faludi, 1991), the 1990s is considered to offer a wider representation of female characters, reflecting cultural shifts throughout the decade (Rehling, 2009). The decrease in female profilers in the 2000s, together with a renewed focus on female victims, suggests a reversal of the 1990s advances. This reversal is also evident in the growth of torture porn, most notably *Saw* (James Wan, 2004) and its sequels, which reframe the profiler narrative within a torture porn aesthetic. *Saw*'s villain, who targets both male and female victims, is revealed to be an educated, wealthy white man whose economic and social privileges enable him to "test" individuals who are often poorer and unable to control space and sight as comprehensively as he can, and whose affluence facilitates his access to isolated warehouses and high-tech surveillance equipment. This imbalance is compounded by the depiction of a Hannibal Lecter / Dexter-like killer "for whom the audience is encouraged to cheer as the figure of the serial killer is utilized in this series as a vehicle of white frustration, anxiety, and vigilantism" (Bernard, 2013, p.102) – a concept that again evokes the "moral message" associated with Victorian Whitechapel's "Ripper" murders.

Conclusion

The profiler film oscillates between constructing the city as a dangerous space requiring masculine supervision and offering women an unusual degree of mobility and power in this space. Some films acknowledge to a limited extent the gendered disparities that regulate the behaviour of women in public space. The specific threat of the serial killer – a criminal who thrives in the urban sprawl – justifies the potentially repressive surveillance of profilers, who discard state-sanctioned procedure in favour of intuition; but that same threat also validates the need to work outside these frameworks, which are themselves often biased against marginalized individuals. However, most female profilers require male guidance, and most women are consigned to the role of victim or threatened dependant (a love interest or daughter of the profiler). Besides bolstering gender norms, many profiler films insinuate that women are exposed to danger in the city and should monitor their behaviour as well as accept the pervasive patriarchal surveillance evident in the films and in discourse around both the city and the serial killer. In depicting these two male agents of surveillance as responsible for urban space, the profiler film frames as benign concepts of surveillance that are in reality repressive and intrusive towards the women they are supposed to protect. Despite being positioned as rational and benevolent, these concepts echo the misogynistic, self-serving advice offered by serial killer Henry Lee Lucas: a lone woman "ain't safe at all."

NOTES

I would like to thank Rob Heynen, Emily van der Meulen, and the University of Toronto Press anonymous reviewers for their invaluable comments and suggestions on this article.

1 The term "torture porn" is used in popular and academic discourse to describe a loose group of horror films, originating in 2004, that feature extreme, aestheticized violence unusually graphic for mainstream cinema (Tziallas, 2010).
2 Interestingly, little effort has been made by the FBI, journalists, and true crime writers to reconcile the framing of the serial killer as a new, nationally specific phenomenon with the globally notorious figure of Jack the Ripper, or even with earlier examples of US-based killers such as 1890s Chicago murderer H.H. Holmes. Instead, the prominent FBI profiler John Douglas marked the centenary of the Whitechapel murders by preparing a psychological profile of the unknown killer, highlighting the FBI's ownership of serial murder (Schmid, 2005).

REFERENCES

Baker, B. (2006). *Masculinity in fiction and film: Representing men in popular genres 1945–2000*. London, UK: Continuum.

Bartky, S. (2003). Foucault, femininity, and the modernisation of patriarchal power. In L. Quinby & I. Diamond (Eds.), *Feminism and Foucault: Paths of resistance* (pp. 61–86). Boston, MA: Northeastern University Press.

Bernard, M. (2013). "LOOK AT ME": Serial killing, whiteness, and (in)
    visibility in the Saw series. In A. Macdonald (Ed.), *Murders and acquisitions:
    Representations of the serial killer in popular culture* (pp. 85–103). London, UK:
    Bloomsbury.

Boyle, K. (2005). *Media and violence: Gendering the debate.* London, UK: Sage.

Bull, S. (2013). Hunting minds, hunting genes: From profiling to forensics
    in TV serial narratives. In A. Macdonald (Ed.), *Murders and acquisitions:
    Representations of the serial killer in popular culture* (pp. 203–225). London, UK:
    Bloomsbury.

Byers, S. (2010). Neoliberal Dexter? In D. L. Howard (Ed.), *Dexter: Investigating
    cutting edge television* (pp. 143–156). New York, NY: IB Tauris.

Cameron, D. (2014). The return of the female serial killer. *Trouble and Strife.*
    http://www.troubleandstrife.org/new-articles/the-return-of-the-female-
    serial-killer/

Cameron, D., & Frazer, E. (1987). *The lust to kill: Feminist investigations of sexual
    murder.* New York, NY: NYU Press.

Caputi, J. (1988). *The age of sex crime.* London, UK: Women's Press.

Caputi, J. (1990). The new founding fathers: The lore and lure of the serial
    killer in contemporary culture. *Journal of American Culture, 13*(3), 1–12.
    http://dx.doi.org/10.1111/j.1542-734X.1990.1303_1.x

Cettl, R. (2003). *Serial killer cinema: An analytical filmography.* London, UK:
    McFarland & Company.

Cornwell, P. (2002). *Portrait of a killer: Jack the Ripper – case closed.* London, UK:
    Little Brown.

Cunningham, D. (2007). Living in the slashing grounds: Jack the Ripper,
    monopoly rent, and the new heritage. In A. Warwick & M. Willis (Eds.), *Jack
    the Ripper: Media, culture, history* (pp. 159–175). Manchester, UK: Manchester
    University Press.

Donald, J. (1999). *Imagining the modern city.* London, UK: Athlone.

Douglas, J., & Dodd, J. (2007). *Inside the mind of BTK.* San Francisco, CA:
    Jossey-Bass.

Dyer, R. (1997). Kill and kill again. *Sight and Sound, 7*(9), 14–17.

Dyer, R. (1999). *Seven.* London, UK: British Film Institute Publishing.

Dyer, R. (2002). *The matter of images: Essays on representation.* London, UK:
    Routledge.

Faludi, S. (1991). *Backlash: The undeclared war against women.* London, UK:
    Chatto and Windus.

Fido, M. (1999). David Cohen and the Polish Jew theory. In M. Jakobowski &
    N. Braund (Eds.), *The mammoth book of Jack the Ripper* (pp. 164–186). London,
    UK: Robinson.

Foucault, M. (1977/1991). *Discipline and punish: The birth of the prison* (A. Sheridan, Trans.). London, UK: Penguin Books.

Gates, P. (2006). *Detecting men: Masculinity and the Hollywood detective film.* Albany, NY: SUNY Press.

Gregoriou, C. (2011). *Language, ideology, and identity in serial killer narratives.* London, UK: Routledge.

Halberstam, J. (1995). *Skin shows.* Durham, NC: Duke University Press.

Harris, T. (1981). *Red dragon.* London, UK: Random House.

Harris, T. (1988). *The silence of the lambs.* London, UK: Random House.

Harris, T. (1999). *Hannibal.* London, UK: Random House.

Harrison, P. (1999). Catch me when you can. In M. Jakobowski & N. Braund (Eds.), *The mammoth book of Jack the Ripper* (pp. 187–203). London, UK: Robinson.

Hollway, W. (1981). "I just wanted to kill a woman. Why?" The Ripper and male sexuality. *Feminist Review, 9*(1), 33–40. http://dx.doi.org/10.1057/fr.1981.18

Jenkins, P. (1994). *Using murder: The social construction of serial homicide.* New York, NY: Aldine de Gruyter.

Kaplan, A. (1998). Introduction to new edition. In A. Kaplan (Ed.), *Women in film noir* (pp. 1–14). London, UK: British Film Institute Publishing.

Keppel, R., & Birnes, W. (2003). *The psychology of serial killer investigations: The grisly business unit.* London, UK: Academic Press.

Knox, S. (2003). The serial killer as collector. In L. Dilworth (Ed.), *Acts of possession: Collecting in America* (pp. 286–302). London, UK: Rutgers.

Lyon, D. (2006). The search for surveillance theories. In D. Lyon (Ed.), *Theorizing surveillance: The panopticon and beyond* (pp. 3–20). Devon, UK: Willan Publishing.

Macdonald, A. (2013). Serial killing, surveillance, and the state. In A. Macdonald (Ed.), *Murders and acquisitions: Representations of the serial killer in popular culture* (pp. 33–48). London, UK: Bloomsbury.

Morgan, J. (2002). Reconfiguring gothic mythology: The film noir-horror hybrids of the 1980s. *Postscript: Essays in Films and the Humanities, 21*(3), 72–86.

Mulvey, L. (1990). Visual pleasure and narrative cinema. In P. Erens (Ed.), *Issues in feminist film criticism* (pp. 28–40). Bloomington, IN: Indiana University Press.

Picart, C. J., & Greek, C. (2007). The compulsions of real/reel serial killers and vampires: Towards a Gothic criminology. In C. J. Picart & C. Greek (Eds.), *Monsters in and amongst us: Towards a Gothic criminology* (pp. 227–255). Cranbury, NJ: Fairleigh Dickinson University Press.

Rehling, N. (2009). *Extraordinary men: White heterosexual masculinity in contemporary popular cinema*. Plymouth, MA: Lexington Books.

Ressler, R. (1992). *Whoever fights monsters*. London, UK: Simon and Schuster.

Schmid, D. (2005). *Natural born celebrities: Serial killers in American culture*. Chicago, IL: University of Chicago Press. http://dx.doi.org/10.7208/chicago/9780226738703.001.0001

Seltzer, M. (1998). *Serial killers: Death and life in America's wound culture*. New York, NY: Routledge.

Simpson, P. (2000). *Psycho paths: Tracking the serial killer through contemporary American fiction and film*. Carbondale, IL: Southern Illinois University Press.

Stratton, J. (1996). Serial killing and the transformation of the social. *Theory, Culture, & Society, 13*(1), 77–98. http://dx.doi.org/10.1177/0263276960013001004

Summerscale, K. (2008). *The suspicions of Mr Whicher, or the murder at Road Hill House*. London, UK: Bloomsbury.

Surette, R. (2007). Gothic criminology and criminal justice policy. In C. J. Picart & C. Greek (Eds.), *Monsters in and amongst us: Towards a Gothic criminology* (pp. 199–226). Cranbury, NJ: Fairleigh Dickinson University Press.

Tasker, Y. (1995). *Spectacular bodies: Gender, genre, and the action cinema*. London, UK: Routledge.

Tasker, Y. (1998). *Working girls: Gender and sexuality in popular culture*. Oxford, UK: Routledge. http://dx.doi.org/10.4324/9780203438152

Tasker, Y. (2002). *The silence of the lambs*. London, UK: British Film Institute Publishing.

Tziallas, E. (2010). Torture porn and surveillance culture. *Jumpcut*, 52. http://www.ejumpcut.org/archive/jc52.2010/evangelosTorturePorn/

Tziallas, E. (2013). The spectacle of correction: Video games, movies and control. In J. Aston & J. Wallis (Eds.), *To see the Saw movies: Essays on torture porn and post-9/11 horror* (pp. 45–72). Jefferson, NC: Mcfarland and Company.

Walkowitz, J. (1982). Jack the Ripper and the myth of male violence. *Feminist Studies, 8*(3), 542–574. http://dx.doi.org/10.2307/3177712

Walkowitz, J. (1992). *City of dreadful delight: Narratives of sexual danger in late-Victorian London*. Chicago, IL: University of Chicago Press. http://dx.doi.org/10.7208/chicago/9780226081014.001.0001

Walkowitz, J. (2007). Narratives of sexual danger. In A. Warwick & M. Willis (Eds.), *Jack the Ripper: media, culture, history* (pp. 179–196). Manchester, UK: Manchester University Press.

Ward Jouve, N. (1986). *The Street-cleaner: The Yorkshire Ripper case on trial*. London, UK: Marion Boyars.

Warwick, A. (2006). The scene of the crime: Inventing the serial killer. *Social &*
   Legal Studies, 15(4), 552–569. http://dx.doi.org/10.1177/0964663906069547
Warwick, A. (2007). Blood and ink: Narrating the Whitechapel murders. In
   A. Warwick & M. Willis (Eds.), *Jack the Ripper: Media, culture, history* (pp.
   71–87). Manchester, UK: Manchester University Press.
Willis, M. (2007). Jack the Ripper, Sherlock Holmes, and the narrative of
   detection. In A. Warwick & M. Willis (Eds.), *Jack the Ripper: Media, culture,*
   history (pp. 144–158). Manchester, UK: Manchester University Press.

FILMOGRAPHY

Angel Heart (Alan Parker, 1987)
Blitz (Elliot Lester, 2011)
The Bone Collector (Phillip Noyce, 1999)
Bone Daddy (Mario Azzopardi, 1998)
Candyman (Bernard Rose, 1992)
Cop (James B. Harris, 1988)
Copycat (Jon Amiel, 1995)
CSI: Crime Scene Investigation (Atlantic Alliance, CBS, 2000–)
The Dead Zone (David Cronenberg, 1983)
Dexter (Showtime, CBS, 2006 – 2013)
Diary of a Serial Killer (Joshua Wallace, 1998)
Eye of the Killer (Paul Marcus, 1999)
Eyes of Laura Mars (Irvin Kershner, 1978)
The First Deadly Sin (Brian G. Hutton, 1980)
Frequency (Gregory Hoblit, 2000)
From Hell (Hughes Brothers, 2001)
Hannibal (Ridley Scott, 2001)
Hideaway (Brett Leonard, 1995)
Jack's Back (Rowdy Herrington, 1988)
The January Man (Pat O'Connor, 1989)
Jennifer Eight (Bruce Robinson, 1992)
Kiss the Girls (Gary Fleder, 1997)
The Lodger (Alfred Hitchcock, 1927)
The Mean Season (Philip Borsos, 1985)
Murder by Decree (Bob Clark, 1979)
Off Limits (Christopher Crowe, 1988)
The Raven (James McTeigue, 2012)
Righteous Kill (Jon Avnet, 2008)

The Rosary Murders (Fred Walton, 1987)
Saw (James Wan, 2004)
Seven (David Fincher, 1995)
The Silence of the Lambs (Jonathan Demme, 1991)
Tightrope (Richard Tuggle, 1984)
Time After Time (Nicholas Meyer, 1979)
The Watcher (Joe Charbanic, 2000)

Surveillance and Gendered Embodiment

Race, Media, and Surveillance: Sex-Selective Abortions in Canada

CORINNE L. MASON

Are some fetuses more equal than others? This debate question was posed to *National Post* columnists in the wake of a 2012 study that found immigrant women in Canada are more likely to practise sex-selective abortions than their so-called Canadian counterparts (De Souza, 2012; Ray, Henry, & Urquia, 2012; *National Post*, 2012). The study, which received wide media coverage upon its publication in the *Canadian Medical Association Journal*, singled out immigrant women for enacting femicide or gendercide (the killing of women and girls based on sex/gender).[1] After the journal published this study, the CBC released a short hidden-camera investigative documentary titled *Unnatural Selection*. Mark Warawa, a Conservative MP, subsequently introduced a parliamentary motion (Motion 408) to "condemn discrimination against females occurring through sex-selective pregnancy termination" (Parliament of Canada, 2012). While Warawa's attempt to criminalize sex-selective abortions in Canada has thus far been unsuccessful, Motion 408 is anything but a failure. In fact, the medical, media, and parliamentary attention to the issue has forever changed the abortion debate.

In this chapter, I work at the intersections of reproductive justice, Canadian critical race feminism, and surveillance studies to demonstrate the ways in which mediated discourses around sex-selective abortion have stigmatized racialized women's access to reproductive health services. Centring on an analysis of the CBC's *Unnatural Selection*, this chapter attends to Browne's (2012) conceptualization of "racializing surveillance" as both a means to uncover the "problem" of sex-selective abortion and as a method to address this issue in Canada. I suggest that the CBC's hidden camera documentary, which specifically focuses on reproductive health clinics frequented by racialized and immigrant communities, is an extension and intensification of Othering surveillance practices in the post-9/11 period.[2] I maintain that in the larger social context of racializing surveillance, the CBC's focus on the reproductive choices of racialized and immigrant women is unsurprising. Yet *Unnatural Section* also generates new questions about the control of women's reproductive access in Canada, especially along the lines of race and citizenship. Along with other interventions in the media by anti-abortion activists and by politicians, the recent focus on sex-selective abortions reflects the possibility that the abortion debate will be reopened in Canada; it also marks the intensification of demands for the surveillance of racialized women's reproductive bodies.

Race, Reproduction, and Surveillance

For Canadian critical race feminists, including Jiwani (2009), Razack (2008), and Thobani (2007), the post-9/11 period has produced political and cultural conditions in which racialized threats to the nation-state have been culturalized. In *Looking White People in the Eye*, Sherene Razack (1998) originally conceptualized culturalized racism through thinking about its "covert operations" (p. 60). In a multicultural and pluralist society in which Canadians are expected to be tolerant of Others, cultural differences are used to explain oppression, inequality, or marginalization between racial groups (pp. 60–1). In the post-9/11 period especially, cultural differences are also used defend dominant races from the supposed threat of Others. In this way, culturalized racism calls attention to the ways in which Others' cultural beliefs and values do not correspond to "ours." Covert racisms operate to differentiate those who do not belong to the Canadian imaginary from those who do. In other words, conceptions of modernity, civility, and human rights are relegated to questions of culture. As Razack, Smith, and Thobani (2010) explain, modern operations of racism (coded as cultural debates) are most often conducted on the bodies of racialized women. To be considered Canadian, Razack argues (2008), even if not possessing "Canadian skin" (p. 3), one must hold Canadian values. Racialized immigrants who flee their so-called backward countries and manipulate Canada's multicultural policies are said to bring the worst aspects of their culture with them. Their "cultural difference" (and our racism) links culture to a chain of another associations about Others (the veil, terrorism, and criminality, for example) that threaten the cohesion of the nation (Razack, 2008). In Canada, racialized communities have been represented as manipulating (at best) or disregarding (at worst) the national value of gender equality in the post-9/11 period. This perspective remains a crucial aspect of national identity.

Racialized women – more specifically, immigrant women – are often conceptualized as victims requiring rescue from backward and inequitable cultures by the masculinist Canadian nation-state. These rescue projects entail extensive networks of surveillance. As Jiwani (2009) maintains, this notion of a rescue mission is not simply about cultural narratives of racial incivility; simultaneously, it "produces and reproduces [a] chivalric code of masculinity that is the inverse of the hard power of the security state" (p. 729). Employing examples of racial profiling and security certificates, Jiwani suggests that "conquest and containment" are legitimatized "through the soft power of intervention through rescue and aid leavened by civilizational discourses" (p. 729). As I will demonstrate in this chapter, the surveillance of racialized women's reproductive bodies is legitimized because the practice of sex-selective abortion among immigrant communities is understood to be an enactment of gendercide or femicide. Surveilling racialized women's reproductive bodies can be understood as one example of how Canada "outsources patriarchy," a perspective in which "some cultures are understood solely through patriarchy while others are seen to have outgrown it" (Grewal, 2013, p. 1).

Within a reproductive justice framework, access to reproductive health services such as abortion is about more than choice. While the notion that women should have choice regarding their reproductive health practices has been long associated with women's autonomy, for racialized women, immigrant women, and Indigenous women, who have been disproportionately targeted by reproductive control measures, reproductive health issues are inextricably linked to broader social justice issues (Smith, 2005; INCITE, 2006; SisterSong, 2012; Native Youth Sexual Health Network, 2012). Smith (2005), for example, argues that attacks on Indigenous women's reproductive rights stem from the historical legacy of colonization that named them "pollutants" (p. 107) to white settler nations. For Hill Collins (1990) and Roberts (1997), the state's interference in the reproductive rights of Black women coincided with the expansion of welfare programs in the United States and with the attempt to deny them access to those benefits. Whether through coercive sterilization, the denial of access to abortion, or rape as a weapon of war, the control of reproduction has been central to state regulation of women's bodies, especially racialized women's bodies

(Smith, 2005). Given that the maternal body is imagined to produce the racialized and ethnic identity of the nation, state policies on reproduction are always already inflected by assumptions and desires concerning gender, race, disability, and class. The racialized maternal body matters to the state insofar as racialized women are the main targets for interventionist policies and programs related to reproduction.

Borrowing from the work of critical race and feminist surveillance scholar Simone Browne (2012), this chapter takes seriously the process of "racializing surveillance" in relation to reproductive justice. According to Browne (2012), racializing surveillance is that where "surveillance practices, policies, and performances concern the production of norms pertaining to race" (p. 72). For Browne, a focus on racializing surveillance not only highlights the intersections of racism and surveillance but also pinpoints "those moments when enactments of surveillance reify boundaries and borders along racial lines, and where the outcome is often discriminatory treatment" (2012, p. 72). Racializing surveillance reflects and shapes racial norms against a backdrop of whiteness where those who deviate from racial norms are considered "abnormal" and, therefore, become the focus of intensified scrutiny. Expanding the work of John Fiske (1998), Browne (2012) asserts that racializing surveillance has the "power to define what is in or out of place" (p. 70). Following Browne's (2012) work, Monaghan (2013) furthers theories of racializing surveillance by claiming that surveillance practices of identification, categorization, and enumeration, for example, aim not only to manage populations but also to "produce racial subjectivities according to prefabricated typologies and normative demarcations held by settler societies" (p. 487). As such, surveillance practices reflect and reproduce processes of racialization as they are employed. In this chapter I advance an analysis of racialized surveillance by demonstrating how it is coded in practices of cultural differentiation that reflect and secure processes of racialization.

By centring mediated representations of sex-selective abortions in this chapter, I focus on the ways in which practices of communication are often also practices of surveillance (Gates & Magnet, 2007). As Gates and Magnet (2007) maintain, "In many respects, surveillance technologies *are* media technologies, and in that sense all forms of surveillance beyond direct supervision involve the use of media, from writing and paper to digital video and audio recording devices" (p. 2, emphasis in original).

Borrowing from Scott's (1999) *Seeing like a State*, Magnet and Gates (2009) argue that the collection of information for the purpose of governance work serves to render citizens legible to the state. The legibility of citizens is also mediated by communication strategies. News media interpret and tell stories in ways that reflect, shape, and secure normative values (Hall, 1990; Jiwani, 2006). Thus, broader media practices of representation suggest how practices of surveillance are embedded in the targeting of racialized communities and women in debates over sex-selective abortion.

An examination of the CBC is especially significant in this respect given that, as I have argued elsewhere, that network is Canada's "voice of the nation" (Mason, 2011, p. 95). Indeed, it communicates more than just the news. With its slogan "Canada Lives Here," it communicates Canada's national identity to its citizenry. Importantly, national media – including the CBC – construct hegemonic discourses. As Foucault (1980) maintains, the creation of knowledge is also the production of power. While the CBC represents a diversity of perspectives, and often counter-hegemonic discourses, national media communicate conceptions of belonging through interlocking lines of gender, race, class, sexuality, and disability; those same media also both reflect and generate dominant ways of knowing about events, histories, identities, and practices. In this regard, *Unnatural Selection* does more than present the issue of sex-selective abortion in Canada – it actively stigmatizes racialized women's reproductive health choices through the practice of watching. By inviting the audience to gaze upon reproductive health access in racialized communities, and by employing hidden cameras aimed at uncovering the problem of sex-selective abortions, *Unnatural Selection* practises racializing surveillance. While it is not the only account of sex selection published or produced by the CBC, *Unnatural Selection* represents the most powerful and widely circulated discourses on the issue.

Importantly, this CBC hidden camera investigation is presented as if it is documenting the "reality" of a "real time" event; thus, it supposedly reflects the "real world." Of course, "reality-based" media spectacles are embedded in racist practices of looking (Hall, 1990; hooks, 1992). In documentary-style news reporting, the aim of gazing upon Others is not just to seize and sometimes incarcerate those who commit crimes; it is also to communicate evidence that "they" (read "criminalized individuals") do not belong and/or that they present a threat to citizens and/or national security. Simultaneously, news reporting positions the viewer to identify and empathize with police, reporters, and even reality TV and documentary makers; the viewer is allowed to voyeuristically gaze and experience pleasure as police and state personnel search for drug dealers, sex workers, non-status migrants, "terrorists," and, in the case of the *Unnatural Section*, racialized women accessing reproductive health services (Andrejevic, 2003; Gates & Magnet, 2007). *Unnatural Selection* enacts surveillance by inviting hidden cameras and audiences to reify citizenship boundaries and borders along racial lines. Immigrants are constructed as guests who must remain under scrutiny since their race (read through culture) presents a threat to the Canadian social imaginary, especially as it rubs up against the values of gender equality.

CBC's Undercover Investigation: *Unnatural Selection*

Unnatural Selection begins with news anchor Peter Mansbridge stating: "What we're about to show you is legal in Canada. When a woman is pregnant, it is her right to decide what happens next – that could include aborting a fetus because it's female" (CBC, 2012c). Narrated by senior investigative journalist Diana Swain, *Unnatural Selection* presents an undercover investigation of private ultrasound clinics, where individuals can pay for an ultrasound outside of provincial health care support, and the role of those clinics in the practice of "gender selection" (CBC, 2012c). In April 2012, CBC producers visited twenty-two such clinics in Ontario and British Columbia. Wearing a hidden camera, a CBC producer (a racialized woman) asked ultrasound providers whether they were willing to do an ultrasound fourteen weeks into a pregnancy and, if not, at what stage they would do it. Significantly, it is possible to determine fetal sex in an ultrasound at fourteen weeks' gestation, and still seek an abortion if it is an unwanted pregnancy. Out of the twenty-two clinics approached, seven insisted they would not provide an ultrasound until after the twenty-week mark, at which point it is often too late to access an abortion in a Canadian clinic or hospital.[3] Some clinics suggested that they would provide an ultrasound at seventeen or eighteen weeks (which would have contradicted their official policy), and one offered to perform an ultrasound on the day the producer first entered the clinic. Testing multiple locations of the UC Baby Clinic, which provides 3D and 4D images of fetuses as keepsakes for parents (and claims to have a strict policy of not revealing sex before twenty weeks), the CBC's Investigations Unit found that many service providers were nonetheless willing to do an early ultrasound to reveal the sex of the fetus. Citing empathy for planning, excitement, and the need to paint the nursery room, most administrative personnel at the UC Baby Clinics waived the twenty-week policy – interestingly, they did not speak to the issue of sex-selective abortions. With one exception, it is not clear whether the CBC producer questioned any doctors or medical personnel about sex-selective abortion procedures.

Unnatural Selection claims that in families where boys are valued more than girls, there can be pressure on women to abort female fetuses. The racialized dimension of this perspective is immediately made evident in the film, which begins with a shot of a Sikh doctor performing an ultrasound, followed by a shot of a visibly pregnant woman of colour. Within the first minute, the documentary thus makes it clear that communities of colour and immigrant communities are the target of this investigation, as both practitioners and patients. Dr Verjinder Uhbi, a family doctor, tells the CBC that while "most patients are happy with either gender," some women pressure him for an "early ultrasound" before twenty weeks' of gestation, when an elective abortion is still possible. He states his belief that an early ultrasound is "not right" and that sex selection has been practised in countries like India for decades, thus suggesting that racialized women, and specifically South Asian women, are the ones seeking early ultrasounds. Moving from a shot of a Canadian medical clinic to the streets of an unnamed city in India, the CBC suggests that more than 12 million female fetuses have been aborted in the past thirty years in India alone; however, the social and political context of Indian sex-selective practices is left unexplored. Demonstrating what Narayan (1997) calls a colonial stance and what Mohanty (2003) terms Third World difference, the documentary presents statements about gender-inequitable population policies in China and India as neutral and quick facts; that is, they are presented without historical explanation or nuanced analysis, which enables them to circulate as culturalized explanations of a complex issue. By using images of India, *Unnatural Selection* sets up a visual and affective contrast between Canadian values at home and gender inequalities abroad. Such representations can be understood through the framework of Razack's (1998) culturalized racism, where cultural differences are coded and covert racisms. As journalist Diana Swain maintains, what the film's audience is about to see will be shocking given the "deeply entrenched gender equity laws" in Canada (CBC, 2012c). Grewal (2013) argues that such narratives of outsourced patriarchy, or the use of patriarchy to describe Other cultures, present "unchanging or ahistorical" cultures of gender inequity that "even mobility or diaspora contexts cannot alter"

(p. 4). Canadians are represented as having "a monopoly on liberal and human values" (Abu-Lughod, 2011, p. 32) and as embodying "free sexuality" and personal autonomy, whereas communities of colour and immigrant communities are characterized as staunchly backward and traditional in their gender relations.

Besides offering these racist depictions, *Unnatural Selection* provides impetus for further surveilling racialized communities regarding their access to reproductive technologies, including ultrasounds and imaging technologies. As Browne (2012) outlines, racializing surveillance involves producing and communicating racial norms through policy and practices. According to the CBC's Investigations Unit, Canada's ethnic communities *are* practising sex selection. While coded as cultural difference, the practices of racialized surveillance shown in *Unnatural Selection* maintain a racial logic: there are those who belong to Canada, and there are those who must be "cast out" (Razack, 2008). In the CBC's account, racialized women are seeking sex-selective abortions because their families prefer sons, and racialized ultrasound providers are providing women with unethical information. Yet the CBC is never able to "catch" someone with its hidden cameras in the act of aborting a female fetus, or seeking a sex-selective abortion, or requesting information on the sex of a fetus; all it does is provide examples of private clinics offering early ultrasounds as evidence of sex selection. Significantly, *Unnatural Selection* fails to acknowledge the complicated process many women are forced to undergo simply to access abortion services in Canadian clinics and hospitals.[4]

According to the CBC investigation, in ethnic communities in Canada such as Brampton, Ontario, there are only 86 girls for every 100 boys under the age of eighteen (CBC, 2012c). Without comparing these statistics to those from other regions, *Unnatural Selection* then interviews ultrasound providers at Punjabi Community Health Services in Peel, Ontario, who suggest that women in the Punjabi community choose sex selection to abort female fetuses due to pressure from husbands and family members. Drawing a connection between sex-selective abortions and violence against women and girls in immigrant communities, the service providers suggest that 10 per cent of women who come to PCHS for services related to abortion have been pressured by family members (CBC, 2012c). By linking sex-selective abortions to the control, pressure, and violence experienced by immigrant women at the hands of family members, the CBC is representing racialized and immigrant cultures as overwhelmingly patriarchal, and racialized femininities as culturally imperilled (Razack, 2008).

In Brampton, the CBC's Investigations Unit brought its hidden cameras to the Modern Non Diagnostic Imaging Centre. While there, the CBC producer spoke to a racialized male service provider (shown sitting behind a single desk in a small room, with bath curtains partitioning the ultrasound space). The provider offered to perform an ultrasound for $600 and encouraged the producer to have one immediately. As the documentary points out, this clinic had recently published an advertisement in a local South Asian newspaper to promote its services that read: "this advertisement is not for gender discrimination." Investigative journalist Swain suggests in her narration that the clinic "must be aware of how its business can be used to determine gender in order to abort female fetuses" (CBC, 2012c).

The CBC investigators assumed that racialized and immigrant women were seeking out gender-determining ultrasounds for the purpose of sex-selective abortion. While coded as cultural, this assumption reflected and reproduced racial grammars of difference. The notion that these women might simply be eager to know the sex of the fetus never entered the frame. Nor did the investigators address feminist concerns about the social construction of gender at the twenty-week mark of gestation. The CBC expressed its concern about societies that value boys over girls, but it did not link the issue of painting a nursery room pink or blue to a concern with gender norms and inequality. I have no interest in arguing that sex selection does not happen in Canada, but I am concerned with how *Unnatural Selection* infers that racialized and immigrant women's access to reproductive technologies should be viewed with suspicion. The documentary's narrator maintains that the question of sex-selective abortions "gets at the heart of women's right to choose" (CBC, 2012c), and the documentary makes it clear that some women cannot be trusted with this choice.

According to *Unnatural Selection*, in the "wrong" hands, ultrasounds (both medical and for entertainment) can be used for gender discrimination, so there should be stricter laws to govern when a woman can be told the sex of a fetus. As Magnet and I have argued elsewhere, given that surveillance practices and their relationship to inequality have a long history, the contemporary surveillance of immigrant and racialized women should be linked to the historical sterilization of racialized women and women with disabilities as part of neo-eugenic programs, as well as to the scrutiny of women receiving welfare aid from the state (Mason & Magnet, 2012). Indeed, state institutions have long policed racialized women's bodies. As other scholars contend, surveillance measures generate not only social sorting but also social stratification, entrenching norms and discriminatory treatment (Lyon, 2003; Browne, 2012). *Unnatural Selection* and its hidden cameras are deeply embedded in a context of ongoing socialization and processes of racialization that mark such surveillance practices as acceptable. Importantly, the surveillance of racialized women's access to reproductive health, and the continued scrutiny of abortion practices in the context of a renewed abortion debate in Canada, may create possibilities for new ways of controlling abortion access. To be sure, when Conservative MP Mark Warawa introduced Motion 408 with the aim of stopping sex-selective abortions, he thanked the CBC for "bringing this matter to the attention of Canadians" (Radical Handmaids, 2012, n.p.).

"It's a Girl"

As noted above, the CBC produced *Unnatural Selection* in response to a *Canadian Medical Association Journal* article that first reported the issue of sex-selective abortions in Canada. According to the *CMAJ*'s former editor-in-chief, Rajendra Kale (2012), "when Asians migrated to Western countries they brought welcome recipes for curries and dim sum. Sadly, a few of them also imported their preference for having sons and aborting daughters" (p. 387). In his editorial, "It's a Girl – Could Be a Death Sentence," Kale argues that female feticide in Canada should not be ignored, even if it is "a small problem localized to minority ethnic groups" (p. 387). While experts have not deemed sex selection a systemic issue, Kale suggests that the medical community ought to pay attention because the issue is about "discrimination against women in its extreme form" (p. 387). Curiously beginning his editorial with concluding remarks, Kale writes: "The solution [to sex-selective abortion] is to postpone the disclosure of medically irrelevant information to women until after about 30 weeks of pregnancy" (p. 387). While women have a right to information about their own bodies when it comes to advice and treatment, the sex of a fetus is deemed by Kale to be medically irrelevant information (except in the case of rare sex-linked illnesses), since the sex of a fetus does not affect care.

Of course, such medicalized narratives of women's bodies are not new, nor is the assumption that medical personnel have expertise and therefore should be able to exert control over women's bodies. Kale in his editorial assumes that women are passive receptors of both knowledge and pregnancy, and he represents masculinized medical experts as the agents of reproduction. His views fit squarely within Western medicalized discourses that have been heavily criticized by feminists for treating women as non-experts and non-agents in their own reproductive health (see Boston Women's Health Book Collective, 2013).

According to Kale (2012), postponing the disclosure of the sex of a fetus to all women is a justified reaction to the problem of sex-selection abortions sought by "Asians – that is people from India, China, Korea, Vietnam and Philippines" (p. 387). In the hands of the "wrong" women, ultrasound technologies are dangerous. Offering little historical, political, cultural, or economic context, Kale in his editorial swiftly mentions population policies in China and India to account for the cultural prevalence of son preference among Asians, and he successfully situates the issue as disconnected from other issues. Indeed, the political and economic variables that could properly contextualize the issue of sex-selective abortions are obscured by Kale's overwhelming focus on culture, curries, and dim sum.

Significantly, Kale's claims about sex selection in Canada come from a "small qualitative study in the US" (p. 387). As such, his assertion that "Asians" are more likely to access sex-selective services in Canada is presumptive at best. That said, the American study, which documents how Indian women face pressure to have sons and how women navigate sex-selective technologies, should not be ignored. Of the sixty-five immigrant women interviewed, 40 per cent had terminated pregnancies with female fetuses, and 89 per cent of the women carrying female fetuses in their current pregnancy pursued an abortion at some point in the gestation period. However, it is essential to note that this study specifically sought out Indian women "who had pursued fetal sex-selection in the United States" (Puri, Adams, Ivey, & Nachtigall, 2011, p. 1169) and that the researchers did not compare Indian women's experience in seeking sex-selective abortions with the Indian population in the United States more generally. The study on which Kale bases his assertion that women should be denied medically "irrelevant" information about their pregnancy in early stages in fact provides little justification for the development of new regulations around reproductive health access.

Lest he "paint all Asians with the same broad brush" (Kale, 2012, p. 387), which would do "injustice to those who are against sex selection" (p. 387), Kale calls for a "disclose sex only after 30 weeks" policy (p. 387). He maintains that this policy "would require the understanding and willingness of women of all ethnicities to make a temporary compromise" (p. 387). This temporary but non-negotiable compromise would be established for all women because racialized and immigrant women, especially Asians, cannot be trusted with information about the sex of a fetus. Further entrenching racist stereotypes of "Asians" as particularly patriarchal and culturally backward – stereotypes that are already free-floating in Canada, Kale adds culturalized sexism in reproductive health choices to his list of what Asian immigrants have "brought over" to Canada.

Following Kale's editorial, the *CMAJ* published the article "Sex Ratios among Canadian Liveborn Infants of Mothers from Different Countries," in which Ray, Henry, and Urquia (2012) discuss a population-based study of 766,688 singleton live births (i.e., births that do not involve twins or other multiples) between 2002 and 2007. While they are less forceful than Kale in pushing for government intervention, nevertheless their study reinforces the demand for greater surveillance of immigrant women. Using birth records provided by Ontario Vital Statistics, a government agency that collects data on births, marriages, and deaths, the researchers compared sex ratios among infants of Canadian-born women with sex ratios in immigrant communities "purported to have the highest rates of preference for a son following the birth of one or more daughters" (Ray, Henry, & Urquia, 2012, p. E492). Referring to Ontario as "Canada's most populated and diverse province" (p. E492), they aimed to determine whether "male:female ratios increased with increasing parity in immigrant communities" (p. E492). In other words, the researchers hypothesized that in some immigrant communities, multiparous women (i.e., women who have given birth more than twice) would be more likely to give birth to a male. After reviewing all registered singleton live births in Ontario between 2002 and 2007, they found that there was a higher male:female ratio among infants of multiparous woman originally born in India than among infants of multiparous women born in Canada. They also found that in contrast to their Canadian-born counterparts, women from South Korea were also more likely to give birth to male children. The researchers claim that their findings raise the possibility that Indian and South Korean women may seek prenatal sex discrimination and sex-selective abortions if the fetus is female (Ray, Henry, & Urquia, 2012, p. E493). Without a thorough analysis of other variables that might explain this finding in greater detail, the authors suggest that sex-selective abortions are likely happening, and require the attention of policymakers and medical practitioners. As the CBC's *Unnatural Selection* similarly makes evident, this is a trend worth watching.

These two *CMAJ* articles note that research that seems to point to the rise in sex-selective abortions among Asian immigrants in Canada is merely preliminary. Even so, the studies have been taken up as offering definitive evidence. This has been facilitated by the fact that, in arguing for greater surveillance of immigrant women, both articles draw on a pre-existing set of racialized assumptions, what Yasmin Jiwani (2006) calls "common sense stock knowledge" (p. 4). Borrowing from Stuart Hall (1990), Jiwani maintains that a news story can only make sense to an audience if it is located within a range of knowable social and cultural identifications. News stories tend to adhere to, rather than disrupt, historical archives of knowledge, and they often mirror already circulating discourses. In other words, the construction of news stories generally relies on what is already popularly known about the subject (Jiwani, 2006). Regarding the coverage of sex-selective abortions, the mediated moral panic surrounding the practice has been fuelled by what is always already known about Others. That is, coverage of the issue re-presents old racial grammars of cultural difference, which the mainstream news media consistently reactivate. More specifically, racialized communities are presented as overly patriarchal in contrast to their so-called Canadian counterparts.

In 2012, coverage of a renewed abortion debate in Canada was widespread by the time the CBC produced *Unnatural Selection*. In February of that year, Conservative MP Stephen Woodworth filed a motion in the House of Commons to form a committee to define the "start of life" (CBC, 2012a). Before Mark Warawa introduced Motion 408 on abortion and gender discrimination, Woodworth's proposed Motion 312 failed to gain parliamentary support. Feminist and pro-choice groups, including the Radical Handmaids (2012), wittily named after Margaret Atwood's dystopian novel *The Handmaid's Tale* (1985), in which women are vessels for bearing children and are enslaved to men of the ruling elite, challenged Woodworth's motion. These groups have dismissed Motion 312 and the definition of the "start of life" as a Conservative attempt to criminalize abortion through a political back door. After Motion 312 failed, the "discovery" of sex-selective abortions among immigrant communities dramatically changed the terms of the abortion discourse. In mainstream and alternative media, heated debates about race, gender, equality, violence against women and girls, and immigration intersected with debates over women's right to choose. Instead of being situated within well-known and opposing frames of choice and life, abortion became increasingly represented as an issue of violence against women and girls in Canada – specifically, violence perpetrated by racialized and immigrant communities.

The shift in the debate is evident in the comments of the former Conservative Minister for the Status of Women, Rona Ambrose, who voted in favour of defining the "start of life," citing sex-selection abortion as her reasoning (Rennie, 2012). When asked to respond to the CBC's *Unnatural Selection*, Ambrose stated: "I think we need to work closely with women's groups who are speaking out about this issue in *certain cultural communities*, and ensure that people understand that girls and boys are equal under the law, that they are valuable and that in *this society*, we don't tolerate discrimination against girls and women" (CBC, 2012c, emphasis added).

Razack (2008) argues that when feminists evoke ideas of cultural difference regarding violence against Other women, "contemporary political conditions ensure that their words will not be taken lightly" (p. 85). Employing feminist principles and the language of gender equality around the rights of girls, Ambrose's comments culturalized the issue of gender discrimination in Canada. This was also the case with Canada's "National March for Life" in 2013, which used the slogan "End Female Gendercide" and directly borrowed from Kale's editorial by declaring that "'It's a girl!' should not be a death sentence" (Campaign for Life Coalition, 2013).[5]

These shifts in the parameters of the debates over abortion have reshaped mediated representations; this in turn has legitimized the growth in media and other forms of surveillance. In particular, discourses of Canadian values around gender equality feature prominently in the popular news coverage of the issue. For example, an online CBC news article describes an epidemic of "disappearing daughters" and "missing girls" (CBC, 2012b) in Canada because of access to sex-selective abortions. An especially inflammatory portrayal of sex-selective abortion that invoked key racist tropes was an opinion piece posted online by the *National Post*, one of Canada's national newspapers, by Father Raymond J. De Souza (2012), who linked honour killings, often associated with Asian immigrant communities in Canada, to sex-selective abortions, and who claimed that "equality between the sexes is the bright line in the multicultural sand" (n.p). Father De Souza maintains that honour killings in Canada – a prime example being what is now ubiquitously known as "the Shafia case" (where four female family members were killed by their father, mother, and eldest brother in 2010) – are "barbaric" and "uncivilized" (De Souza, n.p.) and have no place in Canadian society. Collapsing the differences between sex-selective abortion and honour killings, he argues that Canadian values of women's equality are rubbing up against tolerance for immigrant groups that bring with them cultural ideals from their homes in developing nations. Claiming that sex-selective abortion is connected solely to the cultural undervaluing of girls and women in Other cultures, he suggests that multiculturalism in Canada has "utterly failed" (n.p.) and that, echoing Kale's (2012) earlier editorial in the Canadian Medical Association Journal, Canadians cannot "ignore the cult, enjoy the curry" (De Souza, 2012, n.p.).

While a comprehensive exploration of mainstream and alternative media representations of sex-selective abortions is a much larger task than this chapter can take on, from the debates highlighted here we can see that the issue has enabled new forms of opposition to abortion to emerge, besides generating powerful culturally racialized discourses targeting immigrant women. Specifically, the focus on sex-selective abortion has prompted calls for increased surveillance of immigrant communities by the state and medical authorities. One may speculate that such an increase in racializing surveillance by way of collecting and managing information on racialized women's reproductive choice may represent another gatekeeping mechanism in abortion services. Medical studies like that of Ray, Henry, and Urquia (2012), and editorials like Kale's (2012), have already begun this process by arguing that interventionist practices should pay specific attention to immigrant women. Although parliamentary motions proposed by Woodworth and Warawa aimed at imposing restrictions on access to abortion have thus far failed, the growing media interest in sex-selective abortions has fuelled other forms of surveillance, as evident in the CBC's *Unnatural Selection*, which brought the issue out of academic journals and into the homes of Canadians and thus has invited the further surveillance of racialized and immigrant communities' access to reproductive services.

Conclusion

Canadian MP Mark Warawa's motion to condemn sex-selective abortions (Motion 408) was unsuccessful in 2012. However, at its annual convention in October 2013, the Conservative Party of Canada voted in favour of a motion that "condemns discrimination against girls through gender selection" (Radia, 2013, n.p.), while over 125 anti-choice protesters rallied outside the event. That said, the significance of the CBC's

Unnatural Selection has yet to be fully realized: while the documentary successfully surveilled racialized and immigrant women's use of entertainment ultrasound clinics, and has generated a national rhetoric that is stigmatizing racialized women's reproductive choices through culturalized racism, the impact of racialized surveillance on access to reproductive services for women in Canada remains to be seen. Of course, the prospect of being watched and documented at ultrasound clinics controls individuals' ability to act on their reproductive choices. As surveillance theorist David Lyon (1992) reminds us, accumulating information and supervising activities are closely related and are always a means of acquiring power.

Advocates for reproductive justice should remain concerned about the entanglement of racializing surveillance practices with culturalized racist rhetoric as well as by the criminalization of sex-selective abortions in Canada. In the United States, Oklahoma and Arizona have passed controversial bills that outlaw abortions on the basis of the race or gender of the fetus.[6] In Arizona, a person who knowingly performs, undergoes, supports, pressures, or solicits money for the purpose of sex- or race-selective abortion can be charged with a felony, and a physician, physician's assistant, nurse, counsellor, or medical and/or mental health professional who knowingly does not report suspected race- or sex-selective abortions can be found guilty of a felony. This law further criminalizes patients and practitioners of abortion procedures; it is also a surveillance technique. As quoted by Schwartz (2011), the Planned Parenthood Federation of America suggests that doctors and other medical personal may now feel "compelled to ask their patients the reasons for seeking an abortion" (n.p.), thus eroding women's rights to reproductive health services. Martin (2013) argues that abortion regulations not only heighten surveillance but also generate stigma and project a negative image of abortion patients and providers (National Abortion Federation, 2007). These laws can discourage potential abortion providers from delivering such services, resulting in a loss of access to reproductive services for American women.

In Canada, the sex-selective abortion discourse has specifically targeted racialized and immigrant communities, both as patients and as practitioners. *Unnatural Selection* aimed to shed light on cultures of gender inequity; in practice, however, through its use of hidden cameras, it has intensified racialized surveillance of reproductive access in Canada by creating new social norms around race. The possibility of legislation or further regulation of when an individual can be given information about the sex of the fetus, or other "non-medically relevant" information, is very real. Given the legislative precedent set in the United States and the ongoing surveillance of abortion in Canada, it is possible that even more information will be collected about racialized and immigrant women's access to abortion, thus heightening the surveillance of already marginalized women. Already targeted as bodies to watch, racialized and immigrant communities are being made even more suspect by this focus on sex selection, and this may well intensify existing and interlocking systems of oppression that are already creating systemic barriers and reducing access, before *and* after the twenty-week gestation period. The watching of women, as exemplified in *Unnatural Selection*, is an extension of an already long history of racist surveillance, discipline, and control of racialized women and their bodies.

NOTES

1 While sex and gender can be differentiated by socially constructed and biological characteristics, these terms are often used interchangeably in discourses of sex-selective abortion in Canada. Here, I use the terms as they appear in the mediated texts I study. It is also important to note that the texts that are the focus of this chapter work within a cisgender structure where transgender individuals are written out of questions of reproductive justice.

2 I use the term "post-9/11" here following Puar's (2007) discussion of event-ness to denote the way in which the pre- and post-9/11 periods are discursively demarcated and imagined as separated by the event of the 11 September 2001 terrorist attack on the United States. Using "post-9/11" troubles this imagining and calls for a contextual account of simultaneously linked and disjunctive systems of power present along a historical continuum of the pre- and post- 9/11 period.

3 The Canadian Institute for Health Information's latest data suggest that 0.54 per cent of all abortions take place after twenty weeks of gestation (Abortion Rights Coalition of Canada, 2015, p. 2).

4 While beyond the scope of this chapter, it is important to note that the decriminalization of abortion in Canada does not equate to equal or fair access. For example, despite its decriminalized status, abortions are not accessible to all in Canada. For example, Medicare in the province of New Brunswick does not cover clinic abortions, and abortions obtained outside one's home province may not be covered (Abortion Rights Coalition of

Canada, 2006, p. 1). There are no abortion providers across the entire province of Prince Edward Island. Furthermore, many individuals seeking an
abortion face gatekeeping mechanisms and surveillance practices that create
barriers to services.

5 In the context of insidious and ongoing violence against Indigenous women
and girls in Canada, the mediated moral panic around sex-selection abortion is offensive. Minister for the Status of Women Rona Ambrose's tweet
of support for Motion 408, a motion to criminalize sex-selective abortion,
is especially troubling since she has yet to publicly support calls to end
violence against Indigenous women and girls.

6 Utah, Florida, New York, Indiana, Iowa, Mississippi, Kansas, Colorado, and
North Dakota have all had sex-selection anti-discrimination abortion bills
on the books at some time (Lovelady, 2013).

REFERENCES

Abortion Rights Coalition of Canada. (2015). Statistics – Abortion in Canada.
http://www.arcc-cdac.ca/backrounders/statistics-abortion-in-canada.pdf

Abu-Lughod, L. (2011). Seductions of the "honor crime." *Differences:
A Journal of Feminist Cultural Studies*, 22(1), 17–63. http://dx.doi.
org/10.1215/10407391-1218238

Andrejevic, M. (2003). *Reality TV: The work of being watched*. Landham, MD:
Rowman and Littlefield.

Boston Women's Health Book Collective. (2013). *Our bodies, ourselves*. http://
www.ourbodiesourselves.org

Browne, S. (2012). Race and surveillance. In K. Ball, K. Haggerty, & D. Lyon
(Eds.), *Routledge Handbook of Surveillance Studies* (pp. 72–80). London, New
York: Routledge. http://dx.doi.org/10.4324/9780203814949.ch1_2_d

Campaign for Life Coalition. (2013, 8 May). Thousands of Canadians will
march through Ottawa to "End Female Gendercide." https://www.
campaignlifecoalition.com/index.php?p=Press_Room&id=117

CBC (Canadian Broadcasting Corporation). (2012a, 19 April). Disappearing
daughters – an expert responds. http://www.cbc.ca/metromorning/
episodes/2012/04/19/disappearing-daughters---an-expert-responds

CBC (Canadian Broadcasting Corporation). (2012b, 12 June). *Unnatural
selection*. http://www.cbc.ca/player/Shows/The+National/
About+the+Show/Diana+Swain/ID/2245245694/?sort=MostPopular

CBC (Canadian Broadcasting Corporation). (2012c, 13 June). Ban on
'entertainment' ultrasounds urged: More education is also key, say

politicians. http://www.cbc.ca/news/canada/ban-on-entertainment-ultrasounds-urged-1.1242522

De Souza, J. (2012, 9 May). Canada's crisis of cultural confidence. *National Post.* http://news.nationalpost.com/full-comment/father-raymond-j-de-souza-canadas-crisis-of-cultural-confidence

Fiske, J. (1998). Surveiling the city: Whiteness, the black man, and democratic totalitarianism. *Theory, Culture, & Society, 15*(2), 67–88. http://dx.doi.org/10.1177/026327698015002003

Foucault, M. (1980). *Power/knowledge: Selected interviews and other writings, 1972–1977.* New York, NY: Pantheon.

Gates, K., & Magnet, S. (2007). Communication research and the study of surveillance. *Communication Review, 10*(4), 277–293. http://dx.doi.org/10.1080/10714420701715357

Grewal, I. (2013). Outsourcing patriarchy: Feminist encounters, transnational mediations, and the crime of "honor killings." *International Feminist Journal of Politics, 15*(1), 1–19. http://dx.doi.org/10.1080/14616742.2012.755352

Hall, S. (1990). The whites of their eyes: Racist ideologies in the media. In M. Alvarado & J. O. Thompson (Eds.), *The media reader* (pp. 9–23). London, UK: British Film Institute Press.

Hill Collins, P. (1990). *Black feminist thought: Knowledge, consciousness, and the politics of empowerment, perspectives on gender.* Vol. 2. Boston, MA: Unwin Hyman.

hooks, b. (1992). *Black looks: Race and representation.* Boston, MA: South End Press.

INCITE Women of Colour Against Violence (Eds.). (2006). *The color of violence: The INCITE! anthology.* Cambridge, MA: South End Press.

Jiwani, Y. (2006). *Discourses of denial: Mediations of race, gender, and violence.* Vancouver, BC: University of British Columbia Press.

Jiwani, Y. (2009). Helpless maidens and chivalrous knights: Afghan women in the Canadian press. *University of Toronto Quarterly, 78*(2), 728–744. http://dx.doi.org/10.3138/utq.78.2.728

Kale, R. (2012). It's a girl could be a death sentence. *Canadian Medical Association Journal, 16*(4), 387–388. http://dx.doi.org/10.1503/cmaj.120021

Lovelady, D. (2013). At least 9 states considering bills to ban sex-selective abortions. *Christian Post.* http://www.christianpost.com/news/at-least-9-states-considering-bills-to-ban-sex-selective-abortions-91318

Lyon, D. (1992). The new surveillance: Electronic technologies and the maximum security society. *Law and Social Change, 18,* 159–175.

Lyon, D. (Ed.). (2003). *Surveillance as social sorting: Privacy, risk, and digital discrimination.* London, New York: Routledge.

Magnet, S., & Gates, K. (2009). *The new media of surveillance*. New York: Routledge.

Martin, L. (2013). Enacted abortion stigma: Attempts to delegitimize abortion providers through Targeted Regulation of Abortion Providers (TRAP) legislation. Paper presented at the National Women's Studies Conference, Cincinnati, OH.

Mason, C. L. (2011). Foreign aid as gift: Canada's response to the Haitian earthquake. *Critical Studies in Media Communication, 28,* 95–112. http://dx.doi.org/10.1080/15295036.2011.559479

Mason, C. L., & Magnet, S. (2012). Surveillance studies and violence against women. *Surveillance & Society, 10,* 105–118.

Mohanty, C. (2003). *Feminism without borders: Decolonizing theory, practicing solidarity*. Durham, NC: Duke University Press. http://dx.doi.org/10.1215/9780822384649

Monaghan, J. (2013). Settler governmentality and racializing surveillance in Canada's North-West. *Canadian Journal of Sociology / Cahiers canadiens de sociologie, 38*(4), 487–508.

Narayan, U. (1997). *Dislocating cultures: Identities, traditions, and Third World feminism*. New York, NY: Routledge.

National Abortion Federation (2007). *The TRAP: Targeted regulation of abortion providers* https://www.prochoice.org/pubs_research/publications/downloads/about_abortion/trap_laws.pdf

National Post. (2012, 17 January). Internal dissent: Are some fetuses more equal than others? http://fullcomment.nationalpost.com/2012/01/17/internal-dissent-are-some-fetuses-more-equal-than-others

Native Youth Sexual Health Network. (2012). *Areas of work*. http://www.nativeyouthsexualhealth.com/areasofwork.html

Parliament of Canada. (2012). Mark Warawa - Private Members' Motions - 41st Parliament, 2nd Session. 41st Parliament, 2nd Session http://www.parl.gc.ca/Parliamentarians/en/members/Mark-Warawa(25467)/Motions?sessionId=151&documentId=6253205

Puar, J. K. (2007). *Terrorist assemblages: Homonationalism in queer times*. Durham, NC: Duke University Press.

Puri, S., Adams, V., Ivey, S., & Nachtigall, D. (2011). "There is such a thing as too many daughters, but not too many sons": A qualitative study of son preference and fetal sex selection among Indian immigrants in the United States. *Social Science & Medicine, 72*(7), 1169–1176. http://dx.doi.org/10.1016/j.socscimed.2011.01.027

Radia, A. (2013). Tory delegates say "yes" to gun ownership and "no" to sex-selection abortion and euthanasia. *Yahoo News*. http://news.yahoo.

com/blogs/canada-politics/tory-delegates-yes-gun-ownership-no-sex-selection-192727950.html

Radical Handmaids. (2012). http://radicalhandmaids.com

Ray, J. G., Henry, D. A., & Urquia, M. L. (2012). Sex ratios among Canadian liveborn infants of mothers from different countries. *Canadian Medical Association Journal, 184*(9), E492–E496. http://dx.doi.org/10.1503/cmaj.120165

Razack, S. (1998). *Looking white people in the eye: Gender, race, and culture in courtrooms and classrooms*. Toronto, ON: University of Toronto Press.

Razack, S. (2008). *Casting out: The eviction of Muslims from Western law and politics*. Toronto, ON: University of Toronto Press.

Razack, S., Smith, M., & Thobani, S. (Eds.). (2010). *States of race: Critical race feminism for the 21st Century*. Toronto, ON: Between the Lines.

Rennie, S. (2012, 27 September). Rona Ambrose Motion 312 vote: "Sex selection abortion" played role in decision. Canadian Press. http://www.huffingtonpost.ca/2012/09/27/rona-ambrose-sex-selection-abortion-vote_n_1919845.html?utm_hp_ref=canada-politics

Roberts, D. (1997). *Killing the black body: Race, reproduction, and the meaning of liberty*. New York, NY: Pantheon Books.

Scott, J. (1999). *Seeing like a state: How certain schemes to improve the human condition have failed*. New Haven, CT: Yale University Press.

SisterSong. (2012). SisterSong: Women of color reproductive justice collective. http://www.sistersong.net

Schwartz, D. (2011). Arizona enacts ban on abortions based on gender, race. *Reuters*. http://www.reuters.com/article/2011/03/30/us-arizona-abortion-idUSTRE72T0TH20110330

Smith, A. (2005). *Conquest*. Boston, MA: South End Press.

Thobani, S. (2007). *Exalted subjects: Studies in the making of race and nation in Canada*. Toronto, ON: University of Toronto Press.

Chapter 7

Gendering the HIV "Treatment as Prevention" Paradigm: Surveillance, Viral Loads, and Risky Bodies

ADRIAN GUTA, MARILOU GAGNON,
JENEVIEVE MANNELL, AND MARTIN FRENCH

The medical and public health response to HIV has long provided an important site for empirical and theoretical inquiry. Of particular interest to social science scholars has been the ways actors in the HIV movement have continued to mobilize to improve access to prevention information and lifesaving treatments. An activist slogan from the late 1980s declared the need to get "drugs into bodies." Since then much progress has been made in terms of prevention messaging and the development of more effective drug treatments. Most recently the HIV sector has undergone a paradigm shift to "treatment as prevention" (TasP), which promotes scaling up testing and treatment for people living with HIV with the goal of preventing new infections. Here, individual medical outcomes have become linked to public health outcomes. In this chapter we revisit the AIDS activist slogan "drugs into bodies" within the TasP paradigm and consider the implications for those most affected. While recognizing the importance of testing and the benefits of HIV pharmacological treatment, we consider the potential for TasP to lead to a convergence of medical and juridical power targeted at individuals and communities already subject to myriad forms of control. Specifically, we seek to identify the ways in which TasP is leading to new ways of seeing the body as virally suppressed/unsuppressed, and the implications of this categorization for the securitization of HIV and other infectious diseases globally.

Drawing on Michel Foucault's (2007) conception of governmentality and "arts of government," we identify and problematize the ways that TasP (along with related programs and technologies) is producing new relationships between individuals, communities, and the state through seemingly neutral surveillance strategies. We complement Foucault's broad interest in systems of governance with Armstrong's (1995) writing on "surveillance medicine" (p. 395) and more recent contributions to surveillance studies. Our analysis contributes to the literature by highlighting the role of gender in this project, drawing on a gendered analysis to connect seemingly disparate domains of knowledge and expertise with TasP. We are especially interested in gendered subject positions and how their categorization has become a target of medical and public health surveillance focused on medication adherence, sexual "risk taking," and viral load monitoring and suppression. Here we examine surveillant efforts to track and regulate HIV in bodies as a way of understanding, more generally, the gendered dynamics of the gaze as they take shape in, and in relation to, bodies and embodiment. We ask: Who is being targeted, and to what end?

Drugs into Bodies: A Brief History

In the early years following the identification of the HIV virus, treatments were slow to be developed and often had severe side effects and other adverse effects (Arno & Feiden, 1992). Despite few other treatment options, the available experimental drugs were being withheld because of administrative "red tape" (Epstein, 1996). Determined AIDS activists protested, chanting the slogan "Drugs into bodies!" to challenge the bureaucracy that was preventing promising treatments from reaching those most in need (Smith & Siplon, 2006). This relative inaction by the state, the medical establishment, and pharmaceutical companies has been explained by a misguided belief that the so-called general public was not at risk (Patton, 1990). The people contracting the virus – primarily gay men and people who inject drugs – were viewed as marginal to the rest of society. These groups were blamed for spreading HIV, encountered stigma in the health care system, and were excluded from the decisions made about their care. In response, AIDS activists organized to call for more investment from the state and to demand greater involvement in decision-making about HIV-related matters. They succeeded in expediting the testing of HIV drugs and their release to the market (Epstein, 1996).

A paradigm shift occurred in HIV treatment in the late 1990s, after new classes of protease inhibiting drugs were developed. When prescribed in combination with other classes of antiretroviral drugs (a combination known as highly active antiretroviral therapy, or HAART), these drugs slowed the replication of the virus and radically reduced

HIV-related morbidity and mortality (Sepkowitz, 2001). Antiretroviral therapy (ART) requires people living with HIV to take a combination of drugs daily to maintain their health. While ART presents challenges related to toxicity and cost, these drugs have significantly improved quality of life and health-related outcomes for people in treatment. As people with HIV began living longer, researchers, community-based organizations, and public health officials began asking new questions about them – about their sexual health, reproductive health, mental health, and substance use, as well as how they aged. This led to new "relationships" between AIDS service organizations, researchers, medicine and public health, and the state. This was a noticeable improvement over earlier practices of exclusion and erasure; however, critics have charged that this convergence of stakeholders has resulted in new forms of administrative control (Guta, Murray, & McClelland, 2011).

In recent years the HIV sector has undergone yet another paradigm shift with the emergence of "treatment as prevention" (TasP). TasP has reconceptualized treatment as a cost-effective tool for curbing the HIV epidemic (Montaner et al., 2006). It involves combining treatment *and* prevention in what has also been termed "positive prevention": people living with HIV are given ART to reduce their viral loads and to make them less infectious to others. This is said to benefit individuals by increasing their access to medication, reducing the number of future infections, and curbing the spread of HIV. TasP has been touted as a "game changer" and a "paradigm shift in the management of HIV globally"; the influential journal *Science* called it the scientific "breakthrough of the year" (Cohen, 2011). Prominent organizations like UNAIDS, the World Health Organization (WHO), the Centers for Disease Control and Prevention (CDC), and Canada's British Columbia Centre for Excellence in HIV/AIDS (BC-CfE) have been promoting the scale-up of TasP across North America and internationally.

Interrogating the Seeming Neutrality of TasP

There has been much positive messaging about TasP's ability to achieve an "AIDS-free generation," one in which deaths and new infections are drastically reduced (Granich, Williams, & Montaner, 2013). However, important concerns have been raised by Canadian HIV scholars. Nguyen and colleagues (2011), for example, have argued that TasP promotes "magic bullet" (p. 2) approaches that overlook sociocultural and contextual issues. This has been an unfortunate, and recurring, theme in the global AIDS response. Many of the clinical trials that support the efficacy of TasP have been based on data from heterosexual monogamous couples. Lancaster and colleagues (2013) have questioned the generalizability of TasP beyond people in such relationships to populations with diverse risk profiles – for example, gay and other men who have sex with men (often referred to in the literature as MSM), people who inject drugs, sex workers, and others. We complement this emerging body of literature by problematizing TasP by analysing the ways in which gender is constructed and mobilized. To date, there has been surprisingly little discussion about the gendered dimensions of TasP, except that gay and other MSM and women have been targeted, to varying degrees, as recipients. Of particular interest in our analysis is the pioneering "Seek and Treat for Optimal Prevention of HIV/AIDS" (or STOP) program, which entails mass HIV testing, expanded treatment coverage, and novel approaches to retaining individuals in care (Johnston, 2012, 2013). The STOP program represents an initial $48 million investment by the government of British Columbia, which supports a partnership between Vancouver Coastal Health, Northern Health, the Provincial Health Services Authority, Providence Health Care, and the BC-CfE to "expand HIV testing, treatment, and support services to clinically eligible individuals" in British Columbia (Johnston, 2013, p. 19). Surprisingly, the STOP program "did not have a specific gendered approach, meaning that the pilots were typically designed for all people at risk or the general public, regardless of gender" (p. 39). We question this gender "neutrality," in the STOP program and elsewhere, our interest being in what it makes visible and what it conceals, as well as what its implications are for those who are meant to benefit from TasP. To do so, we next turn to the writings of Michel Foucault.

Governmentality and Foucault's "Tool-Box"

Our analysis draws on Foucault's (1980) career-spanning interest in the historically and socially mediated relationship between power and knowledge. For Foucault (1979), power is exercised on the body through different forms of knowledge that apply strategies of surveillance, examination, and normalization to make it docile and easily governed. Foucault (in Foucault et al., 1991) was interested in the processes, both overt and subtle, through which individual conduct is orchestrated (or "conducted"). Such processes, for him, included formal political systems and structures but also the government "of children, of souls, of communities, of families, [and] of the sick" (Foucault, 2003b, p. 138). Foucault (2007) defined this governmentality as "the ensemble formed by institutions, procedures, analysis and reflections, calculations, and tactics that allow the exercise of this very specific, albeit very complex, power that has the population as its target, political economy as its major form of knowledge, and apparatuses of security as its essential technical instrument" (pp. 108–9).

Regarding economic interests, Foucault (2008) noted the emergence of what is now commonly termed neoliberalism, a political-economic rationality that merges economic analysis with a theory of human capital. Much has been written about how neoliberal ideology has shaped the response to AIDS and constructed people as risky and responsible (Adam, 2005). In Foucault's (1980) terms, population is "an object of surveillance, analysis, intervention, modification, etc." (p. 171). The population's productive potential is assured through seemingly "neutral" social institutions and processes (e.g., the law, public hygiene, statistics, etc.), which together form an "apparatus of security" (Foucault, 2007, p. 6) that continuously monitors threats to the population's well-being. While he was known to redefine his concepts as his thinking evolved, this particular definition of governmentality, with its emphasis on economy, population, and securitization, is especially useful for analysing TasP, which stresses cost–benefit analyses, risky populations, and the convergence of medical, public health, and government authorities to administer a programmatic shift.

Practices of surveillance were central to Foucault's analysis of medicine, mental health, sexuality, and justice. Each of these required a web of strategies and techniques for producing and collecting knowledge about the population. Modern surveillance studies scholarship has focused on how norms are encoded, instantiated, and enacted by and through surveillant processes (Lyon, 2003). In keeping with our interest in surveillance and gender norms, we recognize the important role that medicine plays in constructing, reifying, and perpetuating gendered health differences in terms of women and also sexual minority populations (Epstein, 2008). Building on Foucault, Armstrong (1983) traces how the medical gaze extended from examining individual bodies to mapping social networks and spaces. He notes that "surveillance medicine" is in part a response to the need to manage venereal disease and sexually transmitted infections and that it "requires the dissolution of the distinct clinical categories of healthy and ill as it attempts to bring everyone within its network of visibility" (Armstrong, 1995, p. 395).

Surveillance medicine involves the spatializing of risk to "focus more on the grid of interactions between people in the community" (p. 401). Within these spaces, "self and community begin to lose their separateness," and this enables the deployment of a "surveillance machinery" (p. 403). Yet even within this machinery, surveilled subjects engage in a process of self-stylization (Haggerty & Ericson, 2000). Updating Armstrong's approach, Bauer and Olsén (2009) have observed the growing role of modern medical diagnostic technologies and networks of digital databases in enabling a simultaneously individual- and population-focused gaze. Similarly, Walby and Smith (2012) have observed how surveillance medicine has extended into the construction of "risky" sex and sexuality in public health research and practice, and how it has partnered with juridical forms of surveillance and policing to maintain particular conceptions of order. Next we discuss the specifics of TasP, theorizing the relationship between diagnostics, pharmaceuticals, and surveillance.

Technologies for Medical and Public Health Surveillance within TasP

Haggerty (2006) suggests the potential utility of a governmentality approach for studying surveillance, emphasizing the attention that governmentality scholars have given to the specific rationalities, technologies, and forms of visibility implicated in the execution of governmental ambitions. The rationale of TasP, as described by its proponents, is to improve access to treatment and care for people living with HIV and to reduce future infections. This admirable goal is shared by most people working within the global AIDS movement, but it has included new uses of medical diagnostic technologies that have raised some concerns. Following Haggerty, we can understand the medical and diagnostic apparatus that is being built to support TasP as infused with "governmental technologies," an array of "assorted tools used to achieve those governmental ambitions" (2006, p. 40) associated with TasP. Foucault (1988) differentiated between the technologies of power (which serve to conduct and dominate) and technologies of the self (which individuals use to stylize themselves), characterizing the encounter between the two as governmentality in action (Foucault, 1994). In our case, these technologies are literally biomedical technologies, but they also represent more diffuse technologies of power and domination, and of the self. We now apply this to forms of visibility that have enabled increased HIV testing, early ART initiation, and viral load monitoring and mapping.

Estimates suggest that as many as 25 per cent of people living with HIV in Canada are unaware of their seropositive status (PHAC, 2013a). TasP requires increased testing to identify everyone who is infected and to link them to care. The approach used in the STOP program, called "seek and treat," has involved social marketing campaigns that promote testing across the province as well as through local "testing fairs" and incentivized testing (e.g., offering marginalized people a gift card and food in exchange for "consenting" to an HIV test) (Vonn, 2012). For all who participate, the HIV antibodies test requires confessing one's transgressions (e.g., unprotected sexual intercourse, and possibly drug use and sex work), but for some it is the beginning of a formal process that labels them an infected member of a risk group, enters them into a public health database for follow-up counselling and partner contact tracing, and links them to care. The CDC (2013) argues that "early identification of infection empowers individuals to take action that benefits both their own health and the public health" (n.p.). Conversely, Waldby (2004) has argued that the tests act "simultaneously as a diagnostic technology for clinical medicine, a surveillance technology for epidemiology, and a disciplinary technology for the medico/social management of the infected" (p. 114). It is surprising that the shift to large-scale testing has gone relatively unchallenged, considering that earlier attempts generated considerable opposition from community groups. Gagnon and Holmes (2008) have framed large-scale testing as a way to broadly govern groups deemed at risk, especially pregnant women. Within the logic of TasP, a positive diagnosis is followed by early ART initiation and by linking people with care to avoid losing them after testing. This seems to ignore whether individuals are ready to initiate treatment, and whether they can manage the side effects, as well as factors such as class and stigma, which make accessing and using treatment difficult (Mykhalovskiy, 2008). Yet individual factors like these are often overlooked in discourse that promotes the public health benefits of TasP. This of course raises ethical concerns about potential harms and autonomy (Krellenstein & Strub, 2012).

The HIV antibody test is now only the beginning in a series of ongoing tests to monitor the progress of the virus. Whereas the antibody test seeks to identify antibodies generated in response to HIV, thereby allowing the presence of HIV to be inferred, the HIV viral load test has become a standard diagnostic technology for estimating the number of virus particles within a sample of blood or other bodily fluid (e.g., semen, vaginal secretions, etc.) (Race, 2001). The viral load test provides important information about an individual's level of medical compliance, and possible infectiousness. The goal of ART has shifted from inhibiting viral replication to the more specific goal of achieving an "undetectable" level of the virus in the blood (usually defined as under 50 copies/ml and as little as 30 copies/ml) (Widdrington et al., 2011). Individuals who achieve an undetectable viral load are popularly understood to be non-infectious. However, critics have warned that undetectable levels of the virus in the blood do not necessarily reflect levels in the genital tract, which can spike for a range of reasons (e.g., chronic sexually transmitted infection flare-ups and new infections) (Kalichman, 2013). Despite these limitations, viral load is now being used in public health surveillance in the form of community viral load mapping, which Das and colleagues (2010) describe as "an aggregate biological measure of viral load for a particular geographic location … and for a particular group of people who share socio-demographic characteristics" (p. 2). Viral load is an indicator of individual adherence; it follows that community viral load is a marker of the success of TasP programming (Montaner et al., 2010). This previously clinical marker is being combined with geographic information system (GIS) technology to locate "viral concentration" at the aggregate level through a process of community viral load mapping to identify epidemiological "hot spots" (Gagnon & Guta, 2012a). The CDC (2013) would claim that this knowledge allows for more focused and cost-effective interventions. However, we see this as constituting, in Foucault's (2008) terms, an "apparatus" (p. 70) that seeks to govern people living with HIV through a web of biomedical surveillance technologies. Next we consider the gendered implications of this constellation of technologies.

Targets of HIV Surveillance: Gendering HIV in the Era of TasP

Foucault (1979) wrote about how bodies enter a machinery of power that works to make them docile and easily governed through various systems of discipline and surveillance. Central to this process is the development of "dividing practices" that differentiate between the good and the bad in relation to each other and that open a grid of classification, visibility, and discipline. Race (2001) has argued that viral load testing has increased responsibilization, individualization, and privatization of the experience of living with HIV. Under TasP it also works to promote "community" through shared proximity in spaces of viral concentration, as well as a sense of duty to the Other and new ways of thinking about the self. Haggerty and Ericson (2000) remind us that "Foucault also encourages us to acknowledge the role surveillance can play beyond mere repression; how it can contribute to the productive development of modern selves" (p. 607). In this respect, we can view surveillance as deeply implicated in the sexed subjectivities and in sexuality more generally. Foucault (1978) provided important insights into how modern subjects are produced through confessionary practices that make sexuality visible and knowable through scientific techniques and discourses. While he did not discuss gender per se, he was interested in how certain subject positions emerged in relation to the social construction of mothers and "dangerous" forms of sexuality (i.e., same-sex relations) (Foucault, 2003a). Despite sustained charges of androcentrism in Foucault's writings in some feminist scholarly circles, Butler (1990) has sustained a productive dialogue with his work to show how sex and gender are deployed as technologies of governance and also of self-stylization. In the following section we examine the gendered implications of TasP in relation to gay and other MSM and women living with HIV.

Canada's Gendered HIV Epidemic

Despite broad prevention efforts, HIV continues to be an important health issue in Canada. An estimated 71,300 Canadians are currently living with HIV (PHAC, 2014). According to the Public Health Agency of Canada, specific populations continue to be over-represented in Canada's epidemic: gay and other MSM, people who inject drugs, Aboriginal people, prisoners, marginalized youth and women, and people from countries where HIV is endemic. Gay, bisexual, two-spirit, and other MSM comprise the majority of HIV infections in Canada, accounting for 62.7 per cent of all recent HIV-positive test reports (PHAC, 2014). Women accounted for approximately one-fifth of estimated new infections (PHAC, 2014). These categories are not mutually exclusive; indeed, they overlap in ways that create intersecting forms of risk, stigma, oppression, and marginalization (Logie, James, Tharao, & Loutfy, 2011). For example, among women, nearly 21 per cent had been infected through intravenous drug use, and over 66 per cent from heterosexual contact: 28.3 per cent from contact with someone from where HIV is understood to be "endemic," 23.8 per cent from heterosexual contact with someone from a known risk group (e.g., MSM or injection drug use), and 14.1 per cent from heterosexual contact with no identified risk (PHAC, 2014). These national data do not tell the full story of why gay and other MSM and diverse groups of women are at risk of acquiring HIV, nor how they might be targeted (or not) in TasP related programing. We now explore some of these issues.

Women Living with HIV in the Era of TasP

Early in the epidemic, Patton (1994) noted that women were often the "last served" in HIV programing. As the epidemic became general-ized around the world, a growing number of women and girls became affected, and HIV is now said to have "a woman's face" (Annan, 2003). Women are considered biologically and socially more vulnerable to HIV infection (Roth & Hogan, 2013). That is, factors such as vaginal mucosal receptivity to the virus increase a woman's chance of infection over a man's during vaginal sex. Programs that espouse the doctrine of ABC (abstinence, be faithful, use a condom) ignore the reality that while many women are monogamous, their partners are not; that they may be eco-nomically dependent on their male partners; and that the sex they are having may not be consensual (Dworkin & Ehrhardt, 2007). The United Nations (2013) has recognized that gender inequalities and gender-based abuse and violence increase the risk of HIV transmission, and it promotes programs that address these structural drivers. Unfortunately, to our knowledge these concerns have not been discussed in relation to TasP. Rather, TasP, as it has been promoted in the Canadian context, assumes independent actors who avail themselves of testing and treat-ment (i.e., who are *free* to do so). This gap is surprising, considering that TasP is based on a series of clinical trials focused on preventing transmis-sion through ART in sero-discordant heterosexual couples (i.e., couples where one partner is HIV-positive and the other is not), and on the earlier success of trials preventing mother-to-child transmission (CDC, 2013).

The STOP program's "It's different now" campaign invites us to "change HIVstory" by getting tested for HIV (http://www.itsdiffer-entnowbc.org). The accompanying social marketing campaign features an image of a white woman wearing a low-cut dress and an oversized white mascot rabbit head. Across the image is written "We don't think you're special." This bizarre image is meant to convey that everyone should be tested without consideration for their "risk profile." It is in some ways an attempt to destigmatize testing by inviting everyone to be tested, and not just *those* people who are understood to be at risk. The website is sparse except for a few videos from clinicians describing the importance of the STOP program and the need for testing, as well as how living with HIV is different now. An exception is a video of Denise Becker, a woman living with HIV and an activist, who tells us "you have a duty to get tested ... To save other people, to save your children and your family if you're planning on having children, you have to get tested." Pregnant women are an important target for HIV testing, as diagnoses and early treatment can significantly reduce the chances of vertical transmission. Behind the rhetoric of "you're not special" is an obvious focus on women who are indeed special because they may be pregnant. The rabbit head symbolizes every woman's fertility, but any initial anonymity this affords is quickly lost. Pregnant women and mothers are heavily surveilled and regulated (Root & Browner, 2001). Their every decision is subject to medical and legal scrutiny. Of the two photos in the campaign that feature women, both are white, suggesting that they are the women most in need of testing. However, the epidemiological data in Canada show that Aboriginal women represent one of the fastest-growing risk groups (Varcoe & Dick, 2008). Overall, a woman's duty to her baby provides a strong inducement to engaging in ongoing medical surveillance, along with a justification for it.

While TasP promises that testing and early initiation of ART will result in improved health for people living with HIV, women often have worse clinical outcomes than men in the long term (Meditz et al., 2011). Women have lower access to HIV medications and face greater challenges with adherence and drug-related side effects (Andany et al., 2011; Tapp et al., 2011). A woman's "duty" to her family to get tested and start treatment has overshadowed other considerations. Rosengarten (2005) explains that a number of issues were previously weighed before clinicians recommended ART, including "how to negotiate individual and gender-identified physiological differences that may influence test results, drug absorption, and the manifestation of side effects" (p. 75). Such concerns have been omitted from the popular rhetoric of TasP despite women reporting that managing a drug regimen is difficult because of the side effects and social and cultural pressures of being care providers (including hiding medication use from family) (Sayles, Wong, & Cunningham, 2006). Even in Canada, with its supposed universal access to health care, women must negotiate various social interests, institutional authorities, relations of power, and strategies of social control to actually receive care (Berkhout, 2010). Such challenges to adherence inevitably result in women's decreased ability to maintain viral suppression (Howard et al., 2002). Even those with an undetectable blood plasma viral load may still be infectious (Cu-Uvin et al., 2010). The significance of this viral instability is discussed later.

Returning to pregnancy, the WHO (2012) recommends providing ART to "all HIV-infected pregnant women beginning in the antenatal clinic setting but also continuing this therapy for all of these women for life" (p. 1). A growing concern is that while women may test, they are more likely to disengage from the health care system at later stages (Kerber et al., 2007). Continuous engagement with the health care system, adherence, and viral monitoring are necessary for TasP to work (Gardner et al., 2011). Some recommend more integrated services to ensure that pregnant women can be followed beyond delivery for lifelong care (McNairy & El-Sadr, 2012). Of course, many issues need to be considered: in the United States, geographic location and poverty factor into whether pregnant women will even be prescribed ART (Phiri et al., 2014). As well, women's identities and "risk taking" practices are shaped by more than mothering, and women living with HIV experience a range of barriers to accessing care related to their gendered, raced, queer, and sex-working identities (Logie et al., 2011). Meyer, Springer, and Altice (2011) have situated HIV risk within a syndemic of substance use, violence, and victimization for many women. The literature suggests that women of colour are especially likely to be lost to care (Messer et al., 2013). In Canada, it indicates that Aboriginal women, who live with the ongoing effects of colonization, have especially low rates of adherence (McCall & Lauridsen-Hoegh, 2014). Finally, it observes that queer women (often seen as outside HIV or pregnancy) have been historically excluded from HIV prevention messaging and safe-sex interventions (Dworkin, 2005). We further note the absence of trans perspectives in the TasP messaging and literature, and we worry about how the current articulation of sex, gender, risk, and adherence may further marginalize diverse groups of trans and gender-non-conforming individuals. While the focus on pregnancy opens up long-term surveillance for (some) women, it simultaneously serves to exclude others. Thus, the white rabbit comes to symbolize the reproductive potential of the white heteronormative body politic – an innocence and purity that must be protected.

TasP and Constructing the Insatiable and Predatory Gay Man

While HIV may have a woman's face globally, gay and other MSM continue to be disproportionately affected in North America (Prejean et al., 2011; PHAC, 2012). Some scholars, perhaps inadvertently, evoke a moral panic, suggesting that, despite years of sexual health promotion messages, gay and other MSM will not consistently use condoms (Casalino et al., 2014). It should be noted that across all age, gender, and sex groups, condom use is far from ideal (Reece et al., 2010). However, there has been much focus on why gay and other MSM neglect or refuse to use condoms. Some have explained sex without condoms (or bare-backing) in terms of internalized norms about masculinity (Malebranche, Fields, Bryant, & Harper, 2009), a desire for intimacy, and the logic of contextual risk management (Bourne & Robson, 2009), and as reflective of neoliberal discourses about rational choice (Adam, 2005). But most of the literature fails to consider such explanations and instead produces staggering amounts of behavioural research on MSM (Crepaz et al., 2014). Whatever the venue, pride parade or bathhouse, researchers will be present collecting HIV surveillance data (MacKellar et al., 2007). They vigilantly search for any possible associations that could be used to explain increasing rates of infection within the MSM population and beyond. There has been an especially strong focus on MSM of colour, who, supposedly living on the "down low," constitute a threat to heterosexual women (Bond et al., 2009). More broadly, the epidemic has even been attributed among MSM to a combination of having a large number of male sex partners, nitrite inhalant use, and engaging in receptive anal sex (Buchbinder et al., 2005). Such research may reify conceptions of risk and vulnerability that do not reflect those sampled, let alone the larger population (for an in-depth case study and critique, see Mukherjea & Vidal-Ortiz, 2006). Foucault (1978) famously explained how through new scientific techniques and systems for classification, sexual practices became reified and linked to identity, ushering in the birth of the homosexual as a species. While claiming to be a "neutral category" (for a critique, see Young & Meyer, 2005), the MSM has also become a species, characterized by "compulsive sexual behaviour" (Coleman et al., 2010) and a refusal to engage in prescribed prevention strategies, making it a danger to itself and the public.

After thirty years of supposedly inclusive behavioural interventions, many in the HIV sector are now calling for the use of biomedical prevention technologies (Rotheram-Borus, Swendeman, & Chovnick, 2009). It would seem that ineffective and stigmatizing campaigns have run their course and that it is now time for more drastic measures. For these reasons, the scale-up of ART has been proposed as a way to curb the epidemic among MSM in the United States and Canada (Lima, Hogg, & Montaner, 2010; CDC, 2011). A number of scholars have questioned the logic of applying the results of trials from heterosexual couples in monogamous relationships to gay and other MSM, who may have multiple partners (Fallon & Forrest, 2012). Often overlooked in discussions is that treatment access has already been scaled up for MSM in many areas where HIV incidence continues to increase (Kalichman, 2013). These trends may be attributed to a range of intersecting social factors, including homophobia, racism, and stigma (Smit et al., 2011). TasP requires that MSM get tested and initiate ART to reduce future infections, but any transmission is likely to have already occurred unknowingly before the test. After testing positive, most people reduce their sexual risk-taking practices (Marks, Crepaz, Senterfitt, & Janssen, 2005). It would seem any benefits will come from individuals knowing their status, but it is unclear why they should initiate ART early to prevent infections. Will this even be of benefit to MSM of colour, who, like women of colour, are said to have lower ART adherence (Oster et al., 2011)? Or will it just serve to further construct them as a dangerous hypersexual, racialized, and non-adherent Other? Could this lend credence to Strub's (2012) argument that the TasP approach "contributes to the further demonization of people with HIV, and seeing us solely through our potential to transmit a virus, as viral vectors, as potential infectors" (p. 25)? There are of course men who test positive and who continue to have unprotected sex (often making assumptions about their partner's status, or using risk-reduction strategies), but are these encounters responsible for the high rates of infection in the community? Will TasP make a dent in these numbers? How will these so-called "reckless" men be "encouraged" to start and maintain treatment?

The seek and treat program represents a wide net being cast to reach gay and other MSM and pull them into the medical and public health surveillance web. Through testing, these men are labelled either at risk or already infected, and their data are collected for future epidemiological analysis that may further stigmatize their practices. The infected are entered into a public health database and linked with medical care providers to initiate ART. As discussed earlier, one's viral load will be monitored for treatment success or failure. For individuals who succeed, their undetectable status has become a marker of both viral and social status (in the clinic and in the community). Men are now advertising their status online when negotiating sexual encounters (Race, 2010; Mazanderani, 2012). Providing a community perspective, Zachary Barnett, founder and executive director of the Abzyme Research Foundation, explains that an undetectable status is telling of whether someone is "in relatively good health, in terms of their HIV, and is taking care of himself – and who is extending courtesy to his community by taking care of himself and thereby presenting less chance of transmission to HIV-negative partners" (interview with the San Francisco AIDS Foundation, 2013). As with a woman's "duty" to her family, gay men owe it to their "community" to be on treatment for the purposes of TasP. However, for the individual who fails to achieve viral suppression and undetectable status, this raises questions in the clinic about factors in their life that might prevent optimal adherence, such as substance use. This too can be monitored. Gay men's viral loads may be shared with public health (linked to their postal codes) and used to view patterns in aggregate forms through community viral-load mapping. While queer communities are often well known and highly visible in major cities, such communities become (in)visible in new ways in cities like San Francisco (Das et al., 2010). Represented without names as dark concentrations on viral load maps, they are obvious to anyone who knows these cities, and gay men may live in or near proximity to these "risky" spaces. Stripped of their culture and vibrancy, these communities become viral concentrations targeted for "high impact" interventions (CDC, 2011). Proponents argue that these data can be used to better target prevention and education efforts and to direct funds to care; Gagnon and Guta (2012b) counter that these same neighbourhoods are often already known to have health disparities. What will these maps change for these communities, except to mark them as Other?

The rhetoric of community and duty as an organizing technology harkens back to the beginnings of the epidemic, but with a shift in focus from getting "drugs into bodies" that desperately need them, to getting drugs into bodies that *may* need them, or *will* need them, for the benefits of those not infected. In addition to the issues discussed previously, there remain many unanswered questions, including concern over TasP leading to drug resistance that could undermine treatment success for everyone (Sood et al., 2013). Canadian data show that drug and multidrug resistance is increasing among treatment-naive individuals (PHAC, 2013b). Bayer (2010) has raised an important question: "What level of surveillance would be necessary to assure levels of treatment adherence compatible not only with reducing population level viral loads, but also with the prevention of the emergence of resistant viral strains?" (p. 301). In the next and final section, we reflect on this question by locating the TasP paradigm shift within a broader shift in global public health.

Gendering the Medico-Legal Borderland: Securitizing
HIV in Canada

Foucault (1979) famously claimed that in systems like the prison, successful convergence of power flowed not from an ability to reform the dangerous Other, but as a means to justify the spread of systems of control. Of particular interest for our analysis is the growing convergence of crime and health, in what Timmermans and Gabe (2002) have described as the medico-legal borderland. Patton (2011) has warned starkly that TasP requires "testing and mandatory treatment on a scale seen only in dictatorships" (p. 263). This has led others to question the intersections between TasP, new adherence technologies, and HIV criminalization efforts (Gagnon, Jacob, & Guta, 2013). TasP has justified a massive financial investment in key cities and in partnership with global policymakers to produce new surveillance tools that make people living with HIV visible to medicine and public health, but also to legal establishments. We are especially concerned by the growing criminalization of HIV non-disclosure cases across Canada (Adam, Elliott, Corriveau, & English, 2014) and the United States (Lazzarini et al., 2013). Early in the epidemic Waldby (2004) argued that

> just as the invisible virus is a silent danger to the immune system and the person who does not know they are infected, so too is the invisible HIV seropositive person a danger to the body politic. On the other hand the person who has been diagnosed as seropositive must take on their new identity *as virus* in a way which does not endanger the health of the body politic. (p. 139, emphasis in original)

What about people who are unwilling or unable to be adherent? Strub (2011) has posed this disturbing questions: "Might those who refuse treatment for the 'common good' ultimately be considered criminals? Will they be seen as socially irresponsible, labelled enemies of society, selfish or unconcerned about spreading HIV?" (n.p.). Viral load has made its way into Canadian courts, most recently with the Supreme Court of Canada decision *R. v. Mabior* in 2012. The Court ruled that non-disclosure of one's HIV status to a sexual partner may be legally acceptable when a condom is combined with an undetectable viral load (*R. v. Mabior*, 2012 SCC 47, [2012] 2 S.C.R. 584). Haggerty and Ericson (2000) foreshadowed the way "non-criminal justice institutions" would be increasingly called upon to "augment the surveillance capacities of the criminal justice surveillance system" (p. 617). This recent development has HIV activists, scholars, and legal experts wondering how it will be used in practice. Will this require people living with HIV to subject themselves to ongoing viral load monitoring to produce potential "evidence" about themselves? Not surprising, the spectre of criminalization is not discussed when people are being offered incentivized HIV tests (Vonn, 2012).

Criminalization for non-disclosure in Canada is a complex social and legal issue that exceeds the scope of this chapter. What interests us is the relationship between TasP, criminalization, and new forms of surveillance. We note that women (especially those living in relationships where they are at risk of violence) (Mackinnon & Crompton, 2012) and racialized people have been disproportionately singled out for prosecution (Mykhalovskiy & Betteridge, 2012; Adam, Elliott, Corriveau, & English, 2014). As discussed above, women (especially racialized women) experience greater challenges with adherence and with maintaining an undetectable viral load. Women who use drugs and engage in sex work face additional barriers to adherence and are unlikely to benefit from any single prevention strategy (El-Bassel, Wechsberg, & Shaw, 2012). What will *R. v. Mabior*, which entrenches the importance of viral load testing in the adjudication of non-disclosure cases, mean for these groups? The focus on condoms and viral load is interesting. It has been well established that women have less control over condom use in relationships (East, Jackson, O'Brien, & Peters, 2011), and condom use for sex working women can be even more complicated (Shannon et al., 2009). Should positive women subject themselves to ongoing viral load monitoring to ensure they can "prove" they were virally suppressed at the time of these encounters? While we applaud the recent success of sex workers in Canada who organized to strike down Canada's prostitution laws through the Supreme Court (*R. v. Bedford*, 2013), could such seeming legal advancements converge with TasP in unexpected ways? While purely speculative, could the future legal regulation of sex work lead to mandatory ART for sex workers? What will happen if transmission occurs despite the use of ART? Will the courts separate out those who are able to "prove" their adherence through an evidence trail from care providers? Could all of this be necessitating the production of databases to identify marginalized people through the health care system for use by legal authorities? If so, to what end?

We see TasP as part of a global shift in securitizing infectious disease through militaristic strategies (French, 2009). HIV has been constructed globally as a threat to health and financial security, and if traditional prevention strategies cannot contain the epidemic then new strategies may be in order. Elbe (2009) has argued that the securitization of HIV, besides representing a response to a devastating illness, "is also being animated by a wider assemblage of state and non-state actors who concurrently exercise sovereign, disciplinary, and governmental forms of power in this quest" (p. 13). The trends we have described in Canada and the United States are likely to manifest themselves differently around the world, including in contexts where women have fewer rights over their bodies and where same-sex relations are being criminalized. Elbe (2005) has further suggested that including gender and human rights issues in a discussion of securitizing AIDS could counter the normalizing and racist undertones inherent in the securitization discourse. Racism here is defined as a strategy to differentiate between those whom the state should make live through active investment and those whom it should let die through inattention and neglect (Foucault, 2003c). TasP subtly constructs gender (the dutiful mother and the promiscuous gay man) in ways that drive racism and normalization. Our analysis has highlighted the ways in which various groups have been targeted by TasP programming (to varying degrees and to varying ends), with some likely to benefit and others continuing to "fail." The once diverse range of approaches taken by the HIV sector to reach different populations has been transformed in the logic of seek and treat, with the end goal being particular outcomes – individual and collective viral suppression as defined by specific lab values. We are concerned that this biomedical paradigm shift will continue to ignore the social and structural drivers that have fuelled the epidemic. We are even more concerned that those who fail to succeed in the new logic of viral suppression will be marked for prosecution and further forms of exclusion. The ongoing refinements of viral load measurements, and more sophisticated forms of surveillance, do not seem to be bringing us any closer to understanding the various social and material needs of people affected by HIV. Instead these people continue to be cast as a dangerous Other in need of policing, for individual, public, and now global health.

Conclusion

In this chapter we have identified and examined the intersections of TasP and technologies for medical surveillance. Our goal was to consider the gendered dimensions and implications of this programmatic shift. We see TasP as falling into a macro milieu that is securitizing the treatment of infectious diseases and risky persons. Here treatment becomes the linchpin that makes new forms of surveillance, including the criminalization of "risky" sex, seem necessary and even beneficial. If TasP fails to reduce infections and produces greater drug resistance, this will have truly disturbing implications for the HIV sector, and new and more invasive forms of surveillance will probably be required. The securitization response includes a range of strategies not discussed, including quarantine. While this may seem polemical, we note that growing rates of criminalization are being combined with attempts to reduce the rights of people living with HIV globally. We encourage others to continue the discussion we have started here, with the goal of furthering a gender analysis and connecting it to micro- and macro-level policy changes. Resisting the urge to offer a solely negative reading of the operations of power, we remain hopeful that there will be new possibilities for ethical engagement and opportunities for resistance within the TasP paradigm (Rosengarten, 2004; Race, 2012). Globally, activists and scholars are writing about these issues and organizing to challenge criminalization and improve treatment access (for those who need it but still do not have it). We hope they will also challenge policymakers to ensure that TasP is scaled up in a way that reflects diverse interests and that ensures that privacy, confidentiality, self-determination, and vitality are protected, while continuing to battle the forms of stigma that make this necessary.

REFERENCES

Adam, B. D. (2005). Constructing the neoliberal sexual actor: Responsibility and care of the self in the discourse of barebackers. *Culture, Health, & Sexuality, 7*(4), 333–346. http://dx.doi.org/10.1080/13691050500100773
Adam, B. D., Elliott, R., Corriveau, P., & English, K. (2014). Impacts of criminalization on the everyday lives of people living with HIV in Canada. *Sexuality Research & Social Policy, 11*(1), 1–11. http://dx.doi.org/10.1007/s13178-013-0131-8
Andany, N., Raboud, J. M., Walmsley, S., Diong, C., Rourke, S. B., Rueda, S., Rachlis, A., Wobeser, W., MacArthur, R., Binder, L., Rosenes, R. & Loutfy, M. R. (2011). Ethnicity and gender differences in lipodystrophy of HIV-positive individuals taking antiretroviral therapy in Ontario, Canada. *HIV Clinical Trials, 12*(2), 89–103. http://dx.doi.org/10.1310/hct1202-89

Annan, K. (2003). In Africa, AIDS has a woman's face. *Women and Environments International, 60/61*, 49–50.

Armstrong, D. (1983). *Political anatomy of the body: Medical knowledge in Britain in the twentieth century.* Cambridge, UK: Cambridge University Press.

Armstrong, D. (1995). The rise of surveillance medicine. *Sociology of Health & Illness, 17*(3), 393–404. http://dx.doi.org/10.1111/1467-9566.ep10933329

Arno, P. S., & Feiden, K. (1992). *Against the odds: The story of AIDS drug development, politics, and profits.* New York, NY: Harper Collins.

Bauer, S., & Olsén, J. E. (2009). Observing the others, watching over oneself: Themes of medical surveillance in post-panoptic society. *Surveillance & Society, 6*(2), 116–127.

Bayer, R. (2010). Mass testing and mass treatment for epidemic HIV: The ethics of medical research is no guide. *Public Health Ethics, 3*(3), 301–302. http://dx.doi.org/10.1093/phe/phq022

Berkhout, S. G. (2010). *Social identity, agency, and the politics of adherence to antiretroviral therapy in HIV/AIDS care.* Vancouver, BC: UBC Press.

Bond, L., Wheeler, D. P., Millett, G. A., LaPollo, A. B., Carson, L. F., & Liau, A. (2009). Black men who have sex with men and the association of down-low identity with HIV risk behavior. *American Journal of Public Health, 99*(S1), S92–S95. http://dx.doi.org/10.2105/AJPH.2007.127217

Bourne, A. H., & Robson, M. A. (2009). Perceiving risk and (re)constructing safety: The lived experience of having "safe" sex. *Health Risk & Society, 11*(3), 283–295. http://dx.doi.org/10.1080/13698570902906421

Buchbinder, S. P., Vittinghoff, E., Heagerty, P. J., Celum, C. L., Seage, G. R. I., III, Judson, F. N., …, & Koblin, B. A. (2005). Sexual risk, nitrite inhalant use, and lack of circumcision associated with HIV seroconversion in men who have sex with men in the United States. *Journal of Acquired Immune Deficiency Syndromes, 39*(1), 82–89. http://dx.doi.org/10.1097/01.qai.0000134740.41585.f4

Butler, J. (1990). *Gender trouble: Feminism and the subversion of identity.* New York, NY: Routledge.

Canada (Attorney General) v. Bedford, 2013 SCC 72.

Casalino, E., Choquet, C., Leleu, A., Hellmann, R., Wargon, M., Juillien, G., …, & Bouvet, E. (2014). Trends in condom use and risk behaviours after sexual exposure to HIV: A seven-year observational study. *PLoS One, 9*(8), e104350. http://dx.doi.org/10.1371/journal.pone.0104350

CDC (Centers for Disease Control and Prevention). (2011). *High-impact HIV prevention: CDC's approach to reducing HIV infections in the United States.* Atlanta, GA: Centers for Disease Control and Prevention, National Center for HIV/AIDS, Viral Hepatitis, STD, and TB Prevention, Division of HIV/ AIDS Prevention.

CDC (Centers for Disease Control and Prevention). (2013). Prevention benefits of HIV treatment. http://www.cdc.gov/hiv/prevention/ research/tap/

Cohen, J. (2011). Breakthrough of the year. http://www.sciencemag.org/ content/334/6063/1628.full

Coleman, E., Horvath, K. J., Miner, M., Ross, M. W., Oakes, M., & Rosser, B. S. (2010). Compulsive sexual behavior and risk for unsafe sex among internet-using men who have sex with men. *Archives of Sexual Behavior, 39*(5), 1045–1053. http://dx.doi.org/10.1007/s10508-009-9507-5

Crepaz, N., Tungol-Ashmon, M. V., Higa, D. H., Vosburgh, W., Mullins, M. M., Barham, T., ... & Lyles, C.M. (2014). A systematic review of interventions for reducing HIV risk behaviors among people living with HIV in the United States, 1988–2012. *AIDS, 28*(5), 633–656. http://dx.doi.org/10.1097/ QAD.0000000000000108

Cu-Uvin, S., DeLong, A. K., Venkatesh, K. K., Hogan, J. W., Ingersoll, J., Kurpewski, J., ... (2010). Genital tract HIV-1 RNA shedding among women with below detectable plasma viral load. *AIDS, 24*(16), 2489–2497. http:// dx.doi.org/10.1097/QAD.0b013e32833e5043

Das, M., Chu, P. L., Santos, G.-M., Scheer, S., Vittinghoff, E., McFarland, W., & Colfax, G. N. (2010). Decreases in community viral load are accompanied by reductions in new HIV infections in San Francisco. *PLoS One, 5*(6), e11068. http://dx.doi.org/10.1371/journal.pone.0011068

Dworkin, S. L. (2005). Who is epidemiologically fathomable in the HIV/ AIDS epidemic? Gender, sexuality, and intersectionality in public health. *Culture, Health, & Sexuality, 7*(6), 615–623. http://dx.doi. org/10.1080/13691050500100385

Dworkin, S. L., & Ehrhardt, A. A. (2007). Going beyond "ABC" to include "GEM": Critical reflections on progress in the HIV/AIDS epidemic. *American Journal of Public Health, 97*(1), 13–18. http://dx.doi.org/10.2105/ AJPH.2005.074591

East, L., Jackson, D., O'Brien, L., & Peters, K. (2011). Condom negotiation: Experiences of sexually active young women. *Journal of Advanced Nursing, 67*(1), 77–85. http://dx.doi.org/10.1111/j.1365-2648.2010.05451.x

El-Bassel, N., Wechsberg, W. M., & Shaw, S. A. (2012). Dual HIV risk and vulnerabilities among women who use or inject drugs: No single prevention strategy is the answer. *Current Opinion in HIV and AIDS, 7*(4), 326–331. http://dx.doi.org/10.1097/COH.0b013e3283536ab2

Elbe, S. (2005). AIDS, security, biopolitics. *International Relations, 19*(4), 403–419. http://dx.doi.org/10.1177/0047117805058532

Elbe, S. (2009). *Virus alert: Security, governmentality, and the AIDS pandemic.* New York, NY: Columbia University Press.

Epstein, S. (1996). *Impure science: AIDS, activism, and the politics of knowledge.* Berkeley, CA: University of California Press.

Epstein, S. (2008). *Inclusion: The politics of difference in medical research.* Chicago, IL: University of Chicago Press.

Fallon, S. J., & Forrest, D. W. (2012). Unexamined challenges to applying the treatment as prevention model among men who have sex with men in the United States: A community public health perspective. *AIDS and Behavior, 16*(7), 1739–1742. http://dx.doi.org/10.1007/s10461-012-0258-2

Foucault, M. (1978). *The history of sexuality: An Introduction.* New York, NY: Vintage Books.

Foucault, M. (1979). *Discipline and punish: The birth of the prison* (1st Vintage ed.). New York, NY: Vintage Books.

Foucault, M. (1980). *Power/knowledge: Selected interviews and other writings.* Toronto, ON: Random House of Canada.

Foucault, M. (1988). *Technologies of the self: A seminar with Michel Foucault.* Amherst, MA: University of Massachusetts Press.

Foucault, M. (1994). Technologies of the self. In P. Rabinow (Ed.), *Ethics: Subjectivity and truth* (pp. 223–251). New York, NY: The New Press.

Foucault, M. (2003a). *Abnormal: Lectures at the Collège de France, 1974–1975* (1st Picador USA ed.). New York, NY: Picador.

Foucault, M. (2003b). The subject and power. In P. Rabinow & N. Rose (Eds.), *The essential Foucault: Selections from essential works of Foucault, 1954–1984* (pp. 126–145). New York, NY: New Press.

Foucault, M. (2003c). *"Society must be defended": Lectures at the College De France 1975–1976* (D. Macey, Trans.). New York, NY: Picador.

Foucault, M. (2007). *Security, territory, population: Lectures at the Collège de France, 1977–1978.* Basingstoke, UK: Palgrave Macmillan. http://dx.doi.org/10.1057/9780230245075

Foucault, M. (2008). *The birth of biopolitics: Lectures at the Collège de France, 1978–79.* New York, NY: Palgrave Macmillan. http://dx.doi.org/10.1057/9780230594180

Foucault, M., Burchell, G., Gordon, C., & Miller, P. (1991). *The Foucault effect: Studies in governmentality.* Chicago, IL: University of Chicago Press.

French, M. A. (2009). Woven of war-time fabrics: The globalization of public health surveillance. *Surveillance & Society, 6*(2), 101–115.

Gagnon, M., & Guta, A. (2012a). Mapping HIV community viral load: Space, power and the government of bodies. *Critical Public Health, 22*(4), 471–483. http://dx.doi.org/10.1080/09581596.2012.720674

Gagnon, M., & Guta, A. (2012b). Mapping community viral load and social boundaries: Geographies of stigma and exclusion. *AIDS, 26*(12), 1577–1578. Authors' reply: 1578–1579. http://dx.doi.org/10.1097/QAD.0b013e328354f58a

Gagnon, M., & Holmes, D. (2008). Governing masses routine HIV testing as a counteroffensive in the war against HIV-AIDS. *Policy, Politics, & Nursing Practice, 9*(4), 264–273. http://dx.doi.org/10.1177/1527154408323931

Gagnon, M., Jacob, J. D., & Guta, A. (2013). Treatment adherence redefined: A critical analysis of technotherapeutics. *Nursing Inquiry, 20*(1), 60–70. http://dx.doi.org/10.1111/j.1440-1800.2012.00595.x

Gardner, E. M., McLees, M. P., Steiner, J. F., del Rio, C., & Burman, W. J. (2011). The spectrum of engagement in HIV care and its relevance to test-and-treat strategies for prevention of HIV infection. *Clinical Infectious Diseases, 52*(6), 793–800. http://dx.doi.org/10.1093/cid/ciq243

Granich, R. M., Williams, B., & Montaner, J. (2013). Fifteen million people on antiretroviral treatment by 2015: Treatment as prevention. *Current Opinion in HIV and AIDS, 8*(1), 41–49. http://dx.doi.org/10.1097/COH.0b013e32835b80dd

Guta, A., Murray, S. J., & McClelland, A. (2011). Global AIDS governance, biofascism, and the difficult freedom of expression. *Aporia: The Nursing Journal, 3*(4), 15–29.

Haggerty, K. D. (2006). Tear down the walls: On demolishing the panopticon. In D. Lyon (Ed.), *Theorizing Surveillance: The Panopticon and Beyond* (pp. 23–45). New York, NY: Routledge.

Haggerty, K. D., & Ericson, R. V. (2000). The surveillant assemblage. *British Journal of Sociology, 51*(4), 605–622. http://dx.doi.org/10.1080/00071310020015280

Howard, A. A., Arnsten, J. H., Lo, Y., Vlahov, D., Rich, J. D., Schuman, P., ... & Schoenbaum, E. E. (2002). A prospective study of adherence and viral load in a large multi-center cohort of HIV-infected women. *AIDS, 16*(16), 2175–2182. http://dx.doi.org/10.1097/00002030-200211080-00010

Johnston, C. (2012). The STOP HIV/AIDS project: Treatment as prevention in the real world. *Canadian AIDS Treatment Information Exchange.* http://www.catie.ca/pif/spring-2012/stop-hivaids-project-treatment-prevention-real-world

Johnston, C. (2013). *Shifting the paradigm: The history of the Vancouver STOP HIV/AIDS Project.* Toronto: CATIE.

Kalichman, S. C. (2013). *HIV treatments as prevention (TasP): Primer for behavior-based Implementation.* New York: Springer. http://dx.doi.org/10.1007/978-1-4614-5119-8

Kerber, K. J., de Graft-Johnson, J. E., Bhutta, Z. A., Okong, P., Starrs, A., & Lawn, J. E. (2007). Continuum of care for maternal, newborn, and child health: From slogan to service delivery. *Lancet, 370*(9595), 1358–1369. http://dx.doi.org/10.1016/S0140-6736(07)61578-5

Krellenstein, J., & Strub, S. (2012). The ethical implications of "treatment as prevention" in the United States. *HIV/AIDS Policy & Law Review, 16*, 11–14.

Lancaster, K. E., Nguyen, N., Lesko, C. R., & Powers, K. A. (2013). Generalizability and scalability of HIV "treatment as prevention." *AIDS, 27*(15), 2493–2494. http://dx.doi.org/10.1097/01.aids.0000432468.61626.d4

Lazzarini, Z., Galletly, C. L., Mykhalovskiy, E., Harsono, D., O'Keefe, E., Singer, M., & Levine, R. J. (2013). Criminalization of HIV transmission and exposure: Research and policy agenda. *American Journal of Public Health, 103*(8), 1350–1353. http://dx.doi.org/10.2105/AJPH.2013.301267

Lima, V. D., Hogg, R. S., & Montaner, J. S. (2010). Expanding HAART treatment to all currently eligible individuals under the 2008 IAS–USA Guidelines in British Columbia, Canada. *PLoS One, 5*(6), e10991. http://dx.doi.org/10.1371/journal.pone.0010991

Logie, C. H., James, L., Tharao, W., & Loutfy, M. R. (2011). HIV, gender, race, sexual orientation, and sex work: A qualitative study of intersectional stigma experienced by HIV-positive women in Ontario, Canada. *PLoS Medicine, 8*(11), e1001124. http://dx.doi.org/10.1371/journal.pmed.1001124

Lyon, D. (2003). *Surveillance as social sorting: Privacy, risk, and digital discrimination.* New York, NY: Routledge.

MacKellar, D. A., Gallagher, K. M., Finlayson, T., Sanchez, T., Lansky, A., & Sullivan, P. S. (2007). Surveillance of HIV risk and prevention behaviors of men who have sex with men – a national application of venue-based, time-space sampling. *Public Health Reports, 122* (Suppl. 1), 39.

Mackinnon, E., & Crompton, C. (2012). Gender of lying: Feminist perspectives on the non-disclosure of HIV status. *University of British Columbia Law Review, 45*(2), 407.

Malebranche, D. J., Fields, E. L., Bryant, L. O., & Harper, S. R. (2009). Masculine socialization and sexual risk behaviors among Black men who have sex with men: A qualitative exploration. *Men and Masculinities, 12*(1), 90–112. http://dx.doi.org/10.1177/1097184X07309504

Marks, G., Crepaz, N., Senterfitt, J. W., & Janssen, R. S. (2005). Meta-analysis of high-risk sexual behavior in persons aware and unaware they are infected with HIV in the United States: Implications for HIV prevention programs. *Journal of Acquired Immune Deficiency Syndromes*, 39(4), 446–453. http://dx.doi.org/10.1097/01.qai.0000151079.33935.79

Mazanderani, F. (2012). An ethics of intimacy: Online dating, viral-sociality and living with HIV. *Biosocieties*, 7(4), 393–409. http://dx.doi.org/10.1057/biosoc.2012.24

McCall, J., & Lauridsen-Hoegh, P. (2014). Trauma and cultural safety: Providing quality care to HIV-infected women of Aboriginal descent. *Journal of the Association of Nurses in AIDS Care*, 25(1) (Suppl.), S70–S78. http://dx.doi.org/10.1016/j.jana.2013.05.005

McNairy, M. L., & El-Sadr, W. M. (2012). The HIV care continuum: No partial credit given. *AIDS*, 26(14), 1735–1738. http://dx.doi.org/10.1097/QAD.0b013e328355d67b

Meditz, A. L., MaWhinney, S., Allshouse, A., Feser, W., Markowitz, M., Little, S., ... & Connick, E. (2011). Sex, race, and geographic region influence clinical outcomes following primary HIV-1 infection. *Journal of Infectious Diseases*, 203(4), 442–451. http://dx.doi.org/10.1093/infdis/jiq085

Messer, L. C., Quinlivan, E. B., Parnell, H., Roytburd, K., Adimora, A. A., Bowditch, N., & DeSousa, N. (2013). Barriers and facilitators to testing, treatment entry, and engagement in care by HIV-positive women of color. *AIDS Patient Care and STDs*, 27(7), 398–407. http://dx.doi.org/10.1089/apc.2012.0435

Meyer, J. P., Springer, S. A., & Altice, F. L. (2011). Substance abuse, violence, and HIV in women: A literature review of the syndemic. *Journal of Women's Health*, 20(7), 991–1006. http://dx.doi.org/10.1089/jwh.2010.2328

Montaner, J. S. G., Hogg, R., Wood, E., Kerr, T., Tyndall, M., Levy, A. R., & Harrigan, P. R. (2006). The case for expanding access to highly active antiretroviral therapy to curb the growth of the HIV epidemic. [Review]. *Lancet*, 368(9534), 531–536. http://dx.doi.org/10.1016/S0140-6736(06)69162-9

Montaner, J. S. G., Lima, V. D., Barrios, R., Yip, B., Wood, E., Kerr, T., ... & Kendall, P. (2010). Association of highly active antiretroviral therapy coverage, population viral load, and yearly new HIV diagnoses in British Columbia, Canada: A population-based study. *Lancet*, 376(9740), 532–539. http://dx.doi.org/10.1016/S0140-6736(10)60936-1

Mukherjea, A., & Vidal-Ortiz, S. (2006). Studying HIV risk in vulnerable communities: Methodological and reporting shortcomings in the Young Men's Study in New York City. *Qualitative Report*, 11(2), 393–416.

Mykhalovskiy, E. (2008). Beyond decision making: Class, community organizations, and the healthwork of People Living with HIV/AIDS. Contributions from institutional ethnographic research. *Medical Anthropology, 27*(2), 136–163. http://dx.doi.org/10.1080/01459740802017363

Mykhalovskiy, E., & Betteridge, G. (2012). Who? What? Where? When? And with what consequences? An analysis of criminal cases of HIV non-disclosure in Canada. *Canadian Journal of Law and Society, 27*(01), 31–53. http://dx.doi.org/10.3138/cjls.27.1.031

Nguyen, V.-K., Bajos, N., Dubois-Arber, F., O'Malley, J., & Pirkle, C. M. (2011). Remedicalizing an epidemic: From HIV treatment as prevention to HIV treatment is prevention. *AIDS, 25*(3), 291–293. http://dx.doi.org/10.1097/QAD.0b013e3283402c3e

Oster, A. M., Wiegand, R. E., Sionean, C., Miles, I. J., Thomas, P. E., Melendez-Morales, L., ... & Millett, G. A. (2011). Understanding disparities in HIV infection between black and white MSM in the United States. *AIDS, 25*(8), 1103–1112. http://dx.doi.org/10.1097/QAD.0b013e3283471efa

Patton, C. (1990). *Inventing AIDS.* New York, NY: Routledge.

Patton, C. (1994). *Last served: Gendering the HIV pandemic.* London, UK: Tayor and Francis.

Patton, C. (2011). Rights language and HIV treatment: Universal care or population control? *Rhetoric Society Quarterly, 41*(3), 250–266. http://dx.doi.org/10.1080/02773945.2011.575328

PHAC (Public Health Agency of Canada). (2012). Fact sheet: Gay, bisexual, two-spirit, and other men who have sex with men. 30 August 2012.

PHAC (Public Health Agency of Canada). (2013a). Human immunodeficiency virus HIV screening and testing guide. http://www.phac-aspc.gc.ca/aids-sida/guide/hivstg-vihgdd-eng.php

PHAC (Public Health Agency of Canada). (2013b). Summary of main findings from the Canadian HIV strain and drug resistance surveillance program.

PHAC (Public Health Agency of Canada). (2014). HIV and AIDS in Canada: Surveillance report to December 31st, 2013. http://www.phac-aspc.gc.ca/aids-sida/publication/survreport/2013/dec/assets/pdf/hiv-aids-surveillence-eng.pdf. Retrieved August 12, 2015

Phiri, K., Fischer, M. A., Mogun, H., Williams, P. L., Palmsten, K., Seage, G. R., & Hernandez-Diaz, S. (2014). Trends in antiretroviral drug use during pregnancy among HIV-infected women on Medicaid: 2000–2007. AIDS *Patient Care and STDs, 28*(2), 56–65. http://doi.org/10.1089/apc.2013.0165; http://www.ncbi.nlm.nih.gov/pmc/articles/PMC3926172/

Prejean, J., Song, R., Hernandez, A., Ziebell, R., Green, T., Walker, F., ... & Hall, H. I. (2011). Estimated HIV incidence in the United States,

2006–2009. *PLoS One*, 6(8), e17502. http://dx.doi.org/10.1371/journal. pone.0017502

Race, K. (2001). The undetectable crisis: Changing technologies of risk. *Sexualities*, 4(2), 167–189. http://dx.doi.org/10.1177/136346001004002004

Race, K. (2010). Click here for HIV status: Shifting templates of sexual negotiation. *Emotion, Space, and Society*, 3(1), 7–14. http://dx.doi. org/10.1016/j.emospa.2010.01.003

Race, K. (2012). Framing responsibility. *Journal of Bioethical Inquiry*, 9(3), 327–338. http://dx.doi.org/10.1007/s11673-012-9375-x

Reece, M., Herbenick, D., Schick, V., Sanders, S. A., Dodge, B., & Fortenberry, J. D. (2010). Condom use rates in a national probability sample of males and females ages 14 to 94 in the United States. *Journal of Sexual Medicine*, 7(s5), 266–276. http://dx.doi.org/10.1111/j.1743-6109.2010.02017.x

Root, R., & Browner, C. (2001). Practices of the pregnant self: Compliance with and resistance to prenatal norms. *Culture, Medicine, and Psychiatry*, 25(2), 195–223. http://dx.doi.org/10.1023/A:1010665726205

Rosengarten, M. (2004). The challenge of HIV for feminist theory. *Feminist Theory*, 5(2), 205–222. http://dx.doi.org/10.1177/1464700104045409

Rosengarten, M. (2005). The measure of HIV as a matter of bioethics. In M. Shildrick & R. Mykitiuk (Eds.), *Ethics of the body postconventional challenges* (pp. 71–90). Cambridge, MA: MIT Press.

Roth, N. L., & Hogan, K. (2013). *Gendered epidemic: Representations of women in the age of AIDS*. New York, NY: Routledge.

Rotheram-Borus, M. J., Swendeman, D., & Chovnick, G. (2009). The past, present, and future of HIV prevention: Integrating behavioral, biomedical, and structural intervention strategies for the next generation of HIV prevention. *Annual Review of Clinical Psychology*, 5(1), 143–167. http:// dx.doi.org/10.1146/annurev.clinpsy.032408.153530

San Francisco AIDS Foundation. (2013). How do you talk about it? Two guys take on "undetectable." http://betablog.org http://betablog.org/two-guys-take-on-undetectable

Sayles, J. N., Wong, M. D., & Cunningham, W. E. (2006). The inability to take medications openly at home: Does it help explain gender disparities in HAART use? *Journal of Women's Health*, 15(2), 173–181.

Sepkowitz, K. A. (2001). AIDS – the First 20 Years. *New England Journal of Medicine*, 344(23), 1764–1772. http://dx.doi.org/10.1056/NEJM200106073442306

Shannon, K., Strathdee, S. A., Shoveller, J., Rusch, M., Kerr, T., & Tyndall, M. W. (2009). Structural and environmental barriers to condom use negotiation with clients among female sex workers: Implications for HIV-prevention strategies and policy. *American Journal of Public Health*, 99(4), 659–665. http://dx.doi.org/10.2105/AJPH.2007.129858

Smit, P. J., Brady, M., Carter, M., Fernandes, R., Lamore, L., Meulbroek, M., … (2011). HIV-related stigma within communities of gay men: A literature review. *AIDS Care*, 24(4), 405–412.

Smith, R. A., & Siplon, P. D. (2006). *Drugs into bodies: Global AIDS treatment activism*. Portsmouth, NH: Greenwood Publishing.

Sood, N., Wagner, Z., Jaycocks, A., Drabo, E., & Vardavas, R. (2013). Reply to Gonzalez-Serna et al. *Clinical Infectious Diseases*, 57(3), 479–480. http://dx.doi.org/10.1093/cid/cit261

Strub, S. (2011). Treatment Refusal = Criminal? http://blogs.poz.com/sean/archives/2011/06/treatment_refusal_cr.html

Strub, S. (2012). *Treatment as Prevention: Is It Time for Action?* Paper presented at the International AIDS Conference, Washington.

Tapp, C., Milloy, M., Kerr, T., Zhang, R., Guillemi, S., Hogg, R. S., … & Wood, E. (2011). Female gender predicts lower access and adherence to antiretroviral therapy in a setting of free healthcare. *BMC Infectious Diseases*, 11(1), 86. http://dx.doi.org/10.1186/1471-2334-11-86

Timmermans, S., & Gabe, J. (2002). Introduction: Connecting criminology and sociology of health and illness. *Sociology of Health & Illness*, 24(5), 501–516. http://dx.doi.org/10.1111/1467-9566.00306

United Nations Programme on HIV/AIDS. (2013). *Global report: UNAIDS report on the global AIDS epidemic: 2013*. New York, NY: UNAIDS.

Varcoe, C., & Dick, S. (2008). The intersecting risks of violence and HIV for rural Aboriginal women in a neo-colonial Canadian context. *International Journal of Indigenous Health*, 4(1), 42–52.

Vonn, M. (2012). British Columbia's "seek and treat" strategy: A cautionary tale on privacy rights and informed consent for HIV testing. *HIV/AIDS Policy & Law Review*, 16(May), 15–18.

Walby, K., & Smith, A. (2012). Sex and sexuality under surveillance: Lenses and binary frames. In P. Johnson & D. Dalton (Eds.), *Policing Sex* (pp. 54–66). New York, NY: Routledge.

Waldby, C. (2004). *AIDS and the body politic: Biomedicine and sexual difference*. New York, NY: Routledge.

WHO (World Health Organization). (2012). *World Health Organization*. Geneva: WHO.

Widdrington, J., Payne, B., Medhi, M., Valappil, M., & Schmid, M. L. (2011). The significance of very low-level viraemia detected by sensitive viral load

assays in HIV infected patients on HAART. *Journal of Infection, 62*(1), 87–92.
http://dx.doi.org/10.1016/j.jinf.2010.11.001

Young, R. M., & Meyer, I. H. (2005). The trouble with "MSM" and "WSW":
Erasure of the sexual-minority person in public health discourse. *American
Journal of Public Health, 95*(7), 1144–1149. http://dx.doi.org/10.2105/
AJPH.2004.046714

Under the Ban-Optic Gaze: Chelsea Manning and the State's Surveillance of Transgender Bodies

MIA FISCHER

With few exceptions, gender and sexuality have largely been invisible in surveillance studies. However, non-normative queer bodies – whose identities, sexual desires, and practices fall outside heterosexual and gender-binary norms – have not been invisible to contemporary systems of surveillance (Conrad, 2009). Lyon (2007) defines surveillance as the "the focused, systematic and routine attention to personal details for purpose of influence, management, protection or direction" (p. 14). The lack of attention paid to the gendered practices of surveillance on the part of feminist and queer theorists is surprising, particularly given the long-standing pathologizing of non-normative sexual practices in the West, which Foucault (1978) aptly described in *The History of Sexuality*. Stanley (2011) elaborates that "inheriting a long history of being made suspect, trans/queer people, via the medicalization of trans identities and homosexuality, have been and continue to be institutionalized, forcibly medicated, sterilized, operated on, shocked, and made into objects of study and experimentation" (pp. 7–8). Recently, WikiLeaker and whistle-blower Chelsea (formerly Bradley) Manning's struggles with gender identity and the US military's initial refusal to provide hormone therapy treatment for her desired transition have become highly publicized in the media. Manning's story draws attention to the policing and monitoring that many transgender and gender nonconforming bodies endure at the hands of the state.[1]

Chelsea Manning was found guilty of espionage after the biggest leak of government secrets in US history. Manning, a former US Army intelligence analyst, was convicted for providing the whistle-blowing website WikiLeaks with a July 2007 video titled "Collateral Murder," which depicts a US Apache helicopter attacking and killing

Iraqi civilians, among them two Iraqi war correspondents working for Reuters. She also obtained more than 700,000 sensitive US intelligence documents relating to the wars in Iraq and Afghanistan as well as diplomatic cables from US embassies around the world, which WikiLeaks subsequently released throughout the summer and fall of 2010. These materials painted a highly embarrassing portrait of US might and diplomacy. They exposed not only backstage international diplomacy but also ruthless and ineffective military actions: from night raids gone wrong, to checkpoint shootings of Iraqi civilians, to blunt comments about foreign leaders, to missile strikes accidentally targeting children, to torture conducted by Iraqi forces with the silent approval of US troops (Leigh & Harding, 2011).

Manning was caught through contact with ex-hacker Adrian Lamo, to whom she wrote in an online chat room: "If you had unprecedented access to classified networks 14 hours a day, 7 days a week for 8-plus months, what would you do?" (cited in Reitman, 2013, n.p.). Lamo notified the authorities and began logging his chats with Manning. Lamo would later say that he was afraid Manning's leaking could put US lives at risk (Thompson, 2011). Manning stood trial in June 2013 for twenty-two violations of military law, eight of which fell under Article 104 of the Espionage Act, a 1917 statute prohibiting the sharing of information with unauthorized sources (i.e., "aiding the enemy"). That statute has become key to what some view as the Obama administration's broader "war on whistle blowers." On 30 July 2013, Manning was found not guilty of aiding the enemy but was convicted of twenty other charges – including six under the Espionage Act – and sentenced to thirty-five years in prison. Shortly after her sentencing at the end of August 2013, Manning announced:

> I want everyone to know the real me. I am Chelsea Manning. I am a female. Given the way that I feel, and have felt since childhood, I want to begin hormone therapy as soon as possible. I hope that you will support me in this transition. I also request that, starting today, you refer to me by my new name and use the feminine pronoun. (cited in Gabbatt, 2013)

Whether one views Manning's actions as heroic or treacherous, her treatment in detention, the news media's sensationalized coverage that portrayed her as a sexualized Other,[2] and the US Army's refusal to provide hormone therapy for her gender dysphoria have ignited numerous public debates.[3] Her desire to transition and her treatment in detention have called attention to the state surveillance that transgender communities often face and have made more prominent some of the issues that disproportionally affect (and in most cases harm) trans communities. For example, sex segregation in US correctional facilities based on birth-assigned sex and the (in)accessibility of health care are two such issues. Hence, the story of whistle-blower and WikiLeaker Chelsea Manning and the state surveillance enacted on her non-normative queer body provide grounds for critical engagements with the surveillance of trans bodies within the safety state – defined here as an amalgam of governmental, corporate, and civil entities invested in fostering "national security" and "citizen safety" at the expense of civil liberties.

Using Didier Bigo's (2006) concept of the ban-opticon *dispositif* – which describes how transnational bureaucracies, driven by a "globalized (in)security" post-9/11, work at a distance to monitor and control population movement through surveillance – I engage with Manning's story, particularly her trial, as an entry point for exploring the gendered surveillance practices of the state. Such practices police, monitor, and discipline non-normative queer bodies, thus making them sites of both exclusionary and inclusionary policies. The ban-optic *dispositif* provides a useful theoretical framework for exploring the often overlooked surveillance of gender nonconforming bodies at the hands of the state and for interrogating the political implications of such practices in the formation of policies that strive to inhibit the "free movement" of populations, rendering certain communities abject. Drawing on queer, feminist, and critical race theories, I argue that Manning's trial and incarceration illustrate ban-optic surveillance practices to be inherently racializing and racialized, and that they reproduce and perpetuate systemic inequalities through the intersectionalities of (hetero)sexism and transphobia.

I begin by presenting Bigo's (2006) conceptualization of the ban-opticon. I explore the questionable pre-trial detention practices employed against Manning as indicative of the ban-opticon's "exceptionalism of power" (p. 35) and its exclusionary practices that result in social death. By interrogating advanced imaging technologies as a means of identification, as well as the ambiguous gender reclassification requirements within the US more broadly, I dissect the state's efforts to normalize trans bodies through the production of "normative imperatives" (p. 35). I then move to the military's refusal to grant hormone therapy to Manning, arguing that it is a deliberate act of state violence against gender nonconforming people that seeks to extinguish any potential gender fluidity, which is cast as a threat. Finally, I relate Manning's struggles within the prison industrial complex (PIC) – a site where private, political, and financial interests collude in promoting prison expansionism – to those of other trans bodies caught in similar situations by exploring how the intersectionalities of race, gender, and class harm trans people, particularly those of colour, through a conflation of HIV/AIDS and queerness. The surveillance practices that scrutinize transgender bodies should alert scholars to the fact that surveillance is an inherently gendered and racialized practice that brings certain bodies into view by rendering them "socially significant"; that is, they are cast as threats in need of containment, through either normalization or systematic exclusion. In this way, these non-normative bodies become important sites of ban-optic operations of liberal governance. The policing of transgender and queer bodies is an example of the regulatory practices that the state uses to enforce racialized and sexualized notions of what constitutes proper citizenship.

The Safety State and the Ban-Optic Gaze

Since 9/11, surveillance systems and practices have proliferated. Their novelty lies in the simultaneous emergence of the "surveillance society" and the "safety state," that operate in tandem to create a culture of control in which surveillance becomes the vital means and central component of a politics of personal information (see Lyon, 2007, pp. 195, 197). For Bigo (2006), the discourses around "globalized (in) security" generated by the development of threats of mass destruction and terrorism form a "governmentality of unease" (p. 6) as a complete, connected apparatus, or what Foucault (1980) called *dispositif* – "a thoroughly heterogeneous ensemble consisting of discourses, institutions, architectural forms, regulatory decisions, laws, administrative measures, scientific statements, philosophical and moral propositions" (pp. 194–5). The outcome is not a global panopticon but a ban-opticon – a concept combining Jean Luc Nancy's idea of the "ban" as developed by Agamben, with Foucault's panopticon.

Philosopher Jeremy Bentham developed the idea of the panopticon as a model prison in the late eighteenth century, arguing that criminals could only internalize productive labour habits if they were under constant surveillance by their guards without being able to tell where the warden's gaze was focused (see Davis, 2003, p. 46). Foucault expanded this notion of the panopticon by using it as a metaphor for modern "disciplinary societies" and their eagerness to observe and normalize certain behaviours. Foucault sees power not as a fixed commodity residing in one place, but as disciplines – sets of instruments, techniques, or technologies – that render power automatized and dis-individualized. Hence, the panopticon ("the all-seeing eye") proliferates across all institutions – including schools, the military, and hospitals – surveilling and controlling the population. These panoptic features, moreover, function in such a way that the population soon internalizes these power structures and begins to police itself, thereby becoming the principle of its own subjection (Foucault, 1995).

Bigo argues that with the rise of global (in)securities since 9/11, the *dispositif* is no longer the panopticon as described by Bentham, but rather a ban-opticon: "It depends no longer on immobilizing bodies under the analytic gaze of the watcher but on profiles that signify differences, on exceptionalism with respect to norms and on the rapidity with which one 'evacuates'" (Bigo, 2006, p. 45). In other words, the ban-opticon uses information technologies to grasp the constant process of flux and to channel flows instead of dissecting bodies. Bigo proposes the ban-opticon to indicate how profiling technologies are used to determine who is placed under specific surveillance by institutions such as the Department of Homeland Security (DHS). Further drawing on Agamben (1998), the ban-optic *dispositif* has the strategic function of controlling and surveilling selected groups of people exempted from the majority; by marking them as "unwelcome" and "banned," it creates categories of exclusion – for example, by equating Middle Easterners and Muslims with terrorists. I use Chelsea Manning to explore the three characteristics of the ban-opticon: first, the exceptionalism of power within liberal state societies (states of emergency and their tendency to become permanent); second, the exclusion of certain groups in the name of their future potential behaviour (profiling); and third, the normalizing of non-excluded groups through the production of normative imperatives (especially a belief in the free movement of people). In turn, I examine how these three characteristics are specifically related to the gendered surveillance practices of the safety state through their targeting of transgender communities.

While Bigo emphasizes the deployment of the ban-opticon at a level that supersedes the nation state, I focus here on how the US safety state deploys the ban-opticon through its gendered surveillance of non-normative queer bodies via the DHS as well as detention practices employed within the PIC. Using the figure of Manning and drawing connections to other aspects of state surveillance that trans bodies often face, such as the increased "securitization of identity" (Rose, 1999, p. 240ff.), I aim to expand Bigo's conceptualizations of "unwelcome" populations beyond racial configurations to specifically question the state's gendered surveillance practices and the monitoring and policing of gender nonconforming bodies.

Blowing the Whistle on the Extralegality of Indefinite Detention

Although former JAG officer Tom Kenniff asserted on Fox News that "he's not a terrorist, he's a US citizen, he's in uniform. He's entitled to all the rights anyone would enjoy in this trial" (Fox News, 2013), Manning's treatment in detention and the slow trial proceedings have belied Kenniff's assertion, thus inspiring many debates and gesturing towards Bigo's (2006) ban-opticon as an "exceptionalism inside liberalism" (p. 36). Bigo explains that the exceptionalism of power refers to the relation between the juridical production of "special" laws and their creation of a "permanent state of exception and emergency" (p. 36). The state's constant monitoring and policing of Manning during her pre-trial incarceration is an example of these exceptionalisms within liberalism; she was placed in a "domestic" waiting zone that mirrors the disconcerting status of the detainees held at the Guantánamo Bay prison camp. These practices rendered Manning as an Othered alien enemy who can, and should, be denied many of her rights as a US citizen.

After Manning was incarcerated in June 2010 in Camp Arifjan, Kuwait, the then twenty-two-year-old was repeatedly deprived of human contact and put on a "reverse sleep cycle" as part of "administrative segregation" (the military does not use the term "solitary confinement"). In an article for *Rolling Stone*, Janet Reitman (2013) chronicled Manning's deteriorating health: she was found one night "screaming, shaking, babbling, and banging and bashing his [sic] head into the adjacent wall" (n.p.), according to official documents. Reitman cited Manning as saying: "I just remember thinking, I'm going to die. I'm stuck here in this animal cage, and I'm going to die'" (n.p.). In July, 2010 Manning was transferred to the Marine Corps brig in Quantico, Virginia, and placed on "suicide prevention." In the following excerpts from March 2011, Manning vividly described the conditions of her incarceration:

I was also stripped of all clothing with the exception of my underwear. Additionally, my prescription eyeglasses were taken away from me. Due to not having my glasses, I was forced to sit in essential blindness during the day ... Under my current restrictions, in addition to being stripped at night, I am essentially held in solitary confinement. For 23 [hours a] day, I sit alone in my cell. The guards checked on me every five minutes during the day by asking me if I am okay. I am required to respond in some affirmative manner. At night, if the guards can not [*sic*] see me clearly, because I have a blanket over my head or I am curled up towards the wall, they will wake me in order to ensure that I am okay. I receive each of my meals in my cell. I am not allowed to have a pillow or sheets ... If I attempt to do push-ups, sit-ups, or any other form of exercise I am forced to stop by the guards. (cited in Rothe & Steinmetz, 2013, pp. 285–6)

These techniques of constant observation and frequent interruption are widely used on detainees in Iraq and Afghanistan, as well as at Guantánamo. In 2011 a UN special report concluded that the US government was guilty of subjecting Manning to "cruel, inhuman and degrading treatment" (Pilkington, 2012). A similar conclusion was drawn by some 250 prominent lawyers and legal scholars, among them Yochai Benkler, who in April 2011 signed a letter published in *The New York Review of Books* denouncing Manning's treatment as "illegal and immoral" (Benkler, 2013). These experts also determined that the treatment she received violated the Eighth Amendment's prohibition of cruel and unusual punishment and the Fifth Amendment's ban against pre-trial punishment (see Goldsmith, 2011). After months of public pressure, Manning was transferred to the Joint Regional Correctional Facility at Fort Leavenworth, Kansas. There, she was described by Commander Lt. Col. Dawn Hilton as a "typical detainee" who exhibited no significant mental health or behavioural problems (cited in Reitman, 2013, n.p.). After spending more than 1,000 days in pre-trial detention, Manning's actual court-martial proceedings finally began on 3 June 2013. The prolonged incarceration of Manning vividly demonstrates how the surveillance practices within liberalism post-9/11 have been increasingly extralegal without being strictly illegal, creating a permanent state of exception.

Butler (2003) argues that "when law becomes a tactic of governmentality, it ceases to function as a legitimating ground: *governmentality makes concrete the understanding of power as irreducible to law*" (p. 94, emphasis in original). Therefore, indefinite or "prolonged" detention practices and enhanced interrogation techniques constitute an illegitimate exercise of power – one that has become part of a broader tactic to neutralize the rule of law in the name of security. These techniques do not necessarily signify an exceptional circumstance; rather, in the state of emergency they have been established as the naturalized norm. Agamben (1998) emphasizes that "the exception does not subtract itself from the rule; rather, the rule, suspending itself, gives rise to the exception and maintaining itself in relation to the exception, first constitutes itself as a rule" (p. 18). These illiberal practices at the heart of liberalism, then, constitute one of the contemporary features of the ban-opticon.

Manning's treatment in pre-trial detention, in conjunction with the media's framing of her as a traitor to national security, exemplifies the second defining trait of the ban-opticon: its ability to construct categories of excluded people – "abnormals" – connected to the management of life (Bigo, 2006, p. 38–9). As the safety state authorizes these invasive surveillance and illegal detention practices against Manning, she has been placed in a permanent waiting zone where she lacks legal protections and has functionally been sentenced to social death. Manning becomes the *homo sacer* – the non-subject excluded and banned – not by being placed outside of law, but by being *abandoned* by law, exposed and threatened on the threshold where life and law, inside and outside, become indistinguishable (Agamben, 1998, p. 28). Revealing some of the exclusionary and exceptional mechanisms that the ban-opticon has enacted on Manning allows a closer look at the gendered surveillance practices and mechanisms that the safety state deploys in its efforts to manage the movement of queer and gender nonconforming bodies.

Surveilled Mobility: Advanced Imaging Technologies and the Securitization of Identity

Bigo (2006) describes the ban-opticon's construction of categories of excluded people – "abnormals" – connected to the management of life as a refashioning of policing and surveillance that "is ... capable of enlarging its scope by the use of intensive technologies of biometrics and shared databases" (p. 39). Since 9/11, we have witnessed the rise of new identification technologies that reinscribe existing social norms and inequalities and that aim for the "securitization of identity" (Rose, 1999, p. 240). Previous scholarship has addressed the perpetuation of racial profiling through biometric surveillance (see, e.g., Gates, 2011) but typically leaves unaddressed the implications for the policing of sexuality and gender. Policy changes that have been enacted as part of the "War on Terror" to administer identity verification systems do more than target immigrants and "terrorist Others"; they also function as exclusionary mechanisms that impact and present challenges to trans bodies, particularly through the use of advanced imaging technologies and gender (re)classification policies.

Advanced body imaging technologies, such as the 3D scanners used by the Transportation Security Administration (TSA) at airports, point most clearly to the intersectionalities between racial profiling, the "War on Terror," and (trans)gender surveillance enabled by these technologies. Magnet and Rodgers (2012) explicate how advanced imaging technologies – the "virtual strip search" – disproportionately affect marginalized groups, including trans people, travellers with disabilities, and racialized, ethnic, and religious communities. Notwithstanding the TSA's (2011) assertion that a program called "Automated Target Recognition" is used on all advanced imaging scanners to eliminate the image of an actual traveller and replace it with a generic outline of a person to improve passenger experience and privacy, these technologies single out bodily anomalies that contradict social and security expectations – for example, genitalia, breasts, or prosthetics that are assumed to conflict with a traveller's gender presentation. Thus, they render trans and gender nonconforming bodies particularly vulnerable. Full body scanners are characteristic of the ban-opticon in that they are built to police and "catch" non-normative subjects. Once these "deviant" bodies are detected, they may be singled out and further scrutinized by the TSA to establish their "true" identity, as the example below illustrates. The transgender person may be "outed" by these security measures, and that person's privacy may be invaded even further with a physical pat-down.

The following excerpts from a blog post by Cary Gabriel Costello (2012), a trans man, whose documentation labelled him male and who had not undergone any reconstructive or chest surgery, underscore some of the implications of full body imaging technology. When Costello had to step through a full body scanner for the first time in March 2012, the machine revealed "multiple anomalies" around his chest area:

> I was taken aside for a patdown. I asked that this be done in privacy, and was taken to a room by two TSA (cis)male agents[4] ... The agent doing the patdown seemed concerned that I was concealing something under my shirt ... The TSA agent doing the patdown finally asked me what my

garment was. I said that it was a chest binder, which I wore because I was a trans gender [*sic*] man. The agent said, "A what?" I had to explain what that meant. The agents looked both dubious and uncomfortable. I was extremely concerned that I was going to be asked to remove the binder, but, after some silent staring and thinking, the TSA agent told me he would screen the garment for explosives with swabs while I was wearing it ... After my binder was indeed found not to be a terrorist weapon, I was allowed to leave. The process was not only humiliating, but time consuming, and I had to rush for my plane.

Body imaging technologies, such as those used by the TSA, are deployed by the safety state as "disciplining technologies" (Magnet & Rodgers, 2012, p. 111) that essentialize particular gendered bodies and monitor those that deviate from normative understandings of biological sex and gender presentation. What the state considers normative is, of course, always related to social hierarchies that typically privilege white, cisgender, middle-class heterosexual and abled persons. Gender functions as a regulatory ideal that works performatively to constitute the illusion of binarized sexed bodies, "more specifically to materialize the body's sex, to materialize sexual difference in the service of the consolidation of the heterosexual imperative" (Butler, 1993, p. xii). In addition, these technologies of surveillance are based on a flawed belief in a technological determinism that presumes that verifiable identities can be tracked through gender markers "visible" on identification documents or images. It falsely assumes essential links between sex, gender, identity, and identification: "The idea being promoted by the growing surveillance apparatus is that we can really track people if we just identify their genitals or scan their retinas or have their fingerprints, but every single piece of identity verification technology is very flawed" (Spade, 2009, p. 367). The gendered surveillance practices of the safety state, as experienced by Costello, work to restrict the mobility and free movement of trans and gender nonconforming bodies.

Gender (re)classification policies at the state, federal, and local levels that outline when and how the gender marker on identity documents can be changed, shows that no uniform agreement exists as to what actually constitutes maleness or femaleness. The legal measures for documenting trans people's gender status often clash with one another, even as they all work towards tighter regulation and surveillance of legal gender (Beauchamp, 2009). Some agencies require sexual reassignment surgery before they will change gender classification;

others do not. In 2010 the US Department of State changed its identification requirements for "gender reassignment applicants" for US passports, eliminating the requirement for genital surgery (US Department of State, 2013). In June 2013 the US Social Security Administration followed suit, eliminating the surgical requirement for changing one's sex category on social security records (Snow, 2013). In Minnesota, changing one's gender on a driver's licence is comparatively easy; it is sufficient to provide a letter from a physician that medically certifies "appropriate" clinical treatment for gender transition (Outfront Minnesota, 2013). Other states require amended birth certificates before they will change the gender marker on a driver's licence. Some states will amend these only with documentation of surgery, while others, such as Idaho, Ohio, and Tennessee, outright reject any change of gender classification on birth certificates (Lambda Legal, 2015). These conflicting legal regulations are indicative of ban-optic surveillance practices and exclusionary mechanisms of the safety state. Preventing trans people from obtaining consistent gender markers across all of their identity documents exposes them to more harm and limits their mobility.

The state's emphasis on surgical procedures reflects the ban-opticon's third characteristic – the induction and production of normalizing behaviour. Indeed, the state's surveillance and monitoring of trans bodies by requiring medicalization and surgical treatment aims to eliminate all potential gender fluidity and ambiguity, since those ambiguities are perceived as deviant, dangerous, and threatening. Such requirements firmly reassert the gender binary. The ban-optic gaze of state agencies foists normalizing imperatives on individuals to rid themselves of any residues of non-normative gender in order to avoid state surveillance practices and to blend in and pass – to go "stealth" as Toby Beauchamp (2009) argues. Since going stealth means wilfully concealing and/or consciously deceiving, the state literally creates the behaviour it then regulates, monitors, and often criminalizes. At the same time, the state's systematic policing and exclusion of those who do not have the ability or the desire to go stealth reflects the equation of gender fluidity with a threat. Bodies that defy these normalizing imperatives are labelled "abnormal" and "unwelcome" (Bigo, 2006). This is precisely what lies at the heart of the ban-opticon: certain populations are normalized and allowed free movement, while non-normative bodies are Othered – that is, excluded and rendered abject, aberrant, and threatening.

Hormone Therapy Treatment and the Everyday Violence of the Safety State

The medicalization of transgender bodies by state surveillance is evident in Manning's diagnosis of gender dysphoria and the US military's initial refusal to grant her hormone treatment. The day after her sentencing on 20 August 2013, Manning released a statement announcing that she wanted to live as a woman and expressed her desire to receive estrogen treatments, which would promote breast development and other female characteristics. Her lawyer, David Coombs, emphasized in an interview with Associated Press that Manning had known for a long time that she would make such a statement but had waited "for the media surrounding the trial to dissipate" (Smith, 2013, n.p.) so as not to convey the sense that her announcement was insincere or simply a means to get attention. Manning hoped that Fort Leavenworth would allow such treatment, since she had been diagnosed with gender dysphoria by two Army behavioural health specialists even before her trial (Associated Press, 2013). Manning (2013) indicated that she would pursue a "Request for Treatment Plan of Gender Dysphoria" (p. 1) consistent with the currently accepted standards as outlined by the World Professional Association for Transgender Health (WPATH). Those standards include real-life experience (a period of time in which trans individuals live "full-time" in their preferred gender role) and hormone replacement therapy. If necessary, she would file a writ before a military or civilian court (Manning, 2013). The Army and other branches of the military currently do not provide hormone treatment, and soldiers diagnosed with gender dysphoria are administratively discharged, which Manning cannot be until she completes her prison sentence and/or exhausts the appeals process.[5]

While Manning did not indicate an intent to undergo gender confirmation surgery and is housed in the all-male prison facility at Fort Leavenworth, critics in the media and online were quick to object to the use of taxpayer dollars to fund her treatment. In a *Today Show* interview, hostess Savannah Guthrie (2013) repeatedly asked Manning's lawyer: "Is it the bottom line, you don't think she wants sex reassignment surgery or she doesn't think she'll be able to get it?" A headline in *Military Times* (2013) read "Bradley Manning Wants YOUR TAX DOLLARS to Pay for Hormone Therapy," and a *Rightwing News* blog headline announced "Bradley Manning (Traitor, Male) Wants Taxpayers To Pay For Female Hormone Therapy" (Wurzelbacher, 2013). These comments reflect the hysteria and sensationalism so often encountered in the media regarding the idea of taxpayer money supporting trans people's needs and health coverage. Manning's story illustrates the many difficulties and troubling realties that transgender prisoners face throughout the penal system. The US military penal and legal systems are so premised on the notion of two gender categories – male and female – that they cannot easily grasp when a person moves from one to another or conforms to neither. The ban-optic gaze, further fuelled by the media's preoccupation with pathologizing and transphobic discourses, views gender fluidity as a major threat that must be contained.

In 2011 the US Federal Bureau of Prisons changed its policy on hormone therapy treatment so that inmates in the bureau's custody with a possible diagnosis of gender dysphoria now receive an individualized assessment and evaluation before a proposed treatment plan is developed that promotes the "physical and mental stability" of the patient (GLAD, 2011, n.p.). But the sad reality is that even for those who can overcome the administrative hurdles necessary to receive gender-related care, such care is often inconsistent, featuring incorrect dosages of hormones and arbitrary implementation of treatment (SRLP, 2007). For example, supporters of CeCe McDonald, a young transgender woman of colour who was charged with murder for killing her attacker during a transphobic and racist assault in Minneapolis, had to organize a call-in campaign so that she could maintain her appropriate dosage of hormones. The all-male facility in which McDonald was housed did not provide hormones to her for several weeks and then proceeded to only administer six milligrams of hormones instead of the twenty she had been prescribed. Through widespread social media activism, supporters rallied behind McDonald and successfully bombarded the prison's directors with phone calls requesting the appropriate dosage (CeCe McDonald Support Committee, 2013). Similarly, Vicki, a transgender woman imprisoned in a maximum security men's facility in upstate New York, explained:

> Hormones are sporadic. It's a major chore to get refills. They took me off Premarin [a commonly prescribed hormone] for four months. You have no idea the effect of that. I filed a grievance, wrote letters, finally won them back after four months. Here I have to apply monthly, and they lie about not having them. They're trying to lower my dosage. They treat hormones like they're narcotics or something. (cited in SRLP, 2007, p. 27)

The military's refusal to allow Manning to transition exemplifies the exclusionary and normative regimes of sexuality and gender imposed more broadly by the ban-opticon and its practices of surveillance, policing, screening, and profiling within the PIC.

The Prison Industrial Complex and the Surveillance of Trans Bodies

Describing the PIC as "a set of symbiotic relationships among correctional communities, transnational corporations, media conglomerates, guards' unions, and legislative and court agendas," Angela Davis (2003, p. 107) argues that in "the era of the prison industrial complex" the prison has become "a black hole into which the detritus of contemporary capitalism is deposited" (p. 16). Wacquant (2001) and Alexander (2012) have aptly demonstrated how prisons function as the new Jim Crow, a "substitute apparatus" (Wacquant, 2001, p. 97) for the containment of lower-class African Americans in order to perpetuate their socio-economic marginality. Similarly, reports published by transgender organizations such as the Sylvia Rivera Law Project (SRLP) confirm that transgender and gender nonconforming people, particularly those of colour, are disproportionately criminalized, imprisoned, assaulted, denied medical care, and placed in gender-inappropriate facilities (see SRLP, 2007; Hanssens et al., 2014). A 2011 survey by the National Center for Transgender Equality (NCTE) and the National Gay and Lesbian Task Force (NGLTF) of nearly 6,500 trans and gender nonconforming people revealed that over 54 per cent of respondents had contact with the police, that 16 per cent had been sent to jail, and that 47 per cent of those trans people spending time in jail were African American (NGLTF, 2011). The PIC functions not only as a space of containment, but as a primary site for ban-optic surveillance practices that are particularly harmful to trans bodies of colour.

Spade (2012) and Davis (2003) point out that the intersection of criminality and sexuality continues to be racialized in the PIC, perpetuating a long strain of criminalization processes harking back to the days of slavery. The intersections of race and sexuality were essential to the violence of slavery, and those intersections continue to function as political rationales for state surveillance and disciplining practices. Racialization practices and the construction of gender categories are mutually reinforcing processes. Because US correctional facilities are sex-segregated and house prisoners according to their birth-assigned sex and/or genitalia, trans women who live and identify as women, but who were classified as male at birth, are generally placed in men's facilities. Spade (2012) argues that "sex segregation is a key component of racialized social control, and these institutions focus enormous energy on classifying, policing, harming, and disappearing people who occupy and exceed the borderlands of gender legibility and sexual normalcy" (p. 190). In those facilities transgender women, low-income queers, trans youth, and gender nonconforming people of colour are frequent targets of discrimination and violence, which can include anything from "sexual-identity confusion counseling" to "rehabilitation" into heteronormative and gender-binary moulds, as well as rape, physical and verbal abuse, forced prostitution, xenophobia, homophobia, transphobia, and finally, frisks and strip searches (see, e.g., Spade, 2009, 2012; Ware, 2011; Hanssens et al., 2014).

Of particular concern is the state's criminalization of HIV to police sex, gender, and sexuality. The following story demonstrates that the ban-optic gaze of the PIC particularly targets and manages racialized and sexualized non-normative queer bodies living with HIV or AIDS. Victoria Arellano, a twenty-three-year-old, HIV-positive, undocumented, transgender woman, was arrested in April 2007 for a traffic charge and brought to a detention centre in San Pedro, California. Arellano was in good health at the time of her arrest and exhibited no symptoms of the disease. Once detained, however, her health deteriorated rapidly, because she was not given access to her daily medications, such as Bactrim, which helps prevent pulmonary infections. She repeatedly pleaded with staff at the detention centre to see a doctor, but her requests were routinely ignored. Officials finally relented and sent her to a hospital, where she died only two days later of an AIDS-related infection (Hernandez, 2008). The death of Victoria Arellano, after she had spent eight weeks in a federally operated facility, points to the intersections of the violence and surveillance practices enacted by the PIC against historically marginalized subjects. Her death further illustrates how such practices perpetuate the stigmatization of HIV/AIDS and queerness, as well as how the two are conflated, mirroring a time when HIV was referred to as gay-related immune deficiency (GRID).

In Alabama and South Carolina, the only two US states mandating that HIV-positive prisoners be segregated from the rest of the inmate population, such stigmatization is exacerbated. Potts (2011) aptly notes that "HIV-segregated prisons become the meeting place for sexuality, disease, and deviancy to come together and make the law's violent management of bodies seem like a favor to the nation" (p. 106). After mandatory HIV testing upon arrival, prisoners who test positive are ordered into immediate solitary confinement, where they may have to stay for months until a bed in one of the HIV units becomes available. Prisoners in both states are forbidden access to many prison jobs and educational programs, which can be important for reintegration into society. Because these separate HIV units are located in high security prisons, HIV-positive prisoners often serve their sentences in higher security prisons than their crimes officially warrant, resulting in increased costs to taxpayers (ACLU & Human Rights Watch, 2010). These state surveillance practices clearly aim to police sex, gender, and sexuality through the criminalization and further stigmatization of HIV.

Similarly, Robinson (2011) has demonstrated that the K6G unit of the Los Angeles County Jail, established to protect prisoners who may be targets of violence because of their gender nonconformity and/or sexual orientation, operates as a site for the enforcement of racialized, gendered, and classed constructions of homosexuality. The screening test for determining whether an inmate is eligible for placement in the "protective" K6G unit is based on narrow assumptions about white, affluent, middle-class, gay urban culture and identity, and is applied as a "one-size-fits-all-scheme" for the prison's mostly black, brown, and poor inmates. K6G inmates are publicly stigmatized by being required to wear light-blue uniforms, in contrast to the dark blue uniforms worn by inmates in the general prison population. The staff rely mainly on physical attributes to identify transgender inmates when they are arrested – although not all transgender people necessarily display feminine markers such as breast development – and tend to conflate gender variance with sexual orientation. Thus, the test fails to account for the varied racial and gendered dimensions of queer and/or trans identity. It automatically construes gay and transgender people as equal to "victim," while heterosexuals are "predators." The K6G screening policy constructs gay and transgender identity in a stereotypical fashion and excludes some of the most vulnerable inmates – for example, heterosexual and bisexual men, men who have sex with men but do not identify as gay, and gay-identified men who do not embody white, affluent gay culture (Robinson, 2011). The "protective" K6G unit reflects what Roderick Ferguson (2005) terms the "racing of homonormativity." In recent years, the white homonormative community has been able to claim privileges and access to US citizenship and rights to the detriment of those communities marginalized through race, class, and gender.

And while the LA County Jail is one of the few jails in the country that makes condoms available to K6G inmates, it offers no such protection from HIV infection to its general inmate population (see

Robinson, 2011, p. 1367). Again, this perpetuates the myth that HIV is a "gay disease" and leaves other inmates excluded from access to such health care. LA's K6G unit, then, reveals some of the ironies of civil rights and LGBT organizations advocating for the protection of those "facing the most violent consequences of white supremacy, heterosexism, and gender binarism by achieving recognition or legibility for them in state apparatuses of security that are themselves key locations of that violence" (Spade, 2012, p. 185). The operations of the ban-optic gaze within the PIC point precisely to the crux of modernity: the nation-state's claim to provide freedom from violence depends on its systematic deployment of violence against and surveillance of those perceived as irrational and non-normative. It presents a moment of "freedom with violence" (Reddy, 2011, pp. 37–41) – a unique structure of state violence for social emancipation. These "protective measures," as with the creation of a K6G unit or the segregation of HIV prisoners, enable inegalitarian applications of the very practices that constitute their function as allegedly creating more security.

Even good-willed reform efforts by LGBT advocacy organizations fail to address the structural violence inherent in the PIC and how these special units and solitary confinement measures only expand and legitimize new avenues for the state to administer racialized norms of gender and sexuality. To put it bluntly in the words of CeCe McDonald, "Prisons are not safe for anybody." The denial of adequate medical treatment and the segregation mechanisms employed in US correctional facilities only solidify the gendered and racialized surveillance and violence that the ban-opticon enacts on the bodies and psyches of already vulnerable and marginalized populations.

Conclusion

The US government's long campaign against Manning ended in August 2013 when she was sentenced to thirty-five years in prison. Due in large part to the media attention surrounding her case, more than 1,000 days were deducted from her sentence for her time spent in military custody since May 2010. Additionally, she was "compensated" for the harsh treatment she had endured at the Quantico marine base. Contrastingly, such compensations are at best unlikely, and at worst non-existent, for the vast majority of transgender people subject to the violence of the state. Despite these concessions, Manning's sentence represents the longest ever handed down for a leak of US government information and will put her behind bars for most of her adult life. Her prison term far exceeds other military convictions, like that of Charles Garner, who received a ten-year sentence for his role in the Abu Ghraib scandal. Manning has been strategically placed in a "waiting zone" and assigned an identity "not even lived as such" (Bigo, 2006, p. 45). Clearly, the case of Manning exemplifies Bauman and Lyon's (2013) point that "the principle purpose of the ban-opticon is to make sure that the waste is separated from the decent product and earmarked for transportation to a refuse tip. Once it is on it, the panopticon will see to it that the waste stays there – preferably until biodegradation completes its course" (p. 66).

In September 2014, the American Civil Liberties Union (ACLU) filed a suit on behalf of Manning demanding that she receive treatment for her official diagnosis of gender dysphoria, including psychological treatment, hormone therapy, and gender confirmation surgery. The case is currently pending in a federal court (Grim & Sledge, 2015). In February 2015, *USA Today* obtained an internal memo written by the commander of the Fort Leavenworth Disciplinary Barracks that approved Manning to receive hormone therapy treatment. However, Manning is still prohibited from engaging in "female hair grooming" (Vanden Brook, 2015). In March 2015 an army appeals court ordered the military to stop referring to Manning as male and to employ either gender-neutral language or use feminine pronouns in all of its legal filings (Manning had legally changed her name to Chelsea in April 2014). The military's tentative decision to recognize Manning's gender identity presents a small victory in her continued fight for transgender health care and points to the state violence and bureaucratic hurdles that most incarcerated transgender people face on a daily basis.

The use of advanced imaging technologies as a means of identification, the ambiguous gender reclassification requirements within the United States, and the denial of health care and frequent deployment of violence against trans bodies in the PIC, all underscore how pervasive the state's gendered and racialized ban-optic surveillance practices are. The separation and harvesting of waste – of those who have been marked as nonconforming, disposable, and excluded – into various detention systems depends on the systematic normalization of certain populations through the production of normative imperatives that rely on liberal, universalizing notions of what constitutes proper gender identity. These surveillance practices are repressive, but more importantly they also engender normative modes of behaviour. In short, "exclusions include elimination and its softer sister, assimilation (you can survive among us if you renounce your identity)" (Bauman & Lyon, 2013, p. 151).

What the sexualized Othering of Chelsea Manning and the treatment of transgender people, particularly those of colour within the PIC, shows is that the ban-optic surveillance of the state functions to extract "a skin colour, an accent, an attitude" from the "unmarked masses" (Bigo, 2006, p. 45), and that these practices operate at the intersections of gender, race, sexuality, and class. In other words, the gendering of sexuality and the sexualization of gender is riven with class and race dynamics that make it impossible to detach the constitution of gender or sexuality from the broader contexts of institutionalized power in which they come to cohere (see Valentine, 2007, p. 60). Thus, my analysis of Manning's story and the treatment of trans and gender nonconforming people in the PIC contributes to an understanding of how the state surveillance of gendered and racialized bodies is central to perceptions of both safety and security. As Bauman and Lyon (2013) assert, ban-optic surveillance connects what Foucault split apart – *discipline* and *security*: "Security is surveillance as its ever evolving techniques monitor mobilities in a risk-ridden world. Insecurities are a practical corollary of today's securitized societies" (p. 107). Therefore, Bigo's (2006) concept of the ban-optic *dispositif* presents a useful theoretical framework for queer and surveillance studies to explore the frequently overlooked scrutiny of gender nonconforming bodies at the hands of the safety state and to interrogate the political implications of such practices for the formation of exclusionary/inclusionary policies monitoring the free movement of populations. The policing of transgender and queer bodies is inextricably tied to questions of national security and regulatory practices of the state – in a word, biopower. These practices enforce racialized and sexualized notions of gender identity to firmly assert the state's constructions of citizenship and safety. A ban-optic analysis demonstrates how surveillance practices not only are inherently racializing and racialized, but also (re) produce systemic inequalities through (hetero)sexism and transphobia. An effective critique of the ban-optic structures of the safety state and its gendered and racialized surveillance practices demands that we pay close attention to these interlocking systems of oppression. If we attempt to separate transphobia, (hetero)sexism, and misogyny from racism, xenophobia, and ethnocentrism, we fail to address these pressing concerns adequately.

NOTES

1 Defining identity categories such as transgender – or the commonly used shortened version trans/trans* – is an inherently difficult and contradictory task, particularly as we risk "assigning a normative telos to an identity category that is often employed to oppose this modernist, binary logic" (West, 2014, p. 9). I use the terms transgender and trans to point to a wide variety of gender nonconforming experiences and embodiments that resist the assumed stability of sex, gender, and sexuality. I follow Susan Stryker's (2008) emphasis on the performativity and social construction of identity by referring to transgender as "people who move away from the gender they were assigned at birth, people who cross-over (trans-) the boundaries constructed by their culture to define and contain that gender" (p. 1, emphasis in original). Similarly, I use the term queer here with all its inclusive potential to cover a broad spectrum of people whose identities, sexual desires, and practices fall outside the heterosexual and gender-binary norms. However, I fully recognize that queer oftentimes functions as a false universal, a catch-all umbrella term, that remains narrowly focused on certain gay and lesbian identity politics and that neglects and is oblivious to transgender issues.

2 While it is not the primary focus of this article, I suggest that Manning's pre- and post-transition media coverage was extremely sensationalizing. Initially, the media emasculated Manning as a "troubled" gay man who had discipline problems, was frequently harassed, and was never really "man enough" to be a soldier. Coverage after her sentencing further psycho-pathologized her as the sexualized Other outside the bounds of gender normativity.

3 Following Butler (2006), I am rather cautious of the official diagnosis of "gender dysphoria" (previously known as "gender identity disorder" in the *Diagnostic and Statistical Manual of Mental Disorders*), for it tends to function as an instrument of pathologization that undermines transgender autonomy by establishing gender as a relatively fixed and stable phenomenon.

4 Cisgender and cissexual typically describe types of gender identity where an individual's experience of their own gender is congruent with the sex they were assigned at birth. Biologist Dana Leland Defosse is credited as the first person to put the neologism "cisgender" into public circulation, in the mid-1990s. "Cis-," based on the Latin root, prefixes things that are "on the side of" or do not change a property. In recent years, cisgender has become popular as a label for those "staying *within* certain gender parameters (however they may be defined) rather than *crossing* or (trans-ing) those parameters" (Enke, 2013, p. 235, emphasis in original).

5 The Pentagon is currently reviewing the ban of transgender people in the US military. Secretary of Defense Ashton Carter has commissioned a working group to study the guidelines and regulations needed to welcome transgender people to serve openly. Once that work is completed, it is widely expected that the military's transgender ban will be lifted.

REFERENCES

ACLU & Human Rights Watch. (2010). Sentenced to stigma: Segregation of HIV-positive prisoners in Alabama and South Carolina. *American Civil Liberties Union*. https://www.aclu.org/files/assets/health0410webwcover.pdf.

Agamben, G. (1998). *Homo sacer: Sovereign power and bare life*. Stanford, CA: Stanford University Press.

Alexander, M. (2012). *The new Jim Crow: Mass incarceration in the age of colorblindness*. New York, NY: New Press.

Associated Press (2013, 29 August). Lawyer: Bradley Manning is doing well in prison. *CBS News*. http://www.cbsnews.com/8301-201_162-57600719/lawyer-bradley-manning-is-doing-well-in-prison

Bauman, Z., & Lyon, D. (2013). *Liquid surveillance: A conversation*. Cambridge, UK: Polity Press.

Beauchamp, T. (2009). Artful concealment and strategic visibility: Transgender bodies and US state surveillance after 9/11. *Surveillance & Society*, 6(4), 356–366.

Benkler, Y. (2013, 1 March). The dangerous logic of the Bradley Manning case. *New Republic*. http://www.newrepublic.com/article/112554

Bigo, D. (2006). *Illiberal practices of liberal regimes: The (in)security games. Cultures et Conflits*. Paris, France: Editions L'Harmattan. http://www.people.fas.harvard.edu/~ces/conferences/muslims/Bigo.pdf

Butler, J. (1993). *Bodies that matter: On the discursive limits of "sex."*. New York, NY: Routledge.

Butler, J. (2003). *Precarious life: The powers of mourning and violence*. New York, NY: Verso.

Butler, J. (2006). Undiagnosing gender. In P. Currah, R. M. Juan, & S. Price Minter (Eds.), *Transgender rights* (pp. 274–298). Minneapolis, MN: University of Minnesota Press.

CeCe McDonald Support Committee. (2013). The call-in campaign for CeCe to get her correct dosage of hormones was an incredible success! *FreeCeCeMcDonald*. http://freececemcdonald.tumblr.com/post/27152788583/hello-cece-supporters-the-call-in-campaign-for

Conrad, K. (2009). Surveillance, gender, and the virtual body in the information age. *Surveillance & Society*, 6(4), 380–387.

Costello, C. G. (2012, 25 March). TSA body scanning and the trans body. *TransFusion*. http://trans-fusion.blogspot.com/2012/03/tsa-body-scanning-and-trans-body.html

Davis, A. Y. (2003). *Are prisons obsolete?* New York, NY: Seven Stories Press.

Enke, A. F. (2013). The education of little cis: Cisgender and the discipline of opposing bodies. In S. Stryker & A. Z. Aizura (Eds.), *The transgender studies reader 2* (pp. 234–247). New York, NY: Routledge.

Ferguson, R.A. (2005). Race-ing homonormativity: Citizenship, sociology, and gay identity. In E. P. Johnson & M. G. Henderson (Eds.), *Black queer studies: A critical anthology* (pp. 52–67). Durham, NC: Duke University Press.

Foucault, M. (1978). The history of sexuality. Vol. 1. *An introduction*. New York, NY: Vintage Books.

Foucault, M. (1980). The Confession of the Flesh. In C. Gordon (Ed.), *Power/ knowledge: Selected interviews and other writings, 1972–1977* (pp. 194–228). New York, NY: Harvester Press.

Foucault, M. (1995). *Discipline and punish: The birth of the prison* (A. Sheridan, Trans.). New York, NY: Vintage Books.

Fox News (2013, 11 April). Judge: Bin Laden raid member can testify in WikiLeaks case. [Video File] *Fox News*. http://video.foxnews.com/v/2293646359001/judge-bin-laden-raid-member-can-testify-in-wikileaks-case

Gabbatt, A. (2013, 22 August). "I am Chelsea Manning," says jailed soldier formerly known as Bradley. *The Guardian*. http://www.theguardian.com/world/2013/aug/22/bradley-manning-woman-chelsea-gender-reassignment

Gates, K. A. (2011). *Our biometric future: Facial recognition technology and the culture of surveillance*. New York, NY: NYU Press.

GLAD. (2011, 30 September). Federal Bureau of Prisons makes major change in transgender medical policy. *Gay & Lesbian Advocates & Defenders*. http://www.glad.org/current/pr-detail/federal-bureau-of-prisons-makes-major-change-in-transgender-medical-policy

Goldsmith, L. (2011). Bradley Manning: Rich man's war, poor (gay) man's fight. In R. Conrad (Ed.), *Against equality: Don't ask to fight their wars* (pp. 45–50). Lewiston, ME: AE Press.

Grim, R., & Sledge, M. (2015, 5 March) Court orders army to stop referring to Chelsea Manning as a man. *Huffington Post*. http://www.huffingtonpost.com/2015/03/05/chelsea-manning_n_6811352.html

Guthrie, S. (Host). (2013, 22 August), *Today Show*. New York, NY: NBC. www.lexisnexis.com/hottopics/lnacademic

Hanssens, C., Moodie-Mills, A. C., Ritchie, A. J., Spade, D., & Vaid, U. (2014). *A roadmap for change: Federal policy recommendations for addressing the criminalization of LGBT people and people living with HIV*. New York, NY: Center for Gender & Sexuality Law at Columbia Law School.

Hernandez, S. (2008, 1 June). Lethal limbo. Lack of healthcare turns federal detention into a death sentence for some immigrants. *Los Angeles Times*. http://articles.latimes.com/2008/jun/01/opinion/op-hernandez1

Lambda Legal. (2015, 3 February). Know your rights: Changing birth certificate sex designations: State-by-state guidelines. Lambda Legal. http://www.lambdalegal.org/know-your-rights/transgender/changing-birth-certificate-sex-designations

Leigh, D., & Harding, L. (2011). *WikiLeaks: Inside Julian Assange's war on secrecy*. New York, NY: Public Affairs.

Lyon, D. (2007). *Surveillance studies: An overview*. Cambridge, UK: Polity Press.

Magnet, S., & Rodgers, T. (2012). Stripping for the state: Whole body imaging technologies and the surveillance of othered bodies. *Feminist Media Studies*, *12*(1), 101–118. http://dx.doi.org/10.1080/14680777.2011.558352

Manning, C. (2013, 28 October). Memorandum for "Private Manning Support Network." Subject: Scope of representation by David E. Coombs. *Private Manning Support Network*. http://www.chelseamanning.org/wp-content/uploads/2013/10/Manning-Coombs-Representation.pdf

Military Times (2013, 22 August). Bradley Manning wants YOUR TAX DOLLARS to pay for hormone therapy. *Military Times*. http://forums.militarytimes.com/showthread.php/7599-Bradley-Manning-Wants-YOUR-TAX-DOLLARS-to-Pay-for-Hormone-Therapy

National Gay and Lesbian Task Force. (2011). *Injustice at every turn: A report of the national transgender discrimination survey*. http://www.thetaskforce.org/static_html/downloads/reports/reports/ntds_full.pdf

Outfront Minnesota. (2013). Gender changes on Minnesota driver's licenses. *Outfront Minnesota*. http://www.outfront.org/library/licenses

Pilkington, E. (2012, 12 March). Bradley Manning's treatment was cruel and inhuman, UN torture chief rules. *The Guardian*. http://www.theguardian.com/world/2012/mar/12/bradley-manning-cruel-inhuman-treatment-un

Potts, M. C. (2011). Regulatory sites: Management, confinement, and HIV/AIDS. In E. A. Stanley & N. Smith (Eds.), *Captive genders: Trans embodiment and the prison industrial complex* (pp. 99–112). Oakland, CA: AK Press.

Reddy, C. (2011). *Freedom with violence: Race, sexuality, and the US state*. Durham, NC: Duke University Press. http://dx.doi.org/10.1215/9780822394648

Reitman, J. (2013, 14 March). The trials of Bradley Manning. *Rolling Stone*, 1178. http://www.rollingstone.com/politics/news/the-trials-of-bradley-manning-20130314

Robinson, R. (2011). Masculinity as prison: Sexual identity, race, and incarceration. *California Law Review, 99*(1309), 1309–1408.

Rose, N. (1999). *Powers of freedom: Reframing political thought*. New York, NY: Cambridge University Press. http://dx.doi.org/10.1017/CBO9780511488856

Rothe, D. L., & Steinmetz, K. F. (2013). The case of Bradley Manning: State victimization, realpolitik, and WikiLeaks. *Contemporary Justice Review: Issues in Criminal, Social, and Restorative Justice, 16*(2), 280–292. http://dx.doi.org/10.1080/10282580.2013.798694

Smith, M. R. (2013, 27 August). Chelsea Manning lawyer gives more details on gender change. *Associated Press*. http://www.twincities.com/national/ci_23952628/chelsea-manning-lawyer-gives-more-details-gender-change

Snow, J. (2013, 14 June). Social Security to ease requirements for transgender people. *MetroWeekly*. http://www.metroweekly.com/2013/06/social-security-to-ease-requir/

Spade, D. (2009). Keynote address: Trans law and politics on a neoliberal landscape. *Temple Political & Civil Rights Law Review, 18*(2), 353–373.

Spade, D. (2012). The only way to end racialized gender violence in prisons is to end prisons: A response to Russell Robinson's "Masculinity as Prison." *California Law Review, 3*, 184–195.

Stanley, E. A. (2011). Fugitive flesh: Gender self-determination, queer abolition, and trans resistance: An introduction. In E. A. Stanley & N. Smith (Eds.), *Captive genders: Trans embodiment and the prison industrial complex* (pp. 1–11). Oakland, CA: AK Press.

Stryker, S. (2008). *Transgender history*. Berkley, CA: Seal Press.

Sylvia Rivera Law Project. (2007). *It's war in here: A report on the treatment of transgender and intersex people in New York state men's prisons*. New York, NY: Sylvia Rivera Law Project.

Thompson, G. (2011, 21 December). Last witness for military takes stand in leak case. *New York Times*. http://www.nytimes.com/2011/12/21/us/governments-last-witness-takes-stand-at-bradley-manning-hearing.html?ref=bradleyemanning&_r=0

Transportation Security Administration. (2011, 25 January). *TSA Advanced Imaging Technology: Impact Assessment Update*. Department of Homeland Security. https://www.dhs.gov/xlibrary/assets/privacy/privacy-pia-tsa-ait.pdf

US Department of State. (2013). Identification requirements for gender reassignment applicants. *US Department of State.* http://travel.state.gov/passport/get/first/first_5100.html

Valentine, D. (2007). *Imagining transgender: An ethnography of a category.* Durham, NC: Duke University Press. http://dx.doi.org/10.1215/9780822390213

Vanden Brook, T. (2015, 13 February). Military approves hormone therapy for Chelsea Manning. *USA Today.* http://www.usatoday.com/story/news/nation/2015/02/12/chelsea-manning-hormone-therapy/23311813

Wacquant, L. (2001). Deadly symbiosis: When ghetto and prison meet and mash. *Punishment and Society, 3*(1), 95–133. http://dx.doi.org/10.1177/14624740122228276

Ware, W. (2011). Rounding up the homosexuals: The impact of juvenile court on queer and trans/gender-non-conforming youth. In E. A. Stanley & N. Smith (Eds.), *Captive genders: Trans embodiment and the prison industrial complex* (pp. 77–84). Oakland, CA: AK Press.

West, I. (2014). *Transforming citizenships. Transgender articulations of the law.* New York, NY: NYU Press.

Wurzelbacher, J. (2013, 23 August). Bradley Manning (traitor, male) wants taxpayers to pay for female hormone therapy. *Rightwing News.* http://www.rightwingnews.com/crime/bradley-manning-traitor-male-wants-taxpayers-to-pay-for-female-hormone-therapy

Surveillance and the Gendering of Urban Space

The Spectacle of Public Sex(uality): Media and State Surveillance of Gay Men in Toronto in the 1970s

ZOË NEWMAN

I can pinpoint the very moment it all started to change, when the calm broke: when news that twelve-year-old Emanuel Jaques had disappeared spread through our neighbourhood in the whispered prayers of women returning from Mass ... Worry about what had happened to Emanuel, the Shoeshine Boy, was closing in on us. Our parents had told us to be afraid, warned us of the dangers lurking on the city's main drag. But we wouldn't let their fear stop us. (Anthony De Sa, 2013, pp. 1–2)

On 1 August 1977, the *Globe and Mail*, Canada's newspaper of record, reported that a twelve-year-old boy, Emanuel Jaques "of Shuter Street," had been missing since 28 July (*Globe and Mail*, 1977a, p. 1). The following day, it was front-page news that his body had been discovered "on the roof of Charlie's Angels sex shop at 245 Yonge St. ... The building displays a neon sign that reads Sexy on the top line and Girls, Girls on the bottom" (York & Lipovenko, 1977, p. 1). Police reported that the "12-year-old shoeshine boy," now identified as from Regent Park, the government housing project built in the late 1940s as slum clearance, had died by asphyxiation, and that further forensic testing was being conducted to determine "if the boy had been sexually abused" (York & Lipovenko, 1977, p. 1). That Jaques's body had been found on Yonge Street, one of the city's most visible and contested streets, dramatically boosted the intensity of the coverage the crime received. Conclusive forensic evidence aside, links were being forged to tie Jaques's murder to spatial disorder and sexual deviance, beginning anew the process of justifying surveillance of gay men and sex workers, and displacing them from areas of the city that they occupied.

Four men were charged in Jaques's death: Saul David Betesh had turned himself in to police the day before the body was discovered, and three other men were arrested later in August (Keating, 1977, p. 1). These arrests did not bring closure, however. To the contrary, the case was front-page news in the *Globe and Mail* for four days, and it continued to be followed almost daily for the month of August. Related stories reported a massive public outcry and city-wide mourning for Jaques, as well as legal manoeuvring to increase municipal powers over "sex establishments" (Beddoes, 1977a; Hill, 1977a, p. 5; Porambo, 1977a; Porambo, 1977c; Rogers, 1977). A full-time assistant Crown attorney, Toomas Ounapuu, was assigned the task of clearing up unresolved "morals charges" and managing "a wave" of new charges that the police were laying "on the Yonge Street strip" (Hill, 1977a, p. 5). Simultaneously, a special prosecutor, Morris Manning, was appointed "to seek court injunctions that would close unlicensed body-rub shops and nude encounter establishments" (Baker, 1977a, p. 1). Nine days after the discovery of Jaques's body, the police task force boasted that it had laid approximately 330 charges since the earlier start of its "crack down on prostitution and other criminal activity on Yonge Street" (Hill, 1977a, p. 5). Stories scattered through the paper told of arrests, charges, or closures in sex shop raids and for other sex crimes, until just a "handful of Yonge Street shops" were left open (Hill, 1977b, p. 1).[1]

Readers of the *Globe*, including municipal politicians, would have been reasonable to take as fact that Emanuel Jaques had died, and that his body had been found on Yonge Street. What was not so certain was whether his death was meaningfully related to Yonge Street, Regent Park, gay men, or sex work. Yet those spaces and bodies were readily identified by the media and city officials as somehow relevant, perhaps even causal. The murder of Emanuel Jaques, while a devastating event, quite likely would not have received the kind of widespread attention it did without a larger context of shifting legal boundaries around sexuality and a lesbian and gay community growing in visibility and power. With "homosexuality" already decriminalized in the Canadian Criminal Code, in July 1977 a committee within the Ontario Human Rights Commission had recommended that sexuality be protected against discrimination (Warner, 2002, p. 135).

Saul David Betesh, Werner Gruener, Robert Wayne Kribs, and Joseph Woods stood trial on charges of first-degree murder from 16 January to 10 March 1978. Although Betesh had turned himself in to police on 31 July 1977, admitted that he and Kribs raped and killed Jaques, named two other men he said were involved, and told police where to find Jaques's body, Betesh along with Gruener, Kribs, and Wood initially pleaded not guilty (Keating, 1978, p. 5; Strauss, 1978b, p. 5). Less than a month into the trial, however, Kribs changed his plea to guilty (Strauss, 1978a, p. 1). Ultimately, Kribs and Betesh were found guilty of first-degree murder and sentenced to life imprisonment, with no eligibility for parole for twenty-five years (Carriere & Strauss, 1978, p. 5). Woods was found guilty of second-degree murder, and Gruener was acquitted (Carriere & Strauss, 1978, p. 5). During the court proceedings, a pathologist confirmed that Emanuel Jaques drowned after "being sexually attacked" (Carriere, 1978, p. 5).

The months immediately following the murder of Emanuel Jaques brought a rise in the surveillance and harassment of gay men across the city. In the fall of 1977, there were police raids and "mass arrests" in four Toronto bathhouses (Hannon, 1982, p. 273). In December of that year, charges were laid against *The Body Politic*, Toronto's local gay and lesbian newspaper at the time; the charges followed a raid by Operation P, "a special joint Toronto/provincial police unit set up to investigate pornography" (Jackson, 1982, p. 4). The following December, in 1978, ending a long-standing tacit police acceptance of bathhouses, the Barracks bathhouse was raided. Historian Gary Kinsman (1996) identifies this as "the initiation of a new operational policy" (p. 339) that would unfold with increasing raids in the late 1970s and reach its peak in the early 1980s. As Gerald Hannon (1982), journalist for *The Body Politic*, wrote in his account of the 1981 Operation Soap bathhouse raids and mass arrests in Toronto, "Yonge and Wellesley is turf we've liked to say belongs to us, but realize is ours only grudgingly, and on loan" (p. 274).

In addition to considering how media coverage tied Jaques's murder to cleaning up Yonge Street and regulating gay men, this chapter will point to an element left quite invisible in the *Globe*. At a time when Toronto's downtown was expanding and real estate prices were on the rise, political and business interests were at stake on Yonge Street. While ridding Yonge Street of "filth" and "sin" was touted as a way to safeguard respectability and families, concrete investments were also being protected.

This chapter is drawn from a larger study about how the Jaques murder was politically and culturally mobilized as a means to reassert white heteronormativity in Toronto, largely through spatial regulation. Here, however, the focus is narrowed to surveillance, particularly to the interplay of public visibility and urban space, with mediated gazes and police crackdowns. I understand surveillance as a systematic process involving technologies of state-authorized police tracking of people's movements, communications, and personal data (Kinsman & Gentile, 2010), but I extend that process to include non-state practices of watching and rendering visible, such as those practised and produced by mainstream media coverage. I draw on Thomas Mathiesen's (1997) model of the synoptic gaze, as well as the work of a number of other surveillance studies scholars, to consider the relationship between formal and informal surveillance. Asserting that the gazes of police and the media are parts of a whole reflects one of my central inquiries, about how surveillant processes of constituting and "knowing" a group in categorical terms contribute to plausibly denying that group full civil rights, including protection from state surveillance. To authorize placing a person or group under surveillance (by police) requires some foundation of belief in their threat, criminality, or "subversion," to use the language of Canadian postwar security policing (Kinsman & Gentile, 2010, p. 24).

If being suspected of "subversion" creates the precondition for surveillance (with "subversion" as the evidence surveillance seeks to gather), we might then consider certain media discourses as contributing to the frame through which gays and lesbians came to be defined as socially undesirable, with local and national repercussions. In the post-1969 politics of visible gay sexuality, commercialized spaces of consumption and leisure, and an explicit municipal political campaign to clean up and "save" Toronto's reputation, an aggregation of formal and informal surveillance practices is rendered visible. I begin with an overview of the Jaques murder case and the spatial and moral regulation to which it gave rise, but it is this aggregation and its effects that form the focus of this chapter.

(Un)Covering the Death of Emmanuel Jaques

My attempts to deconstruct newspaper coverage of the events following the discovery of Emanuel Jaques's body are not intended to suggest that his murder did not merit public outrage. Rather, my sense is that under different political and social circumstances, his death might very well have received little press. Jaques worked on Yonge Street, which could easily have produced a construction of him as a hustler, and as one of eight children of an immigrant Portuguese family living in Regent Park, he was marked as racially other. Large-scale Portuguese migration to Canada was in its second decade by the 1970s, and Torontonians of Portuguese descent were economically disenfranchised and often subjected to anti-immigrant sentiment (Iacovetta, 2006, p. 199; Miranda, 2009, p. 111). Regent Park, identified by the *Globe* as "a broken-down end of the city" (Porambo, 1977c, p. 5), had a long history as a stigmatized urban space (Rose, 1958). None of these details make Jaques's life any less important or his death any more acceptable, yet I can only too easily imagine the story that might otherwise have been told about him; it would certainly not have been a story in which he was held up as one of Toronto's own. In so many ways Jaques was an outsider, socially indistinguishable from the people pitted against him. All of the mythical taints that were made to adhere to gay men might readily have been used to negatively distort Jaques and his life. Instead, Jaques and his family were cast as symbols of goodness and respectability for other Torontonians to rally behind, and the figure of the predatory outsider was projected onto another marginalized community. This stark representational contrast formed a link in authorizing formal state surveillance as protection of an imagined public, and as such stands as an example of media surveillance.

Existing literature on the murder of Emanuel Jaques and the campaign to clean up Yonge Street often uses the framework of moral panics. As in the germinal work of Stanley Cohen and Stuart Hall, scholars note that in the aftermath of Jaques's murder, the print media played a significant role in heightening the political mood in Toronto to a moral panic (Ng, 1981; Kinsman, 1987; Brock, 1998; Warner, 2002). Media narratives that bolstered the campaign to clean up Yonge Street made it possible to launch a repressive spatial campaign against particular residents, all the while feeding and reinforcing heteronormative discourses about deviance, as well as about the superiority and respectability of the general population.

These kinds of media representations are what Kathryn Conrad (2009) refers to as a "technology of surveillance ... that extends beyond the state" (p. 5). For people already susceptible to public scrutiny and "exposure" – in Conrad's case also gay men, also accused of public indecency – media narratives combine fear and desire in such a way that surveillance becomes naturalized or culturally "embedded" (p. 6). Thomas Mathiesen's (1997) concept of the synopticon speaks to this surveillant function of the media. As I will elaborate further below, Mathiesen coined the term synopticon to counter Foucault's claim that there was a turn in the late eighteenth and early nineteenth centuries away from forms of spectacle towards a panoptic model of surveillance. Mathiesen contends instead that panopticism and synopticism are symbiotic. By his account, these two modes of watching can be found as aspects of the same institutions, working in tandem to produce "decisive control functions" that shape "behaviour and attitude" and even consciousness (1997, pp. 218–19, 222–3, 228–30). This notion of panoptic and synoptic power working in concert – as mutually sustaining, or even as simultaneous aspects of the same technologies – is often understood through the example of mass media news coverage that contributes to generating public sympathies and even support for increased panoptical surveillance and incarceration (Lyon, 2006, p. 44; Doyle, 2011, p. 287). I would add that publicizing people's sexual lives in the media sometimes functions as an extension of formal state surveillance. These dynamics were very much at play in the case surrounding the murder of Emanuel Jaques.

Almost every *Globe* article about the murder at some point refers to Jaques as "the little shoeshine boy." The emphasis on this aspect of his life contributes to the mythological and moralistic thrust of newspaper accounts of his murder. In Victorian parlance, "shoeshine boys" were orphans who had been rescued by Christian missions and were put to work tending to the boots of London's wealthy (Cohen, 1997, p. 83). According to this "official East End success story," shoeshine boys were evidence of the possibility of redemption and prosperity – thanks to the goodness of liberal society. As the shoeshine boy, Jaques represented proof that Canadians are benevolent and charitable. His death also became part of a narrative of martyrdom and revenge, motivations that continue the biblical theme of evil that must be thwarted by good people. This implicit call to action to protect innocence can perhaps explain the overwrought and invasive journalistic descriptions of his funeral: "the figure of Christ on a black cross ... hung on the wall overlooking the expensive, 64-inch white lambskin casket that was being closed over the angelic face of Emanuel Jaques for the last time. Flowers were everywhere, more than 40 bouquets and wreaths" (*Globe and Mail*, 1977b, p. 5). The pitiable, charity-case quality of the shoeshine trope was transfigured into martyrdom, bolstering the "cause" of taking action against gay men and Yonge Street, the putative guilty parties.

"Protecting the children" is a common note in fear-based media coverage (Keenan, 2014, p. 13). In August 1977, one local invocation of "children's safety" was the warning that if gays and lesbians were allowed contact with children, the latter might be swayed towards sexual deviance, or even be at risk of sexual molestation. Letters to the editor in the 1 August *Globe and Mail* included one given the title "Gay rights." A person wrote "arguing that the Ontario Human Rights code should not protect the rights of homosexuals in employment as teachers, camp counsellors and youth workers" (Hall, 1977, p. 6). The author supported this position by stating that since homosexuality is "an illness which could, in certain circumstances be 'contagious' I feel that those jobs in which the person works with and could influence young people should not be open to homosexuals" (p. 6).[2] Newspaper coverage also used a demonstration by members of Toronto's Portuguese community to underscore a narrative of imperilled youth, as in the *Globe*'s image of a boy holding a sign reading "Am I safe?" (Ng, 1981, p. 54). The *Globe* further reported that twelve-year-old Luis Sequeira presented a petition to Premier William Davis "urging a cleanup of the Yonge Street strip in the wake of the slaying of a shoeshine boy who worked on the strip" (Lavigne, 1977, p. 5). Elsewhere, the heading on the petition is reproduced in capital letters: "STAMP OUT GAYS AND BODY RUBS" (Beddoes, 1977a, p. 8). While such an item may seem inflammatory and certainly homophobic, it mirrored governmental tactics, crystallizing a convergence of synoptic and panoptic forms of surveillance: "Attorney General Roy McMurtry enlarged the province's drive against the Yonge Street 'strip' to include gay hustlers" (Lynch, 1977, p. 4).

While not definitive or uniform in their effect, rhetorical flourishes like these lend themselves to particular ways of knowing. The stories told about vulnerable youth mobilize a sense of common cause, a knowledge of "ourselves" as decent, concerned, and prepared to act to defend our beliefs. An article on whether or not David Crombie, the mayor at the time, would run again in the next election noted that "Mr. Crombie says the clean-up of Yonge Street and its restoration as a family street ... are important to him" (Baker, 1977b, p. 5). Alderman and city budget chief Art Eggleton declared that "the heat is on and it will stay that way until Yonge Street is a safe place for families" (Boyle, 1977, p. 2). This wholesome, vigilant collective identity was significantly conjured through vilifying gay men as a threat; more to the point, public cohesion was secured both *through* a way of seeing (where gay men and visible gay culture were understood as dangerous) and *as* a way of seeing (where being "good" equalled being watchful).

The press implicated gay men in Emanuel Jaques's murder in a number of questionable ways. A 1977 article in *The Body Politic* charged that by "gratuitously" (Lynch, 1977, p. 1) describing people and places as homosexual, "the media seized on the alleged murder story to press home a morality campaign that city officials were already conducting against Yonge Street's exploitative heterosexual bodyrub studios. But they extended it to an attack on homosexuals" (p. 1). The *Globe* used somewhat circuitous tactics to associate homosexuality with criminality, violence, and Yonge Street. Less than three weeks after the *Globe* reported the discovery of Jaques's body, the newspaper devoted space to two stories about Kurt Freund, "an eminent sexologist" (Bruner, 1977b, pp. 1–2; Bruner, 1977a, p. 2) at the Clarke Institute of Psychiatry. A front-page story ran with the headline, "Only cure for dangerous sex sadists is castration, Metro psychiatrist says" (Bruner, 1977b, p. 1). Freund was quoted as stating that removal of testicles "would guarantee that a dangerous child molester ... 'nine months after the operation will never do it again.'" The other related story, titled "An appetite for sex is measured at Clarke," was an account of journalist Arnold Bruner's visit to Freund's clinic. He chronicled Freund's current research on "men with out-of-the-ordinary sexual appetites" (Bruner, 1977b, p. 2), as well as describing the sexologist's work dating back to the 1950s: "He adapted aversion therapy to treat homosexuality ... 'After eight years of trying therapy I realized it didn't work ... There is only one proven way to help people who have a dangerous sadistic problem with which they cannot cope ... testicular enucleation or pulpectomy, which is removal of the sex glands'" (p. 2). These articles reinforced notions of homosexuality as abnormal and even violent, giving these views a sheen of scientific validation even while they ignored much of the research done since the 1950s.

The last of the predators brought into view was Yonge Street itself. In one article, "Yonge Street's sexual sewers" (Beddoes, 1977b, p. 8) were fingered as the underlying cause of Jaques's murder. A positively Victorian letter to the editor blamed "this centre of sexual filth ... the decadence which has resulted in the tragic death of a small boy on Yonge street" (Temple, 1977, p. 6). An article about how "police no longer hassle gays on strip" was placed above a piece making a contradictory claim that "the campaign for gay rights will probably suffer a serious setback because of alleged homosexual involvement in the death of a 12-year-old Manual [sic] Jaques" (Porambo, 1977b, p. 5). This item situated Charlie's Angels, on the roof of which Jaques's body was allegedly found, in the midst of gay sexual activity. The article cuts back and forth between conversations with two men apparently working on Yonge Street: "Riding down the strip toward Charlie's Angels body-rub parlor ... the cab driver said Toronto was fast becoming the biggest hangout for professional homosexuals in North America ... Homosexuals are not popular today in a city that has prided itself on its liberal atmosphere" (Porambo, 1977b, p. 5). Then the narrator takes us "back out on the roof, near where the body was found," and next we're "back at the gay bar half a mile up the strip" (p. 5), leaving no doubt that the spaces of Jaques's murder, of the sex industry, and of the gay community, are one. The article concludes that Jaques's murder was causing "an emotional upheaval unlike any seen in Toronto for years" (Porambo, 1977c, p. 5); the Gothic imagery in the above accounts, of filth and decadence, points to this affective over-burdening. Jaques's death had become both a symbolic threat to "good Torontonians" and the occasion for a cathartic new group identity.

Locating the Crime: Yonge Street as Contested Space

A patchwork of preoccupations and uses, a pawnshop of our several urban dreams, a cacophony of unfinished business ripe for bankruptcy or the quick profit of wallet or soul, a string of little shopping districts and big stores, a street-vendors' haven, a sin strip, a strollers' alley, a mix of ritzy and rubby and rube, [Yonge Street] rambles on and on like a pica-resque novel, one shining or sorry or tawdry or funny adventure after another. (Kilbourn, 1984, p. 21)

There were so many good [bars on Yonge Street] with really great bands, that it was hard to make a choice. Yonge Station was a bit on the rough side and you might have to dodge the odd beer pitcher in order to enjoy the band, but it was an interesting place to visit if you were into studying the nocturnal subhuman or perhaps Nosferatu? (Tassy, 1996, p. 103)

Geographically, Yonge Street serves as the dividing line between east and west in Toronto, running the entire length of the city, from the shore of Lake Ontario almost as far north as Lake Simcoe (Marshall, 2011). Established in the late 1700s along a trail used by the people of the Huron–Wendat Confederacy,[3] colonial histories have it that the street named by John Graves Simcoe was "divided into 'two nations' – rural folks at one end and townspeople at the other" (Berchem, 1996, p. 151). In the mid-1800s, Yonge Street remained a dividing line, sepa-rating "the nefarious St. John's Ward, described as being ... 'the Negro quarter ... of Toronto'" on the west, from "the notorious Stanley Street" on the east (Berchem, 1996, p. 11). According to historian John Weaver

(1979), in the early 1900s, St John's Ward or "the Ward" "was treated by good and proper Torontonians as a blemish whose foreign contagion was best kept away from the sanctity of the suburbs" (p. 43). After the First World War, the popular representation of Toronto's topography was largely unchanged: "On either side of Yonge Street, in the old downtown area, there was little evidence of hope or of prosperity, rather there was utter squalor. The ever-infamous Ward to the west and Moss Park to the east of Yonge Street were described in the report of a Committee on Housing as 'the worst slums of Toronto'" (Berchem, 1996, p. 150). Neighbouring on Moss Park a handful of blocks east of Yonge, Cabbagetown was known at the turn of the twentieth century as an Anglo-Celtic, working-class neighbourhood, with a concentration of "disorderly houses and houses of ill-repute" (Weaver, 1979, p. 46). In the 1940s, Cabbagetown would be torn down and rebuilt as Regent Park, the country's largest public housing project. This was the area where Emanuel Jaques and his family lived, described by the *Globe* as one "where the houses are close together and everybody knows his neighbors" (Beddoes, 1977a, p. 8).

In the summer of 1977, Yonge Street still functioned symbolically as urban wilderness – as the frontier up against which the dominant society could define itself and demonstrate its power. Indeed, a great deal was at stake in the symbolic battle over Yonge Street. In the dozens of articles about Jaques and Yonge Street published in the *Globe* in August 1977, economic interests are rarely mentioned as relevant to the 1977 clean-up campaign. Yet at the very corner where Emanuel Jaques used to shine shoes, and along the surrounding blocks, major change was taking place. Downtown Toronto was in the midst of a building boom, and land on and around Yonge Street was becoming prime real estate. Space and its uses were being contested in a very material sense.

In the mid-1960s, the Eaton family began drawing up construction plans in preparation to return to their old stomping grounds. The first Eaton's had been a dry goods store at Yonge and Queen, opened in 1869, with its annex, mail order warehouse, and factories stretching north up Yonge (Barc, 2010). In 1930 the Eaton family opened a new "upscale" department store at Yonge and College (Belisle, 2011, p. 42). In 1966, John David Eaton, then president of Eaton's, announced that his family intended to develop their old factories and warehouses into a huge indoor shopping mall that would stretch north and west from Yonge and Queen over 22.5 acres (Plummer, 2012). The architects, planners, and business executives associated with the proposed Eaton Centre did their best to make the case for their plan, arguing that the land on and around Yonge and Queen was "underdeveloped with predominantly substandard buildings" (McGiven, 1966, n.p.). They claimed that their project was "the best possible approach to the revitalization of this stra-tegic area" and "the most effective means of stimulating a rebirth of the central business district" (McGiven, 1966, n.p.). But their ambitious proposal encountered considerable resistance from defenders of Toron-to's heritage, for it would require the demolition of both Old City Hall and the Church of the Holy Trinity (McGiven, 1966).

In 1972, the Eaton family, now in partnership with the Bronfmans' Cadillac Fairview Corporation, signed a new agreement that would protect both historic buildings and still create a shopping centre with a flagship department store, more than two hundred additional stores and restaurants, high-rise towers, and eight hundred parking spots (Plummer, 2012). The planned mall, now anchored at Yonge and Dundas and stretching several blocks south and west, was expected to become the premier retail location in Toronto (Ng, 1981, p. 78). Deborah Brock (1998) describes the Eaton Centre project as part of "a renewal of commercial development on Yonge Street" (p. 32) taking place during the mid-1970s. Politicians and business owners hoped that a "transformation" – spearheaded by the $250 million Eaton Centre project – would bring "middle-class shoppers" back to down-town Yonge Street (p. 32). Weighing in on the new commercial com-plex, the city's daily newspaper, the *Toronto Star*, represented Yonge Street as needing rescue particularly from the "smut industry" (Ng, 1981, p. 64), with the Eaton family positioned as the street's likely saviour. In February 1977, the Eaton Centre, "a theatre, a spectacle designed to entertain the public into spending its money" (Finlay, 1977), opened its doors. The CBC's coverage of the opening noted that "to make some of the most expensive retail space on this conti-nent pay for itself, Eaton's is concentrating much more than before on fashions and furnishings for the urban and affluent" (Finlay, 1977). Consider, then, who were the neighbours of this long-planned project that billed itself as "unquestionably chang[ing] the whole character not only of the downtown area, but of the whole city of Toronto" (McGiven, 1966).

By the mid-1970s, gay businesses and political organizations were multiplying in Canadian cities, often forming geographic concentra-tions. In Toronto, that clustering occurred around the downtown stretch of Yonge Street, making the area "the main artery of Toronto gay social life" (Benson, 2012, p. 10). By 1975, there were at least twenty gay bars and clubs on Yonge Street alone, with nineteen more within a few block radius (McLeod, 1996, pp. 281–2). The Parkside Tavern, at 530 Yonge Street, was one of the bars gay men had been frequenting for some time. On 1 January 1977, a new bar opened directly above it: Stages was the city's first "gay disco," as well as a new phenomenon by virtue of being popular – for its great sound and atmosphere – with both gay and straight people (Benson, 2012, p. 11). Dudes, one of the first gay-owned bars, also opened in 1977. It was located just off Yonge behind the Parkside (p. 11). "Gay commercial facilities" (Kinsman, 1987, p. 182) on or near Yonge in the 1970s also included bathhouses, restaurants, and bookstores (see Figure 1).[4]

The spatial and commercial expansion of gay communities in 1970s Toronto was occurring within a relatively new legal and moral paradigm. As a result of liberation movements in the 1960s, Canadian public policymakers were being pushed to acknowledge the public presence and claims of socially marginalized groups. The 1969 reform of the Criminal Code decriminalized homosexual activity provided it took place in private, between adults over the age of twenty-one (Brock, 1998, p. 26). This offered gays and lesbians the protection of domestic privacy, and in doing so, it opened the door to social changes that posed a threat to the moral and financial establishment. In this climate of change, as I will elaborate, a clampdown on visible queer sexuality was activated (Walby, 2009, p. 369; Kinsman & Gentile, 2010, p. 302).

After 1969, even as private homosexual acts between consenting adults were no longer categorized as criminal, the Canadian state extended its powers to regulate public space and behaviour. As Brock (1998) writes, this decriminalizing would actually result in "intensified police persecution of gay men in public spaces" (p. 28). It is to this tension between "private" freedom and "public" persecution of sexualized bodies and practices – and its effects in 1970s Toronto – that I now turn.

The limited and tenuous protection of domestic privacy afforded gays and lesbians in post-1969 Canada reflected a paradox: an imagined "public" characterized by its moral rectitude and therefore its right to privacy was set against a group imagined as threatening the public order with its immorality and therefore as forfeiting its right to privacy. Surveillance of "public" sex and sexuality is often legitimized in the name of protecting a city's image and commercial activities; reshaping public urban spaces into privatized zones of consumption is

Figure 1. The shared space of downtown Yonge Street

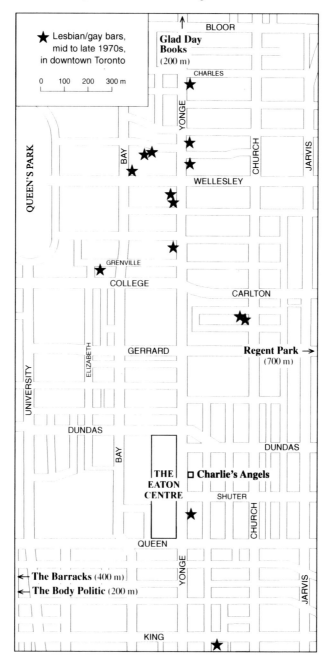

then articulated as for the greater good, rather than being understood as going against the interests of the collective in a free and open common (Conrad, 2009). In this contraction of "the public," the paradox is the simultaneous assertion of "privacy" as perhaps the most sacred of the values that surveillance is said to protect, and the invasion of that privacy in the name of security (Lyon, 2006, p. 51). Breaching the privacy of "the few" (through surveillance), and thereby constraining their right to public space, in order to protect "the many," naturalizes the former's expulsion from that public. This exceptionalism to secure "the public good" can actually make claims about what and who are respectable and therefore "properly" private. In simple terms, then, surveillance is a process of making known (Walby, 2009, p. 376), a process that, as we can see in the intertwined narratives around Emanuel Jaques and Yonge Street, enables the reinstallation of a normative moral order that conditions the possibility of belonging and access to the city.

Making Homosexuality Visible/Making Homosexuality a Visible Problem

As the case of Yonge Street in 1977 suggests, redefining public spaces ultimately involves political manoeuvres and discourses that also redefine who is a citizen, how a citizen may behave, and when a person's behaviour crosses the line into criminality or deviance. I have already mentioned the sweeping closures of "body rub" parlours and the mass arrests in bathhouses on and around Yonge Street in the wake of the murder of Emanuel Jaques; I have also given some background on the Eaton family's large-scale, decade-long property development along Yonge Street, which had finally come to fruition in 1977, in the vicinity of the growing numbers of gay bars. Here I continue to describe the political and regulatory climate for gay men leading to the "cleanup," to trace how gay men and their public visibility were branded as a social problem requiring continued scrutiny. Gay men and lesbians knew that downtown Yonge Street was the place to go for clubs and socializing, but they also knew they would likely have unwanted company in those spaces. At the Parkside Tavern, police spying on patrons in the bathrooms was the norm from the mid-1960s through the 1970s (Benson, 2012, p. 10). Becki Ross (1995) characterizes the police and legal regulation of mid-1970s Toronto as "intrusive, coercive ... state and social repression" (p. 32). In addition to police entrapment of gay men in bathrooms, there were attempts to forcefully erase gay visibility at a representational level. Mainstream newspapers and radio stations refused to carry advertising with gay content, and in 1975, the Morality Squad of the Metro Toronto police ordered *The Body Politic* removed from newsstands (Ross, 1995).

Visibility itself appears as a significant puzzle in the history of formal state surveillance of gay men and lesbians in postwar Canada. In their examination of national security policing from the 1950s into the 1990s, Gary Kinsman and Patrizia Gentile (2010) trace a convoluted strategy change in the late 1960s at the level of the RCMP. Canada's national police force shifted from a policy of surveillance triggered by the "problem" of closeted "homosexuals" (who were deemed vulnerable to blackmail), to RCMP and local police surveillance as necessitated by the "problem" of gay men and lesbians having a public presence (Kinsman & Gentile, 2010, pp. 243–5, 263). In the mid to late 1970s, the public clampdown on queer visibility took a new form: combined RCMP and municipal police surveillance, raids, and mass arrests in Ottawa, Montreal, and Toronto gay bars, bathhouses, and political organizations (Hannon, 1982, p. 273, Kinsman & Gentile, 2010, pp. 304–5, 310–12). This practice of police surveilling and raiding Canadian urban spaces frequented by gays and lesbians was not simply a response to queer visibility; in concert with mainstream media coverage, this formal surveillance both augmented and problematized the visibility of gay men.

The mainstream media contributed to the public criminalization of gay men in the 1970s by forging links in the chain of surveillance at a number of significant points. Articles clipped from mainstream and alternative newspapers found their way into RCMP files, presumably to support surveillance operations (Kinsman & Gentile, 2010, pp. 247, 298). The police leaked information obtained through surveillance and arrests to journalists, who then published articles that named people rounded up during raids – articles that sometimes included hyperbolic and unfounded claims about legal evidence (Kinsman & Gentile, 2010, p. 305). Sensationalist media coverage and security policing thus worked in concert to make gay men and lesbians visible as potential sources of pollution to be "cleaned up" (Kinsman & Gentile, 2010, p. 310).

After the murder of Emanuel Jaques, federal bawdy-house legislation, aimed at prohibiting commercial sexual services from being exchanged in a fixed location, further empowered municipal police to carry out active surveillance of bars, bathhouses, and massage parlours on Yonge Street. Police who witnessed "acts of indecency" such as sex between men could enter a bawdy-house and arrest anyone on site as "found-ins" (Kinsman, 1996, p. 339). Later in 1977 and into 1978, gay men and lesbians in Toronto continued to be subjected to active surveillance, undercover policing, and police raids in connection with local queer political organizing to disrupt a visit by anti-gay activist Anita Bryant (Kinsman & Gentile, 2010, pp. 330, 333–5). Charges and arrests stemming from police surveillance, as well as the previously examined sensationalist coverage in the *Globe and Mail* of Emanuel Jaques's murder, brought gays and lesbians to heightened public visibility as criminal suspects.

Surveillance, Media, and (Sexual) Spectacle

The Emanuel Jaques case in 1970s Toronto opens a window onto the ways in which surveillance and media spectacle regulate forms of sexuality and shape urban social relations. As my discussion has shown, the dynamics here are complex and sometimes contradictory, and demand that we think in new ways about surveillance. In this section, I draw out some of the theoretical implications of my argument through an engagement with others working in the field. I consider the role of formal surveillance in imagining and marking some sexualities as dissident; I also consider how analyses of these processes intersect with theories of media surveillance.

Public belonging and ostracism are common themes in the literature on the surveillance of sexual categories and sexualized bodies. Becki Ross (2010) describes intensified citizen and state surveillance of sex workers from the mid-1970s to the mid-1980s as delineating who was legitimate and who was out of place in Vancouver's West End. She argues that clean-up campaigns often literally dictate who can enter a space and who is "trespassing," besides symbolically assigning differential entitlement to rights of citizenship (Ross, 2010, pp. 208, 202). In his examination of present-day surveillance of men in Ottawa parks, Kevin Walby (2009) describes the multiple effects of patrols by National Capital Commission officers – effects that include "normalization of sexuality" (pp. 368, 376), purification of space, and marking of national belonging. He elaborates that "normalization of sexuality" establishes citizenship as heterosexual; in this way, gay sex comes to be known through a lens that renders it a problem. Writing in the British context, and turning to journalistic practices, Phil Hubbard (2001) points out that in periodic discussions of "national values," when the moral beliefs of a nation are being debated or redrawn, there is a tendency for sexual practices to be held up for questioning in sensationalist, fear-laden media coverage (p. 53). The effect is often a "heterosexual-izing" of the nation, such that some acts and actors are said to be incommensurate with good and therefore full citizenship (Hubbard, 2001, p. 52). For Hubbard, one condition of full citizenship is access to and use of "national" territories. When citizenship is "heterosexualized," so too is public space: when some cis-gendered or gender-conforming man–woman demonstrations of affection are normalized, people who appear or act "gay" or "lesbian" are marked as abnormal. As Kinsman and Gentile, Ross, and Walby indicate, the access of "sexual dissidents" to public space and citizenship thus becomes constrained (Hubbard, 2001, pp. 55–6). In Toronto in the late 1970s, police surveillance, legal regulation, and sensationalist coverage contributed directly to a trampling of civil rights (Ng, 1981, p. 83); more broadly, such actions can be understood as a process of marking sexual dissidence and constraining the right to the city.

What I am tracing here is a cyclical process. At its outset are sexualized bodies marked as suspect, whose movements must be tracked and otherwise contained. But this is also an end point. We come to know those bodies (as sexual and suspect) through a combination of technologies that render them visible and subject to scrutiny. Hubbard (2001) suggests that for sexually marginalized people and communities, access to public space is perhaps not the most pressing issue; more urgent for us is privacy, that is, the ability to evade "the gaze of the state and the law" (p. 65). The surveillant gaze renders the "crime" of sexual indecency publicly visible in order to further mark and expel "sexual dissidents." Having been brought into being and visibility as threats *in* the public and *to* the public, gay men in 1970s Toronto could legitimately be placed under surveillance by the media and the police. As hypervisible and criminalized bodies, they were denied their claims to national belonging and their right to fully occupy public space.

Shari Dworkin and Linda Wachs (1998) provide another take on the role of media surveillance in pathologizing gay men's bodies. In their analysis of the 1990s mainstream coverage of the HIV/AIDS status of US sports celebrities Magic Johnson and Greg Louganis, Dworkin and Wachs (1998) found that articles on Johnson repeatedly reflected shock at the possibility of a straight man becoming HIV-positive, while Louganis's seroconversion was normalized by journalists, consistent with a Christian fundamentalist view of gay men as predisposed to AIDS. Drawing on Foucault, Dworkin and Wachs (1998) suggest that we understand these media narratives as surveillance because they shape what is thinkable (and unthinkable). The stories the media chose to run about Johnson and Louganis, and the ways in which those stories were framed, asserted the natural and unchanging character of identity categories, associated gay men with danger, and attached blame for AIDS to gay men's bodies and sexual practices (Dworkin & Wachs, 1998, p. 3). These methods of rendering publicly visible and knowable both "gay" and therefore "straight" sexualities engage a simultaneous process of casting out and privileging (Dworkin & Wachs, 1998, pp. 12–14).

Thomas Mathiesen (1997), whose work I introduced earlier, provides a historical approach to understanding media surveillance. Twenty years after the 1977 publication in English of Foucault's *Discipline and Punish*, Mathiesen proposed an amendment to one of the most enduring concepts from that text: the panopticon as an architectural design, a (concealed) way of looking, and a schema of modern systems of power. He writes that Foucault was seeking to demonstrate several significant changes in the penal system and in society as a whole. Foucault illustrated this shift with two distinct historical moments in Paris: he opened *Discipline and Punish* with a description of a public execution in 1757, then contrasted it with the highly scheduled routine of one prison inmate in 1838 (Mathiesen, 1997, pp. 216–17). As public spectacles of punishment were modernized, a technique of power was introduced in prisons and more gradually into everyday life. Foucault posited that between the mid-eighteenth and mid-nineteenth centuries, the sovereign's spectacular manifestations of authority witnessed and consumed by the masses were replaced with the daily exercise of panopticism by "the few" within the confines of the prison (Mathiesen, 1997, p. 218).

Mathiesen concedes this proliferation of panopticism, but only up to a point. He does agree that panoptical surveillance has taken hold within the prison system, in policing more broadly, and in social institutions such as schools and psychiatric facilities. However, where Foucault (according to Mathiesen) says that spectacles of power "gradually yield" to hidden panoptical surveillance, Mathiesen insists there was concurrent development of mechanisms for "the many to see and contemplate the few" (1997, p. 218). We might say it is the "from" and "to" – Foucault's suggestion that the emergence of panopticism caused a rupture and displaced spectacle – that raises questions for Mathiesen, given such evidence as pre-eighteenth-century manifestations of panopticism (e.g., the Spanish Inquisition), as well as the expanding, multiplying forms and functions of mass media that accompanied and perhaps even defined modernization. Mathiesen is certainly not alone in contending that the culture of spectacle is alive and well. Douglas Kellner (2003), following on Guy Debord, provides an exhaustive list of early-twenty-first-century examples of "media spectacle ... invading every field of experience, from the economy to culture and everyday life to politics and war" (p. 10).

Just as Mathiesen revised Foucault, others have taken up the former's approach with some caveats. Aaron Doyle (2011), for example, concurs that the panopticon and synopticon are "parallel systems of control" and that "the mass media are often a key institution of social control, especially in the politics of crime" (pp. 287–8, 296), but he argues for greater complexity than he sees in some of Mathiesen's analysis. Specifically, Doyle reads Mathiesen as equating all media coverage with surveillance and as concluding that the prospects for resistance are grim. Instead, Doyle argues that while mass media can indeed generate support for state surveillance (by oversimplifying events and players, failing to provide context, and overdramatizing consequences), media can also mobilize opposition to it. David Lyon (2006) similarly contends that the possibility of resistance was not rendered in Mathiesen's paradigm and that this was an oversight.[5] Nevertheless, we can see that mainstream media coverage of the murder of Emanuel Jaques shows the inseparability of synopticism and panopticism insofar as representations of punishment (arrest, prosecution, conviction, incarceration, deportation) often include images of state/police might (Doyle, 2011, p. 288). Those mediated performances of state authority – the footage of police escorting handcuffed suspects, the staged press conference with a phalanx of uniformed figures around their chief, the overhead photos of anonymous officers in riot gear encircling a crowd of protesters – may be intended to remind us of the force and reach of state power, whether or not that effect is achieved.

Kathryn Conrad's (2009) study of state and media surveillance of queer people in Northern Ireland shows that the Jaques case was by no means unique to its time. Much as in Canada, in Northern Ireland the late 1970s were a period of heightened police activity around popular cruising and public or semipublic sex spots. "Homosexual activity" had been decriminalized in Britain in 1967, yet it remained punishable by life in prison in Northern Ireland until 1982 (Conrad, 2009, p. 14). More than two decades after decriminalization, in 2006, police surveillance of public toilets in Belfast resulted in a raid where twelve men were arrested and ten were fined for sexual offences. Conrad asserts that surveillance did not culminate in the raid; rather, it operated jointly through media spectacle with the publication in the *Belfast Telegraph* of the names, addresses, and photographs of the men arrested. Conrad writes that the newspaper coverage can be connected to serious life-altering consequences that followed for the accused, including loss of home and job, as well as harassment and threats. One of the arrested men ultimately committed suicide.

As we saw in previous discussions of "cleaning up" and heterosexualizing public space, these conjoined processes of synopticism and panopticism have implications for social belonging and participation. Consider what Conrad (2009) calls the "feedback loop": surveillance of already scrutinized groups contributes to "normalizing visibility," which then also regulates queer spatial practices (p. 7). To my mind, expectations about what is "normal" and therefore can occur in public, and what is "indecent" and therefore must be hidden or scrutinized, or both – what Lyon (2006) might call "the politics of visibility" (p. 36) – can certainly be understood as structuring the symbolic closet, but the subtext of those expectations and their broader effects relate to the limits of belonging. With its attendant paradox of discretion and deceit, the closet shapes the accessibility of actual public spaces (for gathering socially, politically, sexually, or otherwise) and thereby conditions the characteristics of the public and inclusion therein (Conrad, 2009, p. 23). For example, Conrad suggests that the social-spatial policing of gay men has shaped "the push toward privatisation" (2009, p. 16) – that is, the late-twentieth- and early-twenty-first-century political strategy whereby some gay activists distance themselves from sexualized (public) culture and present instead an image of respectable domesticity. Kellner (2003), writing about the post-9/11 era, similarly describes news coverage, consumer culture, and the rise of the Internet as spectacles that contribute to alienation, passivity, and depoliticization while generating more corporate profit. We might imagine these spectacles as orienting people inwards, but in shaping our sense of ourselves, they also shape our relations with one another as well as the possibility of collectivity.

What Mark Andrejevic (2005) calls "lateral surveillance" offers another model of collective watching and another bewildering moment of alienation and union. By his account, lateral surveillance entails a disparate collection of individuals each watching its own individual target: "not the top-down monitoring of employees by employers, citizens by the state, but rather the peer-to-peer surveillance of spouses, friends, and relatives" (2005, p. 481). But Internet searches of prospective dates or employees is not simply a third mode of watching (what we might call "the few" watching "the few"), because those individual acts of horizontal monitoring are bound by a sense of collective, almost democratic, responsibility. Andrejevic suggests that this practice of "keeping track of one another" (2005, p. 485) amounts to a meeting place between risk society and governmentality, reflecting a perception of social causation when it comes to danger, and thus a shared burden. This notion of shared accountability for risk can be seen in a distributed or "offloaded" approach to monitoring risk, whereby many "subjects of the gaze" are charged with individually protecting national security at airports, for example (Andrejevic, 2005, pp. 485–6). While not all media coverage is explicitly about reporting risk and so is not necessarily generative of this sideways gaze, the belief in "protective" watching constitutes the group (as imperilled), as well as the self within that collectivity (as responsible or even entitled to be vigilant). This sense of mutual care would be heart-warming, and might seem to offer an antidote to isolationist individualism, were it not for the paradoxical state of privacy vis-à-vis what is and can be public.

In Toronto during the late summer of 1977, newspaper coverage and state surveillance brought gay men into view as a problem, in such a way that this visibility contained within it the justification to remain watchful. State surveillance carried out by police is surely part of a process of marking and expulsion, but it is not the first or only point of departure. Nor is its justification secured only once. Public forms of scrutiny, such as the media, serve as precursors to surveillance, though we might equally consider formal surveillance as an extension of the public hypervisibility that attends marking as sexually, racially, or politically other. To be made a target of surveillance is already to have been shown to be outside of or even against national interests, and in turn, surveillance (re)confirms that suspicion.

Here we have another facet of the process of making known: it was not only gay men who were brought into being through media and state surveillance. Also created was an imaginary collective with a duty to watch, whose members could know themselves as responsible and "not them" by virtue of directly monitoring suspected threats or authorizing representatives to do so. The divisive relations shaped by formal and informal surveillance remind us of another shared facet of work by Foucault and Mathiesen: attention to panopticism and synopticism as mechanisms of power. Perhaps we might consider how individual acts of "informing ourselves," of making public and making *a* public, become tied into securitization that expels those who must be known.

Conclusion

In Toronto newspaper accounts from August 1977, the murder of Emanuel Jaques emerged as a focus for general social unease about changing sexual values. I have situated the portrait painted by the media of Yonge and Dundas within a larger canvas, coloured and contoured by the 1969 changes to the Criminal Code, by the new class of shopper sought for the Eaton Centre, by the increasing numbers of bars on and around Yonge Street, and by proposed amendments to the Ontario Human Rights Code. My contextualizing is a response to what I see as the *Globe and Mail*'s attempt to activate triggers in their representation of the murder of Emanuel Jaques. The mythologizing of Jaques and the crime done to him, and the demonizing of the perpetrators of the crime and the scene of the crime, engaged both a way of seeing and a justification for surveillance. The mood created by sensationalizing his murder provided an opening for the enforcement of dramatic spatial and personal restrictions. In managing the putative crisis, the government and police established themselves as in control and as protectors of the common good. As the limits around the expression of "homosexuality" were redrawn, public space was defined as the arena for the state to articulate and impose its version of Canadian values. It would seem that one of the values espoused through these events was the good citizen's burden to be watchful and fearful, especially of signs of sexual difference.

The murder of Emanuel Jaques was mobilized for political gain because of what it could be made to tap into: tales of gay men as child molesters and murderers, and beliefs about Yonge Street being a slum that menaced good and respectable people and indeed the nation. I am suggesting that newspapers did more than simply report the events as they occurred: newspapers contributed to a campaign of formal and informal surveillance and spatial regulation by sensationalizing the details of the case, and through their choices of stories. The resulting campaign reinforced stereotypes and produced a climate of imperilled heterosexuality and "family" values. I have given my attention here to what was made visible, to how mechanisms of surveillance shape social belonging, but it should also be noted that surveillant visibility occludes as much as it makes known. We should certainly consider how social and political struggles for sexual liberation were displaced in Toronto newspapers in August 1977, but we have a further responsibility to think about how Emanuel Jaques and his family were rendered invisible by the state and media spectacle that supposedly was meant to honour him.

NOTES

I would like to thank Rob Heynen and Emily van der Meulen for their patient and thorough editorial work on this chapter. Gary Kinsman generously answered my questions about security policing in Toronto during the 1970s. I am also grateful for questions and suggestions from Debi Brock, Amanda Glasbeek, and the University of Toronto Press anonymous reviewers. Thank you to Carolyn King for cartographic work.

1 Deborah Brock's (1998) sources indicate that 224 charges were laid against "inmates" and "keepers" of common bawdy-houses in the period from the middle of July to the beginning of September 1977, compared to 16 charges laid between June and July of the same year. In July 1977, there were 40 "adult entertainment" shops on Yonge Street. By November, there were only 4, and in December 1978, "the last body rub parlour on Yonge Street closed its doors" (Brock, 1998, p. 36).

2 Thankfully, in the same issue *The Globe* printed a letter from a man protesting an earlier article about the negative effects of changes to the Ontario Human Rights Code: "Must it be said yet again? Child molesting is almost entirely a heterosexual male problem. Thus openly gay teachers would be no more likely to harm their pupils than openly heterosexual male teachers" (Barnes, 1977, p. 6).

3 See James Bow's work on the Transit Toronto website (transit.toronto.on.ca). Note that the Huron-Wendat are now Wyandot.

4 This spatial expansion of gay culture was gender-specific, according to Becki Ross (1995). Ross notes that lower incomes among lesbians, especially those who were parents, working class, and/or people of colour, translated into fewer specifically lesbian bars and commercial social spaces. She also ties the relative invisibility of lesbian sexuality to there being less police and legal regulation than what gay men experience

(pp. 36–37). Ross thus shows that conditions of visibility are mediated by gender and racialization.

5 Certainly in this moment of celebrating Edward Snowden and criticizing Communications Security Establishment Canada, the media's decrying of state surveillance is a recognizable phenomenon. See for example the following *Globe and Mail* editorials: "Metadata spying is spying" (4 February 2014); "Needed: More eyes on Canada's spies" (2 February 2014); and "2013: The year of snooping" (27 December 2013). See also *Globe and Mail* articles such as "Snowden leaks 'justified,' NSA violated public trust: Media editorials" (2 January 2014); and "The silence over privacy puts our freedoms at risk" (Ann Cavoukian, 27 January 2014). David Lyon (2006) argues that audience reception offers a further level of resistance to the synopticon: because meanings and their effects are contextual, there is no direct, causal relationship between coverage of crime and fear. Audiences can actively generate meaning. However, Lyon also acknowledges that not all forms of watching are equal in their social currency, since "the major media conglomerates monopolize official images" and "some forms of watching carry more weight than others" (2006, p. 39).

REFERENCES

Andrejevic, M. (2005). The work of watching one another: Lateral surveillance, risk, and governance. *Surveillance & Society*, 2(4), 479–497.
Baker, A. (1977a, 12 August). Metro aims to shut down sex shops. *Globe and Mail*, p. 1.
Baker, A. (1977b, 17 August). A long race for mayor: Term of three-time winner Crombie still has more than a year to run but stalking O'Donohue vows his old rival won't get another "free ride." *Globe and Mail*, p. 5.
Barc, A. (2010, 23 December). The origins of the Eaton Centre. http://www.blogto.com/city/2010/12/the_origins_of_the_eaton_centre
Barnes, C. (1977, 1 August). Gay Rights. *Globe and Mail*, p. 6.
Beddoes, D. (1977a, 5 August). In sorrow and anger. *Globe and Mail*, p. 8.
Beddoes, D. (1977b, 10 August). Gays on guilt: Blame media. *Globe and Mail*, p. 8.
Belisle, D. 2011. *Retail nation: Department stores and the making of modern Canada*. Vancouver, BC: UBC Press.
Benson, D. (2012, 4 December). Then & now: Stages. *The Grid*, pp. 10–11.
Berchem, F. R. (1996). *Opportunity road: Yonge Street 1860–1939*. Toronto: Natural Heritage/Natural History Inc.

Boyle, R. (1977, 17 August). Metro Council votes to ask province for ban on nude entertainment where alcohol served. *Globe and Mail*, pp. 1, 2.

Brock, D. R. (1998). *Making work, making trouble: Prostitution as a social problem.* Toronto, ON: University of Toronto Press.

Bruner, A. (1977a, 20 August). An appetite for sex is measured at Clarke. *Globe and Mail*, p. 2.

Bruner, A. (1977b, 20 August). Only cure for dangerous sex sadists is castration, Metro psychiatrist says. *Globe and Mail*, pp. 1, 2.

Carriere, V. (1978, 23 February). Boy drowned after sex attack, pathologist says at Jaques trial. *Globe and Mail*, p. 5.

Carriere, V., & Strauss, M. (1978, 15 February). Accused split boy's $3 after raping, killing him, court is told. *Globe and Mail*, p. 5.

Cohen, P. (1997). Out of the melting pot into the fire next time: Imagining the east end as city, body, text. In S. Westwood & J. Williams (Eds.), *Imagining cities: Scripts, signs, memory* (pp. 73–85). New York, NY: Routledge.

Conrad, K. (2009). "Nothing to hide ... nothing to fear": Discriminatory surveillance and queer visibility in Great Britain and Northern Ireland. In N. Giffney & M. O'Rourke (Eds.), *Ashgate research companion to queer theory* (pp. 1–29). Surrey, UK: Ashgate.

De Sa, A. (2013). *Kicking the sky.* Toronto, ON: Doubleday Canada.

Doyle, A. (2011). Revisiting the synopticon: Reconsidering Mathiesen's "The Viewer Society" in the age of Web 2.0. *Theoretical Criminology, 15*(3), 283–299. http://dx.doi.org/10.1177/1362480610396645

Dworkin, S. L., & Wachs, F. L. (1998). "Disciplining the body": HIV-Positive male athletes, media surveillance, and the policing of sexuality. *Sociology of Sport Journal, 15*, 1–20.

Finlay, M. L. (1977, 23 February). Take 30 [Video]. http://www.cbc.ca/archives/categories/economy-business/consumer-goods/eatons-a-canadian-institution-1/jewel-in-the-crown.html

Globe and Mail. (1977a, 1 August). Search is intensified for missing boy, 12, p. 1.

Globe and Mail. (1977b, 3 August). Services tomorrow: Funeral, burial plot are provided free, p. 5.

Hall, R. (1977, 1 August). Gay rights. *Globe and Mail*, p. 6.

Hill, J. (1977a, 11 August). Assistant Crown assigned to handle Yonge strip charges: 330 offences alleged since July 11. *Globe and Mail*, p. 5.

Hill, J. (1977b, 24 August). Strip is dying but girls are lively. *Globe and Mail*, p. 1.

Hannon, G. (1982). Raids, rage, and bawdyhouses. In E. Jackson & S. Persky (Eds.), *Flaunting it! A decade of gay journalism from The Body Politic* (pp. 273–294). Toronto, ON: Newstar Books & Pink Triangle Press.

Hubbard, P. (2001). Sex zones: Intimacy, citizenship, and public space. *Sexualities, 4*(1), 51–71. http://dx.doi.org/10.1177/136346001004001003

Iacovetta, F. (2006). *Gatekeepers: Reshaping immigrant lives in Cold War Canada.* Toronto, ON: Between the Lines.

Jackson, E. (1982). Introduction. In E. Jackson & S. Persky (Eds.), *Flaunting it! A decade of gay journalism from The Body Politic* (pp. 1–6). Toronto, ON: Newstar Books & Pink Triangle Press.

Keating, M. (1977, 3 August). Suspect in boy's slaying remanded, segregated in jail. *Globe and Mail*, p. 1.

Keating, M. (1978, 17 January). Picking jury slows trial of 4 in boy's slaying. *Globe and Mail*, p. 5.

Keenan, E. (2014, 24 April). Minor threat. *The Grid*, p. 13.

Kellner, D. (2003). *Media spectacle.* New York, NY: Routledge. http://dx.doi.org/10.4324/9780203166383

Kilbourn, W. (1984). *Toronto remembered: A celebration of the city.* Toronto, ON: Stoddart.

Kinsman, G. (1987). *The regulation of desire: Sexuality in Canada.* Montreal, QC: Black Rose Books.

Kinsman, G. (1996). *The regulation of desire: Homo and hetero sexualities* (2nd ed.). Montreal, QC: Black Rose Books.

Kinsman, G., & Gentile, P. (2010). *Canadian war on queers: National security as sexual regulation.* Vancouver, BC: UBC Press.

Lavigne, Y. (1977, 11 August). Male hookers upset McMurtry. *Globe and Mail*, p. 5.

Lynch, M. (1977, September). Media fosters bigotry with murder coverage. *Body Politic*, pp. 1, 4.

Lyon, D. (2006). 9/11, synopticon, and scopophilia: Watching and being watched. In R.V. Ericson & K. D. Haggerty (Eds.), *The new politics of surveillance and visibility* (pp. 35–54). Toronto, ON: University of Toronto Press.

Marshall, S. (2011, April 13). The end of Yonge Street. *Spacing.* http://spacing.ca/toronto/2011/04/13/the-end-of-yonge-street

Mathiesen, T. (1997). The viewer society: Michel Foucault's "panopticon" revisited. *Theoretical Criminology, 1*(2), 215–234. http://dx.doi.org/10.1177/1362480697001002003

McGiven, E. (Host). (1966, March 1). Toronto File [Radio]. http://www.cbc.ca/archives/categories/economy-business/consumer-goods/eatons-extra-clips/unveiling-plans-for-the-eaton-centre.html

McLeod, D. W. (1996). *Lesbian and gay liberation in Canada: A selected annotated chronology, 1964–1975.* Toronto, ON: ECW Press.

Miranda, S. P. (2009). Portuguese women's activism in Toronto's building cleaning industry, 1975–1986. In C. Teixeira & V. M. P. Da Rosa (Eds.), *The*

Portuguese in Canada: Diasporic challenges and adjustment (pp. 109–135). Toronto, ON: University of Toronto Press.

Ng, Y. C. Y. (1981). *Ideology, media, and moral panics: An analysis of the Jaques murder*. (Unpublished masters thesis). University of Toronto.

Plummer, K. (2012, 20 October). The eventful history of the Church of the Holy Trinity. http://torontoist.com/2012/10/historicist-the-heart-of-the-city

Porambo, R. (1977a, 4 August). The next child may be yours: The neighbors march for Manuel. *Globe and Mail*, p. 4.

Porambo, R. (1977b, 3 August). Police no longer hassle gays on strip, homosexual says. *Globe and Mail*, p. 5.

Porambo, R. (1977c, 5 August). Shoeshine boy's funeral tugs at the heart of strangers. *Globe and Mail*, p. 5.

Rogers, B. (1977, 9 August). 15,000 march on City Hall, Legislature over boy's slaying. *Globe and Mail*, p. 1.

Rose, A. (1958). *Regent Park: A study in slum clearance*. Toronto, ON: University of Toronto Press.

Ross, B. L. (1995). *The house that Jill built: A lesbian nation in formation*. Toronto, ON: University of Toronto Press.

Ross, B. L. (2010). Sex and (evacuation from) the city: The moral and legal regulation of sex workers in Vancouver's West End, 1975–1985. *Sexualities*, *13*(2), 197–218. http://dx.doi.org/10.1177/1363460709359232

Strauss, M. (1978a, 9 February). One of 4 men pleads guilty in Jaques case. *Globe and Mail*, p. 1.

Strauss, M. (1978b, 13 February). Accused confessed to murder of shoeshine boy, court is told. *Globe and Mail*, p. 5.

Tassy, M. (1996). Yonge when I was younger. In S. J. Brown (Ed.), *Researching Yonge Street* (pp. 102–106). Toronto, ON: Ontario Genealogical Society, Toronto Branch.

Temple, W. H. (1977, 15 August). Yonge Strip. *Globe and Mail*, p. 6.

Walby, K. (2009). "He asked me if I was looking for fags …": Ottawa's National Capital Commission conservation officers and the policing of public park sex. *Surveillance & Society*, *6*(4), 367–379.

Warner, T. (2002). *Never going back: A history of queer activism in Canada*. Toronto, ON: University of Toronto Press.

Weaver, J. C. (1979). The modern city realized: Toronto civic affairs, 1880–1915. In A. F. J. Artibise & G. A. Stelter (Eds.), *The usable urban past: Planning and politics in the modern Canadian city* (pp. 39–72). Toronto, ON: Macmillan.

York, M., & Lipovenko, D. (1977, 2 August). Body on sex-shop roof: 4 men charged with murder; missing boy, 12, was drowned. *Globe and Mail*, pp. 1–2.

Chapter 10

The Surveillance Web: Surveillance, Risk, and Resistance in Ontario Strip Clubs

TUULIA LAW AND CHRIS BRUCKERT

Notwithstanding contemporary fashion and exercise fads that suggest attitudes towards erotic dance are changing, the Second Wave feminist conception of strip clubs as voyeuristic environments, where women are passive objects of the male gaze (cf. Mulvey, 1975), continues to hold conceptual sway. Indeed, while it is true that strip clubs would not exist but for the patronage of their almost exclusively male clientele, the gaze of clients comprises only a portion of the watching in strip clubs (Murphy, 2003; Egan, 2004). In this chapter we destabilize assumptions about the male gaze by examining what we call the surveillance web. This web of surveillance is composed of lines of sight that pervade the strip club and are filtered through gendered and raced scripts. Although we build on the work of Egan (2004) and surveillance scholars insofar as we explore the links between surveillance, power, and social control, we depart from their emphases on technological forms, suggesting instead that embodied surveillance remains a significant feature of workplaces.

This reflection draws on eleven in-depth semistructured interviews with male third parties[1] working with female strippers (two managers, two disc jockeys, three disc jockey/managers, one doorman/bouncer, two bouncer/managers, and one individual who provided protection and driving services) and two focus group interviews with eight female erotic dancers.[2] Starting from the insights of these participants, who work/worked in Ottawa and/or Toronto strip clubs, we come to appreciate the centrality of gendered risk management in strip club surveillance practices. As Carol Smart (1992) notes, "woman has always been both kind and killing, active and aggressive, virtuous and evil" (p. 36). However, in strip clubs the dualism is informed by stigmatic assumptions predicated on notions of risk – erotic dancers (like sex workers) are conceptualized as simultaneously *at risk* and *risky* (Bruckert & Hannem, 2013). This tension speaks to the "myriad of ways in which risk and morality are entwined" (Ericson & Doyle, 2003, p. 3). On the one hand, erotic dancers' "shameless displays" of sexuality are perceived to pose a threat (risk) to the moral fibre of society and women's equality; on the other hand, the dancers themselves are assumed to be vulnerable (at risk) for assault, sexually transmitted illness, and exploitation. This reading of strippers' gendered bodies exists alongside stereotypical scripts of risks read onto racialized bodies. We argue that these notions of gendered risk/riskiness intersect with racialization and play out in surveillance by multiple actors in strip clubs, not in a technological "surveillant assemblage" (Haggerty & Ericson, 2000) but in a decidedly low-tech surveillance web (but see McCahill, 2002).[3]

As we map and unpack the multiple forms, locations, and subjects of surveillance in strip clubs, we find intersecting and converging lines of sight in which all spaces are (in principle) visible; but at the same time, we find temporal holes where social actors resist and/or are wilfully blind. Unravelling the threads of the surveillance web allows us to explore the complex and at times contradictory ways in which risk and surveillance converge; doing so also positions us to reflect on disciplinary power, governance, and social sorting that pivot on notions of at-risk/riskiness. And it positions us to "see" how social actors negotiate the environment, engaging in resistance and subversion. We begin by sketching the scene in order to provide the necessary context for the conceptual framing and subsequent analysis.

Setting the Stage: Strip Clubs in Ontario

The main attraction of a strip club is of course *the strippers* – indeed, without them the establishment would simply be a dark, gloomy bar serving overpriced drinks. Although it is their presence that makes the establishment appealing to clients, dancers receive little or no remuneration from the club; instead, they earn their income directly from customers, for whom they provide personalized services in the form of twenty-dollar lap dances and/or companionship in (usually) private champagne rooms, also called VIP rooms. Dancers are therefore not (technically speaking) employed by strip clubs; instead, they are contractors who pay a fee (from $10 to $50) to use the physical space of the club and the services it offers (e.g., security), which they require to perform their jobs (Bruckert, 2002; Law, 2012). That said, since strippers must conform to club rules and expectations, their relationship with management is in some ways decidedly employee-like. In real terms, this means that erotic dancers are treated like employees while being denied the rights and protections such workers generally enjoy.

The ambiguous position of erotic dancers as contractors/employees is further complicated by the hyper-regulation of the clubs in which they labour. Although these are lawful establishments, they are subject to directives that facilitate and increase state surveillance over and above the restrictions and oversight imposed on mainstream businesses (Bruckert & Dufresne, 2002). This speaks to their status as *morally* suspect and *risky* enterprises. This structural stigma (Hannem, 2012) is evident in municipal by-laws, premised on the potential for contamination, that severely restrict the spaces that strip clubs are permitted to occupy (van der Meulen & Durisin, 2008; see also Hubbard, 2009). This form of state surveillance extends into and shapes the geography of the club itself: Ottawa's by-laws stipulate that the physical layout of the club must meet the approval of municipal officials (City of Ottawa, 2004); Toronto's by-law exercised similar oversight until it was repealed in 2013 (City of Toronto, 2012). Municipal regulation also includes the licensing of owners, managers, and (in some cities, including Toronto) dancers. Licences constitute surveillance insofar as they require criminal record checks (applicants who have been convicted of prostitution-related offences are refused) and are kept on file and occasionally verified by the municipality.

Most significantly, the by-laws in Toronto and Ottawa prohibit touching between dancers and customers (City of Ottawa, 2004; City of Toronto, 2010, 2013). In effect, this means that lap dancing with physical contact – the principal source of strippers' income – is legally prohibited albeit a common practice. As such, club owners, dancers, and patrons have been charged with contravening municipal by-laws and federal laws (e.g., relating to bawdy-houses) (Lewis, 2000; Bruckert, 2002). Although the by-laws were ostensibly put in place to protect their health and safety (Bruckert, 2002; Bruckert & Dufresne, 2002), dancers are charged disproportionately more often than customers (Lewis, 2000). In short, assumptions about dancers being at-risk/risky underlie state surveillance and enforcement practices. We now turn to examine how these assumptions inform managerial surveillance.

Unpacking Surveillance

Although technological and workplace surveillance has been subject to theoretical reflection and empirical study,[4] little surveillance analysis has been done on strip clubs. A notable exception is Egan (2004), who has examined surveillance as an instrument of social control at a strip club in the United States. Drawing on Foucault, Egan argues that the gaze of the club owner is rendered panoptic via cameras positioned throughout the club. She contends that although this panopticon facilitates surveillance by security and management, as well as self-surveillance by and peer surveillance among dancers, regulatory power is disrupted by dancers' strategic acts of resistance. As a result, the strip club is an environment of simultaneous repression and subversion – an imperfect panopticon.

Egan's analysis of site-specific surveillance effectively challenges and complicates normative assumptions about the sex industry as a locus of oppression. However, surveillance scholars, in theorizing about technological forms of surveillance on a larger scale, have moved beyond the panopticon to take into account the "multiplication of the sites of surveillance [which] ruptures the unidirectional nature of the gaze" (Haggerty, 2006, p. 29; see also Lyon, 2006). For example, focusing primarily on data collection technologies, Lyon (2007) defines surveillance as "the focused, systematic and routine attention to personal details for the purposes of influence, management, protection or direction" (p. 14). Haggerty and Ericson (2000) expand on this, introducing the concept of the technological "surveillant assemblage" that scrutinizes, targets, and intervenes by generating data doubles, through a network that is rhizome-like in its continual expansion and its ability to level hierarchies of observation by integrating disparate systems into a larger whole.

While data doubles are an important part of sorting and classification, which Lyon (2007) insists are both central to surveillance, they are particular to electronic forms. If technological surveillance relies on meticulously collected data to engage in social sorting (Koskela, 2012), everyday surveillance by social actors, in its relatively limited reach, necessarily pivots on social identity (Goffman, 1963) – that is, on the attributes ascribed to an individual by others that are realized in interaction. As a case in point, in this chapter we will see that surveillance practices in strip clubs are informed by the ascription of particular gendered attributes – specifically, by the dualistic conception of women as hypervulnerable and manipulative seductresses, or as both at risk and risky. In this regard, looking at surveillance at the level of human interaction allows us to consider its purposes as well as its consequences (both intended and unintended) through an analysis of how ascribed attributes, gendered and racialized tropes, and stereotypes converge in a particular time and place and play out in the lives of social actors – in other words, the *embodiedness* of surveillance.

Moreover, while we appreciate that the surveillant assemblage moves beyond Foucault's "static, unidirectional panopticon metaphor" (Ball, 2005, p. 93), we require a model that allows not only for multidirectionality but also for divergence. To reflect these concerns, we use the metaphor of a surveillance web made up of networks of actors with particular lines of sight, which overlap but do not necessarily all converge or work coherently together. We must also take heed of Lyon's (2007) reminder that "surveillance is always hinged to some specific purposes" (pp. 14–15) – purposes that in and of themselves are neither inherently negative nor inherently positive. In this way, we retain Foucault's insight regarding the role of surveillance in disciplinary regimes while keeping in mind Mathiesen's (1997) insistence that surveillance may not always play a disciplinary role. We now turn to our data to map and unpack the diverse forms, directions, and tactics of surveillance in strip clubs.

Mapping the Surveillance Web

In a world where surveillance is so often associated with CCTV cameras and, more recently, with governments' sophisticated spying on the online activities of their own citizens (see, for example, the information released by Edward Snowden), most surveillance in strip clubs is decidedly low-tech. At the clubs where Tony (manager/DJ), Reverend (doorman/manager), and Donna and Charlene (dancers) worked, security cameras were used for surveillance, but unlike in the strip clubs Egan (2004) examined, those cameras were not the primary tools of surveillance. Instead, surveillance was distributed through a network: bartenders and waitresses watched dancers' and patrons' alcohol consumption, disc jockeys (DJs) monitored dancers' performances and interactions with customers, and bouncers watched the behaviour of both customers and dancers (see also Murphy, 2003; Lewis, 2006; Price-Glynn, 2010; Lavin, 2013).

Managers organized and participated in this surveillance network, shouldering considerable responsibility. Adam (manager/DJ) described being a manager as follows: "You kind of supervise every-body. You always got your eye on the bartender, the wait staff. Even the cook, if there's a kitchen." This finding echoes DeMichele and Tewks-bury's (2004) insistence that other employees, such as security person-nel, are subject to surveillance – for example, in regard to drug and alcohol consumption (see also Lavin, 2013). Similarly, Gilles (manager) described supervising club workers and customers "all the time, every minute … and they don't know." Moreover, managers employed preventive, reactive, and disciplinary approaches to the surveillance of dancers, who were assumed to be both (potentially inadequate) employees and risky/at-risk.

Although strip club owners and managers couch their surveillance of "dancers' every step, breath and move … in terms of 'protection'" (Egan, 2004, p. 304), they are also preoccupied with the dancers' work ethic. In this regard, Tony (manager/DJ) suggested that his role focused on surveilling dancers to ensure they were acting as reliable employees (notwithstanding that they were not technically employees) to "make sure that the girls are signed in, make sure that the time is accurate, make sure they don't leave before their five hour minimum." In con-trast to Egan's (2004) findings, however, cameras appear not to have been used as disciplinary tools. At Charlene's (dancer) club, for exam-ple, a punch clock or registration with the DJ were the preferred meth-ods for verifying whether dancers were on time for their shifts, in spite of the club having what Charlene rhetorically referred to as "a million cameras."

By contrast, DJs had fewer albeit quite specific surveillance responsi-bilities. They were tasked with ensuring good labour practices on stage:

> I just have to make sure that the girl is there if at all possible, and let management know if they aren't, try to maybe motivate some of the girls if they're running late on shows, maybe encourage them to stay longer on stage, you know, making sure that they take off the right – appropriate amount of clothing per song, that kind of stuff. (Chico, DJ)

The apparent ubiquity of managerial surveillance can foster self-regulation. For example, dancers in the Toronto focus group talked about management posting "signs in the change room that say you have to stay fit and keep your hair and nails and look good" (Jen, dancer); furthermore, "if you're not fit by this date … we'll fire you" (Carrie, dancer). This is a reminder of managerial surveillance (see also

Chapkis, 2000), but it is also a disciplinary tool that presents dancers with a choice between self-discipline (keeping or getting fit) and being sanctioned (getting fired). Leigh (dancer) chose the former: "a lot of people hated it and were really mad ... I ended up losing a little bit of weight as incentive from it."

Managerial surveillance is also informed by the legal "grey area" in which lap dancing is situated, as well as by the heightened surveillance by the state and its agents (including municipal by-law officers and police), which fosters a particular focus on avoiding municipal and criminal charges (see also Bruckert, 2002; Murphy, 2003; Egan, 2004; Hubbard & Colosi, 2013). Certainly, managers and security personnel in our research framed their surveillance of dancers as being informed by intersecting safety and legal concerns, given that dancers, being gendered sexualized subjects, are both agents who use their sexuality and potential victims *because of* their sexuality (or as we have previously framed it, they are both risky and at-risk). It is perhaps not surprising that at times, the primary concern seemed to be that dancers would contravene the law by offering sexual services. George (doorman) put it this way: "We're supposed to walk through [the VIP area] to make sure that they're not doing extras [sexual services]." At Tony's (manager/DJ) club, this meant "no grinding" or "sexual activities," and "if the girls are found to be doing sexual activities they will be escorted out of the premises immediately." Surveilling dancers for their perceived "immorality" and related legal riskiness sometimes meant that "[dancers] can't leave the club for more than 15 minutes at a time ... because we're worried girls might be turning tricks in the parking lot" (Studley, DJ). At the same time, this adjacent space was perceived as potentially risky for dancers: "If I see that, you know, there's guys that are waiting [outside], and a girl can't get out without this guy – you know, then I'll go, and I'll arrange for her to get out the back door" (Fuzzy Pickle, DJ). The ways in which concerns about dancers as at-risk and risky converge can be gleaned from the following narrative by Chico (DJ), who oversaw

> everything from a girl on stage taking a tip from a customer going too far. I try and jump in on the microphone, you know, say, "Hey, look, you know, we can't do that," or, "Put your hands on the stage," or, you know, "A doorman's going to come and whack you in the groin if you don't be careful."

Fuzzy Pickle's and Chico's comments alert us that it is not just dancers who are risky – customers, too, are perceived and surveilled as potential risks: "There's always three or four people in security and they have 'security' written on their sweaters ... and they move around quite a bit" (Tony, manager/DJ). Gilles (manager) applied a preventive approach to surveillance by screening customers before they entered the club: "We keep our eyes open, and if we see trouble, we don't let him in." In other clubs, organized crime was a concern: "No [gang] colours ... Because the [gang] colours scare the rest of the customers away" (Dalton, manager). Surveillance, premised on scripts about the "right" way and reason to patronize strip clubs, also occurred after customers entered the establishment. For example, Dalton (manager) perceived "guys who came in by themselves" as a "real flag ... That's an antisocial behaviour in itself."

Managers and security personnel also surveilled customers to ensure they were behaving "appropriately." Leigh (dancer) recalled one such instance, when a manager "tapped [the customer] on the shoulder and said if he couldn't come up with more complimentary ways to cheer for the girls, then he would ask him to leave." Tony (manager/DJ) told us about "keep[ing] your eyes on the customers" to prevent "guys with cell phones taking pictures." It seems that security cameras, when present, were relied on only as a potential source of verification. Reverend (doorman/manager) and Tony (manager/DJ) described using surveillance footage to provide evidence in cases where customer misconduct (e.g., violence or theft) required police attention. Clients may also be risky in monetary terms, and this requires preventive approaches to ensure the economic security of dancers by keeping track of the amount of time they spend with clients in the VIP areas: "You put their [dancers'] name and their time ... It's $20 a song, four minutes a song" (George, doorman).

Not all surveillance focuses on dancers and clients. Scott, a full-time doorman and part-time manager, also surveilled other employees: "As a manager, my job was to also make sure that sort of [inappropriate] behaviour didn't happen with, say, the shooter girls or the waitresses." He also "had to make sure the other doormen didn't take things too far, whether by physical force or just ... be[ing] an asshole."

At times, the interests of dancers and managers converge, and dancers surveil other dancers in the interest of minimizing risks: "A girl who's not clean [provides sexual services] either has to clean her act up – or usually, you know, the girls assume or deter it to make the girl go away

... The girls sort of police themselves that way" (Adam, manager). In the following narrative, Sasha (dancer) corroborates Adam's perception:

> We had this new girl one time, and she didn't really have any boundaries, and she was just doing whatever customers wanted, so the girls – the schedule[d] girls – kind of got together and shamed her out of doing that ... Her behaviour is [now] more in line with the rest of the girls.

According to Sasha, such peer monitoring, or lateral surveillance (Andrejevic, 2005), in the dancer network can give rise to informal collective strategies such as "gossip campaigns," which can be (though not always) an effective way for dancers to protect their health and business interests by limiting customers' expectations of "extras." Lateral surveillance among dancers can in this respect be seen as an extension of individuals' responsibility for themselves that also serves to "fill in" gaps in the managerial surveillance network (see also Andrejevic, 2005). Notably, at the same time, strippers are also resisting managerial authority and subtly subverting hierarchical scripts when they intervene to manage the behaviour of other workers (Bruckert, 2002; see also Murphy, 2003). We expand on dancer resistance in the coming sections.

The Topography of Surveillance: Place, Process, and Practice

Most of the surveillance described above forms part of the managerial network. But dancers and other employees also engage in surveillance for their own purposes. In these respects, while the *space* of the strip club is criss-crossed with the sightlines of the surveillance web, these lines do not converge at a central point, nor is any one actor all-seeing. The capacity of individuals to surveil is also shaped by the physical layout of clubs: "We have to supervise the girls at times – to the best of our ability because it's difficult to get in there" (Reverend, doorman). Sasha (dancer) confirmed that "there were definitely some [champagne rooms], like, that were sort of tucked away in certain corners that girls who did extras would go there with their regulars." Illumination, or rather the lack thereof, creates another barrier to surveillance: "Because clubs are dark and they're done dark on purpose, it's hard to discern the difference [between appropriate and inappropriate activity]" (Adam, manager).

The layout of strip clubs creates hidden spaces, yet in other respects their physical arrangement is designed to facilitate surveillance. Sasha (dancer) described a club where the DJ booth was adjacent to the change room: "various people like the managers and the DJs would come in and nag us about stuff like, you know, 'Get out onto the floor. Stop taking so long to do your hair.'" This kind of perpetual surveillance means that the dancers are denied private space: "We didn't have a place where us girls could just go and do our makeup and fix our hair and bitch about customers. We always had the male staff around us" (Donna, dancer).

Managerial surveillance of dancers' behaviour may even extend beyond the confines of the club. Tony (manager/DJ) described an informal system that functioned, in effect, as an inter-club surveillance network:

> A couple weeks ago I got a call from the bartender at The Candy Apple saying there's two black girls that gave him terrible attitude, so they were almost physically removed from The Candy Apple, and they called us to give us a heads up, cause they heard, they were overheard saying, "Well lets go to Charlie's" ... So we, you know, watch each others' back.

Such inter-club surveillance can affect dancers' job security. Donna (dancer) told us about dancers being "blacklisted" across Ottawa (see also Bouclin, 2009). Tony's specification that the two dancers with "*terrible attitude*" were "*black girls*" also suggests closer monitoring by clubs of certain populations. We explore the issue of social and racial profiling in greater detail later in the chapter.

Surveillance practices may also affect customer satisfaction, according to Adam (manager):

> If you've got a bouncer wandering around and poking his head in the booths every five seconds to make sure something not right is happening, you've ruined it for the client, who's paying good money to enjoy, you know, a dance.

This poses financial challenges for dancers:

> My customers – they weren't really necessarily looking for extras – they just wanted some privacy and to be able to talk and cuddle and, you know, enjoy my time, and to have a bouncer coming in the champagne room literally every song was very distracting to them ... It impacted my business. (Donna, dancer)

Notably speaking to the at-risk/risky tension, this surveillance, while frustrating, also sometimes increased Donna's feeling of security:

"Sometimes when I was in the champagne room, especially when it was a day shift or a Sunday night … I'd be all alone, so I guess in that way, it was nice to have the bouncer walking around."

Surveillance "Blind Spots"

As we have seen, managerial surveillance strategies are informed by perceptions of legal risk. Managers also implement – though they do not necessarily consistently enforce – rules to protect themselves from being charged with prostitution-related or other infractions (see also Jones, Shears, & Hillier, 2003; DeMichele & Tewksbury, 2004; Egan, 2004; Price-Glynn, 2010; Lavin, 2013). To this end they download legal liability onto dancers by positioning themselves as unaware of sexual activity: "You try to put a front on that you were following all the rules" (Dalton, manager). Such wilful blindness temporarily obscures sight-lines in the surveillance web, creating "blind spots." Managers and bouncers told us that they monitored dancers and customers to control the provision of "extras" and the consumption of illegal drugs, but that they also sometimes purposefully turned a blind eye. Managers and doormen spoke of occasionally relaxing their surveillance practices. Scott (doorman/manager) told us "there are some times, special, you know, permission was made, friend of the manager, whatever. And I was not usually involved in that, I'd walk away." According to Studley (DJ), "it's a lot of, you know, if we don't see it happening, it's not happening kind of mentality … If we catch you doing it, then you're in trouble." Adam (manager) highlighted another potential implication of wilful blindness:

> You would hope that, if someone was practising sex in the strip club, which is supposed to be for entertainment and not for sex, that they would practise safe sex. But that's not really something you can police … because that would imply that you accept the fact that it's happening when it's not supposed to be happening.

Addressing alcohol and illicit drug consumption at strip clubs takes what Lavin (2013) characterizes as "the path of least resistance" (p. 362). This seems to involve not only wilful blindness but also discretion. Adam (manager) acknowledged that "the dancers do drugs, the staff do drugs. Um, it's just a business that caters to that sort of thing … And you just deal with it … So [my attitude is] if you're going to do it, try to be discreet about it." In his capacity as a DJ, Chico surveilled dancers' drug and alcohol consumption insofar as it affected the women's ability to do their job: "Girls can't be, you know, falling-down drunk or, you know, under the influence of some drug that they can't do their [stage] show." Others' attitudes towards monitoring drug consumption in the club were decidedly resigned: "All we can do is try and minimize it [drug use]" (Reverend, doorman/manager). In contrast to most managers, who responsibilized dancers to manage their risk "out of sight," Dalton (manager) employed a risk management strategy. Drawing on highly gendered notions of "respectability" (and the need for dancers to manage their risk in the interests of security), he tried to encourage self-discipline:

> If you see a girl who's, you know, getting too drunk, you know, let her know what's going on ... "Listen, you know, you're better than that. You can't make any money [drunk], you know. This is not the kind of image you want to present of yourself. Think about it." ... Only the bad guys want the, you know, the heavy drunk girls. They got bad intentions. (Dalton, manager)

Resistance and Counter-Surveillance

Up to this point we have presented the surveillance networks we uncovered, mapped the topography, process, and practices of strip club surveillance, and spoken of surveillance gaps. Of course the significance of surveillance is complicated by the ability of social actors to resist; in "contexts where surveillance is perceived as or has the effects of control, the fact that its subjects interact and react with surveillance means that its effects are mitigated or magnified in part in relation to their involvement" (Lyon, 2007, p. 7). In other words, surveillance must be understood as part of a dynamic process that, while speaking to power relations, also has the potential to be subverted. This of course brings us back to Foucault (1978) and his understanding of power as permeating all social interactions – as both an effect and a condition of other relations and processes. It follows that resistance is not just inevitable; it is in a reciprocal and constitutive relationship to power. From this point of departure we can appreciate that while managers' wilful blindness can be seen in part as accepting the realities of drug use and the provision of illicit sexual services, it can also be seen as resistance to state surveillance. Bridget (dancer) and Bobby (dancer), for example, both suggested that clubs where they had worked had arrangements to protect dancers from the gaze of the state:

> [Management] would know an hour in advance that licensing was coming in [to inspect and] ... anybody who was unlicensed would leave and come back in a couple hours, and anybody who was licensed was required to stay so that it didn't look suspicious that half the girls were gone. (Bridget, dancer)

This alerts us to another form of counter-surveillance that speaks to strippers' agency and self-determination (and that implicitly challenges normative gender tropes of women's passivity). Dancers watch managers and DJs in order to determine when they are being observed, largely to minimize the risk of being sanctioned for breaking rules (Bruckert, 2002). This counter-surveillance is sometimes complemented by management's wilful blindness. For example, Charlene (dancer) found that

> if you're going to sell drugs at the club, you follow every other rule – you get there on time; you don't mouth off; you don't complain ... They'll let you break this bigger rule if you don't squeak about the smaller things.

Similarly, Bobby (dancer) suggested: "Just do your job and, you know, keep your nose clean, and then they'll let you do what you want." Like the dancers in Egan's (2004) study, Donna (dancer) told us about "reinscribing" managerial surveillance for her own ends:

> Sometimes clients will try and do things that they aren't allowed like touching between our legs, and it was really easy because I could say, "Oh, I'd love to do that, but, you know, the bouncer would fire me." So then it kind of keeps the fantasy for him. I don't have to say, "I don't want you to touch me between my legs."

In light of the very real possibility of losing their livelihood, dancers in our research did not engage in overt acts of resistance very often. For example, although Donna (dancer) perceived that the manager had overstepped his authority when he admonished her for spending too much time in the dressing room on a slow night, she "knew if I said anything to him, I'd be gone [fired] in a second." Sometimes dancers engage in passive collective resistance. For example, when management increased surveillance in an effort to collect a "cut" of their lap dance fees (cf. Egan, 2004), Sasha and her colleagues "just stopped cooperating, and then the managers never talked about it again."

Other workers also subvert managerial directives. For example, Fuzzy Pickle (DJ) took advantage of a gap in managerial surveillance by cancelling a nightly promotional event that the dancers did not like:

> It wasn't that busy, and I didn't want to interrupt the girls that were making some money to bring them out to do a free dance because at the end of the day, the more money the girls make, the better my night is going to be ... So I just skipped over it.

In other words, here we have behaviour that is counterproductive to the organization, but beneficial to dancers because they can continue to provide lap dances uninterrupted. This can also be lucrative for the DJ, since dancers will be more generous with their tip-out if their shift has been profitable. This is comparable to organizational scholars' descriptions of employees and middle managers misbehaving or cooperating to resist upper management's surveillance measures and subvert the organizational hierarchy (Willmott, 1997; Ball, 2010; Jensen & Raver, 2012). Bruckert (2002) calls this the "informal economy of favors" (p. 43), which in turn suggests that resistance to managerial surveillance may sometimes be financially motivated. According to Sasha (dancer), "girls who did extras ... tipped out the bouncers" to ensure they did not "see" the infraction. Conversely, Reverend (doorman/manager) described "doormen ... who would try to extort from girls, whether it be financial or sexual," when they caught dancers breaking club rules, while Donna (dancer) found that surveillance did not always lead to intervention: "The only time a bouncer would really do anything for me was if I tipped him." In the economy of favours and other strategies enumerated above, it appears as though resistance to surveillance is calibrated in relation to risk.

Sorting and Stereotyping in and from the Periphery

We now consider the final way our research suggests that notions of at-risk/riskiness play out in erotic dance establishments. We have already seen some social sorting in the screening practices used by third parties for security purposes. Strip club actors also engage in and confront social sorting and stereotyping at the periphery of the club, in encounters with the public, the state, and another kind of third party from outside the club, the "pimp." In the reflection that follows, we keep in mind Koskela's (2012) emphasis on "social sorting, in which less privileged populations are disproportionately stigmatized, discriminated against or excluded" (p. 50), as a significant way in which surveillance data are put to use.

Although Eric identified himself as a provider of driving and protection services, in some respects he resembles the "pimp" as described by both the dancers and the (other) third parties we interviewed. As with other aspects of the relationship between dancers and these particular third parties,[5] we cannot be certain about the extent of their surveillance practices. That said, Eric described two such responsibilities: he "would look out for" "his girl" by monitoring her interactions with customers, and he would "make sure that I'm very, very good with the bouncers. They understand that, 'See those girls over there? They are mine … Take care of them, watch out for my girls bro.'" Eric described his surveillance of the customers as follows: "I would sit in the club and I would watch certain things. She'd always ask me to like, not let certain guys go talk to her, or to show certain guys that I am there so that they wouldn't."

In stark contrast to Eric's description of his relationship with strip club staff, most of the third parties we spoke with (who were employed by clubs) were highly suspicious of outside third parties such as Eric, and enacted surveillance strategies to prevent them from entering the establishment or to eject them from it. At the club where Studley (DJ) worked, management surveilled for certain attributes ("black guys") and behaviours in customers ("none of them want a drink, none of them want to pay cover, 'Oh, I'm just waiting to talk to so-and-so,' or whatever, then every girl that walks by, they're calling them over"). Such strategies reflect Koskela's (2012) insistence that the targets of suspicion are gendered and racialized in ways that often result in young men of colour being perceived as suspicious. That this amounts to social profiling – which is, by definition, informed by stereotypical assumptions (CDPDJ, 2009) – was something Fuzzy Pickle (DJ) was quick to point out:

> The club is trying to do what they can to eliminate [the presence of pimps] as far as, you know, there's no hats allowed in the club … You've got a hoodie on, you've got to take off the hood. We want to see who you are, basically. You know, if we ever have to identify you on camera – that sort of thing. No rap in the music. They're trying to – they're trying to do what they can to keep those types of people out, but they're not there for the music, and they're not there to wear hats. They're there to get money [from dancers].

As Fuzzy Pickle's narrative suggests, this strategy is prejudicial and of questionable effectiveness. It could also have a direct impact on the labour opportunities of racialized dancers: the club where he worked imposed a quota of "five black girls," ostensibly "because they're trying to limit the amount of pimps they let into the club, and, I guess, the thought is that black girls will bring in the black guys," who were presumed to be pimps. In other words, the gendered and racialized stereotypes of "pimps" play out in strip clubs to the detriment of racialized dancers.

Also, dancers engaged in social profiling to protect themselves from those they perceived to be "pimps." Charlene, Donna, Carrie, and Bridget had all had experiences with men trying to establish particular sorts of relationships with them. Bridget explained:

> The first month that I started dancing – I became friends with this girl who, like, I didn't realize her boyfriend was her pimp, but he would come into the club and sit and watch her work, and – I talked to him. He was like, "You know, I'll elevate you, and, like, we'll save money" ... and she invited me to live with the two of them, but ... I thought it was suspicious, and so I didn't.

In response to such tactics, Carrie and Leigh (dancers) began watching out for, and avoiding, men in the club who offered to coach them in how improve their financial well-being.

While the interactions between club third parties and dancers with "pimps" highlight the stereotypical assumptions inherent in social profiling, we also see stigmatic assumptions in instances of state surveillance of strip clubs. Our participants had varying opinions and experiences of this. George (doorman) told us that the police

> come in. They don't identify themselves, and they kind of linger around the front door waiting for something to happen. Then they'll just, all of a sudden, walk up, flash their badge, ask for the manager, demand to walk through the bar, and then you have to comply, call the manager over. The manager takes him all through the bar, and – they just give us attitude.

Although Fuzzy Pickle (DJ) did not object to police visits, he felt that "sometimes, they overstay their welcome in the club."

Strip clubs are also subject to public surveillance, which, as Scott (doorman/manager) explains, can be informed by gendered scripts of "appropriate" behaviour and notions of risk:

There was a female dancer who refused to leave the establishment. And this was at 3:00 in the morning ... The bar is closed. But she was high on some drugs. I don't know what she was on, but she was not making sense, was refusing to leave, screaming, just a mess. I had to remove her. And I had had enough. I picked her up and I removed her. Now, as I removed her, there was a crowd outside of the bar, because it's downtown ... Well, the girl's still freaking out, swinging her shoes at random people around her ... Now, I'm in the public's eye. I'm trying to remove her without looking like a, you know, a pimp, bully, whatever stereotype you want to fit, of a bigger man forcing a little girl to do something. And she's not even clothed. She's still in her outfit. So, it looked bad. Somebody had called the police.

Although in that instance the police turned out to be understanding, Scott's story illustrates well that strip club third parties are certainly also the objects of social profiling (cf. Koskela, 2012) pivoting on gendered stereotypes.

Discussion

Our findings suggest that the web of surveillance at strip clubs can be characterized by interconnected (and at times contradictory) sets of practices informed by gendered and raced perceptions of risk. We have surveillance tactics to manage the at-risk/riskiness of dancers and to ensure that the actors in the club interact and behave "appropriately" (according to legal parameters imposed by the state). We also have social sorting informed by stigmatic assumptions to manage risks from the periphery; and we have surveillance as a disciplinary tactic to ensure that strip club staff conform to gendered scripts. The narratives from our respondents focused on the practices and intentions of surveillance; we now consider its consequences.

While the third parties and dancers we interviewed enumerated multiple reasons for surveillance, among them safety and security, mitigation of legal risks, and theft prevention, a significant preoccupation that informed surveillance appears to be proper conduct. Expectations of appropriate performance of femininity and sexuality were eminently discernable in third parties' concerns about preventing dancers from offering "extras," as well as in their expectation that dancers maintain a certain level of fitness and personal grooming. Of course, given that the job itself consists of performing a highly gendered role (see Bruckert &

Frigon, 2003), this is not surprising – ensuring the provision of quality services can be understood as work oversight, and monitoring grooming can be seen as maintaining the image of the business, much like a clean uniform is required in some mainstream jobs. However, the fitness specifications, racial quotas, and emphasis on "non-sexual" behaviour are notable in that the image of appropriate femininity that emerges is one of white, slim, young, middle-class female heterosexuality. Similarly, customers are expected (by both management and dancers) to behave "properly," and security personnel are required to act like "gentlemen" and not like "pimps," who are imagined to be lower-class (wearing "hoodies" and baseball caps), racialized (specifically black) men. In these respects, moral and social norms at the strip club delineate a narrow allowance for "appropriate" appearances of gender, race, and class (see also Koskela, 2012).

Social sorting complements these behavioural expectations: managers, security personnel, and dancers screen for certain customers and dancers. Indeed, our findings support Lyon's (2007) assertion that social sorting is central to surveillance; given that it operates on stereotypical assumptions at strip clubs, it is also problematic. Although the dancers in our focus groups were troubled by racial quotas (which are common in strip clubs and in other sectors of the indoor sex industry [Brooks, 2010; Price-Glynn, 2010; Bruckert, 2012]), they engaged in social profiling in an attempt to protect themselves from men in the strip club who might be "pimps." This social sorting by dancers was less overtly discriminatory than the tactics of some club third parties we spoke with, for whom black men in particular (and, to a lesser extent, racialized and/or under-class men in general), and by association, black women, seemed to raise suspicion. Ironically, strip club third parties are often the objects of the same type of mistrust and social profiling by agents of the state.

The line between "sexy" performances and engaging in acts of prostitution was also relentlessly policed, by management and sometimes by dancers as well. Although some dancers framed this kind of monitoring as a negative use of social sorting to separate the "'in' crowd from the 'out'" crowd (see also Bouclin, 2009), others viewed it as necessary and employed class, race, and gender/sexual stereotypes (linking dancers who provided "extras" to "pimps," for example) to inform their lateral surveillance. In short, we see that the redirection and appropriation of managerial surveillance by dancers is at times no less problematic a tactic.

Given that they were made in reference or reaction to the managerial gaze, it is perhaps not surprising that some of the appropriations

258 Tuulia Law and Chris Bruckert

or reinscriptions of surveillance employed by dancers echoed aspects of management's social sorting and stereotypical assumptions. In the context of the employee-like relationship that dancers have with strip clubs, the costs of overt challenges to the managerial surveillance network and the norms it enforces are too high. So instead, dancers favour covert or everyday acts of resistance (Scott, 1990), including reinscription (Egan, 2004), appropriation, and counter-surveillance.

Conclusion

In this chapter we have seen that two of Lyon's (2007) assertions about surveillance are at play in the web of surveillance networks in strip clubs and in the resistance that circulates within that web: first, social sorting is embedded in surveillance, and second, surveillance and its purposes are neither inherently positive nor inherently negative. Thus, while surveillance can reinforce stereotypes about certain groups involved (or who are imagined to be involved) in the strip club scene in its policing of "inappropriate" behaviour, it can also prevent or stop behaviour that is harmful (such as assault or theft). Moreover, we have seen that without the use of technological innovations, networks overlap and "fill in" surveillance gaps (e.g., through dancers laterally surveilling one another's behaviour). Because they operate through different groups whose interests can fluctuate, coincide, or conflict, these networks can also obscure lines of sight in ways that technological tools would not (e.g., when bouncers accept tips to "turn a blind eye" to dancers offering sexual services). These insights remind us that, even with the growth of the surveillant assemblage (Haggerty & Ericson, 2000), embodied surveillance and counter-surveillance continue to significantly and tangibly affect people's daily lives, and as such warrant scholarly attention. Furthermore, a focus on embodied surveillance has allowed us to highlight the ways in which gender, race, and class – through expectations of "appropriate" behaviour – shape actors' perceptions of risk/riskiness as well as their strategies of resistance.

At the same time, our use of a surveillance framework has allowed us to challenge the Second Wave feminist conceptualization of a male "gaze" exclusively objectifying women. Indeed, if "it is said that analyzing pleasure, or beauty, destroys it" (Mulvey, 1975, p. 8), as voyeurs, customers are merely watching; they are additionally the objects of surveillance by multiple actors in the web. More importantly, strippers' resistance, reinscription, and manipulation of the managerial gaze demonstrates their position as active (though not always critical) subjects.

NOTES

1 Individuals involved in a transaction who are not one of the principals. In a strip club, that would be anyone who is neither the dancer nor the client.
2 The research was undertaken as part of a larger SSHRC-funded research project, titled "Rethinking Management in the Adult and Sex Industry," that interviewed 122 third parties (people who organize(d), facilitate(d) or supervise(d) the work of sex workers) and sex workers who work(ed) in various sectors of the sex industry in eastern and central Canada. For more on the project and methodology, see Bruckert and Law (2013).
3 McCahill (2002) also uses the term "surveillance web" in his book by the same title. However, unlike our low-tech web of sightlines of and alliances between people, McCahill's surveillance web is an electronic network of CCTV systems and communications technologies that are connected via "human linkages."
4 See Hier (2003), Lyon (2006), Koskela (2012), Haggerty and Ericson (2000), and McCahill (2002) for excellent examples of scholars whose work focuses on technological forms of surveillance. For work by organization scholars who have analysed surveillance at the workplace, see for example Ball (2002, 2010), Jensen and Raver (2012), and Sewell (2012).
5 Many of the third parties we spoke with described two kinds of relationships between "pimps" and dancers – one that was characterized by coercion and/or control and/or abuse, and another that they described as more business-associate-like and that included money management. For more on this "associate"-type relationship, see Bruckert and Law (2013).

REFERENCES

Andrejevic, M. (2005). The work of watching one another: Lateral surveillance, risk, and governance. *Surveillance & Society, 2*(4), 479–497.
Ball, K. (2002). Elements of surveillance: A new framework and future research directions. *Information Communication and Society, 5*(4), 573–590. http://dx.doi.org/10.1080/13691180208538807
Ball, K. (2005). Organization, surveillance, and the body: Towards a politics of resistance. *Organization, 12*(1), 89–108. http://dx.doi.org/10.1177/1350508405048578

Ball, K. (2010). Workplace surveillance: An overview. *Labor History*, 51(1), 87–106. http://dx.doi.org/10.1080/00236561003654776

Bouclin, S. (2009). Bad girls like good contracts: Ontario erotic dancers' collective resistance. In E. Faulkner & G. MacDonald (Eds.), *Victim no more: Women's resistance to law, culture, and power* (pp. 46–60). Winnipeg, MB: Fernwood Publishing.

Brooks, S. (2010). Hypersexualization and the dark body: Race and inequality among Black and Latina women in the exotic dance industry. *Sexuality Research & Social Policy*, 7(2), 70–80. http://dx.doi.org/10.1007/s13178-010-0010-5

Bruckert, C. (2002). *Taking it off, putting it on: Women in the strip trade*. Toronto, ON: Women's Press.

Bruckert, C. (2012). Workin' it: Sex workers negotiate stigma. In S. Hannem & C. Bruckert (Eds.), *Stigma revisited: Implications of the mark* (pp. 55–78). Ottawa, ON: University of Ottawa Press.

Bruckert, C., & Dufresne, M. (2002). Reconfiguring the margins: Tracing the regulatory context of Ottawa strip clubs, 1974–2000. *Canadian Journal of Law and Society*, 17(1), 69–87. http://dx.doi.org/10.1017/S0829320100007006

Bruckert, C., & Frigon, S. (2003). "Making a spectacle of herself": On women's bodies in the skin trades. *Atlantis*, 28(1), 48–62.

Bruckert, C., & Hannem, S. (2013). Rethinking the prostitution debates: Transcending structural stigma in systemic responses to sex work. *Canadian Journal of Law and Society*, 28(1), 43–63. http://dx.doi.org/10.1017/cls.2012.2

Bruckert, C., & Law, T. (2013). *Beyond pimps, procurers, and parasites: Mapping third parties in the incall/outcall sex industry*. Ottawa, ON: Rethinking Management in the Adult and Sex Industry Project.

CDPDJ (Commission des droits de la personne et les droits de la jeunesse). (2009). *The judiciarization of the homeless in Montreal: A case of social profiling – executive summary of the opinion of the commission*. http://www.cdpdj.qc.ca/Publications/Homeless_Summary.pdf

Chapkis, W. (2000). Power and control in the commercial sex trade. In R. Weitzer (Ed.), *Sex for sale: Prostitution, pornography, and the sex industry* (pp. 181–201). New York, NY: Routledge.

City of Ottawa. (2004). *Harmonized Licensing By-Law No. 2002–189, Adult Entertainment Parlours – Schedule 11*. Ottawa, ON: City of Ottawa.

City of Toronto. (2010). *Toronto Municipal Code, Chapter 545 Licensing, Article XXXII*. Toronto, ON: City of Toronto.

City of Toronto. (2012). *Minutes of October 30, 31, and November 1 – Item LS16.1*. Toronto, ON: City of Toronto.

City of Toronto. (2013). *By-Law No. 243–2013: To amend City of Toronto Municipal Code Chapter 545, Licensing, respecting adult entertainment parlours.* Toronto, ON: City of Toronto.

DeMichele, M. T., & Tewksbury, R. (2004). Sociological explorations in site-specific social control: The role of the strip club bouncer. *Deviant Behavior, 25*(6), 537–558. http://dx.doi.org/10.1080/01639620490484068

Egan, R. D. (2004). Eyeing the scene: The uses and (re)uses of surveillance cameras in an exotic dance club. *Critical Sociology, 30*(2), 299–319. http://dx.doi.org/10.1163/156916304323072125

Ericson, R. V., & Doyle, A. (2003). Risk and morality. In R. V. Ericson & A. Doyle (Eds.), *Risk and morality* (pp. 1–10). Toronto, ON: University of Toronto Press.

Foucault, M. (1975/1978). *Discipline and punish: The birth of the prison.* Toronto, ON: Random House.

Goffman, E. (1963). *Stigma: Notes on the management of spoiled identity.* New York, NY: Simon and Schuster.

Haggerty, K., & Ericson, R. (2000). The surveillant assemblage. *British Journal of Sociology, 51*(4), 605–622. http://dx.doi.org/10.1080/00071310020015280

Hannem, S. (2012). Theorizing stigma and the politics of resistance. In S. Hannem & C. Bruckert (Eds.), *Stigma revisited: Implications of the mark* (pp. 10–28). Ottawa, ON: University of Ottawa Press.

Haggerty, K. (2006). Tear down the walls: On demolishing the panopticon. In D. Lyon (Ed.), *Theorizing surveillance: The panopticon and beyond* (pp. 23–45). Portland, OR: Willan Publishing.

Hier, S. (2003). Probing the surveillant assemblage: On the dialectics of surveillance practices as processes of social control. *Surveillance & Society, 1*(3), 399–411.

Hubbard, P. (2009). Opposing striptopia: The embattled spaces of adult entertainment. *Sexualities, 12*(6), 721–745. http://dx.doi.org/10.1177/1363460709346111

Hubbard, P., & Colosi, R. (2013). Sex, crime, and the city municipal law and the regulation of sexual entertainment. *Social & Legal Studies, 22*(1), 67–86. http://dx.doi.org/10.1177/0964663912459292

Jensen, J., & Raver, J. (2012). When self-management and surveillance collide: Consequences for employees' organizational citizenship and counterproductive work behaviours. *Group & Organization Management, 37*(3), 308–346. http://dx.doi.org/10.1177/1059601112445804

Jones, P., Shears, P., & Hillier, D. (2003). Retailing and the regulatory state: A case study of lap dancing clubs in the UK. *International Journal*

of Retail & Distribution Management, 31(4), 214–219. http://dx.doi.
org/10.1108/09590550310469202

Koskela, H. (2012). "The other side of surveillance": Webcams, power, and
agency. In D. Lyon (Ed.), *Theorizing surveillance: The panopticon and beyond*
(pp. 163–181). Portland, OR: Willan Publishing.

Lavin, M. F. (2013). Rule-making and rule-breaking: Strip club social control
regarding alcohol and other drugs. *Deviant Behavior, 34*(5), 361–383. http://
dx.doi.org/10.1080/01639625.2012.735611

Law, T. (2012). Cashing in on cachet? Ethnicity and gender in the strip club.
Canadian Journal of Women and the Law, 24(1), 135–153. http://dx.doi.
org/10.3138/cjwl.24.1.135

Lewis, J. (2006). "I'll scratch your back if you'll scratch mine": The role
of reciprocity, power, and autonomy in the strip club. *Canadian Review
of Sociology and Anthropology / La Revue Canadienne de Sociologie et
d'Anthropologie, 43*(3), 297–311. http://dx.doi.org/10.1111/j.1755-618X.2006.
tb02226.x

Lewis, J. (2000). Controlling lap dancing: Law, morality, and sex work. In R.
Weitzer (Ed.), *Sex for sale: Prostitution, pornography, and the sex industry* (pp.
203–216). New York, NY: Routledge.

Lyon, D. (2007). *Surveillance studies: An overview.* Malden, MA: Polity Press.

Lyon, D. (Ed.). (2006). *Theorizing surveillance: The panopticon and beyond.*
Portland, OR: Willan Publishing.

Mathiesen, T. (1997). The viewer society: Michel Foucault's "panopticon"
revisited. *Theoretical Criminology, 1*(2), 215–234. http://dx.doi.
org/10.1177/1362480697001002003

McCahill, M. (2002). *The surveillance web: The rise of visual surveillance in an
English city.* Portland, OR: Willan Publishing.

Mulvey, L. (1975). Visual pleasure and narrative cinema. *Screen, 16*(3), 6–18.
http://dx.doi.org/10.1093/screen/16.3.6

Murphy, A. G. (2003). The dialectical gaze. *Journal of Contemporary Ethnography,
32*(3), 305–335. http://dx.doi.org/10.1177/0891241603032003003

Price-Glynn, K. (2010). *Strip club: Gender, power, and sex work.* New York, NY:
NYU Press.

Scott, J. (1990). *Domination and the arts of resistance.* New Haven, CT: Yale
University Press.

Sewell, G. (2012). Organization, employees, and surveillance. In K. Ball, K.
Haggerty, & D. Lyon (Eds.), *Routledge handbook of surveillance studies*
(pp. 303–312). New York, NY: Routledge. http://dx.doi.
org/10.4324/9780203814949.ch3_4_a

Smart, C. (1992). The woman of legal discourse. *Social & Legal Studies*, 1(1), 29–44. http://dx.doi.org/10.1177/096466399200100103

van der Meulen, E., & Durisin, E. (2008). Why decriminalize? How Canada's municipal and federal regulations increase sex workers' vulnerability. *Canadian Journal of Women and the Law*, 20(2), 289–311.

Willmott, H. (1997). Rethinking management and managerial work: Capitalism, control, and subjectivity. *Human Relations*, 50(11), 1329–1359. http://dx.doi.org/10.1177/001872679705001101

Gendering Security: Violence and Risk in Australia's Night-Time Economies

IAN WARREN, KATE FITZ-GIBBON, AND
EMMA MCFARLANE

On 7 July 2012, eighteen-year-old Thomas Kelly was fatally assaulted in an unprovoked attack in Sydney's Kings Cross nightclub precinct. Kelly was celebrating a friend's birthday when he was randomly attacked by eighteen-year-old Kieran Loveridge. He died two days later from head injuries after hitting the ground during the assault (Frost, 2012). Kelly's death sparked national outrage and calls for several new surveillance and licensing measures to combat violence in the Kings Cross night-time economy (NTE) (Morri & Cuneo, 2012). Loveridge initially received a four-year sentence for manslaughter; this was almost doubled after a successful Crown appeal (*R. v. Loveridge*, 2014). Public outrage over the leniency of the original sentence, and of those imposed in similar cases,[1] prompted the New South Wales (NSW) Parliament to introduce a new "one punch" homicide offence with a mandatory minimum jail term of eight years and a maximum term of twenty-five years' imprisonment where the suspect was intoxicated at the time of the offence (*Crimes Act, NSW*, 1900 s. 25a; Nicholls, 2014).

A year previous, on 3 July 2011, Andrew Dunning was violently restrained while being ejected from Melbourne's Crown Casino due to heavy intoxication (Petrie, 2012). Dunning died four days later from injuries inflicted by three licensed crowd controllers, two of whom were subsequently acquitted of manslaughter while the third was acquitted of criminal assault. At trial, prosecutors argued that Dunning "did not go looking for trouble. His only sin, if you could call it that, was perhaps to have a bit too much to drink" (cited in Petrie, 2012, n.p.). In a separate incident, a crowd controller involved in Dunning's case claimed that his aggressive tactics while ejecting a patron who had been banned for twenty-four hours from the venue the previous evening complied with company training policies (Deery, 2013). The case paralleled the death of former Australian international cricketer David Hookes seven years earlier from head injuries after he had been ejected from a Melbourne nightclub by a licensed crowd controller who was also subsequently acquitted of manslaughter (Moynihan, 2004; Gregory, 2005; Hogan, 2005; *The Age*, 2005).

These cases point to troubling links between security, surveillance, and gender in the governance of Australia's NTEs. Considerable research identifies a strong culture of male values involving honour, status, and preserving one's reputation as a major cause of alcohol-related violence (Polk, 1994; Tomsen, 1997; Connell, 2005; Jacobs & Wright, 2006; Button, 2007; Graham & Homel, 2008; Tomsen & Crofts, 2012). This emphasis has produced two intersecting securitization responses: greater reliance on closed-circuit television (CCTV) and other computerized or biometric mass surveillance technologies (Palmer & Warren, 2013a; Palmer & Warren, 2013b), and the normalized recruitment of male bouncers capable of using superior force or "bodily capital" (Hobbs et al., 2002, p. 357) to counter the generic risks associated with male interpersonal conflict. The prevailing emphasis on broad traits of masculinity silences the nuanced elements of racial conflict (Mason, 2012), homophobia (Tomsen & Mason, 2001; Tomsen & Crofts, 2012), and gender prejudice (Fileborn, 2012) in dominant political debates and media representations of public violence in contemporary Australia, in a way that resonates with similar flawed conceptions of gender, violence, and risk (Batacharya, 2004).

The failure to recognize the intricate dynamics of male conflict legitimizes an equally aggressive form of masculinity and a commensurate reliance on various contentious forms of electronic surveillance as desirable NTE securitization responses. These measures appear blind to the intricacies of male conflict, reinforcing a vague discursive template that focuses on the imprecise or amorphous risks posed by young male "troublemakers," "drunks," "thugs," and "hooligans" (Palmer, Warren, & Miller, 2012, p. 305). The following is a typical example of the contentious security responses in Australia's NTEs generated by this narrow conceptualization of masculine risk:

> The male victim and his friend arrived at the premises at 12:20am where they consumed three alcoholic drinks. At about 1:50am the victim's friend was evicted from the premises because he did not comply with dress regulations. Security guards escorted the victim's friend out the rear door towards the venue carpark and the victim followed. Once outside the victim was

pushed to the ground by a security guard and kicked in the chest and head. The victim was repeatedly knocked down each time he tried to get up. The victim suffered two broken teeth, a broken nose and a small facial laceration in the assault. (Fitzgerald, Mason, & Borzycki, 2010, p. 5)

This chapter argues that a flawed conception of security governance directs surveillance primarily towards the major visible populations associated with alcohol-related violence. This form of risk profiling leads to various surveillance deficits that undermine regulation of the private security industry and the NTE more generally. Foucauldian biopolitical theory recognizes that multiple, intersecting, and at times conflicting forms of regulation and surveillance govern modern securitization practices (Senellart, 2007). When surveillance is devoted to curtailing identifiable risks, other meaningful security and surveillance strategies are likely to be overlooked. In Australia's NTEs, the prevailing regulatory and surveillance focus, which targets violence by young men, has legitimized certain types of technological and human surveillance that have done little to enhance overall levels of security since the mid-1980s, when Australia's liquor industries began to undergo extensive deregulation (Graham & Homel, 2008; Department of Justice (Victoria), 2009; Zajdow, 2011; Tomsen & Crofts, 2012). The gradual normalization of these processes has led to a highly gendered meaning of security in the NTE that wrongly equates harm reduction with more rather than better surveillance. These processes have been backed by increasingly punitive criminal penalties for alcohol- and drug-fuelled violence.

Statistics consistently indicate that up to one-third of reported homicides in Australia occur in recreational settings where alcohol or drugs are consumed (Polk, 1994; Chan & Payne, 2013). Also, between 15 and 30 per cent of reported assaults that occur in or around licensed venues directly involve registered bouncers (VCCAV, 1990; Graham & Homel, 2008; Fitzgerald, Mason, & Borzycki, 2010). Media reports documenting "35 deaths in bars and nightclubs in the past decade in Victoria" – all of these deaths being of young men – have led to calls for "an overhaul of laws and regulations in the security industry" (Lowe, 2011, n.p.). Our argument suggests that these statistics are the product of incremental deficits in directing both technological and human surveillance at the discursively generic problem of violence by young men and that this has produced conceptual "blind spots" associated with racial, homophobic, and sexual violence that compromise the role of surveillance as a key element of NTE securitization.

This argument proceeds in four sections. First, we describe three inter-connected forms of security governance and surveillance described by Foucault to demonstrate how contentious mass surveillance practices become legitimized despite their well-recognized limits. Discernible surveillance deficits associated with any type of security governance have the potential to generate problematic forms of remedial surveil-lance targeting profiled groups, instead of providing enhanced security for the broader population. Second, we apply these ideas to common themes associated with gender, risk, and security that emerge from the literature on governance in the urban NTE. Third, we demonstrate how the criminal law as the standard "juridical mechanism" (Senellart, 2007, p. 5) for dealing with NTE violence constructs a highly restricted notion of liability that reinforces a dominant causal link between confronta-tional masculinity, risk, and harm. This narrow emphasis helps normal-ize male honour as a major cause of interpersonal violence, thus further validating current patterns of technological and human surveillance across Australia's NTEs. Fourth, drawing from interview data examin-ing gender stratification in the Australian security industry, we illus-trate how the self-reinforcing loop of masculinity, control, and physical aggression can be eroded through a more nuanced understanding of routine human surveillance functions undertaken by female security personnel. We conclude by suggesting that the current focus on gen-der in contemporary debates about surveillance, securitization, and governance needs to make way for a more inclusive focus on patron safety and on reducing gender stratification in Australia's NTE security arrangements.

Security, Biopolitics, and Surveillance

Foucault's posthumously published lectures delivered at the Collége De France in 1977 and 1978 examined "a project, a political technique" (Senellart, 2007, p. 23) of urban governance designed to promote mass securitization. While Foucault did not expressly articulate the concept of surveillance, the term emerges frequently in his identification of three intersecting modes of governance that characterize the modern approach to managing urban security. The "juridical mechanism" is commonly enacted through the criminal law and produces "a binary division between the permitted and the prohibited" (Senellart, 2007, p. 5) to encode a particular type of discipline based on punishing wrongdoers and deterring others from the consequences of the state's coercive power.

The "disciplinary mechanism" operates beyond the established binary categories of the criminal law, applying "surveillance, diagnosis and the possible transformation of individuals" through a combination of "legislative ... judicial ... [and] adjacent, detective, medical and psychological techniques" (Senellart, 2007, p. 5). The juridical and disciplinary mechanisms intersect with a broader "apparatus (*dispositif*) of security," one that involves cost–benefit calculations of "probable events," to produce an optimal average of desired intervention within "a bandwidth of the acceptable [rate of behavior and intervention] that must not be exceeded" (Senellart, 2007, p. 6). The actuarial calculus (Harcourt, 2007) used to promote this process of securitization is often susceptible to error due to the temporal and uncertain nature of prediction and pre-emption (Senellart, 2007; Amoore, 2008).

Lyon (2007) is cognizant of the fundamental links between governance, discipline, and security when he defines surveillance as the "systematic and routine attention to personal details for purposes of influence, management, protection or direction" (p. 14). The complex bureaucratic processes associated with Ontario's liquor interdiction system that operated between 1927 and 1975 aptly illustrate how the logic of protection and prevention was contingent on selective forms of technological and human surveillance. A complex bureaucratic system of governance conflated notions of risk, crime, surveillance, and security through a predictive logic managed through early computer technologies that sought to prevent alcohol sales to those with an interdiction notice, in tandem with the centralized monitoring of inventory in liquor outlets. Prominent racial and gender dynamics were associated with the protective motives of the interdiction system, which targeted populations considered susceptible to alcohol abuse or related harm. Thus, common recipients of interdiction notices included Indigenous people, women labelled as "vulnerable," minors, and European-born "foreigners" (Thompson & Genosko, 2009). By invoking various criminal and disciplinary mechanisms to separate safe consumers from those deemed vulnerable and outside an acceptable bandwidth of risk, surveillance and securitization became intertwined through a combination of juridical, disciplinary, and predictive regulatory methods.

Similar processes are discernible in the regulation of Australian NTEs. The widespread perceptions of insecurity generated by frequent incidents of alcohol-related violence have produced various juridical measures targeting nightclub patrons, disciplinary measures applicable to venue licensees and security personnel, and the normalization of surveillance technologies to enhance mass population security. But arguably, these new reforms have often resulted from political expedience and are implemented without meaningful consideration of evidenced-based approaches to reducing alcohol-related harm. In addition, these processes reveal commensurate blind spots in each governance mechanism. For example, biometric surveillance and identity authentication technologies are frequently unable "to identify particular segments of the population" (Magnet, 2011, p. 5) due to embedded design flaws that render certain population groups invisible (see also Pugliese, 2010). Such demographic failures reflect false "biological assumptions about race and gender" (Mason & Magnet, 2012, p. 109) or other population categories that are "not problematized in the scientific literature" (Magnet, 2011, p. 5), such as people with disabilities, or people taking certain medications. Thus, technological infrastructure is frequently unable to recognize the fingerprints, retina hues, gait, or voices of large populations of individuals, and this undermines any protective motive for these forms of surveillance. And these blind spots are strongly underpinned by prevailing cultural presumptions associated with defining risk that influence the logic of various disciplinary methods of human securitization; the consequences of this include poor enforcement of responsible alcohol service and security training requirements (Warren and Palmer, 2014). These sorts of deficits in the disciplinary sphere filter into the expansion of the juridical field, as dominant securitization processes promote certain forms of surveillance that fail "to identify some subjects" yet remain prone "to overselect others" (Magnet, 2011, p. 5). This helps explain the recent introduction of more punitive criminal laws to combat alcohol- or drug-induced violence by young men in contemporary Australia.

Technological deficits in surveillance are only one component of the NTE security *dispositif*. A significant human dimension to surveillance is an inevitable component of urban securitization. In the NTE, juridical, disciplinary, and pre-emptive modes of regulation and surveillance coalesce around the environment of the pub, club, or entertainment precinct, encompassing patrons, restaurateurs, liquor suppliers, entertainers, town planners, and myriad public and private enforcement agencies (Department of Justice (Victoria), 2009), as well as binge drinkers, recreational drug users, young male "thugs" (Palmer, Warren & Miller, 2012, p. 306), serious violent offenders (VCCAV, 1990; Homel & Tomsen, 1993; Hobbs et al., 2000; Graham & Homel, 2008), the mentally ill, the homeless, and actual or prospective victims of alcohol-related assaults. In this diverse context, the privately employed bouncer plays a pivotal order maintenance role that is central to contemporary NTE securitization. We explore these issues in more detail later in this chapter by critically analysing the surveillance implications of juridical processes involving criminal court rulings on alcohol-related violence by young men, and the associated deficits in disciplinary forms of surveillance that inform self-regulation in the security industry. Both of these processes have important gender dimensions that reinforce a narrow approach to contemporary securitization practices in Australia's NTEs. In the next section, we explore how dominant political approaches associated with gender and risk have shaped an unduly narrow security *dispositif* that accepts certain contentious technological and human surveillance methods, despite their commensurate deficits and limited impact in reducing alcohol-related violence.

Risk, Gender, and NTE Security

A consistent discursive pattern informs current securitization practices in Australia's NTEs. In the political sphere, improved security tends to be equated with the introduction of new juridical measures and surveillance technologies aimed at targeting or excluding those considered violent and disorderly. Mirroring trends in several other English-speaking jurisdictions, a growing range of behaviours is open to summary prosecution, heavy on-the-spot fines, and periodic bans from nightclubs or designated entertainment precincts (Hadfield, Lister, & Traynor, 2009; Palmer & Warren, 2013a). Criminal provisions enacted under liquor licensing laws in most Australian states now conflate juridical and disciplinary processes associated with liquor supply, enabling private venue operators and police to issue bans against disorderly patrons for periods ranging from three days to five years (see *Liquor Control Reform Act*, Vic, section 148B(1); Palmer & Warren, 2013a). These measures combine punishment for a detected wrongful act with pre-emption by restricting a person's ability to enter a stipulated venue or urban precinct. Detected breaches of these orders can lead to heavy fines and possible imprisonment, although as a disciplinary process the implementation of the initial ban is immune from conventional juridical review by the criminal courts. These provisions operate alongside an expanded range of liquor control and public order infractions enforceable primarily by the public police, but increasingly vesting surveillance powers on licensed venue operators, private bouncers, and door staff. Also introduced have been a raft of stringent disciplinary measures that include venue management accreditation requirements, liquor licensing laws designed to limit overcrowding and the supply of alcohol to intoxicated patrons, and the mandatory installation of CCTV and related surveillance technologies (Department of Justice (Victoria), 2009). Nevertheless, incremental yearly increases in reported assaults within licensed venues and in the surrounding public areas (Victoria Police, 2010) demonstrate the obvious limits of this range of juridical, disciplinary, and pre-emptive securitization measures.

Additional surveillance technologies, such as mandatory patron identification scanning as a precondition of entry into a licensed venue, or any venue located within a designated NTE precinct (Palmer, Warren, & Miller, 2011, 2012), have also permeated the contemporary security market (Palmer, Warren, & Miller, 2012). As with the Ontario liquor interdiction system, the use of technology to implement identification scanning is contingent on human agency. Studies in Canada (Haggerty & Tokar, 2012) and Australia (Palmer, Warren, & Miller, 2011) document a common "no hands policy" or "selective non-scanning" (Palmer, Warren, & Miller, 2013) applying to certain nightclub patrons, such as bikers, who bypass entry into these systems to expedite patron flows and prevent lengthy queues at points of entry, or who are granted entry by security staff for more clandestine motives. Commonly, those who do not conform to the "standard" risk profile of a young male troublemaker are ushered into a venue through a side door. This demonstrates how the objective of improved securitization through blanket identity authentication produces a surveillance deficit through the manual administration of this technology, while at the same time reinforcing the selective profiling of young male troublemakers and the acceptance of various ancillary risks, particularly to young women, from "identity theft, fraud and information misuse" (Hoey, 2009, n.p.). The gendered dimensions of these processes mirror many of the false assumptions of risk that underpin the development of various biometric surveillance architectures (Pugliese, 2010; Magnet, 2011).

However, the selective profiling of young males also has the potential to overstate the extent of risk in the NTE (Beck, 1992; O'Malley, 2004), while simultaneously undermining security for a large segment of the population considered to be outside the conventional risk profile. The reporting of new incidents of male interpersonal violence amplifies these dominant conceptions of risk and insecurity, which leads to an escalation of related juridical, disciplinary, and security responses targeting the established, albeit extremely broad, risk profile. Harcourt (2007) suggests that this approach to deploying law enforcement and security resources highlights limits in the logic of actuarial prediction. Technological and human surveillance profiles tend to sample *"more* among members of the higher offending group" (p. 147, emphasis in original), and this produces a ratchet effect that increases surveillance and regulation of the targeted group. Simultaneously, the behaviour of non-profiled groups is rendered "elastic" (p. 24) by the disproportionate enforcement focus on the sampled group. This means that aggregate reductions in crime or improvements in overall safety are unlikely, because enforcement and securitization responses are solely devoted to targeting the established risks associated with broadly defined notions of male honour, which are commonly identified through actuarial profiling. Because such processes are unable to recognize the more nuanced dimensions of male interpersonal violence, any securitization responses targeting identified risks will replicate limits evident in the technical development of new biometric technologies that are blind to certain ethnic, gender, and medical traits (Pugliese, 2010; Magnet, 2011).

Elasticity has two major implications in the context of NTE securitization. First, the objectives of technological and human surveillance leave certain risks immune from scrutiny. For example, selective non-scanning has the potential to compromise the rapid identification of female victims of sexual assault, theft, or violence, even though a key rationale for introducing this technology is to promote greater security in licensed venues. Second, many other possible factors contributing to violence in the NTE – in particular, the activities of bouncers – are also immune from the surveillance and security *dispositif*. The elasticity caused by the primary focus on the accepted and generic causes of alcohol-related harm by young men, such as "honour contests," renders other possible safety issues invisible under prevailing juridical, disciplinary, and securitization approaches and their formal and informal operationalization by police, security personnel, and liquor control authorities.

This process has numerous implications for the development of gendered theories of surveillance. As anxieties about insecurity in the NTE produce highly punitive legal and securitization responses (Loader & Sparks, 2007), a popular discourse of increased control and surveillance in locations that encourage "mass alcohol consumption" (Hobbs et al., 2000, p. 707) leads to numerous blind spots or "deficits" due to the overwhelming focus on controlling the visible and "unsavory" risks posed by young men (Hutchinson & O'Connor, 2005; Graham & Homel, 2008). Young women who are outside the established risk profile are potentially subject to lower rates of technological or human surveillance and consequently rendered more insecure. Similarly, in devolved self-regulating markets that are largely "beyond government" (Loader, 2000, p. 328; Rigakos & Greener, 2000), the acceptance of imperfect uses of surveillance technology becomes entrenched. Thus, the conduct of violent or negligent bouncers (Prenzler & Sarre, 2008) remains cast as a commonplace and accepted reaction to the obvious risk of interpersonal violence involving young men. These surveillance deficits have various implications in the diverse environmental settings that constitute the NTE (Lister et al., 2000; Hobbs et al., 2002; Hobbs et al., 2003; DeMichele & Tewksbury, 2004; Hadfield, 2004; Button, 2007; Loyens, 2009; Monk-Turner et al., 2011). Nevertheless, in a context where there is immense concern regarding the ability of state authorities to adequately oversee the juridical and disciplinary requirements impacting on the private security industry (Graham & Homel, 2008), the surveillance of bouncers remains elastic from the overwhelming focus on young male patrons who are without question considered by most to be the major cause of both lethal and non-lethal violence in the NTE.

The male bouncer's physical presence or "bodily capital" (Hobbs et al., 2002, p. 357) is a further legacy of this flawed actuarial, surveillance, and securitization logic. As with new surveillance technologies, the bouncer both deters and reacts to violent confrontation. Physical bulk, aggressive body language, and "an authoritatively intimidating appearance and demeanor" (Hobbs et al., 2002, p. 357) have become primary occupational traits of the bouncer (Monaghan, 2002, 2003). Hence, intimidation, authority, control, and the power to suppress the inevitable risk of physical confrontation are increasingly considered desirable "tools of the trade" (Mopasa & Stenning, 2001; Winlow et al., 2001; Graham & Homel, 2008). Prevailing market forces intertwine with actuarial risk logic in the NTE to shape this approach to human security in a way that supersedes consideration of many equally important occupational functions, such as "housekeeping," "customer care," and non-violent forms of preventative intervention or "rule enforcement" (Wakefield, 2003, p. 165). By disproportionately profiling "the most strident form of expression of masculinity" (Tomsen, 1997, p. 94), the disciplinary approach to private industry self-regulation has led to NTE security becoming dominated by new surveillance technologies and by men with superior bodily capital relative to most patrons. As the next section demonstrates, this process is inadvertently reinforced by juridical discourses that accept a dominant causal risk profile invoking notions of male "honour" in determining criminal responsibility for both lethal and non-lethal assaults in the NTE.

Masculinity, Violence, and the Criminal Law in the NTE

The juridical field employs a specific methodological approach to determining responsibility for allegations of criminal offending (Fielding, 2011). Rather than taking a populist and punitive stance towards the use of intentional, disproportionate, and fatal violence, juridical power strives for a balanced approach based on principles of fairness and impartiality. Interestingly, prior to recent debates and reforms in NSW, excessive and voluntary alcohol or drug consumption was often considered to mitigate criminal responsibility (Tomsen & Crofts, 2012). Although Thomas Kelly's death was instrumental in removing this sentencing concession in NSW, recent judicial decisions in Victoria have reinforced an assumed link between masculinity and violence as a partial excuse for young men involved in alcohol-fuelled confrontations. This form of diminished culpability accepts that a certain degree of male confrontation involving notions of honour and loyalty is to be expected in Australian NTEs. A case analysis of several recent decisions in the Victorian Supreme Court illustrates this tendency.

DPP v Akoteu (2010), *DPP v Seau* (2010), and *R v Polutele* (2011) involved three separate trials for assault and manslaughter after the death of Cain Aguiar outside a hotel in inner western Melbourne in July 2009. Fostar Akoteu told his friends he wanted to assault Aguiar because he had been speaking to a female friend while drinking at the venue. The assault commenced outside the hotel following closing time after all involved had consumed a considerable amount of alcohol. Aguiar died four days after sustaining "a fractured left cheekbone, a fractured skull, brain bruising and bleeding" (*Polutele*, 2011, para. 14) during the attack.

Within the established, albeit highly limited juridical methodological frame, both criminal defence and judicial discourses offer qualified legitimacy to the potential for male honour to reduce culpability for an intentional, unprovoked, and fatal assault. For example, in sentencing Seau, Justice Whelan referred to a statement in Seau's police interview indicating that during the evening he had told Akoteu he would "have his back" (*Seau*, 2010, para. 5). This recognition of solidarity legitimizes an element of male honour, seldom recognized in conventional risk profiles associated with male violence in the NTE, that young men can – and should – be expected to act collectively when a member of their group is threatened. In sentencing Polutele, Seau's co-offender, Justice Williams accepted that this "case of misguided loyalty" (*Polutele*, 2011, para. 31) had a slightly more innocuous honour profile, as Polutele "simply joined in to assist your friends in their alcohol fuelled unprovoked assault on an innocent man" (*Polutele*, 2011, para. 18). The emphasis on honour reinforces a problematic stereotype of contemporary Australian mateship that serves to neutralize the severity of the assault through the logic that drunken "boys will be boys." Furthermore, any ancillary questions associated with surveillance or post–closing-time intervention are beyond the scope of a juridical frame that is confined to attributing blame within established cause-and-effect criteria through a process of reason and neutral testing of the evidence.

The legal acceptance of violence and male values is particularly evident in how Polutele's actions were reviewed in court. Evidence indicated that Polutele "seemed proud of having rendered Mr. Aguiar unconscious with one punch" (*Polutele*, 2011, para. 34). Elsewhere, "one-punch violence" is considered to result from a broader "laxity" (Tomsen & Crofts, 2012, p. 434) associated with justice and political responses to male alcohol-related violence – a laxity that is now turning the other way with the introduction of mandatory minimum jail terms for fatal unprovoked alcohol- and drug-fuelled assaults (Nicholls, 2014). This deficit in the juridical surveillance of male violence reflects a cultural acceptance of "dangerous masculinity" involving self-conceptions of identity that are contingent on honour and physical power (Collier, 1995, 1998). At worst, any negative consequences of violence are overridden by a stronger cultural belief that even slight affronts to one's sense of honour justify the use of retaliatory physical force, a process recognized as a major factor contributing to intimate partner violence (Segal, 1993; Cousins & Gangestad, 2007). Although the "partial but still powerful cultural acceptance ... [of] ... aggressive masculine identity in Australia" (Tomsen & Crofts, 2012, p. 434) is not fully excused within the juridical field, its recognition helps garner acceptance of the prevailing risk profile involving male conflict – a profile that is immune from rigorous forms of social and political scrutiny.

The normalization of honour, solidarity, and violence is also evident with references to competitive sport in formal legal responses to lethal male violence. In *Polutele* (2011), for example, defence counsel argued that there was no evidence of malicious criminal intent as the accused's actions were attributable to "some natural human response to join in group actions out of a sense of loyalty ... [equivalent to] the way young men behave on the football field and elsewhere" (para. 42). While this argument was ultimately rejected, its use implies that group assaults by young men are considered instinctive, uncontrollable, and in some instances a "natural" male response to perceived threats. As with many unproven assumptions that inform the development of various biometric surveillance technologies (Pugliese, 2010; Magnet, 2011), such reasoning dilutes any idea that a young man acting with a sense of honour can resist the innate physical urge to engage in collective and potentially lethal violence. The attempt to use this argument highlights how the juridical mechanism allows for broader cultural notions associated with gender, honour, and risk to feed into the broader NTE security *dispositif* in other ways. Notably, if attempts are made in criminal courts to mitigate collective male aggression through reliance on honour, the rejection of this logic through juridical governance has the potential to re-emerge in other disciplinary or actuarial securitization processes.

The brutality of the fatal assault in *Akoteu* was invariably constructed as a symptom of the broader NTE risk profile involving "violence by young men, fuelled by drugs and alcohol," which warrants a "stern response" from the criminal courts (*Akoteu*, 2010, para. 30). However, the emphasis on honour, mateship, and legitimate collective activity in competitive sport fails to consider the role of surveillance as a vital pre-emptive method for reducing the risk of collective male violence. Juridical methods are arguably not well equipped to deal with these nuanced issues beyond the immediate context of a specific prosecution. However, they do recognize that the use of superior "manpower" as a dominant security approach to countering male violence in the NTE can be open to criminal liability. For example, several deficits in the security response to a confrontation between three nightclub patrons that resulted in the victim sustaining two fractures, bruising, swelling to the head, and concussion were noted in two Victorian sentencing rulings in 2007 (*DPP v Bulut*; *DPP v Terzi*). The crowd controllers initially intervened and ejected the three young men after a physical altercation commenced inside the venue. They later came to the victim's aid after he sustained further injuries outside the venue. The surveillance capacities of the bouncer between the time of the victim's eviction and the time the further injuries were sustained are tempered by a separate series of disciplinary provisions that confine the lawful authority of a security employee to maintain order within the venue itself. This surveillance deficit had little bearing on the legal liability or sentences imposed on the two perpetrators. However, this jurisdictional element of the security role is central to ensuring patron safety in the public spaces around licensed venues. The lack of scrutiny of the bouncers' decision to evict all three patrons, and the potential for this to have escalated the violence on the street beyond their jurisdictional powers and the surveillance of venue managers, is immune from critical analysis in a juridical process that is confined to attributing blame for the harm caused during a fight between three seemingly unruly young men.

Juridical processes can also recognize that victims of violence experience ongoing trauma that impacts on their future involvement in the NTE as a result of poor surveillance by security staff. This is illustrated in the law's response to another Victorian case, *Giannoukas* (2011), which involved a fight that started after the accused requested a group of Australian Rules footballers to stop kicking a spirit glass that had fallen on the floor of a local pub. The footballers instigated a scuffle, and the victim, presumably influenced by a sense of collective male honour, joined in and began "throwing punches" (*Giannoukas*, 2011, para. 3). As the accused fell to the floor he accidentally struck the victim with the beer glass he was holding when the fight commenced. The limits of the binary juridical frame confine discussion of this incident to the respective liabilities of the accused and the harm to the victim, who experienced serious depression and anxiety and who rarely attends "night spots as much now and when I do I don't feel comfortable and are [sic] much more aware of what is happening to me" (para. 8). Whether the issue was captured on mandatory high-resolution CCTV, observed in the monitoring station, or whether the bouncer(s), bar staff, or any others saw the original glass being kicked on the barroom floor, remains unclear. Yet such surveillance deficits have obvious long-lasting impacts for victims and other patrons. As another twenty-nine-year-old struck with a glass by a stranger while celebrating his engagement at a local pub attests: "It was frightening to go through, really. I don't want to go out much any more" (cited in Lowe, 2013, n.p.).

These understandable and ongoing impacts of male confrontational violence are as much about the limits of prevailing NTE surveillance mechanisms as they are about criminal responsibility, honour, and other factors deemed to contribute to male violence in the NTE. As juridical measures deal with the visible symptoms of violence only in terms of blame, liability, and punishment, the broader preventative roles that security and surveillance could or should play are shifted into another regulatory frame. This means the criminal law also legitimizes the causal emphasis of risk profiles identifying male honour, mateship, and violence that inadvertently feed a prevailing securitization approach that normalizes imperfect technological and human forms of surveillance in the NTE. The next section demonstrates how this process contributes to a securitization approach in the disciplinary realm that equates safety with bodily capital, superior force, and coercive control.

Gender, Securitization, and Occupational Roles

Just as violence among male patrons is intertwined with a culture that applauds honour and the use of force (Terrill, Paoline, & Manning, 2003), notions of male chivalry and chauvinism (Loyens, 2009) are embedded standards in the bouncer's occupational culture. Force, physical presence, superior control, and aggressive "bodily capital" are considered necessary occupational traits, all of which are aimed at preventing intoxicated male patrons from engaging in violence. This security profile has significant potential to compromise the safety of all NTE patrons, regardless of gender (Hobbs et al., 2002; Monaghan, 2003), as equivalent notions of honour, power, and status are encoded throughout the NTE security *dispositif* (Graham & Homel, 2008). Thus, while it is considered that the best way to avert the risk of male violence is to "fight fire with fire," this approach to "doing security" has the potential to escalate the prospect of male violence (Graham & Homel, 2008). For example, Tomsen's (1997) detailed ethnographic study of assaults in a sample of pubs in Sydney, NSW, suggested that interactions between bouncers and male patrons reinforce the inevitable qualitative links between disorder, collective drinking, and honour. Over a decade later, these findings were supported by Graham and Homel's (2008) study of an inner Melbourne nightclub precinct. Of particular concern is how these recognized "masculine elements of the NTE security occupation ... create a very great sensitivity to personal slights" (Tomsen, 1997, p. 95) that amplifies violent confrontation between male nightclub patrons and security staff. This has significant implications for both surveillance and security, as only certain forms of behaviour are likely to be watched, or deemed to justify a bouncer's attention and intervention.

In this context, the role of female bouncers in conducting meaningful NTE surveillance and security functions is poorly understood. Profound gender blindness reinforces the view that women are either incapable of undertaking meaningful security roles, or can only succeed by emulating "culturally dominant forms of masculine work behavior" in the security field (Martin & Jurik, 1996, p. 43). Research acknowledges that female bouncers add considerable diversity to NTE security through an approach to surveillance that promotes safety (Wakefield, 2003; Hobbs et al., 2007; Graham & Homel, 2008) rather than the control of identifiable risks. Features such as "alertness," "compassion," "sensitivity," and "understanding" (Holt & Ellis, 1998, in Erickson, Albanese, & Drakulic, 2000, p. 296) are valuable customer care attributes that are frequently subsumed by the dominant occupational value of physical presence and force. Such sex role stratification is another form of profiling, in that it trivializes the proactive and preventive forms of surveillance that characterize research into female occupational practices in the law enforcement field (Heidensohn, 1992; Martin & Jurik, 1996; Brown & Heidensohn, 2000).

However, most private security jobs in the NTE have become gender-categorized as a consequence of market forces that have determined that men are more competent at stereotypically male activities involving assertion, physical presence, aggression, and risk-taking to protect others in the event of physical conflict (Ridgeway, 1997). Gender homophily involves notions of loyalty formed through enhanced social bonds with others of the same sex (Erickson, Albanese, & Drakulic, 2000). This helps explain why, among NTE security personnel, male physical strength and "heavy handed" (Monaghan, 2003, p. 24) collective violence are accepted as the predominant methods of preserving order. Female security personnel are considered incapable of offering adequate individual or collective protection due to prevailing gendered assumptions about their inferior bodily capital.

These false assumptions about the role of gender in the security industry can produce various surveillance deficits that have the potential to undermine the safety of both women (Fileborn, 2012) and men in the NTE (Tomsen & Crofts, 2012). Self-reinforcing homophilic discourses tend to equate violence and physical presence with security. Interviews conducted with a sample of fourteen registered male and female crowd controllers working in the Victorian regional city of Geelong in 2010 unanimously reinforced this embedded gendered component of the bouncer's occupational culture. As the following quote indicates, homophily reinforces the view that the appropriate female security roles involve dealing exclusively with other women:

> All venues should have one [female security employee] especially when you are escorting a female out. There's been ... many times ... you'd have a female throwing up in the toilets, intoxicated in the toilets or something wrong ... That's why you should have a female [bouncer].

This service function is qualitatively divorced from the "real" security work of the male bouncer, who is perceived as better equipped to deal with the established risk profile of violence by disorderly young men. Thus, relegating male bouncers to service activities or "toilet work" is not considered a meaningful surveillance or security activity. In fact, male bouncers are extremely uncomfortable when discussing the seamier elements of NTE service activity or dealing with violence that is not within the recognized male risk profile. As one male respondent commented:

> We have a lot of problems with the females [or] young 18-year [old] girls coming first time out and they get really intoxicated and they don't know the limits and it gets really messy. That is when us blokes have to go in and try and sort it out. If we had a female security it would make our job very easy.

The emphasis on force as an occupational requirement creates a gendered conundrum as "girls are a lot more fragile" than men. Greater care is required to resist physical contact with intoxicated young women, as such contact by a male bouncer is likely to be considered unnecessary, excessive, or inappropriate. As the following quote indicates, male bouncers are invariably tentative when dealing with female patrons, which further reinforces the homophilic preference for female bouncers to undertake the relevant surveillance and security roles that directly involve young women:

> When a girl's had enough to drink and you've got to escort her, you always get the same thing – they don't want to leave and you are standing there thinking okay they don't want to leave, they don't want you to use force or anything – but they don't want to leave ... The only way to get them out is to ... not be real forceful but just sort of guide them out and then you get ... "you can't touch me!!!"

Allegations that any force applied to a female patron by a male bouncer is unnecessary, violent, aggressive, or potentially inappropriate are inevitable by-products of NTE security activities that reinforce gendered role expectations. This view was unanimous regardless of the sex of the interviewees or the violent patrons:

> There was a fight and I ran up and said guys take it easy. One of them then went to punch one of the other guys so I grabbed him and his sister came running in and tried to hit me. So I grabbed her. Now they've tried to say I grabbed her by the throat. I grabbed her by the hands because she grabbed me first.

Homophily also reinforced the undesirability of female bouncers engaging in any physical confrontations, because they are perceived as biologically unequal to their male counterparts. This view serves to reinforce greater loyalty and solidarity among male security workers: "because the other guys that I work with ... are big and tough and can pretty much handle themselves." Thus, even if "the two females I used to work with were both Australian karate champions," it remains an occupational risk for women to intervene to quell violent confrontations between intoxicated men. The following quote demonstrates this perception:

> I don't think if there was female security that she could sort of do a normal role of a crowd controller with males ... I'd hate to see a female security try to break up or get in the middle of a fight because I don't think they could handle it.

Both male and female interviewees endorsed this relationship between gender role stratification and the use of force. Women were perceived to have greater skill in using astute forms of surveillance, such as the "the gift of the gab," to quell actual or potentially violent confrontations, while men were perceived as better equipped to use physical force. The ability to talk to people was seen by one female respondent as valuable: "People respect me more because I am female." This suggests that a subtle form of human surveillance involving observation and reason is a crucial NTE security commodity. In addition, a small number of male respondents endorsed the suggestion that aggressive male patrons are more likely to respond positively to a directive from a female bouncer:

> There'd be these huge guys and if I approached and said it's time to go they'd just tell me to go away, but then she has a word to them and they walk out peacefully, it's fantastic.

This minority view underscores the entrenched nature of sex role stratification, where "some venues will be specific about it and say we don't want to have female security guards" at all. The more common view was that "having one female, probably one's enough at each venue to deal with cases of females." The important surveillance functions associated with "girl work," including deployment as door hosts or clearing empty glasses from tables, was commonly seen as having no security component: "I think on the door that's a good place for it [sic] and that's not being derogative of them [women], it's just how it is."

Finally, the task of operating surveillance technology, such as identification scanning systems, was also stratified by gender. In fact, most respondents considered this technology irrelevant to the security role, largely due to its technical limitations. As one respondent described: "I don't think it helps us at all. I think it's just there to keep a track of things but I don't think it helps." This attitude heightens the value of conventional male traits of verbal aggression, bodily capital, and physical presence as central tools of the trade in NTE security work, while relegating the administration of surveillance technology to a form of "host work" or "door work." Interestingly, the dominant NTE risk profile was so prevalent in all interviews that no respondents in this research pointed out the security deficits associated with the practice of selectively non-scanning certain patrons. Problematically, only one door host recognized that scanners might exacerbate cultural stereotypes by promoting informal methods of visibly profiling "ethnic people" believed to be attracted to a certain R&B nightclub in Geelong "because they actually like to fight." However, other risky patrons, such as "the really intense … scary [bikers] … that the bouncers knew … they'd kind of just let them through the side and you wouldn't think anything of it [though] obviously you couldn't ask questions about it."

Conclusion

The dominant profile of the risky male NTE patron generates various forms of surveillance and regulation as part of a complex security *dispositif*. This matrix increasingly focuses on countering the recognized causes of male violence through equivalent yet legally superior notions of male honour, control, and legitimized force. The nuanced dimensions of human surveillance as viable methods of pre-empting or preventing violence give way to a widely held yet unproven view that new surveillance technologies are necessary to promote safety. However, such technologies invariably target the established risk profile, and male bouncers do not see them as useful supplements to security work. Prevailing juridical, disciplinary, and securitization measures validate the dominant risk template; they also fuel political reactions to new incidents of violence that favour tightening both the legal and technological gaze over the usual male suspects. This logic of NTE security generates a highly problematic elasticity, where female bouncers are relegated to dealing with female patrons, and the excesses of male bouncers become established tools of the security trade.

These problems are legacies of a historical failure to recognize the centrality of gender as a key surveillance and securitization measure in the NTE. This omission has created a self-legitimizing spiral where more juridical methods are deemed necessary to legitimize superior force, control, and exclusion to combat the inevitable and increasing risks posed by drunken young men. Until alternative conceptions of service, dialogue, and safety are considered meaningful occupational traits, sex role stratification will continue to shape the approach to security in the volatile environments of Australia's NTEs. Prevailing juridical and disciplinary discourses render non-technological or confrontational methods of NTE securitization invisible. This chapter suggests that prevailing gendered notions of surveillance, securitization, and risk need to be realigned towards the more inclusive objective of patron safety. This requires acknowledging surveillance as a proactive and nuanced human skill that is "beyond gender," rather than a mere technological phenomenon that continues to tacitly legitimize "security as force" through a flawed regulatory and actuarial logic.

NOTE

1 The January 2014 death of Daniel Christie following a "one punch" assault was also significant in prompting calls for legislative change in New South Wales (Bashan, 2014; Needham & Smith, 2014).

REFERENCES

Amoore, L. (2008). Governing by identity. In C. J. Bennett & D. Lyon (Eds.), *Playing the identity card: Surveillance and security identification in global perspective* (pp. 21–36). London, UK: Routledge/Taylor and Francis.

Bashan, Y. (2014). New Year's Eve coward punch victim Daniel Christie dies but his family do not want his death to be in vain as they call for change, *Daily Telegraph*, 11 January.

Batacharya, S. (2004). Racism, "girl violence," and the murder of Reena Virk. In C. Alder & A. Worrall (Eds.), *Girls' violence: Myths and realities* (pp. 61–80). Albany, NY: SUNY Press.

Beck, U. (1992). *Risk society: Towards a new modernity*. London, UK: Sage Publications.

Brown, J., & Heidensohn, F. (2000). *Gender and policing: Comparative perspectives*. London, UK: Macmillan.

Button, M. (2007). *Security officers and policing: Powers, culture, and control in the governance of private space*. Abingdon, UK: Ashgate.

Chan, A., & Payne, J. (2013). *Homicide in Australia: 2008–09 to 2009–10 National Homicide Monitoring Report*. Canberra, Australia: Australian Institute of Criminology.

Collier, R. (1995). *Masculinity, law, and family*. London, UK: Routledge. http://dx.doi.org/10.4324/9780203421543

Collier, R. (1998). *Masculinities, crime, and criminology: Men, heterosexuality, and the criminal(ised) other*. London, UK: Sage Publications.

Connell, R.W. (2005). *Masculinities* (2nd ed.). Cambridge, UK: Polity Press.

Cousins, A., & Gangestad, S. (2007). Perceived threats of female infidelity, male proprietariness, and violence in college dating couples. *Violence and Victims*, 22(6), 651–668. http://dx.doi.org/10.1891/088667007782793156

Crimes Act NSW (1900).

Deery, S. (2013). Crown bouncer to stand trial in County Court on assault charge. *The Australian*, 13 February. http://www.theaustralian.com.au/news/crown-bouncer-to-stand-trial-in-county-court-on-assault-charge/story-e6frg6n6-1226577118592

DeMichele, M., & Tewksbury, R. (2004). Sociological explorations in site-specific social control: The role of the strip club bouncer. *Deviant Behavior*, 25(6), 537–558. http://dx.doi.org/10.1080/01639620490484068

Department of Justice (Victoria). (2009). *Liquor control reform regulations: Regulatory impact statement*. Melbourne, Australia: Department of Justice.

DPP v Bulut; DPP v Terzi (2007) VSCA 69, 17 April.

DPP v. Giannoukas (7 October 2011) VSCA 296.

Erickson, B. H., Albanese, P., & Drakulic, S. (2000). Gender on a jagged edge: The security industry, its clients, and the reproduction and revision of gender. *Work and Occupations: An International Sociological Journal, 27*(3), 294–318.

Fielding, N. (2011). Judges and their work. *Social & Legal Studies, 20*(1), 97–115. http://dx.doi.org/10.1177/0964663910388857

Fileborn, B. (2012). Sex and the city: Exploring young women's perceptions and experiences of unwanted sexual attention in licensed venues. *Current Issues in Criminal Justice, 24*(2), 241–260.

Fitzgerald, J., Mason, A., & Borzycki, C. (2010). *The nature of assaults recorded on licensed premises. Bureau Brief (No. 43).* Sydney, Australia: NSW Bureau of Crime Statistics and Research.

Frost, C. (2012). Thomas Kelly's girlfriend speaks of horror in the Cross. *Daily Telegraph,* 16 July.

Graham, K., & Homel, R. (2008). *Raising the bar: Preventing aggression in and around bars, pubs, and clubs.* Cullompton, UK: Willan Publishing.

Gregory, P. (2005). Hookes was toppled "like a tree." *The Age,* 23 August. http://www.theage.com.au/news/national/hookes-was-toppled-like-a-tree/2005/08/22/1124562804902.html

Hadfield, P. (2004). Invited to binge? (Licensing and the 24 hour city). *Town and Country Planning, 73*(7–8), 235–236.

Hadfield, P., Lister, S., & Traynor, P. (2009). This town's a different town today: Policing and regulating the night-time economy. *Criminology and Criminal Justice, 9*(4), 465–485. http://dx.doi.org/10.1177/1748895809343409

Haggerty, K., & Tokar, C. (2012). Signifying security: On the institutional appeals of nightclub ID scanning systems. *Space and Culture, 15*(2), 124–134. http://dx.doi.org/10.1177/1206331211430017

Harcourt, B. (2007). *Against prediction.* Chicago, IL: University of Chicago Press.

Heidensohn, F. (1992). *Women in control? The role of women in law enforcement.* Oxford, UK: Clarendon Press.

Holt, C.L., & Ellis, J.B. (1998). Assessing the current validity of the Bem Sex-Role Inventory. *Sex Roles: A Journal of Research, 39*(11), 929–941.

Hobbs, D., Hadfield, P., Lister, S., & Winlow, S. (2002). Door lore: The art and economics of intimidation. *British Journal of Criminology, 42*(2), 352–370. http://dx.doi.org/10.1093/bjc/42.2.352

Hobbs, D., Hadfield, P., Lister, S., & Winlow, S. (2003). *Bouncers: Violence and governance in the night-time economy.* Oxford, UK: Oxford University Press.

Hobbs, D., Lister, S., Hadfield, P., Winlow, S., & Hall, S. (2000). Receiving shadows: Governance and liminality in the night-time economy. *British*

Journal of Sociology, 51(4), 701–717. http://dx.doi.org/10.1080/0007131
0020015334

Hobbs, D., O'Brien, K., & Westmarland, L. (2007). Connecting the gendered
door: Women, violence, and doorwork. *British Journal of Sociology*, 58(1),
21–38. http://dx.doi.org/10.1111/j.1468-4446.2007.00137.x

Hoey, J. (2009). ID scanners "a threat to women." *Brisbane Times*, 7 December.
http://www.brisbanetimes.com.au/technology/security/id-scanners-a-
threat-to-women-20091207-keog.html

Hogan, J. (2005). Lehmann says bouncers "chased" Hookes. *Sydney Morning
Herald*, 24 August.

Homel, R., & Tomsen, S. (1993). Hot spots for violence: The environment of pubs
and clubs. Paper presented to Homicide: Patterns, Prevention & Control.
Canberra, Australia: Australian Institute of Criminology, 12–14 May 1992.

Hutchinson, S., & O'Connor, D. (2005). Policing the new commons: Corporate
security governance on a mass private property in Canada. *Policing and
Society*, 15(2), 125–144. http://dx.doi.org/10.1080/10439460500071739

Jacobs, B. A., & Wright, R. (2006). *Street justice: Retaliation in the criminal
underworld*. New York, NY: Cambridge University Press. http://dx.doi.
org/10.1017/CBO9780511816055

Liquor Control Reform Act, Victoria, (1998).

Lister, S., Hobbs, D., Hall, S., & Winlow, S. (2000). Violence in the night-time
economy: Bouncers: The reporting, recording, and prosecution of assaults.
Policing and Society, 10(4), 383–402. http://dx.doi.org/10.1080/10439463.
2000.9964851

Loader, I. (2000). Plural policing and democratic governance. *Social & Legal
Studies*, 9(3), 323–345. http://dx.doi.org/10.1177/096466390000900301

Loader, I., & Sparks, R. (2007). Contemporary landscapes of crime, order, and
control: Governance, risk, and globalization. In M. Maguire, R. Morgan,
& R. Reiner (Eds.), *The Oxford handbook of criminology* (5th ed., pp. 78–102).
Oxford, UK: Oxford University Press.

Lowe, A. (2011). Bouncers in firing line over 35 deaths. *The Age*, 5 October.
http://www.theage.com.au/victoria/bouncers-in-the-firing-line-over-35-
deaths-20111005-1l83u.html

Lowe, A. (2013). "I had blood everywhere": Face stapled after engagement
party attack. *The Age*, 29 April. http://www.theage.com.au/victoria/
bouncers-in-the-firing-line-over-35-deaths-20111005-1l83u.html

Loyens, K. (2009). Occupational culture in policing reviewed: A
comparison of values in the public and private police. *International
Journal of Public Administration*, 32(6), 461–490. http://dx.doi.
org/10.1080/01900690902861688

Lyon, D. (2007). *Surveillance studies: An overview*. Cambridge, UK: Polity Press.

Magnet, S. (2011). *When biometrics fail: Gender, race, and the technology of identity*. Durham, NC: Duke University Press. http://dx.doi.org/10.1215/9780822394822

Martin, S., & Jurik, N. (1996). *Doing justice, doing gender: Women and the criminal justice system* (2nd Ed.). Thousand Oaks, CA: Sage Publications.

Mason, C., & Magnet, S. (2012). Surveillance studies and violence against women. *Surveillance & Society, 10*(2), 105–118.

Mason, G. (2012). "I am tomorrow": Violence against Indian students in Australia and political denial. *Australian and New Zealand Journal of Criminology, 45*(1), 4–25. http://dx.doi.org/10.1177/0004865811431330

Monaghan, L. F. (2002). Hard men, shop boys, and others: Embodying competence in a masculinist occupation. *Sociological Review, 50*(3), 334–355. http://dx.doi.org/10.1111/1467-954X.00386

Monaghan, L. F. (2003). Danger on the doors: Bodily risk in a demonised occupation. *Health Risk & Society, 5*(1), 11–31. http://dx.doi.org/10.1080/1369857021000069814

Monk-Turner, E., Allen, J., Casten, J., Cowling, C., Gray, C., Guhr, D., ... & Moore, B. (2011). Mandatory identification bar checks: How bouncers are doing their job. *Qualitative Report, 16*(1), 180–191.

Mopasa, M., & Stenning, P. (2001). Tools of the trade: The symbolic power of private security – an exploratory study. *Policing and Society, 11*(1), 67–97. http://dx.doi.org/10.1080/10439463.2001.9964856

Morri, M., & Cuneo, C. (2012). Thomas Kelly king-hit killer caught on camera near Kings Cross crime scene. *Herald Sun*, 17 July. http://www.heraldsun.com.au/news/law-order/thomas-kelly-king-hit-killer-caught-on-camera-near-kings-cross-crime-scene/story-fnat7jnn-1226427632038

Moynihan, S. (2004). Manslaughter trial over Hookes death. *The Age*, 23 November. http://www.theage.com.au/articles/2004/11/22/1100972330568.html?from=storylhs

Needham, K., & Smith, A. (2014). Daniel Christie dies following king-hit punch. *Sydney Morning Herald*,11 January. http://www.smh.com.au/nsw/daniel-christie-dies-following-kinghit-punch-20140111-30ndv.html

Nicholls, S. (2014). Mandatory jail terms for drunken killings. *Sydney Morning Herald*, 21 January. http://www.smh.com.au/nsw/mandatory-jail-terms-for-drunken-killings-20140120-3154k.html

O'Malley, P. (2004). The uncertain promise of risk. *Australian and New Zealand Journal of Criminology, 37*(3), 323–343. http://dx.doi.org/10.1375/acri.37.3.323

Palmer, D., & Warren, I. (2013a). Zonal banning and public order in urban Australia. In R. Lippert & K. Walby (Eds.), *Policing cities: Urban securitization and regulation in a 21st century world* (pp. 79–96). London, UK: Routledge/ Taylor and Francis.

Palmer, D., & Warren, I. (2013b). Surveillance technology and territorial controls: Governance and the "lite touch" of privacy. In G. Galdon & G. Hosein (Eds.), *Privacy and new technologies* (pp. 26–31). Madrid: Novatica/Revista de la Associación Téchnicos de Informática.

Palmer, D., Warren, I., & Miller, P. (2011). ID scanners in the night-time economy. *IEEE Technology and Society Magazine, 30*(3), 18–24. http://dx.doi.org/10.1109/MTS.2011.942311

Palmer, D., Warren, I., & Miller, P. (2012). ID scanning, the media, and the politics of urban surveillance in an Australian regional city. *Surveillance & Society, 9*(3), 293–309.

Palmer, D., Warren, I., & Miller, P. (2013). *ID scanning in the night-time economy: Social sorting or social order? Trends and Issues in Crime and Criminal Justice, 466*. Canberra, Australia: Australian Institute of Criminology.

Petrie, A. (2012). Trial begins over casino death. *The Age*, 15 October. http://www.theage.com.au/victoria/trial-begins-over-casino-death-20121015-27ms2.html

Polk, K. (1994). *When men kill: Scenarios of masculine violence*. Melbourne, Australia: Cambridge University Press.

Prenzler, T., & Sarre, R. (2008). Protective security in Australia: Scandal, media images, and reform. *Journal of Policing, Intelligence, and Counter Terrorism, 3*(2), 23–37. http://dx.doi.org/10.1080/18335300.2008.9686912

Pugliese, J. (2010). *Biometrics: Bodies, technologies, biopolitics*. New York, NY: Routledge.

R v Akoteu [2010] VSC 364 (20 August 2010).

R v Loveridge [2014] NSWCCA 120 (4 July 2014).

R v Polutele [2011] VSC 381 (16 August 2011).

R v Seau [2010] VSC 369 (20 August 2010).

Ridgeway, E. C. (1997). Interaction and the conservation of gender inequality: considering employment. *American Sociological Review, 62*(2), 218–235. http://dx.doi.org/10.2307/2657301

Rigakos, G., & Greener, D. (2000). Bubbles of governance: Private policing and the law in Canada. *Canadian Journal of Law and Society, 15*(01), 145–185. http://dx.doi.org/10.1017/S0829320100006220

Segal, L. (1993). Changing men: Masculinities in context. *Theory and Society, 22*(5), 625–641. http://dx.doi.org/10.1007/BF00993539

Senellart, M. (Ed.). (2007). *Michel Foucault: Security, territory, and population*. New York, NY: Picador/Palgrave Macmillan.

Terrill, W., Paoline, E. A. I., & Manning, P. K. (2003). Police culture and coercion. *Criminology, 41*(4), 1003–1034. http://dx.doi.org/10.1111/j.1745-9125.2003. tb01012.x

The Age (2005). Bouncer cleared of killing Hookes. *Sydney Morning Herald*, 12 September. http://www.smh.com.au/news/national/bouncer-cleared-of-killing-hookes/2005/09/12/1126377250670.html

Thompson, S., & Genosko, G. (2009). *Punched drunk: Alcohol, surveillance, and the LCBO 1927–1975*. Black Point, NS: Fernwood Publishing.

Tomsen, S. (1997). A top night: Social protest, masculinity, and the culture of drinking violence. *British Journal of Criminology, 37*(1), 90–102. http://dx.doi. org/10.1093/oxfordjournals.bjc.a014152

Tomsen, S., & Crofts, T. (2012). Social and cultural meanings of legal responses to homicide among men: Masculine honour, sexual advances, and accidents. *Australian and New Zealand Journal of Criminology, 45*(3), 423–437. http://dx.doi.org/10.1177/0004865812456854

Tomsen, S., & Mason, G. (2001). Engendering homophobia: Violence, sexuality, and gender conformity. *Journal of Sociology 37*(3), 257–273. http://dx.doi. org/10.1177/144078301128756337

Victorian Community Council Against Violence (VCCAV). (1990). *Inquiry into violence in and around licensed premises*. Melbourne, Australia: Victorian Community Council Against Violence.

Victoria Police. (2010). *Annual Report: 2009–2010*. Melbourne, Australia: Victoria Police.

Wakefield, A. (2003). *Selling security: The private policing of public space*. Cullompton, UK: Willan.

Warren, I., & Palmer, D. (2014). Corporate security, licensing, and civil accountability in the Australian night-time economy. In K. Walby & R. Lippert (Eds.), *Corporate Security in the 21st Century: Theory and practice in international perspective* (pp. 174–195). New York, NY: Palgrave Macmillan. http://dx.doi.org/10.1057/9781137346070.0018

Winlow, S., Hobbs, D., Lister, S., & Hadfield, P. (2001). Get ready to duck: Bouncers and the realities of ethnographic research on violent groups. *British Journal of Criminology, 41*(3), 536–548. http://dx.doi.org/10.1093/bjc/41.3.536

Zajdow, G. (2011). Outsourcing the risks: Alcohol licensing, risk, and the making of the night-time economy. *Current Issues in Criminal Justice, 23*(1), 73–84.

Contributors

Jane Bailey is a professor in the Faculty of Law (Common Law) at the University of Ottawa, where she teaches Cyberfeminism and Techno-prudence courses. She has written and spoken extensively on issues relating to gender, technology, and the law, including online child pornography and sexting. She is a co-principal investigator with Valerie Steeves on The eQuality Project, funded by the Social Sciences and Humanities Research Council of Canada. eQuality is investigating the impact of online behavioural targeting on youth, especially how it may contribute to an environment ripe for harassment and "cyberbullying."

Chris Bruckert is a professor in the Department of Criminology at the University of Ottawa. Over the past twenty years she has devoted much of her energy to examining diverse sectors of the sex industry; to that end she has undertaken qualitative research into street-based sex work, erotic dance, in-call and out-call sex work, clients, male sex workers, trafficking, and management in the sex industry. She is an active member of *POWER* (Prostitutes of Ottawa-Gatineau Work, Educate, and Resist), Ottawa's first by-and-for sex workers' rights group.

Mia Fischer is a PhD candidate and Schochet Interdisciplinary Doctoral Fellow in Queer, Trans, and Sexuality Studies focusing on Critical Media Studies in the Department of Communication at the University of Minnesota. Her research explores how media representations of transgender people connect to their surveillance by state institutions, specifically federal and state governments, the military, and the legal system. Her work has appeared in *Feminist Media Studies* and *Sexualities: Studies in Culture and Society*.

Kate Fitz-Gibbon is a senior lecturer in criminology at Deakin University. Her research focuses on the law's response to lethal violence and the impact of criminal law reform in a range of Australian and international jurisdictions. This research has been undertaken with a focus on gender, responsibility, and justice. Recent publications include *Homicide Law Reform, Gender and the Provocation Defence: A Comparative Perspective* (2014) and *Homicide Law Reform in Victoria: Retrospect and Prospects* (co-edited with Arie Freiberg, 2015).

Martin French is an assistant professor with the Department of Sociology and Anthropology at Concordia University with expertise in the areas of risk, surveillance, and social justice. He has examined social and cultural aspects of HIV as well as intersections between public health and the law, and has conducted comparative work between Canada and the United States.

Marilou Gagnon, RN, PhD, is an associate professor in the School of Nursing at the University of Ottawa and director of the Unit for Critical Research in Health. She has done extensive work in the area of HIV treatment side effects, HIV criminalization, stigma, and discrimination in health care settings, community viral load, surveillance technologies, treatment adherence, and HIV testing.

Adrian Guta, MSW, PhD, RSW, holds a CIHR Postdoctoral Fellowship, with a primary affiliation at Carleton University. Dr Guta has expertise in public health, social work, bioethics, HIV, and community-based research. His research focuses on the social, cultural, and ethical dimensions of HIV prevention, care and treatment related programs.

Robert Heynen is a sessional assistant professor in the Department of Communication Studies at York University. His research focuses on historical and contemporary practices of surveillance; visual culture; radical political movements and cultures; critical theories of embodiment; and Weimar German history. He is the author of *Degeneration and Revolution: Radical Cultural Politics and the Body in Weimar Germany* (2015).

Lara Karaian is an associate professor in the Institute of Criminology and Criminal Justice at Carleton University. Her research interests include the pursuit of a positive theory of pleasure and sexuality in law; criminal and constitutional law; critical gender, race, and sexualities theory; critical and cultural criminology; and transformative justice. Her recent Social Science and Humanities Research Council funded project examines how crime prevention and public education efforts simultaneously produce teenage sexting and sexters as objects of thought and as sites of social and legal regulation.

Shenila Khoja-Moolji is a research fellow and doctoral candidate at Columbia University's Teachers College. Her research interests include investigating the constructions of Muslim femininities and masculinities, the entanglement of education with practices of power, and exploring alternative epistemologies from the global South. Her work has appeared in *Signs: Journal of Women in Culture and Society; Gender and Education; Compare: A Journal of Comparative and International Education;* and *Journal of Comparative Studies of South Asia, Africa and the Middle East.*

Tuulia Law is a PhD candidate in the Department of Criminology at the University of Ottawa. Her doctoral research focuses on the performance of gender, race, and class in the work of third parties (e.g., managers, bouncers, DJs), and occupational health and safety through the lens of risk management, in Ontario's erotic dance sector. Her other research interests include stigmatized labour, migrant workers, and sport and masculinities.

Shoshana Magnet is an associate professor in the Institute of Women's Studies and the Department of Criminology at the University of Ottawa. Her books include the monograph *When Biometrics Fail: Race, Gender and the Technology of Identity* (2011), and the edited collections *The New Media of Surveillance* (co-edited with Kelly Gates, 2010) and *Feminist Surveillance Studies* (co-edited with Rachel Dubrofsky, 2015).

Jenevieve Mannell, PhD, is a lecturer in the Institute for Global Health at University College London with expertise in gender-based violence, HIV, and community mobilization. Her research examines the implications of gender-focused policies for everyday experiences of health, including for those living with HIV, surviving violence from intimate partners, and struggling to conform to gender norms.

Corinne L. Mason is an assistant professor in Gender and Women's Studies and Sociology at Brandon University. She conducts transnational critical race feminist analyses of development discourses and popular news media, focusing specifically on representations of LGBTIQ rights, violence against women, reproductive justice, and foreign aid. Her work has been published in *Feminist Formations*; *International Feminist Journal of Politics*; *Critical Studies in Media Communication*; *Surveillance & Society*; *Canadian Journal of Communication*; *Atlantis: Critical Studies in Gender, Culture & Social Justice*; and forthcoming in *Feminist Media Studies*. She is currently working on a book-length project on the "mainstreaming" of sexuality, gender identity, and expression in development.

Emma McFarlane has a Bachelor of Criminology and Honours qualifications from Deakin University. She has worked on several research projects examining security and the reduction of alcohol-related violence in Geelong and Newcastle night-time economies, and a project funded by the Criminology Research Council to examine the use of ID scanners in the Geelong nightclub precinct.

Zoë Newman's research and teaching investigate places where constructions of gender, race, and sexuality shape one another and meet up with ideas about citizenship, neoliberalism, and public space. She is engaged in ongoing work on public celebrations such as Pride and Caribana/Carnival and on the multiple and ambivalent meanings of spectacle.

Alyssa D. Niccolini researches intersections of affect, gender, and sexualities in secondary schooling. Her work has been published in *Journal of Curriculum Theorizing*, *Sex Education: Sexuality, Society and Learning*, *English Journal*, and *Gender and Sexuality in Education: A Reader*.

Jenny Reburn completed a PhD at the University of Glasgow. "Watching Men: Masculinity and Surveillance in the American Serial Killer Film 1978–2008" explores the development of the serial killer film across a thirty-year period with a particular emphasis on the depiction of gender and the portrayal of surveillance.

Valerie Steeves is an associate professor in the Department of Criminology at the University of Ottawa. She has written and spoken extensively on privacy issues and is a frequent participant in the privacy policy process. She is the lead researcher for the Media Awareness

Network's Young Canadians in a Wired World research project, which examines young peoples' online media use. YCWW is funded in part by the Office of the Privacy Commissioner of Canada. She is also the co-principal investigator with Jane Bailey on the eQuality Project, funded by the Social Sciences and Humanities Research Council of Canada. eQuality is investigating young people's experiences of privacy and equality in networked spaces.

Emily van der Meulen is an associate professor in the Department of Criminology at Ryerson University. Her research interests include the criminalization of sexual labour, gendered surveillance studies, and prison health and harm reduction. She is also co-editor of an anthology of writing by sex workers, allies, and academics titled *Selling Sex: Experience, Advocacy, and Research on Sex Work in Canada* (with Elya M. Durisin and Victoria Love, 2013).

Ian Warren is a senior lecturer in criminology at Deakin University. His most recent work, *Global Criminology* (with Darren Palmer, 2015), examines the tensions between global surveillance practices and established legal structures that determine the scope of criminal law and enforcement authority based on geographic territory. He is involved in several ongoing research projects that address issues related to male confrontational violence, the role of technology in assisting the enforcement of geographic or "zonal" bans, extradition, and comparative justice.

Index

Aboriginal women. *See* Indigenous
women
abortion, 135–6, 137–8, 147–8; and
law, 135, 144, 145, 147, 149, 150–1,
151n4, 152n5, 152n6. *See also*
sex-selective abortion
advertising, 8, 12, 73, 227
Agamben, Giorgio, 188–9, 192
agency, 46, 71, 98–9, 252
AIDS, 16; and "drugs into bodies"
slogan, 156, 157–8, 160; and
gender, 173; and media, 229–30.
See also HIV
Akoteu, Fostar, 274
Albrechtslund, Anders, 88, 90,
95, 97–8
Ambrose, Rona, 148, 152n5
Andrejevic, Mark: on "digital
enclosures," 6–7, 20; and "lateral
surveillance," 8, 88, 91, 232–3
American Civil Liberties Union
(ACLU), 202
antiretroviral therapy (ART), 157–8,
162–3, 165, 166–7, 168–9, 173
apparatus, 160–1, 163, 188, 198, 201.
See also *dispositif*
Arellano, Victoria, 199

Armstrong, David, 42, 157, 160–1
Asian immigrants, 146–9
asylum, 7, 9
"at risk," 13, 159, 166–7, 241, 242,
243–4, 245, 246, 249–50, 256.
See also risk
Atwood, Margaret, 147

ban-optic, 6, 187–90, 203; and
biometrics, 193; "*dispositif*," 187,
188–9, 203; gaze, 188–90, 195, 197,
199, 201; and gender, 187, 189–90,
192 195, 198, 199, 202–3; and PIC,
198, 202–3; and race, 187, 194, 200,
202–3
Barnett, Zachary, 169–70
Bartky, Sandra, 106, 107
bathhouses, 215, 224–26, 226–27
bathrooms, 22–3, 226
Bauer, Susanne, 161
bawdy-house, 227, 235n1, 242
Bayer, Ronald, 170
Beauchamp, Tony, 195
Becker, Denise, 166
Belfast, 231–32
Belfast Telegraph, 232
Bell, David, 23

Benjamin, Walter, 20
Bentham, Jeremy, 6, 188–9
Betesh, Saul David, 214–15
Bigo, Didier, 6, 186, 187–9, 190, 195, 203
Bill C-22, An Act Respecting the Mandatory Reporting of Internet Child Pornography (Canada), vii, 51n11
biometrics, 15–16, 18–19, 190; and disabilities, 18–19, 193; and gender, 269, 271, 193–5, 202, 271, 276; and identity, 14, 192–5, 269, 271; and race, 269; and securitization, 170, 192–5, 265, 271; and trans, 18–19, 187, 192–5
biopolitics, 266, 267–70
Black men, 16, 19–20, 119, 255, 257
Black women, 12, 16, 137–8, 249, 255, 257
Body Politic, The, 215, 227
body-rub parlours, 214, 221, 226
borders, 3, 18, 19–20
bouncers, female, 279–82, 283; and NTEs, 265–6, 270, 270–3, 276–7, 278–82, 283; and strip clubs, 244, 249–50, 253, 254, 258
Brighenti, Andrea, 76
Brock, Deborah, 223, 224, 235n2
Brown, Nik, 17
Browne, Simone, 135, 138, 142
Bryant, Anita, 228
Butler, Judith, 12, 164, 204n3

Cadillac Fairview Corporation, 223
Canadian Broadcasting Corporation (CBC), 135–6, 139, 148–50, 223
Canadian Centre for Child Protection (CCCP), 47–9
Canadian Medical Association Journal, 135, 144, 146, 147, 149

Centers for Disease Control and Prevention (CDC), 162, 163
Chase, Sylvia, 109
children, 218–19; and pornography, vii, 36–8, 39, 43, 47–8, 51n4, 51n11
cisgender, 193, 151n1, 204n4, 229
Clarke Institute of Psychiatry, 220
Class. *See* intersectionality
Closed Circuit Television (CCTV), 3, 9, 20, 21–22, 259n3, 265, 271; and strip clubs, 243, 244, 245, 247, 254
"Collateral Murder" (video), 185–86
Communications Security Establishment Canada (CSEC), 236n6
communication studies, 8
confessional texts, viii, 14, 24, 84–6, 86–9, 90–1, 97–9
Conrad, Kathryn, 217, 231
Coombs, David, 196
Cornwall, Patricia, 110–11
Costello, Cary Gabriel, 193–4
counter-surveillance, 251–3, 258
crime, 18, 22, 47, 171
criminal code, vii, 47, 51n11; of Canada, 214, 224, 234
criminalization, viii–ix; of abortion, 135, 147, 150, 151n4, 152n5, 152n6; of HIV, viii, 171–3, 174, 199–201; of gay men, 214, 224, 226–8, 229; of sexting, 36, 44, 48
critical race theory, 135, 136–9, 187
criminology, 15, 16
Crombie, David, 219
Cybertip.ca, 47–9, 51n11

Das, Moupali, 163
"data doubles," 14, 17–18; Haggerty on, 9, 17, 37, 243; and strip clubs, 243–4
Davis, Angela, 198

Davis, William, 219
Debord, Guy, 231
DeMichele, Matthew, 245, 250
Devji, Faisel, 98
Deleuze, Gilles, 7, 37
Department of Homeland Security,
    189–90
Department of State, 195
De Souza, Raymond J., 148–9
detective, and urban space, 108–9,
    116; profiler as, 111, 116
deviance, 13–14, 16, 22–3, 194, 217,
    219–20, 227, 228–9
"digital enclosures," 6–7, 20
disabilities, viii–ix, 10, 12, 18–19, 138,
    139, 143, 193, 269
"disciplinary societies," 189
discipline, ban-optic, 203; and
    control, 7, 48, 57, 88, 151; Foucault
    and, 6–7, 105–6, 163–4, 188–9,
    230, 244, 267–8; and gender, 23,
    194; and HIV, 162, 164, 173; and
    NTEs, 268–9, 270–3, 276–8, 283;
    and panopticon, 73, 75, 105–6;
    parental, 42; and power, 163,
    189, 267–8; and sexting, 48; and
    queers, 187; and the state, 199, 203;
    and strip clubs, 245–6, 251, 256;
    women and, 37, 44, 47–8, 77, 86
dispositif, 268–70, 272, 276, 278,
    282–3; ban-optic, 6, 187, 188–9,
    203. See also apparatus
Donald, James, 107–8
Douglas, John, 113
Doyle, Aaron, 231
Doyle, Arthur Conan, 111
DPP v Akoteu, 274, 276
DPP v Giannoukas, 277–8
DPP v Seau, 274
Dr. Phil, 14, 36, 38–44, 45
"drugs into bodies," 156, 157–8, 170

"duckface" selfie, 62–3, 66, 75
Dunning, Andrew, 264
Dworkin, Shari, 229–30
Dyer, Richard, 118, 119, 121

Eaton Centre, 222–3, 233
Eaton family, 222–3, 226
Egan, R. Danielle, 240, 243, 244, 245
Eggleton, Art, 219
Elbe, Stefan, 173
embodiment, viii–ix, 14–19, 37, 45,
    77, 157, 241, 244; gendered, 5,
    11, 14–19, 258; and surveillance
    studies, 4–5; and trans people, viii,
    19, 187, 198–201
Enlightenment, 10–11, 15, 18
Espionage Act (United States), 186
eugenics, 15–16, 143; "consumer," 17
"exceptionalism of power," 187, 189,
    190, 226, 191–2
exhibitionism, 23, 36, 44;
    "empowering," 85, 98–9. See also
    voyeurism
exotic dancers. See strippers

FBI profiler, 103–4, 110–11, 112–13,
    126n2
Federal Bureau of Prisons, 197
femicide, 135, 137
femininity, 99, 106–107, 256–57;
    online, 63–4, 71–4, 78
feminism, 5, 7–9, 10–14; critical race,
    135, 136–9, 187; and Foucault, 7,
    105–6, 107, 164; and gaze, 8, 240,
    258; and identity, 23–4; and media,
    11–14, 135–6, 139–40, 147–9; and
    memoirs, viii; and penal abolition,
    viii–ix; and objectification of
    women, 44–5; and sex-selective
    abortion, 135–6, 137–8, 147–8; and
    space, 10–11, 20, 23–4; and strip

clubs, 240, 258; and subjectivity, 9–10; and surveillance studies, viii–ix, 10–14, 20–4, 85–6, 86–9, 135, 136, 185; and visibility, 56; and vision, 10, 10–13, 16–17

feminist media studies, 11–14

Ferguson, Roderick, 200

film, 9, 11, 56, 110–11, 122, 124, 125. *See also* serial killer films

film studies, 11, 105

Fiske, John, 138

flâneur, 20–1, 23

flâneuse, 23

Foucault, Michel, 6–9, 110, 164; and apparatus, 160–1, 163; and discipline, 6–7, 105–6, 16–64, 188–9, 203, 230, 244, 267–8; and feminism, 7, 105, 105–6, 107, 164; and gender, 9, 106, 164, 185; on governmentality, 7, 156–7, 159–61, 163, 188, 267; and panopticon, 6–7, 105–6, 10, 188–9, 217–18, 230, 234, 244; and power, 6, 139, 105–6, 159, 162, 163, 171, 189, 230, 234, 251; on racism, 173; and sexuality, 160, 168; and spectacle, 6, 8, 217–18, 230–1

Freund, Kurt, 220

Gagnon, Marilou, 162, 170

Garner, Charles, 202

gay bars, 221, 223–24, 225, 226–27

gay community, 214, 221, 223–26, 225, 226–27

gay-related immune deficiency (GRID), 199

gay men, 16, 229, 169, 213, 215, 227; and criminalization, 214, 224, 226–28, 229; and HIV, 16, 157, 167–70, 229–30; Jaques murder and, 214, 218–20; and media, 23, 218–20, 226–7, 228–34, 234–5; police and, 22, 23, 198–9, 214, 215–16, 220, 224, 226–32, 233, 234; and rights, 200–1, 219, 224, 226, 234; and space, 22–3, 213, 224–6, 225; and TasP, 167–70; and visibility, 215–16, 226–8, 229–30; and Yonge St., 221, 223–6, 225, 226–7. *See also* queers; men who have sex with men

gaze, ban-optic, 188–90, 195, 197, 199, 201; blacks and, 12, 16; and CCTV, 22; and embodiment, 19; and feminism, 8, 240, 258; of *flâneur*, 20; and film, 9; and gender, 8, 11–14, 77, 78, 106, 157, 283; and HIV, 157; male, 9, 11–14, 16–18, 46, 56–7, 58, 71, 77, 90, 93–4, 96–9, 105, 106, 108, 114, 240, 258; managerial, 257–8; and masculinity, 22, 114; media, 216; medical, 160–1; Muslims and, 90, 91, 98; "oppositional," 12; panoptic, 57, 73, 75; and pleasure, 258; of profiler, 103–5, 113–16; and risk, 233; and race, 139–40; resisted, 13; of serial killer, 103–5; and sexters, 37, 43; and social media, 56–7, 58, 71, 77; of state, vii, 229, 252; and strip clubs, 240, 243, 252, 258; synoptic, 57, 73, 216; techno-scientific, 17; and urban space, 215–16; white, 12, 16

gender, 5, 71; and abortion, 19, 143, 145–8, 151n1; and AIDS, 173; and ART, 165; and ban-optics, 187, 189–90, 192, 195, 198, 199, 202–3; and biometrics, 269, 271, 193–5, 202, 271, 276; boundaries, 106–7; and CCTV, 9, 21–2; deviance,

13, 194; and discipline, 23, 194; discrimination, 143, 145–8, 199; and embodiment, 5, 11, 14–19, 244, 258; and the Enlightenment, 10–11, 18; Foucault and, 9, 106, 164, 185; and gaze, 8, 11–14, 77, 78, 106, 157, 283; and governance, 164; and HIV, 19, 157, 164–6, 171–3; homophily, 279–81; and identity, 12–13, 24, 185, 202–3, 243; inequality, 18, 21–2, 140, 141–2, 165; and knowledge, 84, 108, 157; legal, 194–5, 196–7; and media, 5, 10–14, 18, 139–40; and medicine, 160; Muslim women and, 91, 94, 97; and NTEs, 265–7, 270–4, 278–82, 283; and panoptic, 8; and performance, viii, 194, 204n1, 93; of profiler, 119; in "profiler" film, 121–2, 124–5, 125–6; profiling, 279–82; and risk, 241; self-surveillance, 11–12; and serial killing, 104–5, 106–7, 108–9, 121–2; and social media, 12, 14, 57, 59–62, 71–2, 74–5, 99; and spectacle, 11; and STOP, 159; and strip clubs, 240–1, 243–4, 255–6, 256–7; and subjectivity, 9–10, 10–12, 14; and surveillance, 5, 10–14, 24, 56–8, 84, 108, 189, 192–5, 265–6, 276; and surveillance studies, vii–ix, 4–5, 6–10, 13, 15, 24, 56–7, 185, 272–3; and "surveillant assemblage," 17–18, 240, 258; and synoptic, 8; and TasP, 157, 158, 165, 173, 174; and trans, 188; and urban space, vii, 5, 19–23, 108, 123; and vision, 11, 15. See also intersectionality
gender dysphoria, 186, 195, 196–8, 202, 204n3

gendercide, 135, 137, 148
"gender-selection," 140
gender studies, viii
Gill, Rosalind, 86
girls, viii, 13, 37, 44, 47–8, 77, 86. See also Muslim girls
Globe and Mail, The, 213–14, 215, 217, 218–20, 222, 228, 234
governance, 22, 138–9, 160, 266; ban-optic, 188; and biopolitics, 267–70; and gender, 164; liquor, 268–9; neoliberal, 4, 18–19, 160; and NTEs, 267, 267–9; and urban space, 20, 22, 108, 267
governmentality, 7, 156–7, 159–61, 163, 188, 233, 267
Graham, Kathryn, 278–9
Grewal, Inderpal, 141–2
Guantánamo Bay, 190–1

Haggerty, Kevin, 7, 20, 164, 171–2; on "data doubles," 9, 17, 37, 243; on "surveillant assemblage," 7, 17, 37, 76, 243–4, 258
Hall, Stuart, 147, 217
Hannon, Gerald, 215
Haraway, Donna, 16–17
Harper, Brit, 77
Harris, Anita, 87
Hasinoff, Amy, 45
headless selfies, 37–8, 43, 44–7, 49
heteronormativity, 16, 71–2, 73, 78, 89–90, 167, 199, 215, 217
"heterosexuality," 22, 228–9, 232, 234
Hier, Sean, 20
Hill Collins, Patricia, 137
Hilton, Dawn, 191
HIV, viii, 16, 19, 156–7, 162–3, 164–6, 167, 169, 171–2; Aboriginal women and, ix, 164, 166, 167;

criminalization of, viii, 171–3, 174, 199–201; and discipline, 162, 164, 173; disclosure, 171–2; gay men and, 16, 157, 167–70, 229–30; and embodiment, 157; and gender, 19, 157, 164–6, 171–3; and media, 229–30; and medico-juridical power, 156, 171–3; and prison, 164, 199–201; and queer women, 167; and risk, 47–8, 157, 159, 159–61, 162, 164–70, 174; securitization of, 156, 171–3, 174; sex workers and, 159, 172–3; and pathologization, 229–30; trans and, 167, 188; and violence, 165, 167; women and, 164–7, 172. *See also* AIDS
Holmes, Sherlock, 117
homonormativity, 200
homophily, 279–81
homophobia, 266
homo sacer, 192
homosexuality, 22, 185, 200, 219–20, 226–8, 234–5; decriminalized, 214, 224; Foucault on, 168
"honour killings," 148
hooks, bell, 12, 16
Hookes, David, 265
hormone therapy, 185, 186, 187, 196–8, 201
Hubbard, Phil, 228–9
human rights, 136, 173

identification documents, 194–95
identity, 5, 23, 56, 75, 105–6, 194, 230; and biometrics, 14, 192–5, 269, 271; and deviance, 13–14; ethnic, 137–8; and feminism, 23–4; and gender, 12–13, 24, 185, 202–3, 243; and homosexuality, 168, 200; of Muslim women, 85–6, 98, 99;

postfeminist, 86; and public and private space, 23; queers and, 185, 204n1; "securitization of, " 190, 192–5; and selfies, 46–7; and social media, 60–1, 70–2, 74, 98; and surveillance studies, 56–7; trans, 185, 195, 200, 204n1; and urban space, 23; of women, 167. *See also* performance
immigrants, 143–4, 146–7, 149; Muslim, 85, 93–4, 99–100; racialized, 135–6, 136–8, 140, 143–4, 146–9, 150–1; South Asian, 146–9; and sex-selective abortion, 135–6, 141–2, 143–4, 145–9, 150–1
incarceration, viii–ix, 6; Manning's, ix, 187, 190–2, 201–2
Indigenous people, ix, 164
Indigenous women, ix, 137, 152n5, 166, 167
inequality, viii–ix, 4, 58, 59, 69–70, 88, 76–8; and gender, 18, 21–2, 140, 141–2, 165
intersectionality, 12, 79n5, 84, 139, 187, 194, 200, 203, 257, 258; and surveillance studies, vii, 5, 10, 56–7, 173

"Jack the Ripper," 104, 106–7, 108–9, 115, 126n1; and films, 110–11, 122, 124, 125
Jaques, Emanuel (Shoeshine Boy), 213–15, 215–21, 224, 227–8, 230–1, 234
Jiwani, Yasmin, 136, 137, 147

Kale, Ranendra, 144–6, 148, 149
Kelly, Thomas, 264, 274
Kellner, Douglas, 231, 232
Kenniff, Tom, 190

Kincaid, James, 49, 51n4
Kinsman, Gary, 216, 227
knowledge, authoritative, 71;
    "common sense stock," 147; and
    gender, 84, 108, 157; and media,
    147; Muslim women's, 91, 94, 97;
    and power, 139, 159–61, 163; and
    TasP, 157; women and, 144–5
Knox, Sara L., 110, 117–18
Koskela, Hille, 8, 9, 85, 98, 243,
    253–4, 256
K6G unit (Los Angeles County Jail),
    200–1

Lamo, Adrian
Lancaster, Kathryn, 159
lap dances, 241, 246, 252–3
"lateral surveillance," 8, 88, 91,
    232–3; masculinity and, 22, and
    social media, 8–9; and strip clubs,
    242, 243, 248, 257
law, 267–8, 269; and abortion, 135,
    144, 145, 147, 149, 150–1, 151n4,
    152n5, 152n6; bawdy-house, 227,
    235n1, 242; child pornography, vii,
    47, 51n4; constitutional, 191; and
    emergency, 6, 189–90, 192; and
    espionage, 186; and gender, 194–5,
    196, 197; and HIV, 171–3; and *homo
    sacer*, 192; military, 186; and NTEs,
    266–7, 269–70, 270–1, 274–8, 283;
    "one punch," 264, 275, 283n1; and
    public space, 21, 229, 277; and
    strip clubs, 242, 243, 248; and viral
    load, 171–2
Leman-Langlois, Stéphane, 7
lesbians, 23, 93, 198, 204n1, 214,
    224–9, 235n4; Muslim, 93
"liquid surveillance," 7, 201
Loveridge, Kieran, 264

Lucas, Henry Lee, 126
Lyon, David, 150, 185, 231, 236n6,
    243–4, 258, 268; on "social
    sorting," 4, 6

Magnet, Shoshana, 18–19, 138–9,
    143, 193
male gaze, 9, 11–14, 16–18, 46, 56–7,
    58, 90, 93–4, 96–9, 108; and public
    space, 22–3, 34; and serial killer
    films, 14, 105, 106, 114; and social
    media, 71, 77; and strip clubs,
    240, 258
managerial surveillance, 244–8, 249,
    250, 251–3, 254, 257–8, 277
Mansbridge, Peter, 10
Manning, Chelsea, ix, 19, 185–8, 190–2,
    201–3; and "gender dysphoria,"
    186, 196–8, 202; and hormone
    therapy, 185, 186, 187–8, 196–8
Manning, Morris, 214
Martin, Lisa, 150
masculinity, 9, 11, 14, 20, 22–4, 109,
    114, 119, 120, 137; and NTEs, 24,
    185, 265–7, 272–3, 274–8
Mathiesen, Thomas, 8–9, 11–13, 73,
    216, 217–18, 230–1, 234, 244
Mattu, Ayesha, 89, 91
McCahill, Mike, 259n3
McDonald, CeCe, 197
McMurtry, Roy, 219
McRobbie, Angela, 72, 73, 86, 87, 88
media, 5, 8, 10–14, 73, 138–40,
    147–9, 215–16, 217–21, 227, 228–34,
    234–5; and feminism, 11–14, 135–6,
    139–40, 147–9; gay men and, 23,
    218–20, 226–7, 228–34, 234–5; and
    gender, 5, 10–14, 18, 139–40; and
    HIV, 229–30; Jaques murder and,
    213–14, 215, 217, 218–20, 222,

223, 228, 231, 234; and panoptic, 218–19; and the police, 139–40, 216, 233; and race, 143, 146–9; and risk, 233; and sex-selective abortion, 135–6, 139–40, 147–9, 150–1; and serial killing, 109–10; and sexters, 37–8; and spectacle, 8, 139–40, 228–34, 235; and "surveillant assemblage," 18, 37; and synoptic, 216, 217–19, 236n6; and trans people, 196–7. *See also* new media

media studies, 8, 10–14

medicalization, 185, 195–6

medicine, 16, 17, 18, 144–5, 151, 160, 173; "surveillance," 42, 157, 160–1

medico-juridical power, 156, 171–3

medico-legal borderland, 171–3

Melbourne, 274

memoirs, viii. *See also* confessional texts

men who have sex with men (MSM), 159, 164–5, 167–9, 248

Merleau-Ponty, Maurice, 15

Mernissi, Fatima, 99

Meyer, Jaimie P., 167

mind–body dualism, 15, 18

modernity, 15, 20–21, 57, 108, 112–13, 118–20, 136, 201, 266, 267; in Foucault, 6, 164, 189, 230–1

Mohanty, Chandra, 141

Monahan, Torin, 88, 89

Monaghan, Jeffrey, 138

monitoring, 90, 160, 233–4; of gay men, 170; and profiler, 111; peer, 85, 233; of queers, 93, 185, 187; risk, 233; serial killer and, 109–10; and social media, 64–9, 72, 75–7, 85; of state, 185–6, 190, 195; and strip clubs, 256–7; of trans,

185, 187, 190, 195; urban space, 103–5, 107; viral load, 157, 162–3, 170, 172. *See also* "participatory surveillance"; self-surveillance

Motion 312 (Canada), 147

Motion 408 (Canada), 135, 144, 147, 149, 152n5

Mulvey, Laura, 11–12, 56, 58, 105

Murakami Wood, David, 3

Muslim women, 14, 84–6, 86–9; and domestic violence, 94; and gender, 91, 94, 97; and identity, 85–6, 98, 99; immigrants, 85, 93–4, 99–100; and privacy, 96–7, 98–9; sexuality of, 84–5, 89–90, 94–5, 96, 98, 99; self-surveillance of, 84–5, 87, 92, 94; and subjectivity, 14, 84, 86–7, 89–90, 93–4, 94–6; and visibility, 93–4; and watching, 89, 90–1, 97–9

Nancy, Jean Luc, 188

Narayan, Uma, 141

National Center for Missing and Exploited Children, 48

National Center for Transgender Equality (NCTE), 198

National Gay and Lesbian Taskforce (NGLT), 198

National Post, 135, 148–9

national security, 4, 16, 27, 87, 139, 187, 189, 192, 203, 227

neoliberalism, 4, 18–19, 22, 86–7, 160, 167

new media. *See* social media

Nguyen, Vinh-Kim, 158

night-time economies (NTEs), 24, 265–7, 267–70, 272–4, 283; and CCTV, 265, 271; and discipline, 268–9, 270–3, 276–8, 283; and gender, 265–7, 270–4, 278–82, 283;

and governance, 267, 267–9; and homophobia, 266; and law, 266–7, 269–70, 270–1, 274–8, 283; and masculinity, 24, 185, 265–7, 272–3, 274–8; and occupational roles, 278–82; and profiling, 266–7, 271–4, 275, 278, 280, 282; and security industry, 266, 267, 270, 273; and risk, 24, 265–7, 269, 270–4, 275–6, 278, 280, 282, 283; and safety, 267, 272, 277–8, 278–80, 283; and securitization, 265–6, 266–70, 270–4, 278–82, 283; and security, 265–7, 267–74; and sexual assault, 266, 272; and surveillance deficits, 269, 271–3, 277, 279, 282, 283; and violence, 264–7, 274–8, 283

Olsen, Laurie, 93–4
online social media. *See* social media
"on/scenity," 49–50
Ontario Human Rights Commission, 214
Ontario Human Rights Code, 234, 235n3
Ontario Vital Statistics, 146
Orientalism, 84, 97, 98
Orwell, George, 3
Ottawa, 240, 242
Ounapuu, Toomas, 214
"outsourced patriarchy," 137, 141–2

panoptic, 6, 8–9, 11, 57–8, 78, 234; cities, 105–11; Dr. Phil and, 45; gaze, 57, 73, 75; and media, 218–19; spectacle, 218, 230; and strip clubs, 243; "surveillance," 6; and synoptic, 8–9, 11, 13, 73, 76, 217–18, 231. *See also* panopticon; synoptic

panopticon, 6–10, 105–6, 110, 188–9, 217–18, 230–1, 234, 244; and discipline, 73, 75, 105–6; "super-" 6. *See also* panoptic; synoptic
"panoptic sort," 6
"participatory surveillance," 3–4, 8, 12–14, 88, 90; Albrechtslund on, 88, 90, 97–8
patriarchy, 46–7, "outsourced," 137, 141–2
Patton, Cindy, 165
peer surveillance, 85, 89, 91, 92, 233, 243, 247–8
performance, 13, 36, 86–7, 89–90, 93–4, 98; and gender, viii, 194, 204n1, 93; and race, 138, 140–1; and social media, 60, 62–3, 71–2, 73, 74–8, 98; of state, 4, 231; of strippers, 242, 244, 256
Planned Parenthood Federation of America, 150
pleasure, 4, 8, 11, 13, 23, 258; and confessional texts, 84–6, 86–9, 90–1, 97–9; and media, 140; and selfies, 35–7, 43–4, 46, 47, 49–50; and social media, 13, 36, 64, 75, 90–1, 97–9
Poe, Edgar Allan, 111
police, vii, 7, 20, 22; blacks and, 16, 19–20; Jaques murder and, 214, 215–16, 224, 227–8, 230–1, 234; gay men and, 22, 23, 198–9, 214, 215–16, 220, 224, 226–32, 233, 234; and media, 139–40, 216, 233; and NTEs, 270–1; and serial killer films, 14, 111, 123–4, 234, 235n4; serial killers and, 107; sex workers and, 21, 214; and strip clubs, 255–6; surveillance, 216, 229, 231–2, 233; trans and, 198; women and, 21–2

pornography, vii, 14, 36–8, 39, 43–4, 47–8, 51n4, 51n11; torture, 104, 125, 126n1

pornonormativity, 44

postfeminism, 85, 86–9, 93–4, 98, 99

"postfeminist girlhood," 85, 86

power, 4, 6, 58, 150, 240; discipline and, 163, 189, 267–8; "exceptionalism of," 187, 189, 190, 226, 191–2; and femininity, 71–2; Foucault on, 6, 139, 105–6, 159, 162, 163, 171, 189, 230, 234, 251; and knowledge, 139, 159–61, 163; medico-juridical, 156, 171–3; and Muslim women, 97; panoptic and synoptic, 11, 231, 234; and social death, 187

prison, Foucault and, 6–7, 105, 171, 230; and HIV, 164, 199–201; Manning and, ix, 187, 190–2, 201–2; and race, viii–ix, 198–9, 200–1; and trans embodiment, 198–201. See also panopticon

prison industrial complex (PIC), 188, 189, 198–201, 202–3

privacy, 3–4; of Muslim women, 96–7, 98–9; and public space, 224–6, 229, 232–3; and social media, 59, 66–9, 75–6

private space, 23–4; gay men and, 224–6; and social media, 57–8, 76; serial killer and, 117, 122; and strip clubs, 249

private sphere, 23–4, 98–9; and feminism, 10–11, 23–4

profiler, black, 119; as detective, 111, 116; and crime scene, 117–18; FBI, 103–4, 110–11, 112–13, 126n2; male, 119, 120–2, 123–4, 125–6; in popular culture,

110–11; female, 112, 119, 120–1, 125, 126; gaze of, 103–5, 113–16; serial killer and, 104, 105–11; and serial killer in film, 111–25, 125–6; and urban space, 103, 105, 113–14, 115, 119, 123, 124–5; white, 103, 119, 120

"profiler" films, 103–5; and crime scene, 117–18; and domestic space, 110, 121, 123; and gaze, 114; and gender, 121–2, 124–5, 125–6; profiler and serial killer in, 111–25, 125–6; and urban space, 103, 112, 113–14, 115–17, 118–20, 122–5, 125–6; and violence against women, 120–5. See also serial killer films

profiling, actuarial, 272; gender, 279–82; racial, 19–20, 137, 189, 192–3, 198, 249, 253–4, 282; risk, 266–7, 271–4, 275, 278, 280, 282, 283; social, 253–6

property development, 23, 226

prostitutes. See sex workers

Puar, Jasbir, 85, 95, 151n2

public sex, 22–3, 224–6, 226, 231–2

public space, 224–6, 229, 232–3, 234; and feminism, 10–11, 20, 23; gay men and, 23, 213, 225, 226; and law, 21, 229, 277; and male gaze, 22–3, 34; serial killer and, 109, 122; and sexual assault, 21; sex workers and, 21–2, 213–14, 221, 228; and social media, 57–8, 76; trans and, 22–3; and visibility, 215–16, 233; women and, 20–1, 56, 75, 98–9, 123; women's safety and, 9, 22. See also urban space

Punjabi Community Health Services, 142

Quantico, 190, 201
queers, viii–ix, 23; and identity, 185, 204n1; and monitoring, 93, 185, 187; Muslim, 93
queer communities, viii–ix, 23, 220–1, 223–6, 225; visibility of, 169–70, 235n5
queer theory, 56, 185, 187, 203
queer women, 167

R. v. Bedford, 172
R. v. Mabior, 171, 172
R. v. Polutele, 274–6
race, 10, 36, 135–6, 136–40, 142, 149, 150, 198, 258; and ban–optic, 187, 194, 200, 202–3; and biometrics, 269; and cultural difference, 136–7, 141–3, 147–9, 150; Foucault on, 173; and gaze, 139–40; and immigration, 135–6, 136–8, 140, 143–4, 146–9, 150–1; and media, 143, 146–9; and NTEs, 266; and prison, viii–ix, 198–9, 200–1; profiler and, 119; and sex-selective abortion, 19, 135–6, 136–8, 140, 143–4, 146–9, 150–1; and strip clubs, 249, 253–5, 256–7; trans and, 187–8, 198–201. *See also* intersectionality
Race, Kane, 163
"racializing surveillance," 135–6, 138–9, 142, 149, 150
racial profiling, 19–20, 137, 189, 192–3, 198, 249, 253–4, 282; and NTEs, 282; and PIC, 198; and strip clubs, 249, 253–5
Radical Handmaids, 147
Ray, Joel, 146, 149
Razack, Sherene, 136, 141, 148

Reagan, Ronald, 17
"regimes of shame," 44, 98
Regent Park, 213, 216–17, 222
Rehling, Nicola, 119
Reitman, Janet, 190
reproduction, 19, 136–40, 145, 149, 150–1. *See also* sex-selective abortion
reproductive justice, 135–6, 137–8, 147–8, 150–1, 151n1
reproductive rights, 137, 140, 143, 147–48, 150
resistance, viii–ix, 13, 23, 236n6; and "participatory surveillance," 88; of sexters, 36, 44–6; in strip clubs, 241, 243, 251–3, 258–9; and TasP, 174
Ressler, Robert, 113
rights, 54, 136, 190, 214; 216, 228–9; gay, 200–1, 219, 224, 226, 234; reproductive, 137, 140, 143, 147, 147–8, 150
Ringrose, Jessica, 77–8
risk, 22, 161, 233; and children, 47–8; and HIV, 47–8, 157, 159, 159–61, 162, 164–70, 174; and NTEs, 24, 265–7, 269, 270–4, 275–6, 278, 280, 282, 283; and social media, 59, 64–6; and strip clubs, 23–4, 240–1, 242, 245, 246–8, 249–50, 252–3, 255–6, 258. *See also* "at risk"
risk management, 6, 24, 42, 168; and strip clubs, 23–4, 240–1
risk profiling, 266–7, 271–4, 275, 277, 280, 282, 283
risk societies, 94, 233
Roberts, Dorothy, 137
Robinson, Russell, 200
Rosengarten, Marsha, 166
Ross, Becki, 226, 228, 235n5

Royal Canadian Mounted Police (RCMP), 227

safety, 3, 36, 48; and CCTV, 22; children's, 36, 43, 218–19; and NTEs, 267, 272, 277–8, 278–80, 283; serial killers and, 107; strippers and, 242, 246, 254, 256; women and, 9, 21–2
safety state, 187, 188–90, 192, 194–8, 203; and ban-optic, 188–90, 203
scopophilia, 11–12, 37, 38, 48, 49, 51n5. *See also* male gaze
Scott, James, 138
securitization, 187, 234; and biometrics, 192–5, 265, 271; "of identity," 190, 192–5; and CCTV, 21–2, 265; and HIV, 156, 171–3, 174; and NTEs, 265–6, 266–70, 270–4, 278–82, 283
security, "apparatus," 160, 201; and ban-optic, 203; and biometrics, 271; and biopolitics, 267–70; and governance, 266; national, 4, 16, 27, 87, 139, 187, 189, 192, 203, 227; and NTEs, 265–7, 270–4; and privacy, 226; in strip clubs, 249–50; women's, 9, 21–2
security guards, 264–6
security state, 19, 137, 193–5
Sedgwick, Eve, 91, 99–100
"Seek and Treat for Optimal Prevention of HIV/AIDS" (STOP), 159, 162, 165–6, 173
Segal, Judy, viii
selfies, 13, 35–7, 38–47, 47–9, 50n2, 50n3; Cybertip.ca and, 47–9; "duckface," 62–3, 66, 75; and embodiment, 45; headless, 37–8, 43, 44–7, 49; and identity, 46–7;

and pleasure, 35–7, 43–4, 46, 47, 49–50; as pornographic, vii, 14, 47; and scopophilia, 37, 38, 48, 49; and "surveillant assemblage," 37. *See also* sexters
self-surveillance, 4, 9, 11–12, 84–5, 87, 92, 94, 106; and strip clubs, 243. *See also* monitoring; "participatory surveillance"
Senft, Theresa, 77
Brighenti, Andrea, 57, 71, 74, 76–7
serial killer, and crime scene, 117–18; gaze of, 103–5; and gender, 104–5, 106–7, 108–9, 121–2; and media, 109–10; in popular culture, 110–11; and masculinity, 115; police and the, 107; and private space, 117, 122; profiler and the, 104, 105–11; and profiler in film, 111–25, 125–6; and safety, 107; sex workers and, 106–7, 108–9, 117, 122, 124; and urban space, 103, 105, 109, 112, 113–14, 115, 119–20; white, 109, 119
serial killer films, 14, 119, 103–5; and male gaze, 14, 105, 106, 114; police and, 14, 111, 123–4, 234, 235n4. *See also* "profiler" films
sex-selective abortion, 19; *Canadian Medical Association Journal* and, 135, 144, 146, 147, 149; and cultural difference, 136–7, 141–3, 147–9, 150; and disclosure, 144–6; and feminism, 135–6, 137–8, 147–8; immigrants and, 135–6, 141–2, 143–4, 145–9, 150–1; and law, 135, 144, 145, 147, 149, 150–1, 151n4, 152n5, 152n6; and media, 135–6, 139–40, 147–9, 150–1; and Motion 408, 135; *National Post* and, 135, 148–9; and race, 19, 135–6,

136–8, 140, 143–4, 146–9, 150–1;
South Asians and, 141, 145–9; and
surveillance, 135–6, 136–40, 142,
143–4, 150–1; and violence against
women, 142, 147–8, 151n5
sexters, 14, 39–43, 46, 51n10;
criminalization of, 36, 44, 48; and
media, 37–8; resistance of, 36,
44–6. *See also* selfies
sexual assault, 21, 106, 241, 266, 272.
See also violence against women
sex workers, viii, 18; and ART, 173;
and CCTV, 21–2; and HIV, 159,
172–3; Jack the Ripper and, 106–7,
108–9, 122; police and, 21, 214;
and public space, 21–2, 213–14,
221, 228; and serial killers, 106–7,
108–9, 117, 122, 124; and strip
clubs, 246, 257; and TasP, 159, 173
Smart, Carol, 240
Smith, Andrea, 137
Snowden, Edward, 3, 17, 236n5, 244
social death, 187, 192
social hygiene, 16, 21, 22
social media, vii–viii, 3, 12–14,
56–9, 88, 90; as archive, 95–6;
commercial, 8, 61, 72–4, 77, 78; and
embodiment, 77; and femininity,
62–4; focus group on, 58–59;
gaze and, 56–7, 58, 71, 77, 78; and
gender, 12, 14, 57, 59–62, 71–2,
74–5, 99; and identity, 60–1, 70–2,
74, 98; and inequality, 59, 69–70,
78; and "lateral surveillance," 8–9;
monitoring, 64–9, 72, 75–7, 85; and
panoptic, 8; and "participatory
surveillance," 3–4, 8, 12–14, 88, 90;
and performance, 60, 62–3, 71–2,
73, 74–8, 98; and pleasure, 13, 36,
64, 75, 90–1, 97–9; and privacy,

57–8, 59, 66–9, 75–6; and resistance,
13; and risk, 59, 64–56; stalking in,
65–6, 67, 69; and subjectivity, 12,
57, 74, 94–6; and synoptic, 8; and
visibility, 14, 57, 60–3, 70, 71–2,
75–7, 93–4; and women, 58, 59, 74.
See also selfies; sexters
social profiling, 253–7
Social Security Administration, 195
"social sorting," 4, 6, 144, 243, 253–6,
256–8, 258–9
"sousveillance," 23
South Asians, 141, 145–9
Spade, Dean, 198–9
spectacle, 11, 228–34; Foucault
and, 6, 8, 230, 217–18, 230–1; and
media, 8, 139–40, 228–34, 235;
panoptic, 218, 230; public, 6, 8–9,
223, 230; synoptic, 11–12, 218, 230
Stanley, Eric A., 185
stalking, 109–10; in social media,
65–6, 67, 69
state, 4, 231; and discipline, 199, 203;
gaze of, vii, 229, 252; monitoring
of, 185–6, 190, 195; and regulation
of women, 137–8; "safety," 187,
188–90, 192, 194–6, 196–8, 203;
violence, 187, 196–8, 201
"state of emergency," 6, 189–90, 192
state of exception, 187, 189, 190, 226,
191–2
state surveillance, 3–4, 19–20,
185–86, 187, 189–90, 193–6, 218,
226–9, 231–3, 249; and strip clubs,
242, 246, 255. *See also* Wikileaks
strip clubs, 240; and blind spots, 241,
248–9, 250–3, 258; and bouncers,
244, 249–50, 253, 254, 258; and
CCTV, 243, 244, 245, 247, 254;
and counter-surveillance, 251–3,

258; and data doubles, 243–4; and embodiment, 241, 244; and surveillance by employees, 245, 248–9, 250, 257–8; and feminism, 240, 258; and gaze, 240, 243, 252, 258; and gender, 240–1, 243–4, 255–6, 256–7; and "lateral surveillance," 242, 243, 248, 257; and law, 242, 243, 248; and managerial surveillance, 244–8, 249, 250, 251–3, 254, 257–8, 277; in Ontario, 241–2; and peer surveillance, 243, 247–8; "pimp" and, 253–6, 257, 259n5; police and, 255–6; and racial profiling, 249, 253–5; and racial quotas, 254–5, 257; and resistance, 241, 243, 251–3, 258–9; and risk, 23–4, 240–1, 242, 245, 246–8, 249–50, 252–3, 255–6, 258; and safety, 242, 246, 249–50, 254, 256; and sex workers, 246, 257; and "social sorting," 243, 253–6, 256–8, 258–9; and state surveillance, 242, 246, 255; and surveillance webs, 23–4, 240–1, 256, 258, 259n3
strippers, 242, 244–6, 251, 256–7; racialized, 254–5; and safety, 242, 246, 254, 256
Strub, Sean, 169, 171
Stryker, Susan, 204n1
subjectivity, 10–11, 13, 97–8; and confessional texts, 14, 24, 84; and doubled self, 9; and feminism, 9–10; Foucault and, 6–7, 110, 164; and gender, 9–10, 10–12, 14; masculine, 9, 14; of Muslim women, 14, 84, 86–7, 89–90, 93–4, 94–6; and neoliberalism, 86–7; postfeminist, 85, 86; and power, 6; racial, 138;

and selfies, 36; and serial killers, 110; of sexters, 44; and social media, and social media, 12, 57, 74, 94–6; and TasP, 157; trans, 19; women's, 43–5, 57, 74, 85, 86. *See also* Enlightenment
"subjectivity building," 95
"substitute apparatus," 198
"superpanopticon," 6
surveillance, 185, 224–6, 243–4; "algebra of," 44; biomedical, 161, 163, 173; and blind spots, 43, 241, 250–3, 258; and child protection, 36, 43; commercial, 4, 8–9, 57, 72–4; counter-, 251–3, 258; and embodiment, 14–19, 241; by employees, 245, 248–9, 250, 257–8; "flow of," 44; of gay men, 169, 213, 215, 234–5; and gender, 5, 10–14, 24, 56–8, 84, 108, 189, 192–5, 265–6, 276; and HIV, 19, 156–7, 164–6, 167, 169, 171–2; of immigrants, 143–4, 146–7, 149; interpersonal, 74–5, 78; and intersectionality, vii, 5, 10, 56–7, 173; "lateral," 8, 22, 88, 91, 232–3, 242, 243, 248, 257; "liquid," 7, 201; managerial, 244–8, 249, 250, 251–3, 254, 257–8, 277; and media, 5, 11–14, 73, 138–93, 148–9, 216, 217, 228–34, 234–5; medical, 157, 161; and mobility, 192–5; of Muslim women's sexuality, 84–5, 89–90, 94–5, 96, 98, 99; and NTEs, 265–7, 267–70, 272–4, 283; as participatory, 3–4, 8, 12–14, 88, 90, 97–8; peer, 85, 89, 91, 92, 233, 243, 247–8; as performance, 13, 36, 86–7, 89–90, 93–4, 98; police, 216, 229, 231–2,

233; "pornification of," 37–8; prophylactic, 16; public health, 161, 163, 169–70; of "public" sex, 224–26; and queer theory, 56, 185, 187, 203; and race, 136–40, 198, 258; "racializing," 135–6, 138–9, 142, 144, 149, 150; and safety, 3, 36; self-, 4, 9, 11–12, 84–5, 87, 92, 94, 106; and sex-selective abortion, 135–6, 136–40, 142, 143–4, 150–1; social, 91–3; and social media, 3–4, 12–14, 65–6, 88, 90; and spectacle, 11, 231–2; subverted, 44–6; and TasP, 156–7, 161–3, 172–3, 173–4; topography of, 248; of trans people, viii, 19, 187, 198–201; workplace, 241, 243, 247, 259n4; and urban space, 19–24. *See also* monitoring; panoptic; panopticon; state surveillance; surveillance webs; synoptic

surveillance deficits, 269, 271–3, 277, 279, 282, 283

"surveillance medicine," 42, 157, 160–1

surveillance networks, viii, 244. *See also* surveillance webs

"surveillance society," 3

surveillance studies, 4–10, 240; and ban-optic, 203; and embodiment, 4–5; feminism and, viii–ix, 10–14, 20–4, 85–6, 86–9, 135, 136, 185; Foucault and, 6–9, 160; and gender, vii–ix, 4–5, 6–10, 13, 15, 24, 56–7, 185, 272–3; and identity, 56–7; and panoptic, 57, 78; and queer theory, 185, 187, 203; and synoptic, 78; and urban space, 23

surveillance technologies, 3, 161–3, 240

surveillance webs, 23–4, 169, 240–1, 256, 258, 259n3, 259n3; mapping, 244–8; and blind spots, 250, 258

"surveillant assemblage," 17–18, 240, 258; Haggerty on, 7, 17, 37, 76, 243–4, 258

surveilled mobility, 187, 192–5

Sutcliffe, Peter, 107, 109, 124

Swain, Diana, 140, 141, 143, 144

synoptic, 8–9, 11, 58, 78, 218, 230; and child pornography, 48; gaze, 57, 73, 216; and gender, 8; Mathiesen on, 8, 11–13, 73, 216, 234; and media, 218–19, 236n6; and panoptic, 8–9, 11, 13, 73, 76, 217–18, 231. *See also* panoptic; panopticon

Tabor, Phillip, 44

television, 3, 18, 38, 98, 104. *See also* Dr. Phil

terrorism, 85, 87, 188; "sexual," 110, "War on," 96, 193

Thiel-Stern, Shayla, 71–2

Thobani, Sunera, 136

Timmermans, Stefan, 171

Tomsen, Stephen, 278

Toronto, 23, 215, 222–4, 226, 240, 242. *See also* Yonge St.

Toronto Star, The, 223

"Total Information Awareness" program, 17

transgender, viii, 19, 185, 187, 189–90, 193–96, 198–201; and biometrics, 18–19, 187, 192–5; and deviance, 13–14; and embodiment, viii, 19, 187, 198–201; and HIV, 167, 188; and identification, 194–5; and identity, 185, 195, 200, 204n1; medicalization of, 185, 195–6; and media; 196–7; monitoring of, 185, 187, 190, 195; police and, 198; and prison, ix, 187, 189–90, 198–201, 202–3; and public space, 22–3; and race, 187–8, 198–201; and TasP, 167

transphobia, viii, 165, 167, 187, 199–201, 202–3

Transportation Security Administration (TSA), 193–4

"treatment as prevention" (TasP), 30, 156–7, 158; gay men and, 167–70; and gender, 157, 158, 165, 173, 174; and governmentality, 156–7, 160, 161, 163; MSM and, 169; neutrality of, 158–9; sex workers and, 159, 173; and space, 163–4; and surveillance, 156–7, 161–3, 172–3, 173–4; trans and, 167; women and, 165–7

TV, 3, 18, 38, 98, 104. *See also* Dr. Phil

two-spirit people, 164

UC Baby Clinic, 140–1

Uhbi, Verjinder, 141

Unnatural Selection (documentary), 135–6, 139–40, 140–4, 147–8, 149–50

urban planning, 20, 108

urban space, 19–24; and CCTV, 20, 21–2; detective and, 108–9, 116; and embodiment, viii; and feminism, 20, 23; gay men and, 22–3, 213, 225, 226; and gender, viii, 5, 19–23, 108, 123; and governance, 20, 22, 108, 267; and male gaze, 108; and masculinity, 20–3; monitoring, 103–5, 107; profiler and, 103, 105, 113–14, 115, 119, 123, 124–5; and "profiler" films, 103, 112, 113–14, 115–17,

118–20, 122–5, 125–6; serial killer and, 103, 105, 112, 113–14, 115, 119–20; and surveillance studies, 23; and visibility, 215–16. *See also* public space

Valentine, Gill, 21

van der Meulen, Emily, 22

victims, 104–5, 106–10, 117–18, 120–5, 126, 137, 200, 269

Victorian Supreme Court, 274–5

violence, 21, 118–20; alcohol-related, 265–6, 268–9; domestic, 94, 120, 275; and HIV, 165, 167, 199; homophobic, 266; male, viii, 103, 106–7, 119–20, 265–7, 272, 274–8, 283; and masculinity, 24, 109, 120, 267, 274–8; and NTEs, 264–7, 274–8, 283; of PIC, 199–201, 202; police, 16, 19–20; state, 187, 196–8, 201; transphobic, viii–ix, 165, 167, 187, 199–201, 202. *See also* sexual assault; serial killer; violence against women

violence against women (VAW), 21, 120–5, 142, 147–8, 151n5, 275

viral load, 157–8, 162–3, 167, 169–72; and law, 171–2; monitoring, 157, 162–3, 170, 172

virtu(e)ality, 36–7, 42, 44, 50

visibility, 56–8, 60–3, 93–4, 96–7; and biometrics, 269; gay men and, 215–16, 226–8, 229–30; and identity, 56, 194; and inequality, 76; and objectification, 56–7; "politics of," 232; and public space, 215–16, 233; of queer communities, 56, 169–70, 235n5; and social media, 14, 57, 60–3, 70, 71–2, 75–7; and strip clubs, 241;

and "surveillance medicine," 160;
trans and, 19
vision, 10–13, 15, 16–17; "from
below," 27
voyeurism, 11, 36, 43, 44, 46, 76, 98,
258. *See also* exhibitionism

Walby, Kevin, 161, 228
Waldby, Catherine, 162, 171
Warawa, Mark, 135, 144, 147, 149
"War on Terror," 96, 193
watching, 9, 11–13, 16, 34, 36, 56–8,
65–6, 78, 89, 90–1, 97–9, 139, 151,
218; "protective," 233
Weaver, John, 222
web of surveillance, 23–4, 169, 240–1,
256, 258, 259n3, 259n3; mapping,
244–8; and blind spots, 250, 258
"welfare queen," 18
Westlake, E.J., 73
whistle blowers, 185–6, 190–2
Wikileaks, 3, 185–7
Williams, Linda, 11, 49–50
Wilson, G. Willow, 91
women, viii, 13, 15, 43–5, 57, 74,
85, 86; and ART, 166–7; as "at

risk," 13, 166–7, 243–4; bouncers,
279–82, 283; and discipline, 37,
44, 47–8, 77, 86; and gendercide,
135, 137, 148; and HIV, 164–7, 172;
Indigenous, ix, 137, 152n5, 166,
167; and knowledge, 91, 94, 97,
144–5; objectification of, 44–5, 56;
police and, 21–2; and public space,
20–1, 56, 75, 98–9, 123; safety and
security of, 9, 21–2; and social
media, 58, 59, 74; South Asian,
141, 145–9; and state regulation,
137–8; and STOP, 165–6; and TasP,
165–7; as victims, 104–5, 106–10,
117–18, 120–5, 126, 137; and urban
space, 20–1. *See also* Muslim
women
Woodworth, Stephen, 147, 149
workplace surveillance, 241, 243,
247, 259n4
World Professional Association for
Transgender Health (WPATH), 196
Wright, Steve, 107

Yonge St., 213–15, 216–17, 218–21,
221–7, 225, 228, 234–5

Lightning Source UK Ltd.
Milton Keynes UK
UKOW01f2255101016

284893UK00001B/31/P